Religious Poverty
and the Profit Economy
in Medieval Europe

A Dominican and a Franciscan reject offerings from usurers

This scene from a 'moralized' Bible executed at Paris around 1250
accompanies Jeremiah 6:20, 'What good is it to me if frankincense
is brought from Sheba? I will not accept your offerings'.
The moralizing comment says: 'this truly applies to those who offer
alms out of what they've robbed from the destitute'. The preceding
scene shows Christ similarly turning away from
obsequious Jews, suggesting both the Christ-like role of the friars
and the association of Jews with money and usury.

Paris, BN, lat. 11560, f. 138   *Photo:* BIBLIOTHÈQUE NATIONALE

Religious Poverty
and the Profit Economy
in Medieval Europe

LESTER K. LITTLE

Paul Elek London

First published 1978 by
Paul Elek Ltd
54–58 Caledonian Road, London N1 9RN

ISBN 0 236 40109 2

Typeset by Computacomp (UK) Limited
Fort William, Scotland
and Printed in Great Britain by
Unwin Brothers Limited
The Gresham Press, Old Woking, Surrey

Contents

Preface

The history of voluntary poverty as it relates to the new profit economy in Europe between the approximate dates 1000 and 1300 is the subject of this book. It is a story with a long list of characters, including merchants, textile workers, prostitutes, monks, teachers, princes, hermits, and preachers. The setting is Latin—or Western— Christian society, within which, during the period under study, change took place on multiple levels of human activity and concern. The territory is so large and diverse that the evidence has to be highly selective. Whereas in a narrowly defined monograph all relevant materials need to be cited, in a broad, interpretative essay such documentation would weigh too heavily on the reader and risk obscuring the writer's argument.

The main question being asked in this book is 'Why?' Several of the particular problems dealt with briefly here constitute the principal subject of an entire volume or even of several volumes written by others. The very confluence of so many intensive and for the most part excellent studies is what has called forth this investigation, is precisely what renders insistent the question of why things should have happened as they did. Why did Latin Christians react as they did to the development of a profit economy at the start of the second Christian millennium? Why did the relations between Christians and Jews disintegrate so disastrously in the twelfth and thirteenth centuries? Why did voluntary poverty become the key element in renewed forms of the religious life? And, finally, why is it that the voluntarily poor were the ones to work out an ethic justifying the money-making activities of merchants and urban professionals?

The formulation of one person's answers—and that is all they are— has involved the generous patience and wise counsel of others. In cases where I have received help on specific matters, I have made acknowledgement in the appropriate notes. As for those many colleagues and friends who have heard and criticized parts or all of the argument, I would surely commit injustices in trying to list them all. I wish, however, to single out Barbara H. Rosenwein, who in recent years has become a valued collaborator in much of my work, and whose critique of the present text was of the greatest assistance. To her and those many others, I am pleased to express my sincere gratitude.

I have been fortunate in having the collaboration of efficient secretaries and typists, whom I gladly thank; they are Evelyn B. Cannon, Marjorie N. Erikson, Hilda M. McArthur, Margaret A. Van Sant, and Catherine M. Worsley. Moreover, I have been the beneficiary of financial grants for the support of my work. Here I gratefully acknowledge aid received from the College of the University of Chicago and from Smith College. Thanks are also due the Institute for Advanced Study for hospitality and a fellowship in 1969–70 and to the American Council of Learned Societies for a fellowship in 1970–71.

Woven into the fabric of this book is the continuing influence of my teachers. I have studied with many good teachers, none of whom I wish to implicate in my weaknesses and errors. Yet there are three superlative teachers of whom I would like to make special mention. The first is John R. Williams, Professor Emeritus of History at Dartmouth College, where he taught from 1924 to 1964. A student of Charles Homer Haskins, Professor Williams followed that aspect of Haskins' wide range of interests concerned with theology and the schools of the twelfth century. His humane and erudite teaching was my introduction to the field and remains for me today an elusive standard. The second is another student of Haskins, Joseph R. Strayer, Professor Emeritus of History at Princeton University, where he taught from 1930 to 1973. The heir to Haskins' work on Normandy and in institutional history, it was Professor Strayer who gave my original enthusiasm discipline and a capacity for continued renewal. The third is Marie-Dominique Chenu, whose career as a professor of theology is perhaps better defined by his depositions and exiles than by his tenures. I was never in any formal sense a student of Père Chenu, but ever since that day in 1960 when we first met and we talked for an hour, I have claimed him as my teacher. Many of the questions asked in this book can be found in some more or less explicit form in his writings. Thus I acknowledge my good fortune in finding teachers who gave generously of their capacities to encourage, to train, and to question.

Introduction

Marc Bloch's *Feudal Society* spans roughly five centuries of European history, from 800 to 1300. Even while structural in approach it does not present a static profile of that society. Chronological as well as geographical variations are repeatedly introduced to refine the analysis as it is being presented. But since Bloch found so many fundamental and inter-related changes that centred on the eleventh century, he placed a line at A.D. 1050 to serve as an approximate and flexible divider between two ages of feudalism. 'No definite break with the past occurred,' wrote Bloch, 'but rather a change of direction, which despite inevitable variations in time according to the countries or the phenomena considered, affected in turn nearly all the graphs of social activity. There were, in a word, two successive "feudal" ages, very different from one another in their essential character.'[1]

His ensuing description of the first feudal age came under three rubrics: density of population, intercommunication, and trade and currency. With allowances made for the lack of statistics and for the contrasts between one region and another, the fundamental characteristic of the age, according to Bloch, was the low density of its population, a point further aggravated by unequal distribution. In relation to this population the amount of arable land was large, but its productivity low.[2] Among the chief obstacles to communication was the chronic disrepair of bridges and of the old Roman roads, besides the general state of insecurity. Even when travellers got through, travel was slow, no postal service operated, and institutions, in order to function at all, had to rely upon direct contact between individuals. Trade was 'irregular in the extreme'; it was small in volume; and it was made up mostly of luxury items. The balance of trade with the East continued to be unfavourable; the long-term flow eastward of silver and gold left the West with a severe shortage of currency.[3]

Against such a backdrop, Bloch was then able to describe the 'economic revolution of the second feudal age'. Here he stressed the 'intensive movement of repopulation' and the 'incessant gnawing of the plow at forest and wasteland'. The immediate results were a closer association of human groups and the disappearance of the 'vast empty spaces'. Cities, with their distinctive middle class, now took shape, and the manufacture of woollen cloth came to play a central role, similar to that of the making of cotton goods in nineteenth-century England. The West became a supplier of manufactured goods, a key factor in an improved currency situation. The second feudal age, in short, witnessed an accelerated rhythm of circulation and an overall revival of commerce.[4]

The historiographical notion of a second feudal age conforms closely with another abstraction that has been applied to this same period, namely, the 'Commercial Revolution'. The latter is used by way of analogy with the term 'Industrial Revolution' and hence it brings to the history of the period between 1000 and 1300 a well developed set of analytical questions.[5] No one would think a study of the Industrial Revolution complete that was restricted to figures on the amounts of coal dug up and consumed, the lengths of railroad track laid, and the quantity of cotton cloth produced. The history of the Industrial Revolution includes the industrialists who invested in the new machines, the workers who ran the machines, the Luddites, who went about destroying machines, and the Morrisites, who tried to by-pass machines. The Industrial Revolution had a literature and an architecture, a psychology and a spirituality; it was above all rich in politics and in ideologies. Thus questions can and ought to be raised concerning every level of behaviour and thought so that one may appreciate fully the impact on society and on individual lives of a phenomenon so momentous and significant as either the Industrial or the Commercial Revolution. The use of the two abstractions together, moreover, suggests a general scheme for organizing all of European history, in which the centerpiece ('middle age') is the pre-industrial, or commercial, period, stretching from the eleventh century to the nineteenth.[6] Within such a scheme, it will be seen that the basic structural pattern for the entire period had already taken shape by the fourteenth century.[7]

The main problem for the historian in analysing behaviour and thought on multiple, contemporaneous levels is how to make meaningful correlations between one level and another, and ultimately among all of them.[8] Anyone could agree that they are all related—somehow—but it is equally evident that each has a measure of independence and a rhythm of its own. The abrupt modifications common to the level of political relations, for example, are unknown upon the level of ethics.[9] The following study, although making no formal statement on this problem of method, attempts to draw precisely such correlations among the various strata in a specific period of history: the strata of economy, society, and civilization, or, more concretely, those of a monetary economy, an urban society, and a spirituality founded upon poverty.[10]

The first part of this book sets out to delineate the problem of the spiritual crisis of medieval urban culture in terms of a disjuncture between socio-economic change and resistance to adaptation. A brief outline of the main economic developments of the second feudal age does not contradict Marc Bloch, but it takes account of information gathered since he wrote and of a general thesis—applying the concept of the gift economy to early European history—that refines his overall analysis. The 'spiritual crisis' is seen in a growing discordance between new economic and social realities and a traditional, initially unresponsive, clergy and theology.

The second and third parts of this study deal with the responses that this civilization was able to make to this particular crisis. The major responses available were, of course, religious, and they can be divided roughly between those that avoided the issue and those that confronted it. The former, the monks and the hermits, are the subject of Part 2. Part 3 is devoted to those who did not turn away from contemporary problems—the regular canons, various groups of pious laymen, and the Franciscan and Dominican friars.

The friars, who became established during the second decade of the thirteenth century, formulated an intellectual and spiritual ideal properly suited to the new social and economic reality. This growth of an urban spirituality, this resolution of the spiritual crisis of urban culture in the second feudal age, is the subject of the book's fourth, and final, part. The accomplishment of the friars, expressed in the terminology of these introductory pages, was their correlation of the levels of learning, morality, and worship, with those of demography, the system of exchange, and social organization.

PART I

The Spiritual Crisis of
Medieval Urban Culture

1

From gift economy to profit economy

A sixth-century king of the Burgundians named Gunthram once had a dream in which he received directions for finding a cache of buried treasure. He went to the place indicated and while his servants were digging they uncovered 'inestimable treasures' of gold. Gunthram had the gold fashioned into an altar canopy of wondrous size and great weight, adorned with precious gems, his intention being to send it to the holy sepulchre in Jerusalem. When he learned he could not carry out this plan, he had the canopy placed over the tomb of St Marcel in a nearby church at Chalon-sur-Saône.[1]

At Orléans some four centuries later, Bishop Arnoul undertook the reconstruction of the cathedral church of the Holy Cross, which with most of the town had been ruined by fire in 989. One day, when masons were seeking to determine the best site for the church's foundations, they unearthed a formidable quantity of gold, which they estimated sufficient to pay for the new building, however large. They took it to the bishop, who rendered thanks to God and then had it all assigned to the construction project. In the end this gold paid not only for the cathedral but also for several other churches in need of repair.[2]

These two discoveries, apparently fortuitous, can be thought of as historical accidents. But the reactions of people to them and the uses to which the discovered materials were put reflect two markedly different sets of historical circumstances. In the first instance, the reconversion of treasure into yet another form of treasure is typical of the gift economy that flourished in the centuries following the Germanic migrations. The exchange of treasure for building materials and labour in the second instance, however, signals new modes of thought and behaviour upon the very threshold of the eleventh century.

1. PILLAGE AND LARGESS

At the time of the Germanic migrations, the Romans lived within a

3

fixed, well delineated territory. Their age of expansion was well behind them. Their law sanctioned and protected property ownership, and their state controlled markets, buying and selling, weights and measures, and the minting of money.

The Germanic peoples, on the other hand, arrived as migratory bands of warriors, accustomed to living off the lands and people they captured. They were illiterate and, from a Christian perspective, pagan. Their leaders took charge of whatever booty they collected. Some of the booty these leaders kept for themselves, not to hide away or invest but to display, in order to enhance their prestige. Some they gave away as rewards to their companions in arms. Some they offered up at shrines or buried with the dead. And some, to be sure, they traded for luxury items with merchants from the Roman world, whose culture they so strongly emulated. Such luxury items served them in turn for more display and more gifts.

While the Roman type of economic organization, however alien, is relatively accessible to the modern observer, the Germanic type is perhaps better approached via the anthropological model of gift exchange.[3] In a gift economy, goods and services are exchanged without having specific, calculated values assigned to them. Prestige, power, honour, and wealth are all expressed in the spontaneous giving of gifts; and more than just expressed: these attributes are attained and maintained through largess. The act of giving is more important than the thing given. However, this act is less free than the connotation of 'giving' suggests, because one gift obliges the recipient to make a counter-gift.[4] Malinowski's study of the exchange of shell necklaces and bracelets among the Trobriand islanders clearly demonstrated the binding nature of the act and the lesser significance of the value of the materials exchanged.[5] The failure of a recipient to reciprocate properly can lead to the rupture of the social ties involved; it can bring two peoples to war. The offerings made to the deities or to the dead, which in some societies engage a major proportion of the available wealth, are given in anticipation—even if not wholly conscious—of a very real, indeed essential, return.

Within a particular social context, some gifts are obviously more precious than others, and rough estimates of value do enter into gift exchange; the counter-gift is supposed to approximate in value if not surpass the original gift. In the potlach of the Northwest Pacific Coast Indians, some element of evaluation is present because fierce competitions of largess and conspicuous consumption are fought out by rivals.[6] In a market economy, on the other hand, where one expects everything to have an assigned value, haggling, politeness, and fair-mindedness do sometimes have their place. Gift exchange remains as an essential part of social behaviour in modern industrial society, particularly in the areas of philanthropy and hospitality. The assigning of values has become so habitual as to penetrate even these areas of social relations, but it is instructive to see that calculations and the comparing of monetary values can go too far, reaching a point where the spontaneity and generosity of the giver or the host, or else the spontaneity and gratitude of the recipient, are no longer convincing. Likewise in an economy at large, it is with the calculating and assigning of precise values that giving comes to an end and profit-seeking begins. The two forms of behaviour can overlap; they can co-exist; and they can come into direct confrontation, as in the supposed 'purchase' of Manhattan Island.

The entry of the Germanic peoples into the Roman Empire was another such confrontation. Tacitus had already noted how the Germans took particular delight in gifts from neighbouring tribes.[7] The Gothic advance under Alaric, who ruled from 395 to 410, came after the death of the Emperor Theodosius, whom the Gothic historian Jordanes considered a 'lover of peace and of the Gothic race', and after the advent of Theodosius' ruinous sons who deprived the Goths of the 'customary gifts'.[8] In *Beowulf*, the good leaders were those who distributed wealth liberally, like Hrothgar, 'honoured ruler and giver of rings'.[9] Grendel the worm, on the other hand, less a fantastic creature than a bad warrior, was a devourer, and the fire-dragon was a hoarder.[10] The lord's hall, that principal setting for the repose of warriors, witnessed heavy eating and drinking, the recounting of heroic deeds, and the distribution of gifts. Hrothgar decided to have built 'A mightier mead-hall than man had known,/ Wherein to portion to old and young/All goodly treasures that God had given'.[11] Archaeology and poetry collaborate in telling of the ship burials in which the dead were put away with tools and weapons, fine cloths and skins, and precious jewels.[12] The description of the burial of Alaric, in addition to mentioning the treasures that accompanied the deceased, specified that captives were made to dig the grave and were killed immediately afterwards so as to maintain the secret of the gravesite.[13] Germanic art was best expressed in jewelry, and accordingly the goldsmiths and silversmiths held social positions of great prestige. Coins were treated as treasure, serving as items of prestige for the princes who issued and distributed them. Their material value was determined exclusively by weight.

The settlement of the Germanic peoples in the West was accompanied by the simultaneous processes of Christianization and Romanization. The missionaries brought Latin with them and were instrumental in putting the Germanic languages into written form. They were mostly monks, so set up monasteries wherever they went. The monks campaigned against pagan practices, notably the burying of wealth with the dead.[14] The riches that would previously have been sent out to sea or placed in the ground were henceforth diverted into monastic sanctuaries, which in turn became storehouses of treasure. Gregory of Tours tells of the expedition led by Clovis against the Visigoths, from which the Franks returned triumphant and laden with riches, a portion of which Clovis then offered to Saint-Martin of Tours.[15] The Lombard historian, Paul the Deacon, praised King Liudprand for his many generous benefactions, especially at Pavia to the Abbey of St Peter, which was called the 'Golden Heaven'.[16] Thus Christianization hardly put an end to gift exchange but only halted and redirected its least productive forms. Gifts to sanctuaries or to churchmen were made in anticipation of spiritual benefits, although not always as explicitly as in the following letter from an Anglo-Saxon king, Ethelbert of Kent, to the monk and missionary Boniface around the year 750:

By the bearer of this letter I am sending to Your Reverence with my devoted affection a few little gifts: a silver, gold-lined drinking cup weighing three pounds and a half and two woollen cloaks. We are not sending these gifts with the purpose or expectation of receiving any earthly profit or return; but rather on bended knees begging of you what is far more necessary, that in these evil days of manifold and unexpected troubles and in this world so filled with scandals you will deign to aid us with the frequent support of your prayers.

Ethelbert did, though, close with a worldly request, namely, that Boniface send him a pair of falcons of such cleverness and courage that they would without hesitation attack cranes and bring them to earth.[17]

All the characteristic traits of Germanic leaders, from the pillaging of the weak to the endowing of monasteries, are epitomized by Charlemagne (c. 742–814). But the historical importance of his reign is less his traditional behaviour than his attempts to have the Frankish crown take up what he saw to be some of the responsibilities of the Roman state. Part of this overall plan was to establish an effective system of justice that could guarantee peace and order throughout his lands; part was a new policy of minting silver pennies (which had a more practical value than gold coins), as well as a policy of encouraging commerce and of regulating weights and measures. Before these schemes could get translated into durable, institutional realities, the old predatory behaviour of the Frankish lords re-emerged in the generation after Charlemagne's successor; at the same time, the settled Germanic peoples of the West became prey, in their turn, to a new wave of swiftly moving, plundering outsiders.

The first feudal age is a dialogue between these recently settled, nominally Christian, and slightly Romanized Germanic peoples of western Europe, and their non-Christian attackers: the Vikings, the Magyars, and the Moslems. Whereas the Moslems were tied into a sophisticated commercial economy, the Magyars lived by the booty they gathered in their annual spring forays into the central parts of the Carolingian Empire during the first half of the tenth century. Over a longer period of time and a wider area, the Vikings, who had common ancestors with the Germanic peoples they now attacked, made their raids wherever waterways allowed them to go.

A few examples of this interaction between the new besiegers and the newly besieged will suffice. The burial of treasure with the dead in Germanic or western Europe had fairly effectively come to an end in the eighth century.[18] The influence of the Christian clergy in discouraging this practice coincided with the new appreciation of precious metal as specie, the beginnings of a commercial revival, and the enhanced prestige of monastic sanctuaries. A clear step from the gift economy to the profit economy had been taken. Here and there in the West, a profit-making mentality was applied to agricultural production. This was especially true of some monasteries that had the means to organize their lands more efficiently, and it was also particularly true of the Po Valley region. Near the western rim of this region stood Pavia, the Lombard royal capital where the Carolingian market and mint both continued to function even in the ninth and tenth centuries; at the eastern rim stood Venice, which lay within the commercial orbit of the Byzantine Empire. Some of the great monasteries of Lombardy, such as Saint-Ambrose of Milan, maintained warehouses and wharves on the Ticino at Pavia, where they sold surplus produce from their lands.[19] Meanwhile, treasure continued to be buried during the ninth, tenth, and early eleventh centuries, not, significantly, in these areas of precocious commercial activity, but rather in the homelands of the new marauders, in eastern Europe and the Scandinavian North. Not all of the loot gathered in western Europe (most of it taken from monasteries) was carried off to be immobilized in pagan treasure. A portion remained in circulation in the West. The new 'barbarian' chieftains, like those of four and five centuries before, wanted 'civilized' luxury goods. At the fairs organized by the Abbey of Saint-Denis, the Danes purchased wine, which they shipped to England or to Scandinavia and which they there consumed and offered ostentatiously in displays of mutual generosity. The vitality of monetary circulation in the West is suggested by the tribute payments that the Danes extracted from the Anglo-Saxons: in 991 the figure was £10,000; by 1012 it had risen to £48,000.[20]

By the middle of the eleventh century, Europe was effectively free from the pillaging attacks of outsiders. The outsiders had either been pushed back (like the Moslems in the western Mediterranean), or absorbed (like the Northmen in Normandy), or had settled in peripheral areas (like the Hungarians and the Scandinavians); and all of these except the Moslems were being converted to Latin Christianity. It is of considerable interest that the last known buried treasure hoards of eastern and northern Europe date from the 1060s, and that at about the same time in those same regions, the minting of coins began.[21] All of Latin Christian Europe was henceforth able to engage in a system of market exchange where money served as a standard of value for items to be exchanged.

From the late eleventh century onwards, the aggressiveness of European warriors had to be directed against outsiders. There could be no sanctioning of Latin Christians' plundering of each other. Instead the Moslems in Spain, on the Mediterranean islands, on the coast of North Africa, and in the Holy Land were now fair game, as were also the Slavs on Germany's eastern borders. This category of victims eventually included Greek Christians, whose leading city, Constantinople, the Venetians and their warrior allies plundered in the opening years of the thirteenth century. But there were also 'outsiders' within Europe who could be subject to plunder: the Jews, who periodically suffered pogroms; and heretics, whose land, according to canon law, became the legitimate property of the Catholic warriors who conquered it.[22]

A more subtle form of plundering insinuated itself into the new types of activities engaged in by Europeans, such as commerce and banking. Elsewhere, as in the eastern Roman Empire where these activities had had a continuous and much longer history, they were conducted under the eyes of a strong state. This meant that trade was heavily taxed and carefully regulated; moneylending for profit was legitimate and at the same time scrupulously limited. By contrast, European commerce came to maturity well in advance of the state, and as a result nurtured a peculiarly unrestrained aggressiveness, above all when it came to lending money.

Largess no more disappeared after 1050 than did plundering. It remained as a hallmark of the life led by the European aristocracy, and as a model for the life of successful merchants and professionals. It was to be seen not only in their clothes, their homes, their gifts, and their entertainments, but in their works of charity and support of religious institutions. What remained of gift-economy behaviour was thus complementary to commerce; it no longer opposed, or restrained, commercial activity.

2. COMMERCE AND INDUSTRY

Commercial activity made its way into European feudal society along sea coasts and river valleys. The first area of intense commercial activity, as already noted, was northern Italy, an area that united the head of the Adriatic Sea with the valley of the Po. The other main areas were the Mediterranean coasts of Italy, France, and Spain; a river system connecting the Mediterranean with the North Sea via the Rhône, the Saône, the Meuse, and the Scheldt; the Rhine Valley; the English Channel; and the lands bordering on the North and Baltic Seas. The earliest European industries, except for mining, made their appearance in the same areas.

The exchange network uniting these areas did not originate at some point on the Continent between Lombardy and Flanders and then grow outwards. Instead, the earliest significant commercial activity of Latin Christendom was located at the periphery, and was directed outwards to Byzantine Italy, Islamic Spain, and the Scandinavian northern seas. The economic history of the period from the late tenth century through the early twelfth consists, in part, of the tying into one network of these externally oriented frontier areas, of their amalgamation into a single, interdependent economy.

The Byzantine towns of the Tyrrhenian coast, Amalfi, Naples, and Gaeta, as well as Bari on the Adriatic, maintained regular commercial contact with Constantinople in the tenth century and sometimes sent ships on to Syria and Egypt. In return for local produce and naval stores, these ships came back from the East with spices, silk, perfumes, dyes, jewels, and tapestries. Some of this material was unloaded in Italy, to be filtered through to the feudal courts of Europe, while some continued on to the Moslem ports of the western Mediterranean. Venice engaged in the same luxury trade but was effectively free of Byzantine imperial authority and traded to the West, not with Moslems but with the Po Valley towns as far inland as Pavia. In the eleventh century, the leadership of north-western Italy passed from Pavia to Milan, which, with its new canal system, was to become a major industrial as well as commercial and financial centre. It came to share with Venice the distinction of being the largest city in Latin Christendom.[23]

The Christian reconquest of the western Mediterranean in the eleventh century was led by Pisa and Genoa, whose successful raids on Moslem ports provided the capital for their earliest commercial ventures. Subsequently they competed with each other—often violently—for the trade that passed through the ports of Provence, Languedoc, and Catalonia. By the thirteenth century, Marseilles, with the best natural port on the southern French coast, with the Provençal salt marshes to exploit, and with control of the Rhône delta traffic, could deal on its own terms with the Pisans and the Genoese. Narbonne and Barcelona also emerged as powerful, independent ports, as the rivalry between Pisa and Genoa became at times mutually destructive.[24]

Nearly all the Mediterranean ports of western Europe profited from the crusades. The focus of historical attention on the major expeditions, which set out at a rate of about one per generation from the end of the eleventh century to the end of the thirteenth, tends to obscure the fact that a regular traffic between Europe and the Levant was established in the interim. The evolution of this traffic is noteworthy for its increasing sophistication as well as its growth, as can be seen by comparing the First Crusade, which had virtually no logistical organization at all, with those of the thirteenth century, for which detailed contracts were drawn up by shipping agents at Venice, Genoa, and Marseilles.[25]

In the North, as the Vikings established trading colonies and then made a few major settlements, piracy and looting gave way to commercial exchange. From the latter half of the tenth century to the early fourteenth, the northern economy assumed its peculiar shape: countless local economies were amalgamated into a complex trade area that united the coasts of the English Channel, the North and Baltic Seas, and the Atlantic Ocean as far south as Bordeaux and as far north and west as Iceland.[26]

The pivotal point of this trade area was at the outlet of the Rhine and the Scheldt into the North Sea. There in Flanders, Brabant and the Low Countries the first pressures of a population expansion were felt in the tenth century because of the low crop yield of that country's broad sandy estuaries. Sheep could thrive where crops could not; and the presence there already of sheep, the unfailing water supply, the labour surplus, and the critical location combined to make the region specialize in the production of woollen cloth. This high-population area traded labour-intensive goods (cloth) with less densely settled areas for land-intensive goods (grain, wine). The grain at first came from the immediately adjoining countryside, and then more and more from northern France and, to a lesser extent, England. These areas remained the principal suppliers of grain to northern Europe until the fourteenth century, at which time the newly opened lands east of the Elbe started to export wheat and rye. All of the northern waters yielded fish, but commercial fishing came to centre on the fishing grounds off Iceland, England, and Sweden. The salt for preserving the fish came principally from the deposits at Lüneburg, which had access to the North Sea via Hamburg and to the Baltic via Lübeck, or else from the Atlantic coast between the mouth of the Garonne and the Isle of Oléron.[27]

The production of wine affords a clear example of the specialization that was the essence of this economic integration. Previously there had been attempts to make wine virtually everywhere in Europe. But in this age of specialization—when cloth was sent from Flanders to the Parisian basin; grain from the Parisian basin to Scandinavia; timber from Scandinavia to the Low Countries; cheese from the Low

Countries to Iceland; fish from Iceland to Germany; salt from Germany to England; beer and bacon from England to Flanders—the well-known wine-producing districts of modern Europe took shape. One of these was described by the Franciscan chronicler Salimbene, who in 1247 spent some time at his order's convent at Auxerre (in the northern reaches of Burgundy, sixty miles from Paris via the Yonne and the Seine). He had been told before leaving Italy that Auxerre had more wine and more vineyards than Cremona, Parma, Reggio Emilia, and Modena put together. What he was not prepared to see was that every bit of the land around was devoted to the culture of grapes. 'The men of this land do not sow or reap, nor do they store anything in barns, but they send wine to Paris, because they have a river right at hand that goes to Paris, and they sell it for a good price, from which they get all their food and all of the clothes that they wear.'[28] By Salimbene's time, the great vintages of Burgundy, Gascony, the Moselle, and Epernay (the phrase *vin de Champagne* came into use only in the late seventeenth century) were held in high esteem and consumed at commensurate cost. They had not driven all local wines out of production, but they had restricted them, along with beer and ale, to the tables of the relatively poor.[29]

The northern trade was held together by a steady cycle of fairs. The oldest known fair of the region was that of Saint-Denis, a Carolingian fair long interrupted, now revived in the eleventh century, and greatly expanded early in the twelfth century. The fairs of Flanders were of eleventh-century origin. Eventually they became fixed into a pattern with six fairs lasting thirty days each: first Ypres, then Bruges, Ypres a second time, then Torhout, Lille, and finally Messines.[30]

The economies of the western Mediterranean lands and of the territories of the North that centred about the Low Countries linked up at the fairs of Champagne. Ancient in origin and for long inoperative, these fairs were revived in the twelfth century; by 1191 they had become organized into an annual pattern with six stages spread out from spring to early winter and with locations at Troyes, Provins, Lagny, and Bar-sur-Aube. Jurisdiction over the fairs rested with the Count of Champagne and, after 1285, the French king. Merchants from Italian and Provençal towns formed associations to facilitate travel to and from the fairs, to assure adequate protection of their lives, their goods, and their rights, and to be able to bargain effectively with the fair officials. In like manner, seventeen of the woollen-cloth-producing towns of Flanders, Picardy, Champagne, Hainault, and Ponthieu established a league for the purpose of strengthening their bargaining position at the fairs.[31]

A major difference between North and South is revealed by examining the function of the fairs of Champagne. These fairs fulfilled for the North a function adequately assured in the South by towns. When the trade revival started, the Italian towns, however depressed and contracted, already existed. The new trade, including fairs, could develop only within the framework of these towns. In the North, on the other hand, urban development lagged behind the revival of trade. At no place between northern Italy and Flanders were there towns with experienced dealers and bankers who had adequate facilities for big-time international trade or for feeding, sheltering, and entertaining well-travelled merchants. The fairs filled precisely these functions. At the time they went into decline in the early fourteenth century, Bruges and Paris had become year-round commercial centres, year-round fairs, as it were, and competing fairs had been organized in the towns of Chalon-sur-Saône, Geneva, and Frankfurt.[32] Thus Italy had towns from the start, but in the North, as permanent towns were maturing, temporary towns called fairs were set up to facilitate commerce. When Chrétien of Troyes—the name is so familiar that we may forget to associate it with one of the Champagne-fair sites—sought to impress on his readers the view that a certain town was lively and rich, he said that it was as if a fair were held in that town every day.[33]

Our definition of commerce and our description of its revolutionary expansion must be broad enough to include the mobility of people as well as of spices, fish, cloth, wine, and iron. In the 1070s Pope Gregory VII referred to the many Italian merchants who went to France; perhaps they had gone to visit the fair at Saint-Denis. In 1127 there were 'Lombards' at Ypres. In 1190, when the Genoese arranged to take the Duke of Burgundy on crusade, part of the arrangement specified safe conduct for Genoese merchants passing through Burgundy on their way to Champagne, the same promise as the one shortly before granted to merchants from Asti. There were Milanese merchants at the fairs by 1172, while during the thirteenth century this steady parade of Italians to northern Europe included a greater proportion of Tuscans.[34]

Traffic originated in the North as well. The notarial records of Genoa attest to the presence in that town, between 1200 and 1342, of merchants from thirty-six different northern towns; still others were recognizable only as being from Flanders, France, England, Germany, Burgundy, and beyond the Alps (*de Ultramontis*).[35] Flemish cloth merchants also headed south-west to Perpignan, just as merchants of Perpignan had travelled to Champagne and Flanders. Some of the cloth sold at the late-August fair at Perpignan continued on a south-westerly course to the markets of Catalonia and Aragon. The modern route from Narbonne to Bordeaux via Toulouse was not fully operative, but the Mediterranean and the Atlantic were none the less connected by the slightly longer route: Montpellier–Cahors–La Rochelle.[36] Perpendicular to this axis and intersecting it at Cahors was one of the principal routes connecting northern France with Spain. The Lyons–Bordeaux route also passed through Cahors. Thus fortuitously located, the Cahorsins went out to explore the world that had been opened to them. By the closing years of the twelfth century, they were at La Rochelle and beyond Montpellier to Saint-Gilles and Marseilles. In the second decade of the thirteenth century they appeared in Aragon; others of them went to Italy or the Holy Land. Some sent wine by river down to Bordeaux. But in reputation, the Cahorsins were above all bankers. By the late thirteenth century they held a position of influence throughout northern Europe commensurate with that of the Lombards.[37]

The roads were open to scholars as well as to merchants. Gerbert of Aurillac's extraordinary tenth-century itinerary (Aurillac, Catalonia, Rome, Reims, Pavia, Bobbio, Reims, Aachen, Magdeburg, Ravenna, Rome) would have seemed fairly common for a thirteenth-century scholar. Besides scholars it was now the pilgrim who took to the road. No longer did conditions limit one to visiting the shrine of a local saint; the way was open to the shrine of Mary Magdalene at Vézelay, to the shrine of St James at Compostella, and to the countless sacred sites at Rome and in the Holy Land. Moreover, the late twelfth century produced the shrine of Thomas Becket, saint and martyr.[38] Lawyers and litigants, pilgrims and crusaders, professors and students, merchants and bankers—all participated in a new mobility during and after the eleventh century.

Less dramatic but no less important than the trade and travel that involved long distances and high prices was the increase in the size and number of local markets. Throughout Europe, not just along the international trade routes, the market supplanted simpler modes of economic exchange. From Poland to Portugal, new markets were set up, the number of days per week that markets operated increased, and the physical arrangements for the markets took on a more permanent look and reality.[39]

This period of commercial expansion also saw the appearance and modest development of industry, of what one perhaps has to call 'pre-Industrial-Revolution industry'. There is nothing here of heavy industry. The largest and in every other way most important of the early industries was the manufacture of woollen cloth. A full range of quality, from the most coarse to the most fine, became available throughout Europe. This cloth covered not only people but tables, beds, and even walls. There was probably no greater stimulus to the new commerce than the textile industry, not only because of its end product, but because of the great numbers of people whom it drew away from the land, whom it concentrated in small areas, and whose energies it absorbed. Moreover, the finer cloths produced in the West gave that area its first high-quality manufactured item for export, thereby adding valuable weight to the western side of the east-west trade balance.[40]

The centre of the textile industry, which engaged a hierarchy of talent ranging from crude, physical labour to highly refined skills, was Flanders, neighbouring Brabant, and northern France. Already in the third quarter of the eleventh century, a poem entitled 'The Quarrel of the Sheep and the Flax' argued that Flanders was producing fine cloth, much superior to that of other regions, and exporting it to France, Germany, and England.[41] The area industrialized rapidly in the eleventh and twelfth centuries, with virtually every town engaged in textile manufacture, importing raw materials and food, and exporting cloth. The opening of the world to the south via the fairs stimulated this expansion.

Many of the same natural and social conditions prevailed in England, with the important difference that English wool was of superior quality. England thereby became the purveyor of raw wool to the continental textile industry during the twelfth century and thus lagged behind in developing a domestic industry. The plains that drain into the Humber and Wash became the English counterparts to the great estuaries directly across the Channel, though virtually every area of England supported some cloth-producing towns. Even so, the great age of English cloth production, when England kept most of that fine raw wool at home, began only after the fourteenth century.[42] The main source of raw wool in the Mediterranean region, for cloth-making towns like Toulouse, was Castile, where, as in England, the export of wool took precedence over the making and exporting of cloth.

While the Flemish and their neighbours dominated the textile industry, the Italians, who produced an inferior grade of wool and of woollen cloth, dominated the cloth trade. They could even profitably import French or Flemish or English woollen cloth and then re-work and re-finish it with superior techniques and superior dyes.[43] They also imported and re-finished Flemish linen.[44] A monastery near Brescia apparently produced some silk as early as the tenth century, but silk continued to be a precious import from the East. Only in the thirteenth century did a silk-cloth industry get established in Lucca, whence it would later develop into one of the leading industries of Tuscany and Lombardy.[45]

Among the principal adjuncts of the textile industry was the trade in dyes. Three basic dyes—madder, weld, and woad, which give red, yellow, and blue respectively—were conveniently abundant in the cloth-making districts of north-eastern and southern France, Flanders, England, and northern Italy. Mills for crushing woad leaves and madder roots were common in such districts. The production of dyestuffs followed the common trend toward specialization, with

Picardy and Languedoc the leading centres for woad. The great fortunes of Amiens were made in woad, a fact to which the statues of the *waidiers* on the cathedral of Amiens give testimony. Next to wine, woad was the chief commodity shipped out of Bordeaux to northern Europe. Precisely because these dyes were so abundant in Europe, the Italians were able to enhance their expertise in cloth-finishing by importing rare dyes, mineral as well as vegetable, from the East.[46]

The building trades constituted an industry once workers were gathered into large teams and paid to work on complex projects that necessitated a high degree of planning and coordination. The three centuries under study constituted a great age for the construction of churches, castles, town walls, communal palaces, covered market-places, and bridges. The master of a building job had to lease or in some other way procure the use of a quarry; and he had to deal with such specialists as masons, carpenters, smiths, plumbers, glaziers, mortar mixers, and barrowmen, depending on the demands of the job.[47] Already in the early years of the eleventh century, Ralph Glaber commented on how, in addition to the many new churches that were being built, churches everywhere, in monasteries and towns and villages, were being enlarged and rebuilt, whether they needed it or not.[48]

Another type of project requiring large amounts of capital and extensive specialization was mining. Between the sixth and tenth centuries, mining in Europe consisted in the removal of superficial ores. But in the tenth and eleventh centuries, silver, gold, copper, lead, and iron mines were opened in various places in the Harz mountains, as well as in the Alps and the Pyrenees. Sweden, Hungary, Westphalia, Lombardy, and the Basque provinces all became exporters of iron and of such ironwares as grills, gates, keys, locks, hinges, tools, weapons, and ploughshares.[49] The precious metals were fashioned into decorative objects or, for the most part, coins.

3. MONEY AND BANKING

The period of expanding commerce and industry was both paralleled and facilitated by an increase in the amount and use of money in the European economy. The sources of this new money supply, in addition to the recently activated mines, were the Italo-Byzantine trade, the successful Christian advances against Islam (which produced either booty or tribute), and the thawing out of previously frozen wealth. Monasteries, which held the greatest stores of treasure, were among the leading suppliers, in the eleventh century, of funds for investment. Eleventh-century Italian contracts, which usually specified the form in which payment was to be made, reveal an outpouring of hoarded wealth, mostly gold and silver jewelry, into the economy.[50] And, as mentioned at the outset, the reconstruction of the cathedral church of Orléans close to the year A.D. 1000 was financed by buried treasure. Whereas at Chalon in the sixth century King Gunthram had no other thought than to have the unearthed treasure re-shaped so that he could offer it to a religious shrine, at Orléans the bishop dedicated the gold his workers found to a large, unproductive religious shrine without tying up the gold itself in a religious object; the bishop got his church—more than one, in fact—but also released the gold into the economy.

From Carolingian times right through to the twelfth century the only type of coin minted was the silver penny (*denarius*). The early Germanic practice of regarding coins as so much precious metal, a practice that blinded them to the abstract values of money and led them to weigh it instead, gave rise to the designation 'pound' for the standard unit of account. The pound of silver was divided into twenty shillings and the shilling into twelve pennies; a mark was equal to two-thirds of a pound. But these pounds, shillings, and marks were mere numerical units. An actual payment of a pound of silver consisted of 240 pennies. There are strong indications that even though documents of the first feudal age very often specified payments in monetary terms, payments were in fact more likely to be made in goods and services. In such cases the monetary terms served as a standard of account.

At the time when Carolingian order and institutions disintegrated, the minting of silver pennies, just as so many other prerogatives of public authority, devolved more and more on to small, localized, even private rather than public, jurisdictions. One of the few pennies to maintain its value and reputation from Carolingian times right into the twelfth century was the one minted at Pavia. The pontifical mint, on the other hand, closed down in about 975 and a Roman penny did not appear again until 1180. One of the critically important new pennies of the mid-twelfth century was issued in the Champagne-fair town of Provins. But the history of coinage in feudal Europe is not as simple as the mention of a few well known mints such as Pavia, Rome, and Provins would make it seem, for minting experienced the same fragmentation and interruptions that every other social activity underwent.[51]

The first silver coin minted that was larger than the penny was the *grossus denarius*, equivalent usually to twelve pennies and variously designated as groat, grooten, groschen, gros, grosso, ducat, solidus, or shilling. Venice issued the first grosso (but worth twenty-four pennies) in the year 1202. The launching of this coin was probably stimulated by the payment of 51,000 marks of silver to the Venetians by the knights of the Fourth Crusade, who convened at Venice in 1201.

Verona followed Venice with a twelve-penny shilling within a year and Florence and Milan a few decades later. By the close of the thirteenth century a corresponding coin was being minted by virtually every important government in western Europe. The continued growth of silver mining and the continued consolidation of feudal governments lay behind this development.[52] The minting of gold coins began in Castile in 1175, and in both Florence and Genoa in 1252. The French and English kings tried to issue similar coins in the middle of the thirteenth century but both failed; Philip IV succeeded only in 1290 and Edward III in 1344.[53] The market was served not only by these coins that were larger and more valuable than the silver penny but by smaller ones as well, like the light coins issued at Pavia, Lucca, and Milan in the middle of the eleventh century, which were more convenient for local commerce.[54]

The great variety of new coins being issued gave the economy a vitality and versatility that a coinage consisting exclusively of silver pennies could not afford. Still, perhaps the most significant development was that the worth of these new coins was not based exclusively on their intrinsic values but on the values attributed to them by the issuing governments.

In order both to amass capital and to spread the risk in a business venture, merchants—with those of northern Italy well in advance—devised various kinds of partnership agreements to regulate the proportions to be contributed by the contracting parties, the responsibilities of each in carrying out the enterprise, and the proportions of any resulting profit each was to get. Every venture involving more than one person necessitated the drawing up of a formal, notarized contract. Merchants held money on deposit from other persons; they exchanged money in varying currencies; and they sometimes extended credit to their depositors by allowing them to overdraw their accounts. In such a way were certain of the essential functions of banking served by merchants, some of whom, as the economy became increasingly specialized in the twelfth and thirteenth centuries, became full-time bankers.[55]

The desire for stability and security, particularly in the banking business, encouraged the formation of lasting—as against *ad hoc*—partnerships, i.e. companies. Italian companies, notably those in Siena, Lucca, and Florence, were the earliest to establish representatives in other places where they sought to do business, initially at fairs but then in cities. The Paris tax rolls for 1292 list over twenty such Italian companies.[56] It is with the formation of the company (in Italy in the twelfth century, north of the Alps by the early thirteenth), which amassed money in order to invest it for profit, and which did not disperse it impulsively in fits of generosity, as individual merchants were wont to do, that an essential element of the capitalist economy made its appearance.[57] A related development took place in commercial accounting, whose critical tool, double-entry book-keeping, was invented in the latter part of the fourteenth century. The narrower profit margins imposed by the contracted economy of that period probably contributed to the need, if not the invention itself, of such accounting.[58]

The bothers and risks of transporting money were minimized by a system that allowed a merchant to deposit a sum of money with a banking firm in one city and to carry a letter of credit to one or several of its branches or correspondents in other locations.[59] Banking thus served the new economy in still another way by creating fiduciary money. Such money was never minted by governments, but on the basis of public confidence in the institutions that said it existed and had value, it was just as useful as if it had been minted.[60]

Bloch's assertion that the middle of the eleventh century marked a turning point can thus still be instructive if, like all such abstractions, it is used with restraint. This turning point marked the end of the invasions in Europe, with their accompaniment of pillage and ostentatious redistribution. It marked the emergence of a wholly different attitude, one that calculated values to see whether any particular activity or transaction would be profitable. It marked the promotion of commerce and industry from their status as marginal activities to the level of key elements in European economic life. Finally, it marked the recognition and use of money as tool instead of as treasure, the release of new types and of vast quantities of specie into circulation, and the appearance of new techniques for the expeditious handling of money.

2

Adapting to the profit economy

The advance of the new economy had reverberations in virtually every institution, social group, geographical area, and nexus of ideas in Latin Christendom. One major problem that arose concerned the size of communities that people lived in and the number and kind of individuals with whom they dealt. Quantitative change in population brought with it qualitative changes in human life. A second problem concerned the kinds of work people did and the nature of the rewards they got for it. The spread of monetary transactions, previously very restricted, into most types of relationship and most areas of activity brought distress to individuals and institutions alike. And a third problem arose from the obsolescence of prevailing Christian morality. It was difficult for some people to adapt to a new social and economic reality when their religion interposed a clearly articulated and divinely sanctioned morality appropriate to an earlier age. Thus life in the new profit economy raised acute problems involving impersonalism, money, and moral uncertainty.

1. URBAN LIFE

During the first feudal age, life at all social levels was conducted in relatively small communities. Most persons were peasants, and the characteristic form of social organization in which they played out their lives was the village. The cities of the age were the shells and reminders of earlier cities; few of them functioned any longer as centres of administration, ceremony, or commerce. The size of village population depended upon factors such as the size and quality of the available arable land, the tools, the animals, the system of land use, and the demands of the non-productive ruling class. Ploughing was done with the superficial scratch plough, suitable to Mediterranean lands but not to the wetter, heavier lands of northern Europe; the principal draught animal was the ox. The lack of good communications and of well organized markets encouraged a tendency toward self-sufficiency, meaning that much of what was produced had to be produced inefficiently. A tentative generalization of agrarian history is that crop yield in this early period was on the order of 2:1, in other words, that it was at bare subsistence level, with one-half of the crop harvested being used as seed for the next crop. Barely a few hundred people could be huddled together in a village, so far did they have to go to reach their furthest fields, so inefficient were the tools and animals at their disposal, and so unproductive were their lands and their own efforts.[1]

The principal social trait of village life derived directly from this fact of small size: every individual in the village knew every other individual in the village. Work bound the community together, for the heavier, more difficult kinds of labour necessitated cooperation. The community was united spiritually in a single church congregation. Often a village was assured further solidarity by the veneration of a local saint. Likewise local variations of speech and custom underscored both identity and solidarity. The village was thus not an agglomeration of so many individuals; it was instead an integral social organism, apart from which none of its individual members could have existed. Except for the pastoral and wood-gathering activities that took peasants away from their homes temporarily, it was not safe for them to go anywhere, at least not far, and there was rarely any place to go.[2]

Members of the land-controlling class lived in large households made up of their families and retainers. Members of the secular clergy, depending on their social status, lived in either a peasant village or a knightly household. As for the regular clergy, the weaker and poorer monastic communities were like modest manors or villages. The monks were not related by blood but they swore fraternal love to one another and filial obedience to their father the abbot. The community had one will only and spoke with one voice; and the monks, notwithstanding the work of God, worked in the fields six days a week. The more powerful and wealthy monastic communities had serfs to work the fields, so with them the style of community was more akin to that of the knightly household. Most monastic communities had between 20 and 30 members; a few reached 100; the largest, Cluny, never exceeded 400.[3]

When the powerful and wealthy travelled, they depended on the hospitality of their peers and vassals. Monks were supposed not to travel at all, except under very special circumstances and strict limitations. At the same time the Benedictine *Rule* emphatically provided for the charitable reception of strangers.[4] But in using the argument that in each stranger whom they received, they in fact received Christ, the Benedictines gave emphasis to the mysterious quality of strangers. Thus the people of pre-commercial Europe, regardless of their social level, typically lived in small, closed groups, typically did not travel about, and typically did not often have dealings with strangers.[5]

The take-off of the European population in the eleventh century was sustained—if not actually caused—by an 'agricultural revolution'. The Commercial Revolution, that is to say, no less than the Industrial, was assisted at the outset by major developments in agricultural technology that made it possible to feed a burgeoning population. The innovations of the eleventh century (not all newly discovered then but only then gaining general currency) consisted in the use of horses (with horse-collars and horseshoes), the use of deep, mould-board ploughs, and the use of systematic crop rotation in combination with improved fertilizing techniques.[6] Specialization, as in the case of wine production mentioned earlier, led to increases in both quantity and quality. These many innovations brought about an overall increment in the crop-yield ratio from 2:1 to 3:1 (a profit increase of 100 per cent).[7]

In spite of these changed agricultural techniques and of the general demographic expansion, village populations did not change appreciably. All aspects of the work to be done were carried out more efficiently than before. The same land was made to yield more; the same number of peasants, with better tools and animals, could cultivate more land; but as a rule there remained the same, general upper limit on the feasible size of a village. At the peak of the population crest of the second feudal age, European villages had on an average between 20 and 30 households, or hearths, i.e., between about 150 and 200 inhabitants. In very exceptional cases the figure might have run as high as 500 or 600.[8]

There are cases on record of villages where, in the twelfth and thirteenth centuries, newcomers were kept away, not because these persons themselves were offensive but because their livestock, so it was feared, would overpopulate the common pastures.[9] Sabina and Latium, the regions to the north, east, and south-east of Rome, afford an example of delicate ecological balance and of the problems created by population expansion. The landlords of those regions reorganized the patterns of habitation and of land use during the tenth century, enclosing the peasants in several hundred small, fortified villages (*castra*). There is a pattern to how the land surrounding each *castrum* was exploited, from the gardens immediately adjoining the walls to the vegetable fields a little further off, and thus on to the orchards, the vineyards, the dry-grain fields, the olive groves, and, ultimately, to the winter pastures below and the summer pastures above. The narrow restriction of space within the *castrum* and the delicate balance between the nutritive needs of its inhabitants and the modest productivity of its lands dictated restraint on demographic expansion. There are some indications of the cultivation nearer to the *castrum* being allowed to expand, and thus to infringe upon the next circle of cultivation, but any more drastic change in this system risked upsetting it entirely. Several *castra* failed utterly and were abandoned even within the age of expanding economy and population, but the causes of failure, which may include ecological imbalance, remain to be studied carefully. In the *castra* that survived, the population was not allowed to expand.[10]

The overall demographic increase of the second feudal age was of the order of about 300 per cent. This figure represents little more than a projection from the rough estimates that have been made for England, with its relatively good documentation, where the population seems to have increased more than three times between the Domesday survey of 1086 and the coming of the Black Death in 1348.[11] Over the same period of time, the amount of land under cultivation in Europe probably doubled and, as already noted, agricultural productivity then improved greatly.[12] These observations, together with the fact that villages did not grow appreciably, impose two further observations. First, wherever new lands were opened up, new villages were set up. This type of internal colonization absorbed the greater share of the population increase. We know for example that in the first decade of the twelfth century, forty planned villages were organized in lands newly open to exploitation near Toulouse.[13] Secondly, a modest but highly significant proportion of the increased population of the period between 1000 and 1300 settled in towns and exercised clearly urban functions; it was then that the urban configuration of pre-industrial Europe took shape.[14]

Urban population figures for this period are not known with precision, but the orders of magnitude and the relative sizes of different towns do seem to command general agreement. In Italy prior to the Black Death, Milan and Venice each attained a population that demographic historians estimate to be around 100,000. Next came a group of cities with a population of 50,000–75,000—Florence, Genoa, Rome, and Bologna. A score of towns, among them Cremona, Brescia, and Padua ranged between 10,000 and 50,000. Over 150 other communities, scattered up and down the peninsula, attained populations of between 2,000 and 10,000.[15]

In France, the largest city was Paris. The miniscule tenth-century community huddled on the island spread to both banks of the Seine and by the mid-fourteenth century had a population close to 100,000. Narbonne reached a peak of 30,000 and Toulouse of 25,000. France had a group of towns with a population of about 10,000 that included Rouen, Bourges, Dijon, and Bordeaux; below that came another 50 towns with a few thousand people.[16]

The leading towns of the Iberian peninsula, Barcelona, Cordova, and Seville, all had populations over 35,000; Lisbon and Valencia over

10,000. The greatest town of Germany by far was Cologne, with as many as 50,000 people, while altogether about 50 German towns had populations over 2,000.[17] Ghent, with over 55,000 people, was the largest town of the Low Countries, that area of Europe other than Lombardy with the highest proportion of people living in urban communities. Brussels and Bruges were close behind Ghent. Ypres had perhaps 20,000 and other towns such as Louvain and Liège around 10,000. In England, the figures for London rose to about 50,000, while those for York and Bristol followed at 15,000.[18] The evidence for this growing urban population comes from such diverse sources as tax records based on the unit of the hearth (historians are obliged to estimate a fixed number of people per hearth), town-wall construction and repair (which reached their respective peaks in the late twelfth and late thirteenth centuries), and the foundation charters and speculators' advertising that attest to completely new villages and towns. This was the age of the Newtown, Newport, Niewpoort, Neustadt, Villanova, and Villeneuve.[19]

As with the village, the definition of a town or city (the terms are here used interchangeably) rests upon two separate but related factors: the number and the occupations of its inhabitants. The community wholly devoted to agriculture had, as we have seen, a naturally and culturally determined upper limit in population size of a few hundred. The numerical limit for a town, on the other hand, is a minimum, best expressed vaguely as a few thousand. We must explain why this is so and then add a word about the communities that fell into neither category.

European towns had (and some still have) gardens within their walls, besides other gardens and vineyards immediately outside the walls. Town-dwellers who worked in such gardens or vineyards were part of the primary (i.e., food-producing) sector of the economy, along with nearly everybody who lived in the countryside. Another rural function closely related to agriculture, i.e., tool-making and repairing, also found a corresponding place in towns; indeed, the manorial workshop all but disappeared in the twelfth century as town artisans rendered it obsolete.[20] But the determining characteristic of a town is the presence there of people engaged in many other specialized kinds of work: industrial workers, merchants who dealt in long-distance trade and travelled to fairs and to other towns, petty traders who retailed in local shops and markets, lawyers and notaries, school masters, entertainers, government officials, servants, waiters, porters, butchers, and bakers. Toulouse had 177 butchers; Frankfurt, which was about half the size of Toulouse, had 88 butchers and 101 bakers. Montbrison, a market town of 2,000 people near Lyons, supported twelve butchers in the thirteenth century.[21]

The bakers obviously produced something by their labour, and no one questioned that butchers, servants and water-carriers did hard work. They and the artisans and the industrial workers constituted the secondary sector of the society. The utterly new sector, however, consisted of those engaged in tertiary occupations: the merchants, the bankers, the industrial entrepreneurs, and the professionals. This sector was dominant in urban life, not because it constituted a majority of the population in any one city, but because it was in command of the new market economy and eventually derived therefrom considerable wealth and commensurate political power.[22] The people in this sector did not appear to 'produce' anything. Ancestors of the modern 'white-collar workers', they manipulated words, or in some instances they sought to manipulate people through the use of words. They argued, they kept records, they drew up contracts, they negotiated, they bought and sold, they hired and fired, they told stories and sang, they lectured, and they wrote books and letters.[23] They also listened and read, watched and were entertained.

The borderline between village and town, between the purely agricultural community and a community dominated by people engaged in tertiary occupations, is thus defined numerically as somewhere between a few hundred and a few thousand. This may seem to blur the focus on those communities that fall within the intervening category. But in fact the attempts of historical geographers to identify and characterize the 'small town' (under 2,000 people) leads to a sort of limbo (*Agrarstädte*, agrarian towns), where there is a market but no very thriving business, and where agriculture retains the dominant role in the community's income.[24] Contemporary urban sociologists set the minimum population for the communities they wish to study at various levels, depending on the needs of their investigations, from 10,000 down to 2,500;[25] the International Commission of Urban History has set the figure at 2,000.[26]

A revealing indication of the size of urban communities in Latin Christian society comes from the administrative organization of the Dominican Order. One of the basic purposes of the present study is to define precisely the connections between urban society and the Franciscan and Dominican Orders, and an argument will be developed to show that the spirituality of the orders was directly and concretely determined by the essential characteristics of thirteenth-century society. It may seem tautological to introduce into this discussion of the quantitative definition of towns a rule about how big a community had to be for one of the mendicant orders to establish a convent there. Our main purpose, after all, is to define the religious groups in terms of urban society and not *vice versa*. However, the early friars were innocent of numbers. They settled only in urban communities, to be sure, and did so with a considerable, and conscious, sociological awareness. Yet they were still, as Jacques Le Goff has said, of a pre-statistical mentality. By the early fifteenth century, on the other hand, when the Dominicans and Franciscans had existed for more than two centuries and when Europeans had become far more agile in the manipulation of numbers, the organization of a Dominican convent in the Breton town of Guérande was petitioned and granted on the grounds, among others, that the level of population—more than 3,000 inhabitants—was above the necessary minimum. Well after the sociological, urban fact, therefore, the friars gave a numerical definition of the communities in which they settled.[27]

A community where everybody could not know everybody else on a face-to-face, personal basis by name offered both the opportunities and risks of anonymity. 'City air makes one free after a year and a day' (*Stadtluft macht frei nach Jahr und Tag*), said the twelfth-century German legal adage, meaning that a serf who escaped to town and was able to stay there for a year and a day without being caught was henceforth legally free of his servile status and obligations.[28] Yet studies have shown that people who emigrated to towns came from no greater distance than about fifteen miles (the length of a day's journey).[29] Whole urban neighbourhoods were often made up of people from the same village or at least the same section of the countryside. The parish church became the focal point of social and spiritual life, thus in many ways assuming the functions of a village community. The guilds also served an important social function, for apart from their protection of the collective economic interests of the members, guilds provided a sense of identity and a full range of social security measures for their members. Conviviality and fraternity, overlaid with some form of religious identity, appear to have motivated the early formation of guilds.[30] Therefore neighbourhoods, parish churches, and guilds provided groups in which urban dwellers could gain feelings of belonging, friendship, and identity in the midst of an environment where they had daily contact with strangers.

Anonymity can breed crime, or at least allow it to flourish. Brigands formerly had only the forest in which to hide; now they had towns as well. Old villages presumably had the protection of a feudal lord. Villages newly formed in the twelfth century had to have adequate protection guaranteed by a powerful individual or institution. In towns the gates were controlled and the streets patrolled at night, but these efforts did not prevent towns from being either a rich source or a welcome haven for criminals, especially thieves.[31] Prostitution also thrives on anonymity, that is, the anonymity that protects its clients. Victorian social reformers who wrote histories of prostitution confused extra-marital sex of many sorts with prostitution. But prostitution is meant here in the narrower sense of an organized profession in which women are sold to men for fixed periods of time. Statutes forbidding, or more commonly regulating, prostitution appear in Castile and France and Italy and Germany and England in the twelfth century. Mid-thirteenth-century statutes at Avignon specified the neighbourhoods where prostitutes could operate. The same can be said for Mainz, Toulouse, Sandwich, Barcelona, Pistoia, or Hamburg. Prostitutes, whether formally organized in a guild or not, typically venerated Mary Magdalene as their patron saint.[32] London, with fewer than 30,000 people at the close of the twelfth century, was described by Richard of Devizes, who in turn relied heavily on Horace's *Satires*, as abounding in seamy, squalid types, from the pimps and gamblers to the belly-dancers and the 'infinite number of parasites'.[33] Rome, as pilgrimage site, combined the anonymity of a large city with the anonymity of travel; the Eternal City lived off transiency.[34]

A new style of education also found a healthy climate in the towns. The critical factor was not so much anonymity as the concentration of population and of surplus wealth. The pre-commercial European village offered no formal instruction. There the education of children was a spontaneous and continuous activity of all members of the community, directed, though not consciously, towards making children assume the same abilities, feelings, and points of view as those held by their elders, towards making them, in other words, literally replace their elders. Formal instruction for a few young people could be found in monasteries, but the goal there was to indoctrinate novices into the life and thought of the monastic tradition. At its most abstract level, monastic education encouraged reflection on and elucidation of a given truth, but not a quest for new truth.[35]

The formal education provided by the urban, usually episcopal, schools, which began in Italy early in the eleventh century and in the northern countries later in the century, served the rational and impersonal goal of training students to develop their intellectual capacities and of imparting to the more capable ones a competence in some particular discipline. This was mainly accomplished through the emphasis placed on training in dialectic. The distinctive mode of teaching and learning was the disputation. This exalting and disciplining of contentiousness inside the classroom was reinforced by the organizing of competitive sports within and even between schools (some trade and labour groups also had teams), such as the football games in London mentioned by one of Thomas Becket's biographers.[36] Whereas the earlier forms of education provided for the full integration of the young into society as it then stood, the education of the schools prepared some young people for the contentious situations in which they would later find themselves in their society; the schools also prepared students to criticize contemporary practices and institutions and to seek their reform. The earlier style of education reinforced the solidarity of the given primary group, the village, or of the adopted primary group, the monastery. The city schools, on the other hand, were a crucial factor in breaking down the integration of traditional life.[37]

Masters and students congregated in towns and also travelled about from one town to another. The monastic scholar Rupert of Deutz was scandalized both by the life led by masters and students in town and by their continual moving about. He recalled with evident satisfaction that he had never gone wandering from town to town, like some itinerant merchant, in search of the latest intellectual fads.[38] Peter Abelard (died 1142), on the other hand, epitomized the wandering scholar of the type Rupert had criticized. When some of his work had been condemned and he went off into the wilderness, Abelard in a sense proved the sociological rules concerning the urban schools by violating them. He observed that his rivals, those who had done their utmost to hurt him, now lamented his obvious success. Success had followed him even far away from cities and the market place, from controversies and the crowded ways of men.

Secretly my rivals complained and lamented one to another, saying, 'See how the whole world runs after him; we have accomplished nothing by persecuting him except to increase his fame. We tried to extinguish his name, but we have only made it shine still brighter. While in cities students have got everything at hand that they could need, instead they spurn the pleasures of city life, seek out the barrenness of solitude, and willingly make themselves wretched.'[39]

Formal education and formal prostitution were present in towns for separate reasons, yet the two were sometimes related. Such a connection did not escape the attention of James of Vitry in Paris: 'In one and the same house,' he wrote, 'there were schools above and brothels below. On the floor above, masters lectured; below them, whores exercised their depraved profession. In one part the whores quarrelled among themselves or with their pimps, while in the other clerks engaged in their disputations.'[40] Again, it is not the sexual behaviour itself that is of interest but the quintessential urban fact of the simultaneous development of two temporary professions, prostitute and student, which both drew on young people separated from family, household, priest, or village, and which were related to each other by the anonymous, impersonal medium of money. When St Louis set up a home for girls rescued from the wayward life, he initially intended to lodge them in the Latin Quarter, but then decided his venture would have a greater chance for success if carried out beyond the walls of the right bank.[41]

Town life engendered problems of physical as well as of moral health and safety. The high concentration of persons and dwellings led to a persistent danger of fire. 'The only plagues of London', wrote William fitz Stephen in the course of a panegyric that strains credulity as much as the diatribe by Richard of Devizes, 'are the immoderate drinking of fools and the frequency of fires'; indeed London was among the first towns to organize fire-fighting.[42] The rationalizing and specializing society also removed some of the sick from their homes in order to isolate them in hospitals. Toulouse alone erected seven leproseries and twelve hospitals, the first in 1080 and most of the others about a century later.[43] An especially acute urban problem concerned the removal of waste. Whereas the low density of rural population minimized the health hazards of waste and the unpleasantness of barnyard odours, the accumulation of waste in town threatened health and offended sensibilities. The most unpleasant, and therefore lowly, of the foul trades was that of the latrine cleaners.[44] City air could make one sick, or at least uncomfortable.

Another characteristic of town life was the presence of the poor. The term 'poor' is relative, referring to such conditions as weakness in relation to power, illness in relation to good health, or a lack of money. The urban poor had characteristics of their own. Even in strictly material terms, the sources of urban poverty differed from those of rural poverty, for the wage-earner in a city was vulnerable to the fluctuations of an uncontrolled market economy. Particularly on the lower levels of the urban economy, work was not only low-paid but irregular. To be sure, some of the urban poor had immigrated from the countryside. The immediate proximity of those who were successful in the tertiary occupations to those, wherever they came from, who lacked a fixed domicile and a steady supply of food made the problem of urban poverty all the more apparent. Thus the presence of mendicants became a fixture in the city and in the consciousness of city-dwellers. Richard of Devizes included beggars in his list of types that made up London's 'infinite number of parasites'.[45]

The problems raised by leaving village life for that of the town were not reserved to a single generation of eleventh-century immigrants but were faced by every generation throughout the second feudal age. On the basis of the limited evidence available and of a few case studies made thus far, town populations not only did not expand but could not even remain stable by themselves, having to rely instead upon immigration.[46] The average age of females at marriage, some studies have shown, was just slightly higher in cities than in the country (fifteen years as against thirteen), while instead the average age of males at marriage was dramatically and significantly higher in cities (late twenties or early thirties as against early twenties). Men apparently perceived wives and children as assets in a rural setting, whereas in towns they had to establish fortunes more on their own. In any case, urban males had available during their bachelorhood forms of distraction and entertainment less readily available to their rural counterparts. The overall population, in the terms used by demographic historians, had a high sex ratio (number of males per one hundred females). At birth the ratio was c:105, and at forty 120–30 (accounted for by the very high death rate among women in the child-bearing years). But the larger the community, the lower the sex ratio. There being an average age difference of nearly fifteen years between husbands and wives, widows became a characteristic feature of the urban population. Thus the adult population of cities had a considerably greater number of females than males, on the order of 1,200 women to 1,000 men, or, expressed in terms of the sex ratio, 83.3. To sum up, in those cases where detailed studies of urban populations have been carried out, the evidence shows that at any given time a large part of the population of a city (perhaps one-third or even one-half) consisted of people who had immigrated from the country, and thus the individual experience of encountering and then having to cope with urban complexity and impersonalism was a continually recurring phenomenon.[47]

2. THE USES OF MONEY

Once money was no longer buried with the dead or hoarded as treasure it became an instrument of exchange that worked its way into every type of human activity and transaction. A few examples from government, the church, the rural economy, and the urban economy will illustrate this point.

The keystone of feudal government was the personal agreement between lord and vassal to exchange protection for advice and military support. By the early twelfth century, this personal agreement began to be replaced by a money payment. The old obligation of an annual forty-day period of military service was not practical in some new jurisdictions that embraced distances of several hundred miles. But a knight could now fulfil his military obligation by paying scutage (shield money), and his lord in turn could hire mercenaries when and where and for as long as he wanted.[48] The *fief-rente*, an annual income of money granted by lords to men in return for their loyalty and services, is an institution that shows an old relationship redefined in monetary terms. It had its beginnings in the eleventh century in those areas of north-western Europe where a money economy early became dominant; soon it was found throughout western Europe.[49] The amalgamation of feudal principalities into national kingdoms is mostly a story of wars and strategic marriages, but in France there is the odd case of the county of Mâcon, which the crown bought outright from the count in 1239.[50] A decade and a half later, the pope had the crown of the Kingdom of Sicily to dispose of and he offered it at a price to various princes.[51]

On a more regular basis, the encroachment of the profit economy on government is apparent in the development of bureaucracy. Feudal vassals had long served as advisers and judges without any formal training whatever; now, just as certain military obligations were commuted by money payment, the vassals' unpaid counsel gave way to a system that involved the levying of taxes and the hiring of specially trained, salaried bureaucrats by governments. Bureaucrats were perhaps expensive, but they knew their work well and their interests were not opposed to the growth of their employers' prerogatives and powers. The same could not be said for the advisory service rendered by vassals, however well-meaning. The law was becoming too complex for them to understand and the anti-feudal agressiveness of central governments too strong to allow vassals their customary ease and utility at court.[52] The feudal opponents of centralization, too, resorted to hiring lawyers of their own.[53]

Ecclesiastical governments, in particular that of the Bishop of Rome, whose judicial business increased immensely between 1050 and 1300, sought capable administrators. The papal chancery of the twelfth century was considerably in advance of other European chanceries. Papal government generally was so advanced that in many areas of administration it set the style for other governments to follow.[54] Above all, the administration of justice changed Rome from a mere pilgrimage site, however important, to the seat of an extensive and enormously expensive bureaucracy; and nearly every operation of the papal government required a money payment, whether a salary, a tax, a fee, a fine, or a bribe. The papal court was a labyrinth in which every corner and curve was jealously guarded by a toll-keeper, so that proctors who came there on behalf of far-off ecclesiastical corporations soon found themselves rolling in what one historian has called 'the tangled briar-patch, the sticky tar-pit, that surrounded the holy purpose of the Roman curia'.[55] Even if the system were completely honest, and only inefficient, a proctor's biggest problem consisted in getting through to a competent and responsible official in the court and, while waiting, staying alive in Rome. A proctor could, over a period of a few months, quite helplessly dissipate a substantial allowance on food, lodging, and bribes to doorkeepers and secretaries. So expensive and so uncertain were proctors' missions, that some corporations preferred to engage the services of professional resident proctors in Rome. By the second half of the thirteenth century such specialists had taken over a considerable proportion of the lobbying activities at the court.[56] By their experience with the complexities of the system and of the individuals who ran the system, resident proctors were able to get better results for their clients. But like guides who take pilgrims or tourists around to a number of carefully selected and expensive restaurants, the resident proctors had an interest in perpetuating the system.

The sale of church offices, a major preoccupation of ecclesiastical reformers in the eleventh century, was less a new practice than a new perception. The granting of an office in return for a payment was the old gift and counter-gift, newly seen in the eyes of the eleventh century as a sale and hence identified as the heresy of simony. Similarly the established tradition of making a gift to a monastery upon the entry of a new member, a 'gift' that often involved lengthy negotiations between the abbey and the entrant's family, had henceforth to be called into question and its legitimacy examined.[57]

At the same time there was indeed corruption, as in the case of the canons of Arezzo, who were reported to be so busy getting rich that they had to hire mercenary priests to conduct services of worship.[58] A twelfth-century complaint mentions those faint-hearted clerics with benefices who cannot get out of bed when offices are to be sung but who later show up at *spectacula*.[59] The blatantly simoniac Archbishop Manasses of Reims is supposed to have said: 'The archbishopric of Reims would be a good thing, if only one did not have to sing mass because of it.'[60] In 1139 the Second Lateran Council condemned clerics who accept money for administering sacraments; just over 75 years later, the Fourth Lateran Council repeated the condemnation.[61] Some thirteenth-century councils attest to companies of mercenary priests who contracted with bishops to take over the preaching of parishes or even of entire dioceses for extended periods. The councils condemned and tried to curtail the activities of these pulpit condottieri.[62]

The pilgrim had a special association with money, for the very symbols of his condition were the staff he held in one hand and the purse he carried over one shoulder. His mobility depended in part on the convenient transferability of some of his wealth. Such sculptured figures appear in churches all along the great pilgrimage routes.[63] Jesus, too, is transformed into a pilgrim, complete with staff and purse, in an eleventh-century relief at Silos, in Spain, and in a twelfth-century fresco at Sant'Angelo in Formis (near Naples), when he

31

appears in the traditional scene on the road to Emmaus and meets two of the Apostles.[64] Some churches and monasteries organized fund-raising confraternities that secured funds for church construction and spiritual benefits for their members. The practice first appeared in England when Bishop Gilbert Foliot planned the completion of St Paul's in 1175.[65] Around 1200, Robert of Marmion gave £500 to the monks of St Mary of Barbery so that they could build a church and so that he would not have to go to Jerusalem as he had vowed he would, and also so that his soul and those of Philippa his wife and of all of his ancestors and descendants would be saved.[66] Five hundred pounds went a long way. At Canterbury in 1186, Archbishop Baldwin launched a seven-year campaign for construction of a church to honour St Thomas. Those who contributed annually received a one-third reduction on all penances. The treasurer's accounts for Canterbury show that, between 1198 and 1206, the monks received an average annual income of £1,400, of which £426 came from offerings, of which in turn £349 were collected at the two Becket shrines. Overall, the martyr produced one-fourth of Canterbury's income.[67]

In addition to government and the church, the rural economy became imbued with money. The new urban populations had to be fed, and this fact spurred the countryside to turn away from subsistence farming in order to organize for the market. Land values and the prices of the main agricultural products rose three times and more, so that the landlords were among those who benefited most from the new economy. Land in the hands of secular lords along with that of monasteries, moreover, was used as capital for some of the original ventures in trade.[68] The obligations of peasants to supply their lords with fixed quantities of certain agricultural products came increasingly in the eleventh and twelfth centuries to be expressed in terms of a money payment. Similarly, peasant obligations of service to the lord could be and often were commuted, at least partially, by money payments. The payments generally covered the cost of hiring labourers and left something in the way of a profit for the landlord.[69]

Greatly improved techniques of farming gave the peasant some chance of growing a surplus, which he then exchanged at the market for cash. In such a way some peasants were able to purchase their freedom from servile obligations; henceforth they paid rent. The activities of peasants who could be considered manorial artisans were, as previously pointed out, largely superseded by the work of urban craftsmen, who exchanged their products on the market for money. Those peasants who left the soil to work in the new types of industry not only worked for wages but, unlike the craftsmen, were not able to accompany the artifact on which they worked through all its stages.

The complexity and differentiation of industrial processes removed the workers further and further from any sense of close and creative ties with their work.[70]

The role of money in the urban economy is self-evident, at least in trade and finance, but it was also essential to the other activities that thrived in an urban setting, for example learning, and the concomitant opportunities for social advancement. Here, indeed, were commodities not available in the feudal, monastic world. A new profession of specialists in teaching, the *magistri*, appeared and along with it the problem of how the masters were going to be supported. The schools, under episcopal control, and later the universities, under papal control, charged fees.[71] The families of students had to pay these fees, although some bishops provided scholarships for worthy and promising, but needy, young men.[72] Of course only a very few people ever got into the schools and even fewer continued beyond the arts course into the advanced sciences of theology, law, or medicine. They soon found out they could continue only if sufficient money was available.[73] The trouble with such a system was that student motives had now to be questioned. 'They consider that riches only are the fruit of wisdom,' lamented Master John of Salisbury.[74] Indeed, the medical doctors, notaries, and lawyers who completed their schooling then did their work, like teachers, in return for cash fees.[75]

What is it about the character of money that made it so universally pervasive and useful? There is nothing random or casual about the substitution of a money payment for a payment in kind or for a personal relationship of trust. Money is a medium of exchange with very particular characteristics: it is concentrated, mobile wealth. A quantity of agricultural produce surely represents wealth and can for some time be stored or chemically preserved. But that time is limited, whereas money by definition is wealth in safekeeping; it is, in relation to the chronological scale of human life, adequately durable. Moreover, even if the chemical transformation of some products could guarantee them a lengthy duration, money would still have the important advantage of being compact and mobile.

The relationship between money and urban society follows directly from the definitions thus far presented. Urban society is a society so large as to include total or at least partial strangers. The reason that these strangers can deal with one another is that they are willing to receive money in exchange for goods they give others or services they render others. 'Money', said Max Weber, 'is the most abstract and impersonal element that exists in personal life.'[76] This impersonal medium of exchange, which even a stranger would accept, is the vital fluid of the urban organism.

The technical effect of money on the enormous bulk of material goods in the economy of the eleventh century is not unlike the effect

33

of computers on the bulk of information in our own society. Both involve reduction in size, standardization of measurement, and depersonalization. Just as computers, despite their demonstrated usefulness, often provoke a hostile, or at least ambivalent, reaction, money was not everywhere greeted with enthusiasm and joy. It is indeed impersonal, as Weber emphasized, and it can have corrosive, ultimately destructive, effects. For this reason money can be repulsive at the same time as it is attractive. Such a dual nature was fully appreciated in a society whose entire mode of thought was markedly dualistic. The same society was accustomed to the trickery of the devil, who would lure the unwary with sweet smells that turned to foul stenches, or with shiny coins that turned to excrement. A goliardic poem advised bloated wallets to go to Rome, where there was physic for constipated purses.[77] An English sermon rationalized the pecuniary penance as a laxative for purses.[78] Walter of Châtillon advised that no one could get anywhere in an episcopal court if his purse had not yet vomited.[79] Peter Damian denounced simony as 'the first of all the heresies to burst from the bowels of the devil'.[80] A priest named Alberic at Fourgères in Brittany was exposed for stealing the collection money in his own church. He would slip coins up one sleeve and catch them in his garments. Further investigation revealed that this surreptitious accumulator of coins had laid a cross on the altar and then smeared it with human excrement.[81] By the end of the thirteenth century or very beginning of the fourteenth, the pictorial theme of men and also of apes defecating coins made its appearance in the margins of gothic manuscripts. In one of these drawings a worried-looking ape, with his right paw under his chin and his left paw under his knee, defecates three coins into a golden bowl.[82] Another shows a hybrid man defecating coins into a bowl held by an ape.[83] A similar notion of money as filthy and disgusting waste, while not anal in imagery, is seen in the picture of a monster-head vomiting gold coins into a golden bowl.[84] How different was the mentality behind these drawings from the one that, in the ninth and tenth centuries, used depictions of royal and imperial coins to decorate sacred books.[85] An Ottonian Gospel book, or entire Bible, like so many gold coins bearing the portraits of emperors, was more a sacred object to be treasured than a tool to be used. But where money was treated by everybody as an everyday object, it was more subject to disdainful expressions of disgust on the part of those who depended on it. Freud directed modern attention to the association of money with excrement and his findings have been corroborated by psychological anthropologists working in some twenty-five different cultures. Ambivalence towards money has therefore hardly been limited to Latin Christian society, but it was notably pronounced there during the early generations of the profit-seeking monetary economy.[86]

3. CHRISTIAN MORALITY

The accelerated specialization of functions and permeation of specie into the society of the second feudal age marked the passage from what Durkheim called 'mechanical' to 'organic solidarity'.[87] In the former, most people did the same things in life, and they did so without careful reflection or formal training. The morality in such a society was relatively simple, fixed, and, by its own definition, unchanging. In the latter, though, more akin to the second feudal age, individuals laboured at highly differentiated tasks and often confronted problems of choice; hence morality in such a setting was relatively complex, discussable, and impermanent. In the second feudal age, a major moral issue was that the leading urban professions, like money itself, were simultaneously pursued and scorned. The received tradition was in fact biased against all the main elements of the new economy: against cities, against money, and against the urban professions.

From the sixth through the eleventh centuries in the West, when the separate and self-sufficient Benedictine rural estate remained the ideal setting for living the religious life, any flight from cities existed only in traditional Christian and Benedictine rhetoric. At most, the complexities of subsistence, protection, marriage, and other such worldly involvements—but not urban life—were avoided by monks. There were virtually no cities from which to flee. The socio-religious novelty of the second feudal age is that a virtually all-Christian society, liking it or not, underwent urbanization. The guardians of conscience were not prepared with an ideology or an ethic favourable to urban life. On the contrary, we see, for example, St Bernard, the most energetic religious figure of the twelfth century, storm into Paris and with Old-Testament passion and imagery urge students to get out of town. The origins of cities were traced back to Cain by several writers, and one made the specific complaint that town life forced on people the economic imposition of weights and measures and military imposition of walls; the first ended the innocence of pre-urban exchanges and the second substituted segregation for familiarity.[88]

Attitudes towards money did not shift abruptly from one of awe before precious treasure to one of habitual acceptance of it as a practical, everyday tool. In something of an intervening stage, money was seen as an instrument of exchange that had devil-like, magical powers of luring people and then of corrupting them. The traditional theological programme of the virtues and vices invested in avarice some of these same powers. The major sources of our knowledge about attitudes towards money include the writings about and representations of avarice, and an abundant satirical literature of the twelfth century complements these quasi-official viewpoints.

Until the end of the tenth century, pride was unreservedly dominant as the most important vice; writers who dealt with avarice tended to reduce it to a sub-category of pride.[89] But in the eleventh century, Peter Damian heralded a significant change when stating unequivocally: 'Avarice is the root of all evil.'[90] Peter advised the archbishop of his native city of Ravenna in 1043 that avarice was the most serious problem in the church at that time.[91] Over two decades later he characterized the leading problem in contemporary monastic life as the love of money. For the individual monk the question was how best to preserve his treasure, which was Jesus Christ, and the answer, which we will look at more closely further on, began: 'First of all, get rid of money, for Christ and money do not go well together in the same place.'[92] These themes were picked up again and again in the following generations. 'There is no worse vice than avarice,' wrote John of Salisbury.[93] It impeded the pure worship of God, in the view of Peter Lombard.[94] To St Bernard, cupidity was a serious sin that could be found behind every crime. 'An avaricious man,' he said, 'is like hell.'[95] And towards the end of the twelfth century, Alan of Lille wrote: 'Avarice weakens friendship, generates hatred, breeds anger, plants wars, nourishes controversies, and ruptures the bonds of children to their parents.'[96] Pride in the meantime did not surrender its place of pre-eminence but was henceforth constrained to share that place with avarice.

The personification of avarice had several guises. He could appear as a small, crouching figure, his distorted mouth open, at the ready to devour, while he retains the matter accumulated in moneybags. In this connection, Innocent III later observed that avarice and hell were similar in the way they both consume but do not digest. Avarice also appeared with his mouth tightly closed, his fists clenched desperately about two sacks, and with a cat-headed serpent licking one ear. This anal compulsive accumulator also appeared as a fat monster stooping over an enormous bag suspended from his neck. But avarice himself was not always grotesque. At Chartres, *avaritia*, for grammatical reasons a female, sits by a money chest sorting and counting coins. Avarice can even be represented as a rather distinguished-looking person, both handsome and well-dressed, but with a moneybag pulling at his neck and with a dragon-serpent lurking nearby or a grotesque devil right behind. Where avarice is shown being punished in a sculpted relief on a church near Parma, his neck is bent by the weight of a huge moneybag, another bag hangs from each shoulder, by his side stands a devil who yanks out his teeth with pincers, and above him another devil presses down the weight of a treasure chest that he carries on his back.[97]

A theme closely related to that of avarice is the one of Lazarus and the rich man (Luke 16:19–31). Lazarus was a beggar who stood by the door of a rich man's house, waiting in vain for a scrap from the sumptuous table inside; only the rich man's dogs showed compassion, licking the sores on his diseased body. When Lazarus died, his soul was taken to heaven to the bosom of Abraham, whereas when the rich man died, his soul went to face eternal torment in hell. The attributes of the rich man are similar to those of avarice, for when the rich man dies, we see under the bed his moneybags with big, slimy serpents coiled about them. The rich man's soul, moreover, is poked into a gaping hell mouth by a devil who gleefully wields a pitchfork.[98]

Avarice and the Lazarus story appear together on the porch of the monastic church at Moissac. On the right side of this porch, the pilgrim newly arrived sees at eye level the tall, distinguished figures of the Annunciation and the Visitation. Above them he sees the Adoration of the Magi and the Holy Family. And in the top layer of these scenes, all dealing with the infancy of Christ, he sees the fall of the idols of Heliopolis, the Flight into Egypt, and the Presentation in the Temple. Another world awaits this pilgrim on the left-hand side of the same porch, executed in the second decade of the twelfth century. Here the movement is from top to bottom. One sees the sumptuous banquet of the rich man and, lying on the ground outside, Lazarús, poor and sick, with the two compassionate dogs licking his painful sores. Still at the top, Lazarus is shown at rest, comfortably nestled in the bosom of Abraham. Half way down, the rich man dies. Grotesque monsters yank out his soul, while another grasps his moneybags. Then we see the demons punishing him. The rich man is weighted down with a moneybag; the demons press and pull his twisted body. At the lowest level, finally, the story is further abstracted. While on one side the erogenous zones of unchastity are devoured by lizards and snakes, on the other side avarice is punished. A seated miser, with his legs crossed and an air of self-satisfaction, has his hands in a moneybag. There is a devil perched on his shoulders, perhaps pounding on his head. In front of the miser (but badly mutilated in its present condition) stands a beggar.[99] The two sides of the Moissac porch clearly portray a view of reality made up of two utterly opposed and contrasting, but rather evenly balanced, universal forces.

The satirical approach to dealing with the corrosive power of money was in full force by the early twelfth century in the *Translation of the Relics of Saints Gold and Silver*. This is the story of the Archbishop of Toledo's visit to the papal court in search of a favour. He came laden with relics of the saintly martyrs Albinus and Rufinus (white and red, standing respectively for silver and gold), and at each stage of his progress through the court, he had to produce some of these relics—kidneys of Albinus, ribs of Rufinus—in order to get what he wanted.[100] A similar spirit pervades both the roughly contemporaneous *Gospel According to the Mark of Silver* and a version of the traditional acclamation, 'Christ conquers, Christ reigns, Christ rules the world', in which money takes the place of Christ: *Nummus vincit, Nummus regnat, Nummus imperat.*[101]

In the early stages of the profit economy, the received tradition was as unfriendly to commercial activity as it was to cities and money. Canon law had consistently maintained that it is difficult to avoid sin in the course of buying and selling. The particular formulation, however old the ideas, occurred in a letter of Pope Leo the Great (440–461) to the bishop of Narbonne.[102] It is quoted in all the early compilations of canons, and remains in all the great works of the eleventh and early twelfth centuries, including the *Decretum* of Gratian in 1140.[103] Canon law also perpetuated this dictum: 'A merchant is rarely or never able to please God.'[104]

Gratian's distinction between clergy and laity specifies that the former should have no personal property, but instead hold everything in common, while the latter may possess temporal things, but only to the limit of what they can use.[105] A tenth-century monk reported on one of the Frisian merchant settlements near the mouth of the Rhine. He described the merchants as wicked and lawless men, who habitually pooled their resources to pay for unbridled orgies.[106] The clear moral preference of the age was for agricultural and pastoral labour, with the subsequent place of honour given to house-building (after food comes shelter).[107] An anonymous eleventh-century work refers to the base profession of merchants (*ignobilis mercatura*).[108] In his dialogue on Christian theology, Honorius of Autun (early twelfth century) has a disciple ask the master about the various states of lay life and their relationship to salvation. When asked about the chances that merchants have, the master says they have only a slight chance because virtually everything they have they get by fraud, lies, and selfish desire for gain. Asked what he had to say about those who till the soil, the master said that for the most part they would be saved, because they live simply and they feed the people of God by the sweat of their brows.[109] Peter Lombard (*c.*1100–60), whose work had such widespread currency, also reiterated that merchants cannot perform their duties without sinning.[110]

The effect of these general views in a specific case can be seen in the refusal of the Bishop of Arezzo in 1033 to grant the local merchants an exemption they sought from paying a particular tithe. He pointed out to them: 'How grave a sin it is not to give tithes to God (which the poorest peasants never dare withhold from the just labour of their hands), from the profits of your trade, which you rarely if ever exercise without dangers of grave fraud and without the crime of perjury.'[111] Thus peasants do work that is just and they are steadfastly loyal; neither of these things could be said of merchants.

The increasingly common presence of usurers in towns from the eleventh century onwards inspired a wealth of moral condemnations of moneylending that had accumulated since the time of Moses. The fathers of the Third Lateran Council (1179) noted that usury was flourishing nearly everywhere as if it were a licit enterprise.[112] 'Peter has gone travelling,' wrote John of Salisbury about the papacy, 'leaving his house to the moneychangers.'[113] Peter the Chanter's denunciation covered not only the usurers but also those who protect them: 'The detestable usurers are now the bosom companions of princes and prelates, who surrender to the blandishments of the moneybags and promote their sons to the highest posts in Church and State.'[114] William of Auxerre referred to usury in the early thirteenth century as an intrinsically vicious traffic, practised constantly and without cessation as if it were a proper business or way of gaining a living.[115] Robert of Courçon was aware of usury 'universally infecting society', and not without the interested protection of lay and ecclesiastical authorities.[116]

Tradition was less unreservedly hostile to other urban activities but still it cast doubt on their legitimacy. It did not, for example, regard the practice of law as dishonourable, but once lawyers started to collect fees some people wondered if lawyers had the right to sell advice and information. An analogous dilemma faced the masters who taught in the city schools; had they the right to sell knowledge, it was asked, since tradition taught that knowledge is a gift of God, whence it may not be sold?[117]

The punishments depicted in sculpture and literature dramatize the moral risks taken by the new urban professionals. A realistically carved scene on the cathedral of Reims shows a dishonest cloth merchant at work, and in subsequent scenes shows him being apprehended and accused and begging for forgiveness from the Virgin. In the late twelfth century, when Roman documents attest to the organization of a professional group of moneychangers (*cambiatores*), the theme of Jesus chasing the moneychangers from the temple is depicted with compelling force at Saint-Gilles du Gard; Jesus, solid and muscular, shoves with one hand and raises the other menacingly, while the four astonished moneychangers clutch their moneybags like so many personified figures of avarice. Elsewhere a moneychanger shown cheating a pilgrim has a flying devil hooked on to his shoulder. At the cathedral of Piacenza, usury and avarice are condemned to squat in a most precarious and uncomfortable position and with their heads and necks to hold up the lintel over the central door.[118]

The English chronicler Roger of Wendover had a peasant named Thurcill tell about the theatre of devils he had seen in a vision. One of the characters present was the soul of a lawyer who had accepted bribes. He was forced to put burning coins into his mouth and then swallow them. Then the devils placed an iron cart-wheel, studded with spikes and nails, against his back and whirled it around, tearing and burning his back. This compelled him to vomit up the money. He then had to collect the scattered coins and submit to the same process all over again.[119] A monk of Evesham, again in Roger of Wendover, tells about a goldsmith who had cheated his customers on earth. This evil creature was thrown into a heap of burning gold coins. Once burned externally, he next had to swallow the coins. And once burned internally, he had to disgorge the coins in order to count them and to begin the punishment again.[120]

In another English historical work, we hear of the vision experienced by a priest named Walkelin. In the midst of a procession of suffering souls, William of Glos, a great noble in life, appears before Walkelin. He is suffering, he says, primarily on account of his usuries. In particular, he once lent money to a poor man, receiving a mill as security. The man was unable to pay back the debt, and so William kept the mill, thereby disinheriting the man's heirs. As punishment, he holds in his mouth a bar of hot iron from the mill, the weight of which he feels to be more oppressive than the tower of Rouen.[121] A similar form of punishment is shown in an English manuscript illumination of the first half of the fourteenth century: a usurer is shown in a cauldron over a fire with a devil shoving a gold roll into his mouth.[122]

Against such odds one could understandably be tempted to abandon the attempt to make money, an attitude that may explain the sudden popularity in the twelfth century of a very old story, the *Life of St Alexis*. The nucleus of the story is the report of a spiritually heroic 'man of God', born of wealthy parents in the fifth century at Constantinople, who left home on his wedding day and lived the rest of his life as a beggar in Edessa. A Greek version of the story added the name of Alexis, moved the parents' home to Rome, and had the hero return from Edessa to Rome where he spent the final seventeen years of his life as a beggar living unrecognized under the staircase of his own father's house. The story arrived in the West only late in the tenth century when a group of Greek monks organized a monastery in Rome. They named it in honour of St Alexis and soon, not surprisingly, they found the earthly remains of their patron. The cult spread, with all the proper accoutrements: liturgy, pilgrimage, church dedications (in Italy, England, Poland, and Germany already in the eleventh century), Latin versions of the story, an early twelfth-century fresco at San Clemente in Rome, and, in that same century, versions in all the major vernacular languages of Europe. This widely popular tale contained two quite specifically new themes, that of the voluntary renunciation of wealth and the adoption of what was hitherto the exclusively eastern practice of religious mendicancy.[123]

This exaltation in legend of a voluntarily poor man was combined with: (1) the moralists' warnings against the wickedness of city life and the sordid character of the people who gather there; (2) the disgust that money could arouse; (3) the reports of corruption in practically every institution, including the most sacred, in society; (4) the denunciations by theologians and canonists of the virtually inevitable dishonesty of merchants; (5) the prohibitions against moneylending; (6) the serious doubts raised about the legitimacy of professional fees; and (7) the graphic warnings against the moral dangers involved in striving to accumulate money. Together these elements suggest the tension that developed between the innovative sectors of the second feudal age and the morality inherited from the earlier age. So uncompromising was that morality that virtually any participation in the upper levels of the commercial economy involved the dangers of sin and conjured up visions of appalling punishments.

Adaptation to the profit economy was therefore fraught with difficulties. It created tensions between morality and behaviour, between theology and society, between religion and life itself. And in the time before this spiritual crisis could be analysed and resolved, the new tensions found occasional release in old-fashioned pillaging raids against the only 'outsiders' near at hand, namely, Jews.

3

The Jews in Christian Europe

In the eleventh century, when Latin Christendom for the first time achieved a self-conscious unity, there remained within its borders one group of people, the Jews, who were immune to the moral condemnations by the clergy of those who engaged in monetary transactions. It was in the same century that European Jews began to settle in towns, to engage extensively in commerce, and to specialize in the money trade. They gained such a reputation for expertise in the handling of money that they eventually became identified with money and moneylending in the Christian consciousness. And since these were the objects of profound ambivalence on the part of Christians, such an identification carried dangerous risks.

1. MONEYLENDERS

The first millennium of Christian-Jewish relations was marked by an uneasy coexistence, at times tense and hate-filled but rarely violent. In territories controlled by Germanic tribes, where Roman law no longer afforded its protection, the Jews' legal status depended entirely upon the will of the king. During the post-Carolingian period, the Jews came under the control of various feudal lords, ecclesiastical and lay. When the meagre urban and commercial activity of the Carolingian era waned, withdrawal to the land became nearly complete. This was necessarily as true of Jews as of anyone else.

While the Jews did not, of course, lose their identity in this period, they probably came nearer to merging into the rest of the European population than at any other time before the nineteenth century. Everywhere Jews settled, they used the local language. If their well-educated leaders knew Hebrew, the fact is no more remarkable than the fact that a few Christians learned Latin; it had little to do with separating a Jewish from a Christian community. Whereas Jews tended to adopt local names, many Christians favoured the use of Old Testament names. Jews did not distinguish themselves by wearing any special clothing, nor did they look different from their Christian neighbours. The historical record, at least, shows that Christian writers did not describe Jews as having any peculiar physical characteristics, and Christian artists did not render Jewish subjects, such as members of the Holy Family, with what they thought to be peculiarly Jewish attributes. There is no trade or profession of the period that one can identify as either a normal or the exclusive Jewish occupation.[1] There were some Jews engaged in commerce—like those mentioned in a tenth-century charter on behalf of 'Jews and other traders' at Magdeburg—just as there were some non-Jewish merchants, as the same phrase from the same charter attests.[2] Like other early merchants, Jewish merchants gave credit and performed rudimentary banking operations. Other Jews owned rural properties and were integrated into the rural economy.

With the fundamental changes in the economy that we have been discussing came a changed status for the Jews, who were selling their rural lands (which had most likely undergone a notable increase in value) and moving to towns. The concern of ecclesiastical authorities as to whether property actually or formerly owned by a Jew is subject to the payment of a tithe testifies to the importance of Jewish property ownership.[3]

In towns the Jews lived together in one street or neighbourhood, as at Worms, where there was a Jewish quarter by the close of the tenth century. The first walled Jewish neighbourhood on record was provided in 1084 by Rudiger, the Bishop of Speyer. In the following century the walled ghetto became a standard feature of the European town.[4] While the Jews continued to know and use the prevailing local language, just as their ancestors had done, many Jewish communities in the twelfth century decided to give instruction in Hebrew to all of their children, girls as well as boys.[5] In such ways the Jewish identity became increasingly distinct.

The same age gave rise to distinctive forms of dress for Jews, such as the tall, conical hat. Christian ecclesiastical legislators sought to remove all doubts and ambiguities by imposing certain external badges as a way of indicating a Jew. Circular yellow patches or else six-pointed stars, about the size of a man's hand, were to be worn conspicuously. The fact that Jews were generally not recognizable by either physical appearance or clothing is confirmed by the insistent demands of church councils, beginning with the Fourth Lateran in 1215, that Jews identify themselves with these badges.[6]

This newly sharpened identity aids in the sketchy process of assembling a notion—it can be little more than that—of the size and locus of the European Jewish population. From before the start of the *reconquista*, there had been Jews in Christian Spain. In the tenth century, there were Jewish communities in Catalonia, in Castile, and in the far western part of the peninsula, near Coimbra. Jews owned rural properties in every major principality. In the eleventh and twelfth centuries, they also appeared everywhere engaged in various professions and trades alongside Christians. The most important urban settlements were at Barcelona, Zaragoza, Burgos, and Toledo. Only during the thirteenth and fourteenth centuries did Jews become more and more involved in professional moneylending, and even then not exclusively.[7] Most Italian Jews were concentrated in a few relatively large communities in the South, while the rest were spread thinly over the central and northern sections. When Peter Damian agreed to write a treatise against Jews, he did so reluctantly, preferring to write against the vices of the age, 'for these enemies are always with us, while Jews have now almost ceased to exist.'[8] A traveller to Italy in the 1160s found only two Jews at Genoa, while he claimed that there were twenty Jewish families in Pisa and about 200 in Rome. The number of Jewish people in Venice is set by historians at about 1,000. Prior to the middle of the thirteenth century, there were relatively few Jews in the important communities of northern Italy. From that time on they appeared from countries north of the Alps, often as bankers.[9]

Without interruption since Carolingian times there had been concentrations of Jewish people in the towns along the Rhine and the other rivers of western Germany. They owned and managed arable land; they worked as artisans, merchants, and—already in the eleventh century—moneylenders. The spread of Jews eastward in the twelfth and thirteenth centuries was part of the German drive to colonize the lands to the east; afterwards it resulted from the expulsions from the western kingdoms. The Rhenish communities were also responsible for colonizing the Netherlandish towns. There were Jews in Louvain by 1220 at the latest, and in several neighbouring cities within a few decades; they all seem to have emigrated from the Rhineland and, barring a few medical doctors, all were professional moneylenders.[10]

Two hundred and forty twelfth-century Jewish communities have thus far been identified in the territories that comprise modern France. Most of the important northern and north-eastern towns had Jewish residents.[11] The Jews established in England by the Norman conquerors apparently came from Rouen; those still at Rouen in 1096 experienced one of the early pogroms.[12] Reims had a Jewish quarter at least as early as 1103. A Jewry Street with a synagogue and 24 houses owned by Jews ran for a block in the centre of the Ile-de-la-Cité in Paris. Yet there were far more important Jewish populations in the southern towns, especially in Provence and Languedoc. The heaviest concentration of communities was in the Vaucluse; 26 communities lay within a 30 mile radius of Carpentras. Arles, with several hundred Jews, was known for its many distinguished rabbis. Jews figured prominently in the commerce of Marseilles, though for raising capital they had to seek out Christian moneylenders. One of the oldest, largest, and wealthiest communities in the region flourished at Narbonne. At Perpignan, where there is no reference to Jews prior to 1185, a Jewish community appeared and increased to about 300 or 400 people by the late thirteenth century, giving Perpignan one of the largest communities north of the Pyrenees. A very few of these Perpignan Jews were artisans or merchants; nearly all were moneylenders. Perpignan, and Rousillon generally, underwent a considerable expansion at this time, and a large part of the capital and financial talent required was apparently coming from southern French Jewish communities. In a case brought before the court of a small Provençal town in the thirteenth century, the accusation against a Christian usurer stated that there were many Christian usurers in that place who were worse than the Jews. Thus moneylending—hardly an exclusive preserve of the Jews—was becoming the virtually exclusive occupation of Jews.[13]

In England, the Jews held a more conspicuous position in financial matters but could never surpass the Christian moneylenders or escape the immediate and strict control of the king. The strongest European monarchy had been established in England before the effects of the Commercial Revolution were felt there. When the Jews arrived in England, they did so late in the eleventh century under the aegis of the Normans and were made to live together in London near the Tower. Only during the disorderly reign of Stephen (1135-54) did they start to settle elsewhere. When most widely dispersed, towards the middle of the thirteenth century, the Jews were settled in 21 towns and altogether made a community of perhaps 3,000 people. As elsewhere, a few of these people were artisans and merchants, but most heads of families were moneylenders. The principal development for the English Jews came around the year 1180. Until then, Henry II borrowed from them on a modest scale in order to compensate for a lapse in his regular income or to cover an extraordinary expense; apparently Henry repaid these loans. After 1180, Henry tallaged the Jews, that is, he taxed them arbitrarily. An exchequer of the Jews was organized; each Jewish community was to have a leader, a 'priest (or bishop) of the Jews', as he was called, whose duties probably included negotiation of tallages with the royal government. The genius behind this method of collecting revenue lay in the confluence of the following facts: (1) virtually every class and group in English society held loans from the Jews; (2) the Jews had no choice except to pay a tallage; (3) the only way they could get their money was to insist on payment of debts due; (4) while this insistence would perhaps provoke hostility, the Jews remained under royal protection; and (5) the Jews could thus drain off a layer of money from the population at large and pass it on to the royal treasury without the king's having to get approval to levy a tax or his having to pay the costs of collecting a tax. Therefore the Jews, prior to the development of a general and regular system of taxation, had in effect, if unofficially, become royal tax collectors. Under Henry II and Richard, the arrangement gave satisfaction to all parties involved; its abuse by John eventually frustrated all parties. Considerably smaller tallages were taken from the Jews by Henry III and Edward I; meanwhile these kings sought ways to get taxes by consent and Edward began the policy of borrowing regularly from Italian bankers.[14]

With allowances made for local variations, remarkable changes, begun in the eleventh century, had thus taken place in the condition of European Jewry. Jews entered virtually every phase of the new commercial activity, including moneylending. 'All Jews,' observed Her‑nann of Cologne in the following century, 'are becoming involved in commerce.'[15] But that streak of exclusiveness that began to appear in various merchant guilds had the effect of restricting Jews more and more to the field of finance, where they were allowed to operate, though not without competition and a strong measure of control.[16]

By the thirteenth century, the Jews had become a people—still very small in number—living in the midst of Latin Christian society and almost exclusively in towns; practising a religion different from the prevailing one; being distinguished by certain forms of clothing and badges; increasingly self-conscious about its own spiritual and cultural heritage; and in disproportionate numbers deeply involved in the money trade. This involvement placed the Jews in a peculiar situation vis-à-vis Christians.

2. INFERIORS

The relative stability and charity that characterized Christian-Jewish relations in the post-Carolingian era began to deteriorate in the eleventh century. This deterioration is seen in numerous instances of unrestrained physical violence directed against individual Jews or against entire Jewish communities. Deterioration is seen, also, in the practice of forced baptism and its concomitant executions and suicides. It is seen in the many varieties of insult that Christian society added to the injuries it had inflicted upon the Jews. Some insults were sanctioned by popular myth, others by formal public ceremony. Finally, an age relentless in its pursuit of precise legal definitions gave expression to these deteriorated relationships in the form of new laws, new constitutions, and new legal principles.

In the years 1009 and 1010 the Jews of Orléans and Limoges were ordered to choose either to go away, to be converted to Christianity, or to be killed. Practically none was converted but many apparently fled, and a few took their own lives.[17] The unusual phenomenon of a Christian being converted to the Jewish religion was itself the cause of an expulsion. When a duke's chaplain was converted in 1012, the Emperor Henry II expelled the Jewish community from Mainz. Henry's gesture can be interpreted as a warning to potential Jewish proselytizers, but perhaps it was also an angry admission of humiliation at the fact that a relatively important cleric had given in to the 'errors of the Jews'.[18]

At Toulouse in the eleventh century, there was a legend about some Jewish traitors who, more than a century earlier, had given over their town to the advancing armies of Islam. One can understand that civic pride might keep alive such a story of defeat, if there were a clearly established case of treachery involved. But it was a curious civic pride that at Toulouse invented a defeat—for the Moors never took Toulouse—in order to punish the descendants of the supposed traitors. In any event, to perpetuate the memory of this tale, tradition ordained that a Jew stand before the Basilica of St Stephen on Easter Day and be ceremoniously struck in the face; one year the appointed Jew died from the blow. This cruel practice came to an end early in the twelfth century, but only through commutation by an annual money payment to the clergy. Similar traditions and their commutations are recorded at Béziers, Arles, and Chalon-sur-Saône.[19]

In Castile, in a moment of governmental weakness shortly after the death of Sancho the Great in 1035, the burghers of Castrojeriz launched an attack against the neighbouring town of Mercatillo. They killed 60 Jews and forced the remaining Jews to return with them to Castrojeriz.[20] The Spanish Reconquest provided the occasion for knights to pass through southern France and Catalonia; a group of knights on their way through in 1063 attacked several Jewish communities, killing and despoiling as they went. At Narbonne, the archbishop's Jewry was open to these armed pilgrims; indeed the archbishop apparently did nothing to deter them in their cruel mission. The viscount, on the other side of the city, protected his Jews against the outsiders, as did members of the Spanish clergy generally. Pope Alexander II condemned the behaviour of the Archbishop of Narbonne and the knights, and he lauded the viscount and the Spanish clergy. He reminded all parties of God's displeasure at any person's spilling of human blood. Yet he went on to distinguish the case of the Jews, who live peacefully among Christians and whom the mercy of God had predestined to be saved, from that of the Saracens, who had persecuted the Christians and driven them out of their own cities and lands. There could be no condoning of the knights' behaviour, whether caused, as Alexander said, by rash ignorance or by blind cupidity. Still, such behaviour became part of every major

47

expedition against the Saracens, and so in this respect as in virtually all others, the Spanish experience of the eleventh century served as a model for the crusades.[21]

The best known of the attacks on the Jews that coincided with the first crusade took place in the Rhine Valley. Like the Viscount of Narbonne 30 years before, Bishop John of Speyer stood by the Jews of his city in May 1096. He assembled an armed force to protect the Jews, whom he gathered in a castle, and in this way effectively frustrated the designs of the crusading bands. A few weeks later the Jews of Worms faced a similar test but with a less helpful bishop. Whether in their own homes or in the episcopal palace, the Jews of Worms were slaughtered. Cologne, Metz, Mainz, Trier, Bamberg, and Prague were among those cities where this pattern was repeated.[22]

From the description given by Guibert of Nogent of the massacre at Rouen in September of 1096 comes the classic formulation of the crusaders' rationale: it would be putting things in the wrong order for them to set out first to travel great distances eastward to fight the enemies of God when the greatest enemy of all was there before their very eyes. They herded the Jews together in a place of worship (*ecclesiam*)—a church perhaps, but more likely a synagogue—and then slaughtered them all, sparing only those willing to accept Christianity.[23]

Greater emphasis has been placed traditionally on the German rather than the French massacres, perhaps because of the imbalance in extant source materials on the subject. Yet recent study has yielded specific details about a massacre inflicted by crusaders from Languedoc and Provence upon the Jews of some Provençal community, perhaps Monieux, a small town in the Vaucluse. Such a case gives some credence to the assertion of Richard of Poitiers that the crusaders, before going off to the Holy Land, exterminated in many massacres the Jews of virtually all Gaul, apart from those who were willing to be baptized.[24]

The Second Crusade followed the pattern established by the First, with the addition of an influential crusade preacher, who urged attacks against Jews. A Cistercian monk named Ralph travelled throughout 'those parts of Gaul that touch the Rhine and inflamed many thousands of the inhabitants of Cologne, Mainz, Worms, Speyer, Strasbourg, and many other neighbouring cities, towns, and villages to accept the cross. However, he heedlessly included in his preaching that the Jews whose houses were scattered throughout the cities and towns should be slain as foes of the Christian religion.'[25] St Bernard had to be called in to silence this Ralph, a task he succeeded in accomplishing only with great difficulty, due to the fervour of Ralph's popular following. Bernard flatly opposed the pogroms but in his own way he helped foster the mentality that was so receptive to the preaching of Ralph. He argued that Christians should not kill Jews 'for they are living tokens to us, constantly recalling our Lord's passion'.[26] This was a traditional argument, but a provocative one also, and as such it represented a significant choice on Bernard's part. Moreover, his intervention in the disputed papal election of 1130 reveals a deeply hostile attitude towards Jews. The candidate he opposed, Anacletus, was the great-grandson of a Jew who had been converted to Christianity. Jewish ancestry had not prevented the future Anacletus from being a student at Paris, a monk at Cluny, a priest, a loyal supporter of the papal reform party, a cardinal, a papal legate, or the leader of the majority in the college of cardinals. None the less, Bernard wrote to the Emperor Lothair, saying: 'it is well known that Jewish offspring now occupies the see of St Peter to the injury of Christ.'[27]

The Second and Third Crusades added several English towns to the list of localities that experienced pogroms. In the autumn of 1189 a wave of persecution broke out in London and spread throughout most of the country. In March 1190, virtually the entire Jewish community at York was wiped out. Their houses were pillaged, their records destroyed, and the streets were strewn with their corpses.[28]

The signs of things to come can be seen in the policies of Philip Augustus. Shortly after the coronation in 1180, as Rigord tells it, he had 'the Jews throughout all France seized in their synagogues and despoiled of their gold and silver and garments, as the Jews themselves had spoiled the Egyptians at their exodus from Egypt'.[29] The Jews of the royal domain were imprisoned and then released only upon payment of a ransom of 15,000 marks. Next Philip cancelled four-fifths of all debts owed by Christians to Jews, and had the remaining one-fifth paid to the royal treasury. The final step, taken in 1182, was the confiscation of all Jewish property and the expulsion of the Jews from his lands. Philip readmitted the Jews under very carefully regulated conditions in 1198, but the pattern of future treatment of the Jews had been set.

The trampling underfoot of European Jews took place on an intellectual as well as a physical plane. Works by Peter Damian, Gilbert Crispin, and Peter of Blois, to name just a few, follow a well established pattern of citing Old Testament texts, especially Messianic passages, and then trying to prove that the Messiah had come.[30] The *Tractatus contra Judaeorum inveteratam duritiem* ('Treatise Against the Unyielding Obstinacy of the Jews') by Peter the Venerable, Abbot of Cluny from 1122 to 1156, contained a chapter on 'the Absurd and Utterly Stupid Tales of the Jews'.[31] Consistent with his remarkable achievement of having the *Koran* translated into Latin, so that Christian scholars would no longer need to rely on nonsensical notions about the religion of Islam, but rather could give serious attention to the authentic text of Islam, Peter here dealt at length with Talmudic scholarship. He showed how Christian and Jewish understanding on particular biblical passages was at variance and then attacked the Jewish interpretations.

One of the allegorical themes of romance literature was the contrasting relationship of the Old Law with the New, and of Synagogue with the Church.[32] In the thirteenth century the legend of the wandering Jew came to the West, first in an Italian chronicle entry for 1223 and then in Roger of Wendover's *Flores historiarum* five years later.[33] Liturgy also registered a shift in attitude around 1200 when in the Good Friday service the congregation was instructed not to kneel during the prayer for the Jews (urging their ultimate conversion); the faithful continued to kneel, however, for the other solemn prayers.[34]

The inferior status of Jews was intellectualized by Christians in pictures as well as words, with the use of such signs as the tall pointed hat and the circular badge, but more significantly with the use of such attributes as the hook-nose and the crafty eye. In representations of Christ's passion, Jews are implicated at every stage. Not only are the soldiers who take Jesus in the garden prominently hook-nosed Jews; Pilate is shown as a Jew, and the same is true of those who nail Jesus to the cross, of the one who puts the sponge with vinegar to his mouth, and of the one who pierces his side. The allegorical figure of Synagogue found in several hundred works in France and Germany suffers an astonishing array of indignities; and in the thirteenth century, the theme of Jews sucking at the teats of a sow first appeared in Germany.[35]

The legal position of the Jews declined in the course of the second feudal age from an insecure but negotiable status of virtual equality to one of abject servility. This same decline coincided with the period of the coalescing of feudal principalities into entities that in everything but name were sovereign states. Papal lawyers in about 1120 drew up a *Constitutio pro Judaeis*, which established basic guarantees for Jewish life and religion, but with the ambiguous provision that papal protection was reserved for those Jews who did not plot against the Christian faith.[36] Beginning in the late twelfth century, most of the urban charters in Aragon and Castile asserted that 'Jews are the slaves of the crown and belong exclusively to the royal treasury'.[37] Similar statements were formulated by French, English, and imperial lawyers.[38]

In such a climate of thought it is not surprising to find Abbot Peter the Venerable wondering 'whether a Jew is a human being, for he will neither accede to human reasoning nor yield to authoritative statements that are divine and from his own tradition. I do not know, I say, whether that person is human from whose flesh the heart of stone is not yet removed'.[39]

The treatment accorded Jews, the money-specialists of Christian society, was thus in thought as well as deed increasingly cruel in the course of the eleventh, twelfth, and thirteenth centuries. As justification for this cruel treatment, Christians added the insult of regarding the Jews as inferiors, as some class of sub-human beings. They wrote tracts to prove the point, extended the argument with pictorial and plastic representations, and fixed the point by law. All of these themes, depictions, and laws are understandable in the light of Christian violence against the Jews. But why did all of this violence occur in the first place?

3. SCAPEGOATS

Any attempt to explore the motives behind Christian violence against Jews must take into account the evolution of attitudes and feelings, as distinguished from overt actions and carefully reasoned theological and legal statements. These are revealed indirectly through such sources as the charges made against Jews, the associations made between Jews and filth, or the changing image of Judas.

The charge of ritual murder is made in the story told by Chaucer's prioress. In her story, a pure, fair-haired, golden-throated, seven-year-old choir-boy, son of a poor young Christian widow, is set upon in the ghetto by a filthy Jew who lives in a dark alley, who slits the boy's throat, and then dumps the body in a latrine, which the Jews continue to use.[40] Whereas Chaucer was writing in the latter part of the fourteenth century, the first actual charge of ritual murder was made in Norwich in 1144, when the body of a young boy was found on Good Friday and the story quickly spread that the boy had been crucified by Jews. This crucifixion was not the random act of a few local Jews but, according to the story, the carefully contrived action of the collectivity of European Jewry, carrying out a plan conceived at an assembly of rabbis held at Narbonne in the previous year.[41]

Similar charges were made at Gloucester in 1168, Bury St Edmunds in 1181, Winchester in 1192, Norwich again in 1235, and, most notably, Lincoln in 1255. The English did not monopolize the ritual murder charge: it is encountered at Blois in 1171 and at Pontoise and Zaragoza in 1182. At Würzburg, in 1147, the body of a Christian was discovered in the Main and the Jews bore the blame and cost of this unexplained Christian death with several Jewish lives. These are but a few of the charges that were made, and they continued as persistently in the thirteenth century as in the twelfth.[42] Many of them coincided with preparations for crusading expeditions, and these expeditions were in turn, as previously pointed out, almost invariably accompanied by massacres of Jews. Every few years and in various places there would be an eruption of Christian hostility towards the Jews. Then Christians would create the fantasy that Jews had murdered a Christian child, a point usually embellished with hideous detail. The convenience of such a charge was that Christians could then project their own guilt on to the Jews and accordingly punish the Jews, as befits murderers. At Blois, in 1171, 38 Jews were burned at the stake. At Bray-sur-Seine, in 1191, there were 100 Jewish victims. Nineteen Jews were hanged without trial in connection with the Lincoln affair of 1255.[43]

The charge of profaning the sacred host was made against some Jews at Belitz, near Berlin, in 1243; the local Jews were taken into custody and burned to death. There were many such cases in Germany, but relatively fewer in other parts of Europe. The charges vary in detail, although the main point is that the Jews got hold of a consecrated wafer and then subjected it to some iniquitous treatment.[44] The charge of host profanation fulfilled two functions for Christians. First, it permitted them to project on to Jews their doubts about transubstantiation, a doctrine long in the making and finally declared dogma only as recently as the year 1215. There was never a period in which this doctrine enjoyed universal acceptance. The feast of Corpus Christi was established in 1264 to foster its propagation and little more than a century later Wyclif launched his frontal attacks against it; these attacks were kept up by others right through to the Reformation. The Corpus Christi plays also served to bolster popular belief in the miracle of transubstantiation. They showed Jews driving nails into consecrated wafers, thus making them bleed. The dramatic tension was built around this very point, but of course Jews did not have to wonder whether a consecrated wafer were really the body and blood of Christ; that was a problem, instead, for Christians.[45] The second function fulfilled by the charge of host profanation was that it marked an improvement over the ritual murder charge, for it dispensed with the problem of finding a corpse and of identifying the victim.[46]

The charge that Jews contaminate wells and streams was heard in Germany occasionally before 1300, but more generally coincided with the natural disasters that struck Europe during the fourteenth century.[47] By then there was an old tradition of associating Jews with filth and of considering them to be filthy. Peter the Venerable complained to King Louis VII that when a church was robbed of a chalice, the thief would sell the stolen object to a Jew and the Jew would in turn do things to the chalice 'horrendous to contemplate, detestable to mention'.[48] The government of Louis' son and successor included in its rationale for expelling the Jews in 1181 a charge that Jewish pawnbrokers committed disgusting acts with Christian liturgical vessels that had been pawned with them.[49] Matthew Paris recorded the tale of a wealthy English Jew who kept an image of the Virgin inside his latrine where he defecated on it repeatedly.[50] A French counterpart of this story told of a Parisian Jew who fell into the public latrine; he reminded the friends who rushed to help him that it was the Sabbath and thus that they should wait. When the king heard of this he ordered his guards to keep the friends away from the latrine on the following day so that the Lord's day would not be violated. And when the Jews came to the unguarded latrine on Monday, their friend was dead.[51] A thirteenth-century Austrian poet claimed that thirty Jews could saturate even the largest principality with their stench; and a contemporary Flemish poet related the murder of a Christian boy by 'the dirty Jews, the stinking dogs' (*die vule Jueden, die stinkende Honde*).[52]

The association of filth and faecal matter with one's enemies, a common enough phenomenon, takes on special significance in the present case in two ways. First, it places the Jews in the company of that foul-smelling creature the devil. At a critical moment when a converted Jew was baptized, that is, when he abandoned his allegiance to the devil and became a servant of Christ, he was thought to lose his foul smell in the purifying waters of baptism.[53] The personified figure of Synagogue is often shown with the devil; the Church of Christ is set in opposition to the Synagogue of Satan. Secondly, this association calls to mind the connection between filth and money, and indeed one often finds a representation of avarice, seated before his coffer and counting coins, a devil with his tongue sticking out lounging nearby, and he, avarice, bearing the standard attributes of a Jew.[54] One of the twelfth-century dialogues between Synagogue and Church had Synagogue make the charge that Christian rulers and clerics did not demonstrate in their own lives what was generally regarded as Christian holiness. The reply given by Church was notable by the way it ignored this point and also by its counter-charge to Synagogue: 'one could never calculate the extent of your avarice; there is no limit to your evil-doing.'[55]

The personage who more than any other became the epitome of an avaricious man was Judas. 'Judas sold Christ,' explained Thomas of Froidmont, 'out of cupidity.'[56] Matthew Paris distinguished between the burdens of guilt borne by Paul and Peter on the one hand, and, on the other, by Judas. With Paul the problem was ignorance; with Peter it was a matter of weakness, which in turn generated fear; with Judas the problem was iniquity, and in particular, cupidity.[57] All of the standard forms of dress for identifying a Jew were applied to Judas, while at the same time he absorbed the attributes of avarice as well.[58] He was also referred to in the Holy Thursday *tenebrae* service, as 'that most vile of merchants'.[59] Little was known about the early life of this person until a Latin 'Legend of Judas' was composed in the twelfth century (followed shortly by vernacular versions throughout Europe). The legend includes accounts of fratricide, patricide, and incest (with his mother), all as a prelude to his betrayal of Christ.[60] The importance of these amplifications of the story of Judas lay in the fact that he served, for Christians, as a symbol of all Jews; in the words of one monastic author: 'these things that have been said concerning Judas the traitor extend to the entire Jewish people'.[61]

The principal mechanism at work in the complicated web of Christian–Jewish relations was projection. This is easy to see in a statement such as Guibert of Nogent's claim that the Jews were responsible for clerical immorality in his time, giving the reason that Jews were known to introduce clerics to the company of the 'villainous prince' and to teach them to serve him.[62] The charge of ritual murder, although more complicated, can be examined in the same light. There are no extant records of widespread killings of Christians by Jews in this period; all that we have in this connection are the elaborately fanciful tales of ritual murder, filled with their airs of conspiracy and perversion. Meanwhile, there is the long, irrefutable record of the pogroms, and since, as previously pointed out, the ritual murder charge usually accompanied a pogrom, we are permitted to see that charge as a projection of guilt (and at the same time a justification) for the pogrom. Christians, not able to justify and accept the reality of their violent behaviour towards the Jews, and thereby feeling guilty, projected their guilt on to them rather as one casts an image on to a mirror, and then they attacked in them that which they had found intolerable about themselves.

But reports of pogroms usually included mention of destruction done to property as well as harm done to persons. Some accounts specifically state that the financial records of the Jews were destroyed.[63] When official pogroms or expulsions took place, governments were careful to preserve Jewish financial records, for the pattern in such cases was for the governments to demand payment into the royal or seigneurial treasury of a portion of the amounts previously owed the Jews.[64] No such interest restrained the perpetrators of the relatively unorganized pogroms. Blind hatred based on religious fanaticism might have stimulated the flow of energy in many of those who attacked Jews and Jewries, but the fact remains that these attacks—whether consciously or not—served the common end of destroying the written evidence of Christian indebtedness to the Jews. The attacks on Jewish communities—against both property and persons—consisted of more than a cycle of violence, guilt, projection, and more violence. Christians hated Jews because they saw in Jews the same calculating for profit in which they themselves were deeply and, in their own view, unjustifiably involved. It was above all the guilt for this involvement that they projected on to the Jews. The Jews functioned as a scapegoat for Christian failure to adapt successfully to the profit economy.

Peter the Venerable's complaining to the king about what Jews did to stolen liturgical vessels reveals a concrete case of such projection. First of all, he did not emphasize the stealing as a problem; otherwise the discussion would presumably have turned to the protection of churches and the punishment of thieves. Further indication that this was not a critical problem is the rationale for expulsion later promulgated by the royal government, in which theft was not mentioned; the problem was purely one of what Jewish pawnbrokers did to liturgical vessels. In the second place, what Peter did emphasize was the imaginary problem of what Jews did to pawned objects, 'imaginary' not because it could not happen but because he made no specific charge and because there are no such formal charges extant against Jews. And third, Peter's statement diverts attention from the reality that liturgical vessels were being pawned. The reality was that treasure was being transformed into specie. The reality was that someone was undergoing the experience of taking sacred vessels to a perhaps sordid shop and haggling over their precise monetary value in order to realize that treasure in the form of cash.

This reality, moreover, was not hypothetical. The abbey of Cluny, as we shall see, ran heavily into debt in Peter's time, to Jewish moneylenders among others, and when one of the abbey's most generous benefactors passed by there in 1149 to help reduce their debt again, he found that a cross he had presented to the abbey some years before had been stripped of its outer layer of gold.[65]

Peter the Venerable did not participate in pogroms or advocate them. People less well educated and less morally responsible than he gave vent to their feelings of anxiety in all-out attacks against Jewish communities. But Peter in his own way, through the terrible bitterness that his writings display, gave expression to an inner confusion that he could hardly have understood or explained. Little wonder, then, that he doubted whether Jews were human. When Louis VII was preparing to go on crusade (and the Jew-baiter Ralph was preaching), Peter wished the king well but also expressed doubt about whether the expedition, even if successful, would be useful, because enemies far worse than the Saracens lived in their very midst. Immediately he added that he was not suggesting that these worse enemies, the Jews, be killed, for God had condemned them to be preserved in a life worse than death. His idea, though, was that the Jews be made to pay the costs of the forthcoming expedition. And this was just, he argued, because the Jews were wealthy and yet they did not work. Their storage bins were filled with produce and their cellars with wine. Their purses were filled with money and their chests with gold and silver. Yet they did not earn this great wealth by working on the land, nor did they get it from serving as soldiers or in any other honourable and useful position. They got it by stealing from Christians and by receiving goods stolen from Christians by thieves.[66] Apart from the gratuitous accusation about stealing, this was an essentially accurate, if rough, description of those who were successful in the new economy. The other great monastic leader of the twelfth century, St Bernard, explicitly identified the entire money trade with the Jews. He knew but could not fully accept the reality of Christian involvement in the money trade. 'We are pained to observe', he wrote, 'that where there are no Jews, Christian moneylenders "Jew", or "Judaize" (*judaizare*), worse than the Jews, if indeed these men may be called Christians, and not rather baptized Jews.'[67] Bernard thereby gave new significance to a hitherto innocuous Latin verb, *judaizare*, which meant merely to proselytize and to convert people to Judaism, a counterpart to the verb 'to Christianize'.[68] The money trade, the crucial activity of the Commercial Revolution, was thus now considered to be exclusively the work of the Jews. Christian moneylenders were really Jews.

It was both inaccurate and unfair to regard commercial activity, especially moneylending, as the exclusive preserve of Jews, for the Jews always formed a tiny minority of the people so engaged. And yet the main function of the Jews in the Commercial Revolution was to bear the burden of Christian guilt for participation in activities not yet deemed morally worthy of Christians. Christians attacked in the Jews those things about themselves that they found inadmissible and that they therefore projected on to the Jews. Guilt led to hostility, and hostility to violence, which led to a need for rationalizing the violence, and this rationalization led to a deeper hostility and still more violence, and so the fateful cycle turned.[69] Joined to this guilt that was felt by some was a more simple anxiety about the disorders and uncertainties of urban life and about the behaviour of those increasingly separate, marginal people, the Jews; anxiety itself, quite apart from guilt, can breed hostility. And simpler still was the anger of those who felt oppressed by moneylenders.

Religious enthusiasm alone would not have constructed the elaborate device of limiting the Jews to occupations thought by Christian moralists to be sinful and then harassing the Jews for doing their jobs. The particular occupations chosen are themselves most revealing. Presumably the Jews could have been forced to haul water or clean the streets or till the soil. But more complicated Christian feelings were responsible for setting the Jews up in finance and then attacking them bitterly for their involvements in finance.

Early in the twelfth century, Rupert of Deutz inquired: 'Tell me, who are they who gather wicked avarice in their homes more than the Jewish people'?[70] Rupert's prudently rhetorical question remained undisturbed by the obvious answer. Midway through the century, St Bernard made his revealing assertion that all moneylenders, even Christian moneylenders, are Jews. By the late twelfth century, the new needs of both business and government for a system of credit collided head on with the old moral and legal prohibitions against usury. As there was still no yielding on the side of morality or legality, certain Christian princes, in particular the kings of France and England, who remained in firm and exclusive control of 'their Jews', created the fiction that some of the Christian moneylenders, clerical as well as lay, living under their jurisdiction, were Jews—'their Jews', of course—thus enabling them to operate at the prince's pleasure, free from harassment by any other authority.[71] Political power in this way brought to the surface and lent support to a myth that had originated in projection.

PART II

Avoiding the Crisis:
Monks and Hermits

4

The old order

The religious life experienced one of its most dynamic periods in Europe between the early eleventh and early thirteenth centuries: it sparkled with inventiveness and experimentation, with intellectual vigour and spiritual integrity, and with intense rivalries as well. Each of the various forms then taken by the religious life has been studied in detail, but it is desirable to group these many forms together in order to compare them, in particular to be able to observe the ways in which they responded to the development of the profit economy. The earliest of these responses were evasive, tending towards either unthinking involvement or total rejection. The tenth century fostered one form alone of the religious life, that of the monastic community. This type of life had been so disrupted by the Viking, Magyar, and Saracen raids, as well as by the violent internal disorders of the Carolingian Empire in the late ninth century, that it had virtually to be founded all over again. Whether in establishing wholly new communities or in re-establishing old ones, religious leaders of the tenth century thought of their task as a matter of restoring the religious life of the time of Emperor Louis the Pious and his religious adviser, Benedict of Aniane (751–821). This Carolingian monastic ideal was in turn a mixture of the *Rule for Monks* (*Regula monachorum*) composed by Benedict of Nursia in the sixth century; the Cassiodoran view (from the same period) of the monastery as a bastion of erudition ; Germanic notions of authority in which princely and spiritual powers were closely linked; and a hierocratic vision of society, based on function, that exalted the liturgical role of the monks and thus placed them well above the peasants who had the task of working the monastic lands.

The hierocratic vision became social ideology in the thoughts of those authors of the ninth and tenth centuries who wrote about the three orders of society: the order of those who pray (*oratores*), the order of those who fight (*bellatores*), and the order of those who work (*laboratores*). In this sense of 'order', based on social utility, all monks of the time together constituted the monastic order. They also shared the designation 'black monks' (*monachi nigri*), on account of the woollen habit dyed black that was their standard dress.[1]

There did not exist, however, a Benedictine Order, with a constitution, a headquarters, a table of organization, or other such structural paraphernalia. It is, therefore, difficult to know even how many monasteries there were. Each monastery was an independent corporation, yet communities did establish ties of various types among themselves. One type was a formal exchange of prayers such as the one arranged in 942 among the monks of Saint-Martial, Fleury, and Solignac, an act of literally incalculable value in the manner of the gift economy. This became in some cases a confraternity, extending associate membership not only to other monasteries, but to secular clerics, especially bishops, as well.[2] Another type stemmed from the common practice of founding new communities or reforming existing ones by transplanting a group of monks from an already thriving monastery. The affiliations established in this way varied from vague memories of a former influence to strong institutional bonds. Many of the communities reformed by Cluny did not become full-fledged abbeys, that is independent houses each under its own abbot, but remained priories, each under a prior and each considering the Abbot of Cluny as its abbot. The size and importance of these Cluniac priories varied so greatly that estimates of their number range between 1,000 and 2,000.[3] The Castilian monastery of Oño was established on the model of Cluny in 1033; it did not maintain any official tie with Cluny, but instead soon became the master house to over 70 dependent houses.[4] Hirsau in Swabia, which asked for and received a copy of the customs of Cluny late in the eleventh century, in turn radiated a reform programme based on these customs to over 60 other German monasteries within a few decades.[5] In Lorraine, the monastery of Gorze set a pattern of reform that was utterly independent of that of Cluny, indeed that differed from it on many points, and this pattern was followed by some 160 monasteries in the Low Countries and in north-western Germany.[6] A historical geography of the entire monastic order, although clearly desirable, is yet far from being realized; the part of it most complete so far concerns England and Wales, which in the year 1100 had a total of 133 abbeys and priories.[7]

Monastic communities lived mainly from their landed endowment, which had been donated to them by members of the powerful, land-controlling class. The popes and the Ottonian emperors were instrumental in the revival of Roman monasticism. There had been an eighth-century monastery dedicated to St Boniface on the Aventine hill, but, after a lengthy decline, the regular life died out there completely by 950. It was on this site that Pope Benedict VII (974–83) encouraged and aided the establishment of the mixed Greek and Latin monastery of St Alexis, to which he gave land in the Aventine quarter and in various regions around Rome. The Emperor Otto II (973–83), with his Byzantine wife and his Greek intellectual interests, also showed a special concern for this exceptional exercise in coexistence, in which the Greeks regarded Basil as their leader and the Latins regarded Benedict (of Nursia) as theirs. Otto III (983–1003), like many of the popes, drew on Roman monasteries for well-disciplined men to undertake special tasks, in particular the mission to the Slavs, which was so basic to overall imperial policy.[8] In England King Edgar (959–75) convoked the Council of Winchester, which gave unity and direction to the efforts of various reformers trying to re-establish the regular life in that kingdom.[9] Likewise the kings of Navarre, Aragon, Leon, and Castile built and encouraged monastic communities. To them, the monasteries were centres for propagandizing and legitimizing the *reconquista*. Moreover, the Aragonese kings made the monastery of S. Juan de la Peña their mausoleum, granting it in about 1020 a charter of privileges modelled after that of Cluny.[10] The Capetians, prior to establishing close ties with the Abbey of Saint-Denis, treated Fleury, home of the prestigious remains of St Benedict, as if it were a private chapel. Hugh Capet patronized Fleury and advised his son Robert the Pious to keep on the good side of St Benedict. When king, Robert went beyond his father's advice by making his brother Gauzlin Fleury's abbot, and Gauzlin remained in that post from 1005 to 1030. A century later, King Philip I was buried at Fleury, in fulfilment of his desire to be laid to rest near the patriarch of monks.[11]

More numerous than the kings were the dukes, counts, and other high-ranking nobles who built, protected, prayed in, retired to, and were buried in the new and renewed monasteries. Duke William IX of Aquitaine provided the necessary land and assurances for the establishment of Cluny under Abbot Berno.[12] Berno in turn, who was a nephew of King Louis the Stammerer, provided in his will that Cluny should receive La Frette, a priory of another monastery of which he was abbot, together with its village and its lands, plus one-fourth of the salt mines of Lons-le-Saunier.[13] He favoured Cluny in his will because, of all his monasteries, Cluny was especially 'poor in possessions but rich in brotherhood'.[14] Berno's successor, St Odo, was summoned to Rome by Prince Alberic to advise on and effect monastic foundations. Alberic set up generous endowments and members of all factions of Rome's nobility followed his lead.[15] Demetrius Meliosi, Roman aristocrat and a major benefactor of Subiaco, gave Saint-Alexis islands in the Tiber with attendant fishing rights.[16] The historian of the reform programme that flowered and spread out from Gorze remarked that the Gorze reform was something of a family affair among the Lotharingian aristocracy.[17] The dukes of Normandy were characteristically active in fostering the growth of monastic houses, which numbered 25 by 1066, Cluniac practices having been introduced by William of Volpiano, Abbot of Dijon, in the early years of the eleventh century.[18] Besides all of this external support for the monastic order, the upper classes of feudal society supplied most of the monks and virtually all of the abbots in the tenth and eleventh centuries.[19]

Gifts of land usually came with rights as well: fishing rights as in the case already cited, or rights over mills, houses, bakeries, animals, servile labour, and churches (with their tithes).[20] Monasteries assumed or were given franchises for conducting fairs.[21] Norman and Anglo-Saxon monasteries provided knights for ducal and royal armies respectively.[22] Not least important was the jurisdiction that so often accompanied the land. In all parts of Europe abbots gave aid and counsel to their secular superiors. The Abbot of Cluny got his own tribunal as part of the devolution of the authority of the counts of Mâcon.[23] The Abbot of Pomposa, a prince of the empire and lord over large estates of cultivated land as well as of salt marshes in the Po estuary, handed down judicial decisions from the loge of the handsomely refined hall of justice, which stands not far from the monumental abbey church.[24]

Thus in region after region the monastic order was one of the principal landlords. Such was the case with the several monasteries in and around Rome, with Farfa in Sabina, with Subiaco in Latium, and with Cluny in Burgundy.[25] A map showing the centres of power, jurisdiction, communications, and erudite culture in Europe in the tenth and eleventh centuries should not emphasize cities but rather the great monasteries; the big lettering should be reserved not for towns like Milan, Paris, Cologne, but for Monte Cassino, Nonantola, Saint-Martial of Limoges, Reichenau, and so on. It was natural for Pope Urban II to refer to Cluny in the 1090s as 'the light of the world'.[26]

With a seemingly limitless generosity that continued for several generations, the *bellatores* kept up the old traditions of largess. Monastic cartularies show that the busiest period for the making of donations of land was the one embracing the decades just before and after the year 1000.[27] But gifts of precious objects and of specie came to monasteries as well. The success of the eleventh-century Christian offensive against Islam yielded stores of booty that got rapidly redistributed in Europe, especially to monastic establishments. Most of the goods taken by the Pisan raiders from Bona, on the coast of North Africa, went to Cluny.[28] The main source of Moslem wealth that came into Europe was Spain, where the leading power to emerge in the eleventh century was the Kingdom of Leon. King Ferdinand I of Leon (1038–65) proclaimed in about 1060 that an annual gift of 1,000 gold metcales be sent to Cluny, to be used specifically for the clothing of the monks. In 1077, Ferdinand's son, Alfonse VI (1066–1109), doubled the amount of this annual gift.[29] The money came directly from the Moslems into the Leonese fisc as booty when there was fighting or as tribute when there was a truce. In 1087 the Leonese army suffered a crushing defeat at the hands of the Almoravids, thus instantly cutting the flow of specie. Abbot Hugh of Cluny sent Seguin the chamberlain as his emissary to Alfonse's court in 1088 to urge the king to send money. Alfonse apparently still commanded impressive resources, for Seguin returned triumphantly with 10,000 dinars. Then in 1090 Abbot Hugh himself travelled to Burgos to meet with King Alfonso, and he came away with still more Moorish gold.[30] There remain extant some fragments of two account books of Cluny from around 1100 (and much fuller records for the years from 1148 to 1155).[31] These and other sources show that Cluny had so much wealth and so much experience in fiscal administration that it had a formative influence on the accounting system employed at the papal treasury.[32]

Mention was made earlier of the Lombard monasteries that sold surplus produce for cash on the pier at Pavia. It is known, in addition, that some of the earliest landlords to receive payments in specie rather than in kind were monks in the region of Lucca.[33] Another indication of the changes coming about was the shift in importance, and in complexity of function, within monasteries, from the cellarer, who had charge of the storage of produce, to the chamberlain, who had charge of finances. Monastic administrators discovered that it was advantageous to have produce from their distant properties sold locally, and money instead of the produce sent to the abbey.[34] The chamberlain's office also became involved in moneylending: monasteries lent money to nobles, merchants, and crusaders.[35] Between 1090 and 1110, after those important missions by the chamberlain and the abbot to Spain, Cluny lent over £900 to Mâconnais nobles alone.[36] In the same period Farfa began to borrow regularly, and Saint-Denis became deeply indebted to a Jewish financier named Oursel of Montmorency.[37]

The monks were precocious not only in their handling of money but in their involvement with city life. Abbeys that had been built within or on the edge of old cities could not avoid being part of the busy world that began to function before their very doors, as, for example, at Saint Paul's-Outside-the-Walls, Saint-Ambrose, Saint-Germain-des-Près, or Westminster Abbey. A pilgrim from northern Italy vividly described the scene at Saint Paul's-Outside-the-Walls during the first Holy Year (decreed by Boniface VIII in 1300): two clerics stood day and night by the altar holding rakes in their hands, raking in 'infinite money' (*die ac nocte duo clerici stabant ad altare Sancti Pauli tenentes in eorum manibus rastellos rastellantes pecuniam infinitam*).[38] The intrusion of urban life into the cloister could be felt by monastic communities in small towns as well, like Tournus, on the Saône, where the monks of Saint-Philibert had taken refuge from the Vikings; while, a few miles away, Cluny represented another type of monastery, one that was totally rural at the time of its foundation but later on, because of its enormous wealth, fostered the growth of a town right outside its gates. The abbots of both Saint-Philibert and Cluny, given the continued weakness of the counts of Mâcon, gained full control over their respective burgs and of the commercial activity that took place in them. Each abbot controlled markets and fairs, levied taxes, held a monopoly on the sale of salt, and received the homage of local merchants.[39] At Cluny in the late eleventh century, the Jews ceased to be peasants and instead became involved in the new commercial activities in town. Between 1060 and 1075, an identifiable group of burghers appeared, distinct from the knights and peasants. The signatures of these burghers appeared on subsequent Cluniac documents dealing with town affairs. And they in turn became benefactors, like the twelfth-century merchant who donated to Cluny a gold cross decorated with gems, a cup, a chalice, gold and silver candelabra, and 24 marks of silver.[40] Such urban ties did not escape the author of a book on the various forms of religious life in the early twelfth century, for he classed the Cluniacs and others like them as monks who live in or near towns.[41]

The monks of Christ Church, Canterbury, as we have seen, drew a considerable income from the shrine of Thomas Becket, but they received higher amounts from rents on their urban property holdings. By the end of the twelfth century, the monks had become lords of between one-third and one-half of the domestic property of the town of Canterbury, with over 400 separate holdings. They owned 25 dwellings in London and ten in Dover. A remarkable series of surveys and rent-rolls from the period 1160–1206 has preserved these details.[42]

What did the monks do with all this wealth? In their own terms, they prayed; their own social ideal defined them functionally as *oratores*. In terms of the gift economy, they displayed, and consumed, and gave away. The connection between these two replies is that monastic spending was justified by the demands of the liturgy, which required an elaborate setting and was expensive to maintain. John of Salerno described Saint-Martin of Tours in the early tenth century as 'a place full of virtue, remarkable for miracles, overflowing with riches, excelling all in the practice of religion'. Over two centuries later it was the same at Battle Abbey, which claimed to be second to none of the monasteries of England in religion or in the abundance of all good things.[43] 'Overflowing riches' and 'good things' did not impede 'the practice of religion', that is, the liturgy; on the contrary they enhanced it. The old traditions of offering precious gifts to the gods lived on in the monumental abbey churches with their elaborately carved façades and capitals and with the frescoes and tapestries that decorated their walls; it lived on notably in the altars with all their apurtenances: altar cloths, retables (sometimes of gold), candle holders, plates, pitchers, chalices, crosses, statues, books, and, above all, reliquaries. In Benedict's *Rule*, the liturgy took up about one-fourth of a monk's waking hours; by the late eleventh century it had expanded to fill practically the entire day. The original number of psalms to be recited each day was 40; by the end of the ninth century the number had increased to 138; and two centuries later it had reached 170.[44] An important item, therefore, in calculating the cost of the liturgy was the maintenance of the monks (150 at Hirsau and at Christ Church, Canterbury; twice that number at Cluny), who no longer spent any of their time in productive labour.[45]

The psalms and prayers that were recited, especially those added to the original liturgical programme, were recited on behalf of the benefactors of monasteries. The best available means of assuring eternal salvation was to have the monks intercede for the living and to commemorate the dead. The commemoration of departed faithful involved both liturgical solemnity and robust feasting.[46] The agreement concluded at Winchester in about 970 provided for prayers on behalf of the king and his family at all of the offices of the day in all of the English monasteries.[47]

The dominant place of the liturgy in monastic spirituality suggests that charitable assistance to the poor was of secondary importance. Yet there was no tension between the demands of liturgy and those of charity, for the latter was completely absorbed in the former; charity itself was a ritual. The customs of Cluny provided for the maintenance of eighteen paupers-in-residence, with clear specifications of what they were allowed, such as meat on 25 days of each year.[48] The customs also specified a number of meals for poor people as part of spiritual honours the community conferred on persons of high rank and on especially generous benefactors. There were two principal grades of such honour: the *magnum anniversarium* and the *anniversarium mediocre*, the latter in turn divided into three classes. The *magnum* was reserved for abbots of Cluny, and for kings and emperors 'who made large donations to the church'. The various categories of anniversary celebrations differed in such details as the number of bells that were rung, the quality and number of candelabra placed on the altar, the liturgical content of the office and the mass, and finally, the number of poor fed by the sacristan. A *magnum* included the feeding of twelve paupers with a hearty meal of bread, wine, and meat.[49]

At that moment when Leonese gold temporarily stopped flowing to Cluny, and the chamberlain and the abbot hastened to Spain to visit

King Alfonse, Cluny had just undertaken construction of a new church, Cluny III, the largest building in Europe prior to the new St Peter's basilica, which was built in the sixteenth century. It was a critical moment indeed, and we find that Abbot Hugh was able to offer the king honours even greater than those the *magnum anniversarium* already accorded him. A maundy of 30 poor was to be provided on Maundy Thursday; foot-washing was included along with feeding. At Easter the chamberlain was to feed at least 100 poor. Each day at the high table of the monastic refectory, a meal such as the king himself would have been served if dining there was to be served to a poor person; and this practice was to last until King Alfonse's death. Furthermore, a maundy of twelve poor was to be provided on Maundy Thursday in honour of Alfonse's wife.[50] Distributions of food and clothing to the poor did take place at the gates of monasteries. But such distributions did not constitute a sharing of all that the religious community had; they were hand-outs of what the monks chose to give away. The monks, with their formidable wealth, were secure in the knowledge that they performed the noblest and most important function in their society, and also that they—and they alone—were Christ's poor, the poor in spirit. The essential meaning of 'poor' before the triumph of the commercial economy was 'weak' in relation to the powerful. The particular forms taken by monastic spirituality had developed in connection with the problems of power and violence in late Carolingian society. The monks, who were recruited from the warrior class, were men who had surrendered their weapons, who had made themselves voluntarily weak—or 'poor', who thus felt no disturbing contradiction between 'wealth' and 'poverty' while living by a rule in the setting of a materially comfortable, in some cases even magnificent and luxurious, monastery.[51] So solidly established, both materially and spiritually, was the monastic order that the transition made by monasteries from gift economy to profit economy was made without worry or reflection.

In the long run, unthinking acceptance of this transition was costly for the old monastic order. The successful abbots of the twelfth century were of necessity fiscal administrators rather than saints, like Suger of Saint-Denis, who wrote a book on administration and took charge of the royal government during Louis VII's crusade, or like Samson of Bury St Edmund's, who inherited an enormous debt upon his accession and spent his reign wiping it out (with the help of a pogrom in the town of Bury, which he controlled).[52] Another successful abbot was Henry of Blois, brother of King Stephen and, all at one time, Abbot of Glastonbury, Bishop of Winchester, Dean of St Martin-le-Grand in London, and papal legate to England. By careful reorganization of estates, he made Glastonbury the wealthiest abbey in England and Winchester the wealthiest episcopal see after Canterbury. It was Henry of Blois, former monk at Cluny and personal friend of Abbot Peter the Venerable, who once found that the gold had been stripped from a cross he had previously given to the Abbey of Cluny. The same Henry of Blois tried to help pay off some of Cluny's debts with a gift of 2,000 marks in 1149 and, only six years later, another gift of 7,000 marks.[53]

Cluny, rather like the Spanish Empire of the sixteenth and seventeenth centuries, lived so well and so long on money that flowed in from outside, that it neglected the upkeep of its own, more traditional resources and thus suffered a sharp decline when the flow stopped. Neither a Suger nor a Samson nor a Henry of Blois, Peter the Venerable imposed an austerity programme on the monks, which included manual labour, but meanwhile continued to exacerbate Cluny's debts.[54] It is not difficult to understand why, in 1147, Peter denounced so vehemently those vile Jews, who do not work with their hands, in fact who do not work at all, who take advantage of the weak and the poor, who have full storage bins and wine cellars, and who amass great quantities of riches.[55] Surely Peter thought he was describing the Jews, but, as pointed out earlier, he was also, quite unintentionally, describing those most deeply involved in the money economy, and in particular, we might now add, the monks of the old monastic order. In Peter the Venerable's bold plea for money from King Roger II of Sicily, one hears a faint, inverted echo of Abbot Berno's phrase two centuries earlier, 'poor in possessions but rich in brotherhood'. 'Cluny has many debtors,' complained Peter in 1146, 'but few benefactors.'[56]

5

The new Egypt

To get away from the complicated and pressing burdens of running Cluny, Peter the Venerable occasionally sought refuge in the wooded hills of the Charolais. There he would join a small group of monks from his own abbey who were temporarily living as hermits. Not many monks ever chose to live this way, but apparently some abbots permitted those few monks who wished a life of greater solitude and severity to live apart from their communities.

For Peter, such retreats brought a limited measure of relief. 'Wearied with living in towns,' he wrote to a friend, 'we live in the forests and love the meadows.'[1] In the same letter, he quoted with sympathy Horace's preference for quiet Tivoli or peaceful Tarentum over Rome the busy capital. But stature and fame afforded him little privacy, and Peter's retreats call to mind the efforts of the French kings to escape from the crowds and the demanding schedule of Versailles' courtly ritual to the Grand Trianon, and from there, for the same reasons, to the Petit Trianon. 'In what sense are we solitaries,' one of the abbot's companions inquired, 'who after entering the spacious silence of this hermitage, have attracted so many people that we seem not really to have built a hermitage at all, but rather a town?'[2]

The eremitic life had had neither a continuous nor an influential role in the Latin West.[3] Although the example of the Desert Fathers was imprinted in the thought of the founders of western monasticism, a flourishing eremitical movement first appeared in Europe only in the eleventh century, at the very time when the new urban society was taking shape and the old monastic order was reaching its peak of power and prestige. The eremitic movement constituted a rejection of both the new cities and the old monasteries; it avoided the problems of the one and the compromises of the other, in favour of an ideal based on the model of the Egyptian hermits. This movement had noteworthy institutional progeny, but its aspirations and achievements are better studied through the careers and writings of its famous leaders, those who articulated their discontent with the existing monastic order and who brought forth alternative forms of religious life. Six famous leaders worthy of study are Romuald of Ravenna, Peter Damian, John Gualbert, Bernard of Tiron, Robert of Arbrissel, and Stephen of Muret.

1. ROMUALD OF RAVENNA

Romuald (*c.* 952–1027) came from a noble family of Ravenna. He left no writings but he is known to posterity mainly from the biography written by Peter Damian. At the age of twenty, Romuald entered the nearby monastery of Saint-Apollinaris at Classe to do a penance of 40 days on behalf of his father, who had killed a kinsman. Romuald imbibed the monastic life enthusiastically, took monastic vows, experienced a vision of Saint-Apollinaris, and remained in that same monastery for three years. Romuald lived the monastic life too correctly in the opinion of some, and he did not shrink from denouncing the laxity of his fellow monks. For this they conspired to kill him and he barely averted an early death. Romuald fled Saint-Apollinaris and began to live as a hermit, sometimes alone and sometimes in the company of other hermits. He found his way to the Pyrenees, to the great Catalan monastery, Saint-Michael of Cuxa, whose abbot allowed him to live near the monastery as a hermit. For ten years he lived near Cuxa, and at some time during this period he read the lives of the Egyptian Desert Fathers.[4]

Upon returning to Italy, Romuald went to Pereum, a solitary place in the salt marshes about twelve miles from Ravenna. The abbacy of Saint-Apollinaris fell vacant and Emperor Otto III, after consulting the monks there, appointed Romuald as abbot. There followed a stormy, one-year abbacy, and then Romuald withdrew again to Pereum. Here he and his companions built individual cells and truly began the style of eremitic life that Romuald would spend the rest of his days organizing in northern and central Italy.[5]

The most important of these foundations was Camaldoli, high in the Tuscan-Romagnese Apennines, on land given by the Count of Maldoli (*campus maldoli*), probably in the second or third decade of the eleventh century.[6] There was both a cenobitic community and, higher up in the hills, an eremitic community.[7] The place was described as having rushing streams, seven pure fountains, green fields, and paths to and from the mountain ridges.[8] Romuald's influence spread also by way of the important eremitic community of Fonte Avellana, a place that Romuald almost certainly knew but the details of whose foundation remain unknown. Peter Damian said that at Sitria, another of Romuald's settlements, Romuald and his disciples seemed to have founded—not just because of the similar name but the similar way of life—another Nitria,[9] the desert to which St Anthony (*c.* 260–356) fled from Alexandria.

Inspiration came, too, from still further back in time. When Prior Rudolph set down the customs of Camaldoli in 1080, he wrote at length in praise of the solitary life, 'the life that purges the mind and clears the conscience, purifies reason, creates wisdom, sharpens the intelligence, leads to God'. There were so many fine examples and authorities to whom Prior Rudolph thought that one could turn, yet time and space limited him, he said, to listing only Moses, David, Elias, John the Baptist, the Saviour, the ancient Fathers, the philosophers, St Benedict, and St Romuald.[10]

2. PETER DAMIAN

The conversion of Peter Damian (*c.* 1007–72), the most famous and influential hermit of the eleventh century, began with the refusal of a gift. Youngest son of a moderately well-to-do family from Ravenna, Peter lost both his parents when he was about two and subsequently suffered a miserably unhappy boyhood. Salvation lay in formal studies, which he pursued with formidable success at Faenza and at Parma when he was an adolescent. He eventually became one of the most accomplished writers and generally best educated persons of his time.[11]

From student life Peter passed directly into a teaching career, where he was no less successful than before. His biographer, John of Lodi, who was a personal companion in Peter's later years, said that Peter attracted many students and gained 'copious riches' from his work. But a crisis developed for this young man in his early to mid twenties, for he no longer could rely on the discipline of student life and seemed unable to deal with the freedom afforded him by his fees. The resolution of his crisis came when he met and talked with two hermits from Fonte Avellana. He learned of St Romuald from them, and out of admiration and gratitude he offered them a silver vase to take back to the hermitage. To his astonishment, they refused the gift; but rather than take offence, Peter began to perceive that these men were 'truly free and truly happy' (*vere liberi vereque beati*), and the events leading to his entry into Fonte Avellana were thus placed in motion.[12]

In about 1035 he became a hermit and also a priest.[13] He continued to teach but not to be paid for it, in his view a compromising and troubling experience. He taught at the Abbey of Pomposa for two years and afterwards taught in the monastery of Saint-Vincent near Urbino. Virtually all of his writings were markedly didactic, beginning with the biography he wrote of St Romuald.

In 1043 Peter was elected prior of Fonte Avellana. He became actively engaged in church reform by writing to prelates about what he thought to be problems in need of attention. Pope Stephen IX named Peter a cardinal in 1057, a position that thereafter frequently demanded his presence in Rome. While still remaining in his hermitage as much as he could, he dealt with three sensitive political issues on the pope's behalf: the affair of the Patarines at Milan (1059), the dispute between the Bishop of Mâcon and the Abbey of Cluny (1063), and the marriage problems of the Emperor Henry IV (1069).

During and after his mission to Milan, Peter underwent an experience that crystallizes much that is significant about his career and about his perception of society. He was offered a gift of silver by an abbot. He tried to turn it down on the grounds that a papal emissary could not accept gifts from interested parties in the matters under investigation. But the abbot assured Peter that he had no interests whatever to press; then Peter argued that between clerics there was no need to exchange gifts the way laymen did. Still the abbot persisted, this time convincing Peter to use the gift to help support a new eremitic foundation. Peter accepted, but when he returned to Fonte Avellana, he became troubled still again by his acceptance of this gift; at night, when he was trying to recite psalms, his head swirled with dizziness and his intestines seemed to undulate with a swarm of vermin. He had ultimately to return the silver, and to vow never again to accept any gift whatever. In this very personal experience of 1059–60, we see Peter Damian's definitive rejection of gift-economy behaviour in connection with the religious life, behaviour that he had interpreted not in its own terms but in terms of the commercial environment in which he had grown up, studied, and taught. In his administrative capacity as cardinal-bishop of Ostia, Peter favoured releasing his church's accumulated treasure into the economy as specie.[14]

As an active church reformer, Peter participated vigorously in the fight against clerical marriage and concubinage, as also against simony ('first of the heresies to burst from the bowels of the devil', as we noted earlier), and lay possession of tithes ('a deadly poison').[15] Worldly priests necessarily have worldly cares, especially about money, which gives birth to envy and chills the love one has for one's neighbours. The worldly priest has unavoidably to be compared with Judas, who sold the Saviour for a sum of 'vile money'.[16] The task of clerical reform meant depriving clerics of comfortable incomes and getting them to live from the labour of their own hands.[17] And the goal of such reform was not to remove clerics from society but precisely to qualify them for an active role in society: 'The only men fit for the office of preaching (*officium praedicationis*) are those who lack the support of earthly riches and who, because they possess nothing at all of their own, hold everything in common.'[18]

The monastic life, in Peter's view, did not require monumental churches and disciplined choirs. Even though the responses were written in the plural, a single hermit could recite them because the church is everywhere and because all Christians everywhere are united by love.[19] Each monk, he thought, should gauge his own capacities with great frankness and honesty, so as not to indulge needlessly in all the latitude permitted by the rule. At the very least, all monks should avoid costly and comfortable garments.[20] In the hermitage, extensive learning had no place; a knowledge of the Gospels and of the deeds and sayings of the Desert Fathers would suffice.[21] The superfluities of the Benedictine life, with their prolonged chanting, their sounding of bells, their flashy ornaments, were misguided and misleading, where true spirituality was concerned.[22]

But Peter was not permitted the luxury of remaining always in his eremitic retreat whence he could launch attacks against the monks. He had to go to Cluny in 1063. There is a full report of this expedition written by one of the clerks who accompanied him. Also there are letters written by Peter upon his return to Fonte Avellana directed both to Abbot Hugh and to all the monks of Cluny. Peter spoke highly of all that he had seen and experienced: how modest the monks looked and behaved, how moving their liturgy was, how well equipped they were to have running water in concealed conduits passing through all parts of the community where it was needed, and how very kindly he had been received.[23]

Some would interpret Peter's reaction to Cluny as unreserved praise, but the trip there did not alter his way of life and he made very clear how happy he was to return subsequently to Fonte Avellana.[24] Nothing he wrote of Cluny can match his praise for the hermitage, praise in which we hear echoed the language of an eleventh-century Po Valley town:

O warehouse of heavenly merchants, in which are found the best of those wares for whom the land of the living is prepared. Happy marketplace, where earthly goods are exchanged for those of heaven, and things eternal substituted for those that pass away. Blessed market, where life everlasting is set out for sale and may be bought by any man, however little he possesses; where a little bodily suffering can purchase the company of heaven and a few sparse tears procure everlasting gladness; where we cast aside worldly possessions and enter into the patrimony of our eternal inheritance. You, O solitary cell, are the wonderful workshop of spiritual labour, in which the human soul restores to itself the likeness of its creator and returns to its pristine purity, where the blunted senses regain their keenness and subtlety, and tainted natures are renewed in sincerity by unleavened bread.[25]

Peter was not making light of the problems engendered by the monetary economy. He said that the treasure of the individual hermit or monk was Jesus Christ and in the following way he began his advice on how best to keep that treasure:

First of all, get rid of money, for Christ and money do not go well together in the same place. If you were to close both of them in at the same time, you would find yourself the possessor of the one without the other, for the more abundant your supply of the worthless lucre of this world, the more miserably lacking you are in true riches.[26]

If Romuald is credited with founding the Italian eremitic movement, then Peter Damian can be considered its leading theorist and propagator. From his experience in Ravenna, Faenza, and Parma, and later, from his language, Peter appears a person belonging entirely to the new society. With the perspective of that society, he could hardly have avoided interpreting the exchange of gifts among clerics as payments, indeed as illegal payments, or bribes. And with the schooling he got, in these same northern Italian towns, he had the capacity to criticize the behaviour of secular clerics and of monks alike. Both the traffic in money and the display of wealth in the hierarchy and the monasteries were offensive to him, and led him therefore to seek an alternative to the monastic life of his time. 'O eremitic life,' he exclaimed, 'you are the soul's bath, the death of evil-doing, the cleanser of filth; you make clean the hidden places of the soul, wash away the foulness of sin, and make souls shine with angelic purity.'[27]

3. JOHN GUALBERT

John Gualbert (c.995–1073) came from a noble family of fighters who lived in the Florentine countryside. His father was described as a *vir militaris*. When John was a young man, a series of events took place that seriously altered the course of his life. A kinsman, it seems, was murdered, and the family knew who was responsible. The prevailing mores imposed the responsibilities of vengeance on all of the dead man's kin. John was the first to encounter the murderer, and the meeting took place in such a way that the latter was taken completely by surprise. The murderer was defenceless; fearing the worst, he stood before John Gualbert, the honour-bound young knight, with hands outstretched in a cruciform. The day was Good Friday; John let the man go, and himself went into the nearby monastery of Saint-Miniato to contemplate his very Christian but dishonourable deed. The crucifix to which he addressed himself gave him a sign of approval, so he asked if he could enter the community, and he was received.[28]

John worked into the Benedictine life with zest and success, so earning the respect of his adopted brothers that when their abbot died, he was their unanimous choice as successor. The real power lay not with the monks, however, but with the Archbishop of Florence, who sold the abbacy to a wealthy office-seeker. John left Saint-

Miniato, sought advice from a pious and venerable hermit, and then went into Florence on the offensive. He chose what was probably a market-day, in any case 'a day on which he knew there would be a huge crowd of people'. Before a crowd, he denounced both the abbot and the archbishop as simoniacs. The reaction of the crowd was mainly hostile; cries demanding his death were heard. So John and his companions withdrew, and went in search of 'a monastery where they could freely serve Christ'.[29]

They went to Camaldoli but stayed only a short while. The community made them welcome but the prior was insistent upon their adhering strictly to a vow of stability.[30] The formula was not right because Gualbert wished to return to town often in order to preach, and so they left. The year was about 1030. They went to a place closer to Florence, about 22 miles from the city, and there undertook an eremitical style of life. They had arrived at Vallombrosa.

To carry on the business of the monastery, to make all the necessary connections with the secular society beyond the monastery, for Vallombrosa was not nearly so remote or independent a place as Camaldoli, John introduced at some time between 1039 and 1051 a special category of monk, a sort of second-class monk, or lay brother, who looked much like a full-fledged monk, with slight differences in clothing and lacking the tonsure. These lay brothers, called conversi, did the work for the rest of the community, leaving the monks free, not for a full programme of liturgy in the Cluniac manner, but for a life of eremitical contemplation. These conversi took essentially the same vows as the monks, except that they were not bound to remain silent when they went to market or otherwise busied themselves in the world outside the cloister.[31]

John's ideal was something of a reformed Benedictine life tempered with active church reform and St Romuald's eremiticism. When he learned that a rich man had entered one of Vallombrosa's monasteries in the old Benedictine way, by bringing his family fortune with him, John went there right away, asked to see the charter of donation, tore it up, and trampled on the shreds. As he left in anger, he called upon the vengeance of God. Immediately a fire broke out in the monastery, but John did not even look back.[32]

4. BERNARD OF TIRON

Bernard of Tiron (*c.*1046–1117) was born and raised in Abbéville, a town in north-eastern France, where he received a sound education in grammar, dialectic, and the literary arts. At about the age of twenty, he went off to join the monastery of Saint-Cyprian, near Poitiers.

When a fellow monk named Gervais was elected abbot of the nearby monastery of Saint-Savin, he took Bernard along as prior, and together they directed the affairs of Saint-Savin for two decades, until Gervais' death. Bernard was the obvious successor, but to avoid being elected, he fled to the forests of Maine and Brittany to become a hermit. For a while he lived on the Channel island of Chausey (located between Jersey and Saint-Malo), to be 'separated from the bothers and commotions of men'.[33]

Eventually he was called back to his original monastic home of Saint-Cyprian to serve as abbot, and he accepted. But shortly he found himself embroiled in a struggle to maintain Saint-Cyprian's independence against a Cluniac take-over. The struggle dragged on through several stages at the papal court, with the Cluniacs apparently the complete victors at one point, having taken Saint-Cyprian and secured the deposition of Bernard. But in a final, compromise settlement, Saint-Cyprian remained independent and Bernard remained deposed. His biographer says of him after this unpleasant period: 'Boiling over with love of poverty and solitude, he returned to the seclusion of the hermitage, from which he had been drawn away by fraudulent violence, and he found his own mind, which had remained behind there.'[34]

Bernard found himself again, and yet it was not really his old self that he found. 'He found his own mind' in the true sense of self-discovery, because now he did not take up again the simple life of a hermit, but he combined such a life with an active programme of itinerant preaching. He teamed up with two other famous hermits, Robert of Arbrissel and Vitalis of Savigny, whom he had perhaps met earlier in Brittany, and together 'they wandered about bare-footed in various sections of France, preaching the word of God in villages, at castles, and in the cities....'[35]

When he attempted to settle once more and to organize a monastic community, he found Cluny prepared to pounce on him again. Then his friend and protector, Ivo of Chartres, got him a place on the river Tiron, a place without Cluniac connections, and there Bernard at last set up his Abbey of the Holy Trinity.[36] He was helped and patronized by many important and wealthy people, including King Louis VI (1108–37). He organized a school in the monastery and placed it under the direction of Geoffrey (like Louis VI) the Fat, subsequently his biographer. The influence of Bernard and his monastery spread to other monasteries, new and reformed, so that eventually Tiron was an order of ten abbeys and over forty priories.[37]

Among those who flocked to Bernard's communities were a great many people already committed to the religious life. They left their monasteries, some of them doubtless attracted by Bernard's generally great reputation for holiness, but many for the specific reason that they recognized in him 'the new Anthony', and therefore wished to be associated both with him and with his style of poverty.[38]

Bernard was 'a lover of poverty and solitude'; more specifically, a critical facet of his programme was that the monk live from the labour of his own hands.[39] The monasteries that Bernard established had adequate but simple, unostentatious buildings. Bernard himself was loathe to accept or handle money. When Bernard left the forest on his first expedition to Chausey, a well-intentioned fellow hermit gave him eighteen coins to take along. Bernard was upset (*non mediocriter indignatus*), and took the occasion to deliver a brief lesson on true Christian poverty.[40]

Finally, Bernard's spirituality was clearly marked by a socially active conception of the apostolate: the need to go about preaching God's message.[41] And preaching, Bernard had come to understand, was intimately tied to poverty. At Coutances, Bernard got himself entangled in an argument when he attacked clerical marriage. A priest, apparently sensitive to the point being made, challenged Bernard's right to preach to the living since, as a monk, he was supposed to be dead to the world. Bernard replied that a preacher in order to be effective must lead an exemplary life, and that precisely one who is dead to the world, that is to the sins and vices of the world, is better qualified than anyone else to preach.[42] By such thought and action did Bernard and his followers believe that they were helping to create and inhabit 'another Egypt'.[43]

5. ROBERT OF ARBRISSEL

Robert of Arbrissel (*c.*1055–1117) was a Breton who had been a student in Paris and a priest at Rennes before going to Angers to teach philosophy. In 1092 he left Angers for the forest of Craon to give himself over completely to contemplation, that is, to live as a hermit. Apparently there were many other hermits in the wood during the final decades of the eleventh century. Robert, in the usual fashion, attracted others, including monks, people who sought to live regularly 'in the manner of the primitive church'. His first monastic foundation, Saint-Mary of La Roë adopted the Rule of St Augustine, steering clear of any Cluniac influences.[44] Pope Urban II was then travelling in France, and he met Robert and heard him preach. So impressive was the sermon, and Robert's reputation generally, that the pope gave Robert an extraordinary commission to go about as a preacher of the Gospel. It was among the poor especially that Robert carried out the assignment: 'This man preached the Gospel to the poor, he called the poor, he gathered the poor together.'[45]

While continuing as a preacher, Robert's other achievement was the foundation of the monastery of Fontevrault, for both men and women, all under the direction of an abbess, in about 1101. The site itself was wild and inhospitable, 'hidden away from where people lived'; it had to be so, for proximity to castles and towns and neighbours generally tended to negate the effectiveness of the religious life. Men and women, laymen and clerics, came there and worked to build a new home in the desert, a place 'in which the new family and new army of God might live and work'.[46]

Among the men, laymen and clerics were mixed together in the same quarters, but the difference between them was that the priests sang psalms and celebrated masses, while the laymen willingly gave themselves over to work. Silence was observed at all times by everyone.

The peculiar arrangement of a double monastery—not the first ever but very unusual at that time—demonstrates Robert's concern for the salvation of women. The female community was open to women of all conditions, but Robert took special care of the lowliest of the low in the new society: prostitutes.[47] These he hoped especially to bring to the religious life. No person was too low or too miserable to experience the charity of Robert. He established colonies for lepers, and indeed as he lay dying, he directed his thoughts to 'his beloved sick ones' and to 'his lepers'.[48]

As a reformer and preacher, he took on all the powerful sinners of his day. He recognized simoniacs among the learned doctors, the bishops, abbots, priests, and princes of his day. He attacked the adulterous and incestuous, indeed all who ignored the laws of God.[49] But for these people he did not propose ways to cope with the complex social realities of the twelfth-century monetary economy. Instead, he sought to create a refuge for that 'new family and new army of God'.

6. STEPHEN OF MURET

Stephen of Muret (*c.* 1052–1124), whose followers established the Order of Grandmont, came from a noble family in the Auvergne. When Stephen was about twelve, he fell sick in Italy during a pilgrimage and underwent a long convalescence in the house of the Archbishop of Benevento. This prelate was much in sympathy with the reform party then in control of the papacy; moreover he looked favourably on the many Greek Christian hermits living in his region and he often commended their example in his sermons. Stephen's Italian experience also included a stay in Rome, between approximately 1076 and 1080, after the death of Peter Damian but during the pontificate of Gregory VII.[50]

Stephen returned home and shortly afterwards went into the forest of Muret where, for the remaining 40 or so years of his life, he lived as a hermit. He was probably never completely alone; there were other hermits and there were always visitors. A group of disciples gathered about him, living principally by his example, and at no time during Stephen's lifetime did they organize any kind of formal monastic structure. Only after Stephen's death in 1124 did his disciples give institutional shape to the kind of life they led. They removed to a nearby hill, Grandmont, taking with them the remains of their leader, and they built there a monastery and a church, and they elected a prior. Their customs were solidified into a rule during the tenure of the fourth Prior of Grandmont (1139–63), and this rule received papal approbation in 1189 at the same time that Stephen was canonized. The biography of Stephen was similarly assembled over the years by his followers; nearly 20 of its final chapters record miracles, a fact suggesting that the definitive form of this *Vita* was a sort of brief prepared for the canonization.[51]

The lateness of the rule is not to be understood as oversight on the part of Stephen; he would never have written or approved of any rule. He agreed that there were several monastic rules, one for example that is called the Rule of St Basil, another the Rule of St Augustine, and yet another called the Rule of St Benedict. But none of these is the origin of a religion; they are only its preservers and propagators. 'They are not the root, but only the foliage. For there is just one first rule of faith and salvation, one principal rule of rules, from which all the others flow like streams from a spring, I mean of course the holy Gospel, taught by the Saviour to the Apostles, and faithfully announced by them to the entire world.'[52]

The best available source on Stephen is significant for its form as well as its content. The work is a loosely assembled collection of Stephen's teachings and of anecdotes about him, the *Liber de doctrina* or *Liber Sententiarum*. The form of this book is the same as that used in gathering and preserving the wisdom of the Desert Fathers. And so the preferred literary genre as well as the style of life that once flourished in the Egyptian desert was reborn in the years around 1100 in the French wilderness.[53] The *Vita* records that when Stephen and his companions dined together, he had them sit in silence, while one of them read from saints' lives or *The Lives of the Desert Fathers*. Furthermore, Stephen behaved like the Egyptians particularly in the way he received visitors. Rich and poor, strong and weak, saintly and sinful, strange and familiar, all of these came to see the holy man. Like Robert of Arbrissel, Stephen showed a special concern for the welfare of prostitutes; and to these Stephen added actresses. To all he gave an equally patient hearing; some he advised, others he consoled, others he admonished. But to all he gave hope. 'He was a father to them all.'[54]

When he became a hermit, Stephen rejoiced at the solitude, which in his judgment he had found suitable to the life of poverty. The true poor people of Christ were those who utterly renounced the world, claiming and having nothing for themselves; thus the hermitage was the ideal setting for the evangelical life. And as survival was promised to the *pauperes Christi* by God, they would have no need to return to the world.[55]

God's promise did not imply a life of idleness. To a prospective hermit, Stephen put the matter squarely: 'Will you be able, brother, to be a farmer, to carry wood and manure, and to serve all of your brothers?'[56] The Rule of Grandmont, which, although composed at a later time, would on no account be expected to prescribe stricter behaviour than did the founder, specified that there were to be no animals, either for work or consumption.[57] The rule also clearly specified that the church and indeed the other monastic buildings as well were to be of the utmost simplicity, with no pictures, no statues, nothing superfluous; in short, they were to be 'as plain and simple as our religion'.[58]

The charge that Stephen put to a prospective companion was not simply to choose between his rude style of life and a layman's secular life, but between his life there at Muret and life in a Benedictine monastery. 'Look, you can go into any monastery whatever, where you'll find huge buildings and first-rate cuisine all properly prepared and served on time. There you will find animals and great expanses of arable land, but here you will find only the cross and poverty.'[59]

Gerard Ithier, seventh Prior of Grandmont (1188–98), and the one responsible for getting the rule approved and Stephen canonized in Rome, made a significant addition to Stephen's notion of the Gospel as the only religious rule. If someone were to point out that St Benedict wrote a rule for monks, the reply, according to Gerard, ought to be that the Gospel is a rule for everybody. 'All Christians who hold consistently to the faith can be called monks,' said Gerard; and he continued in this way:

As for the rule of God, anyone who follows it can be saved, no matter whether he be married or not; that's something you won't find in the Rule of St Benedict. ... Therefore understand that there can be only one rule and that the Son of God said, 'Apart from me, you will be able to do nothing' [John 15:5]. Thus anyone is judged to be outside the rule who draws away from God's precepts, and in the same way, one remains always within the rule who fulfils His commands.[60]

Gerard's suggestion went far beyond the usual notion of a reform of the religious life, for he was suggesting a radical alteration of the very concept of the religious life, expanding it, ultimately, to embrace all people. This idea was going to recur often in the following century.

7. OPPOSITION TO THE HERMITS

The hermits of the eleventh and twelfth centuries, at least those well known to posterity, did not withdraw quietly from society and stay away forever. They used the eremitic life instead as a vehicle for reform. Not only in making explicitly critical statements but by their very manner and behaviour they represented a severe critique of the existing order, so that they in turn attracted hostile criticism.

A principal issue was the itinerant preaching engaged in by the hermits. By their itinerancy, they challenged Benedictine stability; by preaching to the laity, they challenged the silence of the secular clergy. Marbode, Bishop of Rennes, felt that Robert of Arbrissel's attacks on the clergy were too negative to merit the name of preaching.[61] Ivo of Chartres tried to restrain Reginald the Hermit's attacks on the monks, which he believed to be indiscriminate, especially by reminding Reginald of such positive aspects of the cenobitic life as the opportunities it affords to exercise charity and the protection it affords against the exertion of the individual will.[62] Ivo based most of his appeal on the form of life practised in the primitive church.[63] The same theme served Reginald in replying, but his understanding of the phrase *forma primitivae ecclesiae* differed from Ivo's. With three brief citations from the Gospels on perfection and limitless charity, Reginald arrived at the heart of his argument: 'You know as well as I that cenobitic cloisters rarely or never include this standard of perfection ... because they exclude as much as possible the poverty that Christ the pauper preached.' The monks show deep concern for personal comfort, good food, and protection of their property, if necessary through litigation; in these and in other ways, they are clearly not imitators of Christ or the Apostles but of the Pharisees.[64]

By often appearing in public, the hermits left themselves open to the charge of being part-time, or false, hermits. Around 1135, a priest of Chartres wrote a lengthy poem against these 'false hermits'. The themes he evoked included the unjust attacks made by hermits, their selfishness, their mingling in society and their appearance. The hermits have seized upon some of the less important aspects of black monasticism, went the argument, and they have made exaggerated charges about its laxity, but these same critics understand nothing of the true value of the cloistered life of prayer and spiritual reading. The hermits are similarly lacking in charity towards and understanding of the secular clergy. For all their talk about poverty, the hermits are in reality rapacious wolves; they call themselves enemies of avarice but they are as insatiable as they are grasping. They are parasites, not hermits. As for their removal from society, they in fact spend most of their time wandering about towns, trying to attract attention and donations. 'Get out of the woods and head for the towns' would seem to be their motto. Finally, the appearance of these hermits is offensive. In part, this is because they affect the clothing of the truly religious, and this deception misleads simple people. But on the other hand, they tend to be sloppy: they wear baggy togas and their untonsured hair hangs down over their foreheads and their ears. 'This evil plague,' according to the outraged priest from Chartres, 'has already polluted nearly the entire world.'[65]

One does not have to agree that the hermits 'polluted nearly the entire world', but it is apparent that the leaders among them were familiar with the world they chose to abandon: a world of cities and of monasteries. Romuald was familiar with Ravenna; Peter Damian also knew Ravenna, in addition to Faenza and Parma; John Gualbert knew Florence; Bernard of Tiron, Abbéville; Robert of Arbrissel, Paris; and Stephen of Muret, Benevento and Rome. Moreover, Romuald had his life threatened at Saint-Apollinaris; Peter taught at Pomposa; John believed himself unjustly deprived of the abbacy of Saint-Miniato; Bernard engaged in desperate struggles with Cluny; Robert set up a monastery that was pointedly different from any other at the time; and Stephen posed as a condition to anyone who wished to join him that he explicitly renounce the comforts and ease of the monastic life. Thus in all these cases, neither the new form of economy nor the old form of spirituality—which had reached such an easy, unthinking accommodation with the new economy—was acceptable. The solution proposed was a return to the form of another age of discontent with cities, a revival of third- and fourth-century Egyptian eremitism. Just as this earlier eremitism led to the formation of monastic communities, the rise and expansion of Camaldoli, Fonté Avellana, Vallombrosa, Tiron, Fontevrault, and Grandmont show that the revived eremitic ideal led not to a wave of individual and isolated ascetics but to a reformed cenobitic monasticism.

6

The new monastery

The careers of Bruno of Cologne, Norbert of Xanten, and Robert of Molesme resembled in many essential particulars those of the eremitic leaders. Only historical hindsight justifies their isolation in a separate category; it shows that the institutions that eventually grew out of their efforts far surpassed in lasting importance the eremitic communities. Moreover, these institutions, the orders of the Carthusians, of the Premonstratensians, and of the Cistercians, were not founded upon the Egyptian model, to evolve then almost accidentally into cenobitism; instead, out of a dissatisfaction with the existing monastic order no less pungent than that which drove the hermit leaders, they were intended from the start as reformed monastic communities.

1. CARTHUSIANS

Bruno of Cologne (c.1030-1101) was for twenty years master of the episcopal school at Rheims. Towards the end of this period the archbishopric passed into the hands of the notorious simoniac Manasses, mentioned earlier for his views on the burdensome nature of pastoral responsibilities. After Bruno took part in the papacy's successful campaign to remove Manasses from office, the general expectation was that he would become the next archbishop. But Bruno and three of his colleagues had vowed earlier to get out of Rheims and to go live as hermits. Although one of these colleagues now stayed behind, Bruno and the other two headed south in search of a new life. After a few unsatisfactory attempts to settle down, they went to Grenoble—the year was 1084 and their group now numbered seven—where the bishop, named Hugh, was a former student of Bruno at Rheims. Hugh made available to this band of pilgrims a place called Chartreuse high in the Alps: altitude 3,500 feet, a desolate, rocky place extremely difficult to reach, and during much of the year buried deep in snow. The hermits at first lived two-by-two in little huts, but later on each hermit had his own hut; they also built themselves a small oratory.[1]

In 1090, another former student, now Pope Urban II, sought the services of Bruno as an adviser in Rome. Bruno left, at some risk to the stability of the settlement at Chartreuse, and eventually settled in Italy. After turning down the episcopal see of Reggio, Bruno founded another hermitage in Calabria, on land given by Count Roger. He named his new home Santa Maria della Torre, and it was there, after founding still other monasteries, that he died in 1101.

The initiative taken by Bruno and the inspiration he gave the Carthusians have never been in doubt. But since Bruno stayed at the Chartreuse for only six years, and since the Carthusian customs were reduced to writing only in the late 1120s, during the time of the fifth prior, Guigo I (1109–30), no one knows precisely how Bruno envisaged the structure of the monastery and the relations between it and other monasteries.[2] In Guigo's time, an order was beginning to take shape, and the priors of newly established houses were asking to have the customs of the original house in writing. Monks were sent out from that original house to assist in the organization of new houses, but each of the latter was fully independent from the start, under the leadership of its own prior. By contemporary standards, the order grew very slowly. The priors assembled in a general chapter, presided over by the Prior of the Grande Chartreuse, for the first time in 1141.[3] By the close of the twelfth century, the order consisted of thirty-nine monasteries.

Each of these houses was small by contemporary standards. The number of monks was set at the apostolic figure of twelve; in addition, there was the prior and a maximum of sixteen lay brothers.[4] The Carthusian monks thought of themselves as combining the Benedictine life with some of the earlier eremitic elements. In the preface to their customs, both St Benedict and the eastern hermits, especially St Jerome, were singled out as sources.[5] The choice of a very remote place was carefully thought out; the monks maintained nearly always a strict silence; they continually evoked the memory and example of the Desert Fathers.[6] Carthusian documents characteristically use phrases such as 'eremitic order', or 'eremitic life'.[7] Some though not all of the monks were priests. One of these celebrated mass for the entire community on Sunday.[8] The monks were mostly literate, because apart from their major occupation of prayer and contemplation, they spent their time copying manuscripts. Great care, they said, had to be taken in this work because they were thereby preaching the word of God with their hands instead of their mouths.[9] The detailed list of contents for each cell included all the requisite tools for a copyist.[10]

The material welfare of the community was assured by the lay brothers, under the supervision of one of the monks, called the procurator, who was in general charge of the estate's management and was directly responsible to the prior.[11] The conversi lived a short distance down the hill from the hermitage. There they led a simple, cenobitic life, taking vows and reciting part of the monastic schedule of offices, though their major responsibility lay in making cheese, baking bread, repairing sandals, milking goats, and other such mundane activities.[12] While the conversi acted as a sort of buffer between the hermits and secular society, the conversi themselves had such a buffer in hired servants who negotiated the community's affairs at mills and vineyards and markets.[13] The monastery also hired shepherds to tend its flocks in the mountain pasture.[14]

The Carthusian's church was utterly simple. 'In our church, we have no gold or silver ornaments whatever except for the chalice and reed, in which the Lord's blood is gathered, and we have nothing to do with tapestries and rugs.'[15] In celebrating the office of the dead, there were to be no distinctions made reflecting the status of the person being honoured. Precisely the same formula was to apply in all cases, whether for a priest or a simple monk, a prelate, the prior, or a lay brother.[16] One of their most pointed criticisms of contemporary monasticism was the provision that the monks not write the name of any donor in their martyrology nor perform an *anniversarium* for anyone.[17] Moreover, they insistently tried to restore what they saw as essential elements in the original Benedictine ideal: total obedience, total surrender of the individual will, and rigid maintenance of stability.[18]

While they did not necessarily turn away guests, the Carthusians did not encourage guests indiscriminately. They claimed to be unwilling to care for any visitor's horse, for they had no horses of their own and with this regulation they could be sure that anyone who came to them really felt he wanted or needed to come there.[19]

Guibert of Nogent, who visited the Grande Chartreuse in about 1112, told what happened to another visitor, the Count of Nevers.[20] This count, apparently impressed by the simplicity and piety of the monks, delivered a speech to them warning against the dangers of worldy cupidity. After returning home, and evidently still insensitive to the inappropriateness of his speech, he sent some precious gifts to the monks as a gesture of thanks. Only when the monks returned these gifts did he appreciate the gap between his words and his behaviour. The story, though, does not end with a sensational conversion, but with the count sending the monks some skins for manuscript-copying, which he thought would 'be almost inevitably a necessity for them', a gift, in other words, they would not refuse. He was right.

Guigo gave warnings against 'insane cupidity' and 'vicious avarice'.[21] Bruno himself gave a sermon against worldly riches, in which he explained the image of the camel having difficulty passing through the eye of a needle as a way of indicating how difficult it would be for an avaricious man to get himself out of the belly of avarice. 'In order to eliminate all occasions for cupidity, as far as possible with God's help, both for us and for posterity,' wrote Guigo, 'by this document we order that the inhabitants of this place possess nothing beyond the limits of their desert, neither fields, nor vineyards, nor gardens, nor churches, nor cemeteries, nor offerings, nor tithes, nor anything else whatever of this sort.'[22]

The sites of Carthusian monasteries were selected so that the monks would not suffer any of the confusion or contamination of urban society. One side effect of this voluntary isolation was their key role in developing iron works in the forests and mountains of Dauphiné and in thus making Grenoble the centre of an iron trade.[23] Another effect—in this case intentional—was that they were not bothered much by beggars. The Carthusians not only rejected the old monastic formal charity, they showed an awareness of a more spontaneous form of apostolate potentially open to them, but they explicitly rejected it, too. Guigo stated the principle in the twentieth chapter of the Customs:

To the poor people of this world we give bread or anything else that our will or our means suggest, but rarely do we take one of them in under our roof; instead we send him into town. For after all, we have taken refuge in the isolation of this hermitage not in order to take worldly care of other people's physical needs but for the eternal welfare of our own souls. Thus no one should be surprised if we show greater openness and concern for those who come here on account of their souls than for those who come on account of their bodies. If it were otherwise, then not in harsh and remote and nearly inaccessible places (to which whoever comes for the sake of bodily care will more suffer from physical exertion than attain by way of remedy) ought we long since to have settled down, but rather in busy streets.[24]

The Carthusian programme was thus consciously anti-urban and consciously opposed to the established monastic order; in positive terms, it combined eremitism with poverty and a pared-down monastic rule.

2. PREMONSTRATENSIANS

The founder of Prémontré was Norbert of Xanten (c.1080–1134), a nobleman of high standing (his father was a vassal, and perhaps a kinsman, of the emperor) who got his schooling in the household of the Archbishop of Cologne. He was drawn into the circle of imperial politics and in 1111 participated as a courtier in Henry V's descent into Italy and entry into Rome. His presence at the humiliation of

Pope Pascal II on that occasion was later a source of deep regret.[25]

Between the ages of about 30 and 35, Norbert experienced a profound conversion. His biographers record that he barely escaped being struck down by lightning and thereupon he became a hermit. He lived in the vicinity of the Abbey of Siegburg, about twelve miles from Cologne. Whatever the precise truth of his Luther-like experience with lightning, Norbert found at Siegburg in Abbot Conan a spiritual counsellor such as Luther was to have in Johan von Staupitz. During this time of turmoil and transformation, Norbert was made a deacon and a priest, and then a canon, by the Archbishop of Cologne. At one point Norbert went to Xanten to try to reform his fellow canons. He dressed simply and preached publicly. While he drew a sympathetic popular response, he managed to offend his colleagues. Their day came at the Council of Fritzlar in 1118 when Norbert was reprimanded for usurping the office of preaching, for not dressing and acting in the manner suitable to a canon, and for affecting a monkish habit without having taken vows. Norbert was thus not formally condemned but he understood his colleagues' intention; he responded by advancing to a yet more radical stage.[26]

Norbert resigned his prebend and sold his considerable property, giving the money he received to the poor or to the monks of Siegburg, who had befriended him in his moment of crisis. He set out as an itinerant preacher, though first getting permission from Pope Gelasius II who was sojourning at Saint-Gilles in Languedoc.[27]

Norbert undertook his now official mission as a preacher in the northern provinces of Artois, Hainault, and Brabant. When word reached him of the death of Gelasius and of the election of a successor, Norbert went to Rheims to see that successor, Calixtus II, in order to seek confirmation of his mission. At first he was denied access to the new pope and left Rheims disappointed. But then he met Bartholomew, the Bishop of Laon and a nephew of the pope, and this man was able to arrange Norbert's desired interview. Calixtus, together with Bartholomew, prevailed on Norbert to let himself be elected provost of a little collegiate church, Saint-Martin of Laon, on the outskirts of that city. His modest task was to reform Saint-Martin's clergy, but the clerics there were unwilling and Norbert was basically uninterested.[28]

Norbert now seemed to clarify his desires, with the result that he undertook to settle in the forest with a group of hermits. Bartholomew cooperated by offering a number of alternative sites within his diocese. The one chosen was Prémontré; the year was 1120. In a little more than one year, a substantial community of 40 monks, several of them priests, had gathered there. The need for a formal constitution became increasingly apparent. Late in 1121 Norbert decided that the Rule of St Augustine best suited their needs and accordingly, on Christmas day, all present took a vow to adhere to that rule.[29]

Norbert himself did not remain in solitude at Prémontré. Within even a few days of his arrival there, he quickly went into Laon where, at the famous school of that city, he sought men and money for his new community. He returned to Prémontré with seven of the wealthiest students and a great quantity of money.[30] In 1121, Norbert attended the Council of Soissons, the council at which Abelard faced hostile critics, and journeyed to Cologne to collect relics for the church already under construction at Prémontré. He was actively engaged in 1122 in the founding of the second house of what was to be a new order, at Floreffe near Liège, securing the land with an endowment from Count Gottfried of Namur.[31] In 1124 he preached so effectively against the heretic Tanchelm at Antwerp that people there undertook to establish another daughter house of Prémontré.[32] During this period he did not remain aloof from imperial politics, so that, in 1126, Lothair III designated him to be the Archbishop of Magdeburg.[33]

Between 1131 and 1134, Hugh of Fosse, Norbert's successor at Prémontré and the house's first official abbot, put through a constitution providing the essentials for a federation of monastic houses and for a general chapter.[34] By the middle of the twelfth century, this federation consisted of nearly 100 houses. In 1188, the order received a special commission from Pope Clement III (1187–91) to engage actively in the parish ministry and in charitable enterprises such as hostels, hospitals, and schools.[35] By the middle of the thirteenth century, the order had become a vast agglomeration of over 500 abbeys and priories.[36]

At Prémontré, no monk could possess anything of his own; the adopted dress was the coarse, undyed woollen habit. The customs adopted under Hugh in the early 1130s made no mention of preaching or of the parish ministry.[37] Premonstratensians took the traditional vows of stability and obedience. Adam the Scot, who composed a description of the order, devoted an entire chapter to stability and one to obedience, but gave no such attention to the care of souls.[38]

An analysis of the monastic and clerical life written between 1125 and 1130 places the Premonstratensians unequivocally among those who live far away from concentrations of population.[39] This view seems to confirm something St Norbert is reported to have said in 1120. The occasion of the remark was the combined papal and episcopal request that he take over and reform Saint-Martin of Laon. Although, as we have seen, Norbert made at least a formal attempt to fulfil that request, he is quoted as saying: 'I did not give up the greater splendours of Cologne just to seek the lesser ones of Laon. I do not wish to stay in cities, but rather in wild, deserted places.' Norbert got his wish: Prémontré was a place 'far removed from all habitations of men, and close only to wild boars and wolves'.[40]

3. CISTERCIANS

The most spectacular success of twelfth-century religious life, the Cistercian Order, grew out of the troubled spiritual quest of Robert of Molesme (c.1027–1110). Robert had served as prior in two monasteries of his native province of Champagne and as abbot of a third. His fourth religious home was in the company of some hermits whom he led in 1075 to Molesme, where they fashioned a monastic community out of the wilderness and adopted the Rule of St Benedict. The Bishop of Troyes visited them and, finding them extremely poor, became a generous benefactor. Others did likewise and soon the community prospered. Gifts and converts flowed in until, once again, Robert had to go elsewhere in search of austerity.[41]

In 1098, Robert led 21 of his fellow monks on the famous exodus to Cîteaux where they set up a 'New Monastery'. The prosperous and powerful community of Molesme was apparently hurt by the sudden departure of many of its leaders and decided to press for a papal order to make Robert return to his post as abbot. After only a year and a half at the New Monastery, Robert returned to the old one, where he spent the remaining decade of his life.[42]

Included in the group of exiles from Molesme were the immediate successors to Robert at Cîteaux: Alberic (1099–1109) and Stephen Harding (1109–33). The presence of these exceptionally capable monastic administrators in the exile group and the lack of extant writings by Robert raise questions about who had the ideas for Cîteaux and who should properly be considered its founder. The monks of Molesme were so successful in arguing that Robert had violated canon law by leaving his post that not only did they get him back to Molesme but the Cistercians played it safe by considering Alberic, not Robert, their founder and first abbot. The delicate legal question remained unresolved for a century, until Innocent III ruled that a monk, out of a desire for perfection, could transfer from one monastic order to another one that was more austere. There followed a rehabilitation of Robert and a reconciliation of Molesme and Cîteaux; a monk of Molesme wrote a biography of Robert; the Cistercians began to regard Robert as their founder and first abbot; and in 1221 Robert was canonized by Honorius III.[43]

The century of jealousy and hostility between Molesme and Cîteaux demonstrates rather clearly one aspect of the crisis of Latin monasticism. In its first fifteen years Molesme had become a rich, powerful, handsomely endowed monastery of the old, Cluniac type. Monks there and at Cîteaux, as well as outsiders, were aware that at Cîteaux, something new and different was taking place.

The fortunes of the New Monastery are well known; the small and unprosperous, even declining, community of Cîteaux received its greatest gift on that day in April of 1112 when Bernard (c.1090–1153) arrived and sought admission along with about thirty of his relatives and friends.[44] Cîteaux's subsequent growth far outdid any previous expansion in monastic history. First she established her four 'daughter' houses: La Ferté (1113), Pontigny (1114), Clairvaux (with Bernard as abbot, 1115), and Morimond (1115). Then from Cîteaux and her four daughters the order spread throughout France and into Italy (1120), Germany (1123), England (1128), Austria (1130), and Spain (1140). At the time of Bernard's death the order consisted of 343 houses and by the end of the twelfth century the figure had passed 500.[45] A disproportionate share, nearly one-half, of these houses derived from Bernard's Clairvaux. Towards the end of Bernard's career, Clairvaux alone had nearly 70 daughter houses and over 90 indirect dependencies. This dominant position of Bernard and of his house led at least one scribe, consciously or not, to refer to the Order of Cîteaux as the Order of Clairvaux.[46]

The complements to Bernard's powers of attraction and persuasion that made secure this mighty development of the entire order were the administrative and legislative talents of Alberic and of Stephen Harding. Alberic had been the Prior of Molesme and presumably continued in that position under Robert at Cîteaux before Robert's forced departure. The customs of the New Monastery were set down in the time of Alberic. An account of the secession from Molesme and of the early years of Cîteaux to 1115, the *Exordium parvum*, is thought to be the work of Stephen. Stephen's great monument, the *Charter of Charity*, evolved in several redactions, probably beginning at the time of the foundation of La Ferté in 1113. It set down the basic laws governing the relationships between mother and daughter houses and among all Cistercian houses. Stephen presided over a meeting of abbots from the daughter houses in 1116, though Bernard could not attend because of illness. Ten abbots attended the general chapter in 1119; 69 attended in 1133. The regulations governing the conduct of these annual meetings were formally codified in 1134. Eventually a hall large enough to accommodate over 300 abbots was built at Cîteaux.[47]

The basis of the original Cistercian programme was a strict and literal adherence to the Rule of St Benedict, and this can be ascribed to Robert. In reminding his brothers of their vow to follow the rule, Robert observed: 'But we do not hold to it fully. We observe many practices that cannot be found in it, while at the same time we neglect

91

many of its provisions.'[48] The Cistercian tradition of manual labour for all monks went back as far as the settlement at Molesme, when without any outside help the monks, 'working with their own hands', made the place inhabitable.[49] In imitation of Benedict, the Cistercians chose not to settle in towns, burgs, or villages, or even near any such centres of population. Such was the deliberate rationale expressed in the *Instituta* drawn up by or under the direction of Alberic.[50] From Yorkshire to Portugal, the Cistercians had villages that they considered too close to their properties uprooted and moved.[51]

The life of the Cistercians in fact had many features not in conformity with the rule; for example, like the Vallombrosians and the Carthusians, they relied heavily on the labour of conversi, or lay brothers. On the other hand they did not admit children. They added the office of the dead. The superstructure of the general chapter and the powers given abbots over the abbots of daughter houses were all matters totally foreign to Benedict's legislation.

Cistercians occasionally praised the eremitic life. Bernard once encouraged a restless hermit to remain a hermit, but out of loyalty to the principle of stability and not out of any admiration for eremiticism. Indeed he said that people became hermits out of a lightness and instability of spirit.[52] Similarly he opposed any itinerancy, including that of itinerant preachers.[53] To these he opposed an ideal far more subtle than a simple adherence to the cloistered life. He was able to agree with the notion that the rule was a programme for beginners, and that the more adept should try to surpass it, although he would not have agreed that hermits are superior to cenobites. The religious person should live in a cloister, and therein build an interior solitude capable of securing all the worthy aspects of a hermit's life.[54] Like so many of his contemporaries, Bernard invoked the Egyptian model, yet he made his ideal an anchoritic life lived within the cenobium.[55] William of Saint-Thierry stressed the theme of the desert in his biography of Bernard, for example, when he reminisced about his first visit to the great man at Clairvaux:

Although unworthy of so great a privilege, I remained with him for a few days, and as I looked about me I thought that I was gazing on a new heaven and a new earth, for it seemed as though there were tracks freshly made by men of our own day in the path that had first been trodden by our fathers, the Egyptian monks of long ago.[56]

A yearning for peace and solitude, far away from the busy ways of society, is common to all the great Cistercian writers, including Bernard, William of Saint-Thierry, Aelred of Rievaulx, and Peter of Celle. Bernard urged the masters and students of Paris to flee the

Babylon in which they lived: 'You will find much more in the forest than in books. The woods and rocks will teach you more than any master can.'[57] Similarly Peter of Celle gave warning about deceptive, ravenous, and sophistic Paris. Against that dangerous place and school, he set the Cistercian monastery, which he and others referred to sometimes as the 'school of Christ'.

O blessed school, where Christ teaches our hearts by the word of his virtue, where we learn without studying and reading how we ought to live blessed lives eternally. No book has to be bought there, the master of the scriptorium does not get paid, there is no onslaught in disputations, no weaving of sophistries; it is free of passing judgment on all questions, free from involvement in all reasoning and argument.[58]

The economic organization developed by the Cistercians was one of the marvels of the century. At its simplest, this organization called for the direct exploitation by the monks of their respective monasteries' lands. The estates of black monks had been organized in the same way as those of any lay or ecclesiastical lord, with a division between demesne-land, worked by those peasants, free and servile, who owed service to the lord, and the remaining land, lived on and worked by the lord's tenants. All Cistercian land was in a sense demesne-land, only there were neither free peasants nor serfs. There were instead the conversi, who were full-time farm workers, to assist the monks, who could spend only part of their time in the fields. Properties not contiguous with a house's principal site were similarly organized as single, demesne-like entities, called granges, but worked exclusively by conversi.[59]

The success of this system is legendary, as is also the embarrassment of riches it produced. By the end of the twelfth century, the wealth of the Cistercians had given rise to popular clichés about being as wealthy or as crooked as a Cistercian, and about the Cistercians being the new Jews of Europe. When Gerald of Wales told Walter Map about the two Cistercians who had become Jews, Walter observed that it was too bad that, since these two had resolved to improve their lives, they did not go one step further and become Christians.[60]

The Cistercians of Chiaravalle (Clairvaux), near Milan, built the first permanent irrigation system in northern Italy in the late 1130s.[61] At Casamari and Fossanova in Latium, they specialized in the expensive (but commensurately rewarding) process of raising horses.[62] In England, the Cistercians assumed a central role in the production of wool, not only by raising sheep on their own land but also by marketing the wool produced on the lands of others. They borrowed money, from both Christian and Jewish moneylenders, sometimes against the following year's wool crop, or even against the crop of the following five years.[63]

In 1191, the general chapter forbade the purchasing of landed property, but many houses went ahead with rounding out their patrimonies by purchase.[64] When they lacked a labour force sufficient to work their lands, they leased out their relatively unproductive lands. The ruling of 1208 granting this option was extended to entire granges in 1224. The practice of speculating in stock-raising was approved in 1226.[65]

The foregoing suggests in a variety of ways how the early Cistercian ideals of simplicity, poverty, and manual labour were dissipated in an orgy of wealth in less than a century. The common fault of monastic historians has been to ascribe this wealth to the weakened resolve of late twelfth-century Cistercians,[66] whereas the real fault lies in the original conceptions, if not of the very first Cistercians, then of St Bernard and of his contemporaries in the order.

The settlement in the forest of Cîteaux took place on lands owned by Viscount Rainaud of Beaune. Later on he gave the monks a part of the forest. More significant is the fact that Odo, the Duke of Burgundy, bought out the rest of the forest for the monks, and that he also gave them a vineyard and helped them construct their first buildings. For these benefactions he was regarded by some as the founder of the order and he was buried in the monastery church.[67]

Bernard, who sometimes referred to himself as the 'servant of the poor of Christ at Clairvaux',[68] believed that the kingdom of heaven belongs by right to those who are voluntarily poor.[69] But these cannot simply be poor, tend to their own affairs, and inherit heaven; the transaction is more complicated. Those who possess worldly goods have an obligation to help these poor people of Christ. Moreover, they should use their wealth to make of these people friends who will intercede for them on the day of judgment. And so for example, he commended a group of monks, sent from Clairvaux in 1140 to found a house in Sicily, to the care and generosity of King Roger.[70] The king's response was indeed generous; he gave them food and shelter at first and then productive land on which to settle. Bernard wrote to Roger again, this time to express his gratitude for these blessings. 'These are material things, but they can be traded with in return for heavenly things. This is the way to heaven; by such sacrifices God is won. For to these men belongs the kingdom of heaven and, in return for your material gifts, they will be able to render you everlasting life and glory.'[71] This could as well be a letter from the Abbot of Cluny to the King of Leon. The fact that the general chapter decided in 1180 to permit the burial of kings, queens, and bishops in their churches should not be seen as a sign of decadence on the part of third-generation Cistercians, but as a logical and sensible outgrowth of St Bernard's ideas and behaviour.[72] In thanking the Archbishop of York for material help given fellow Cistercians, Bernard drew a distinction between types of charity in such a way as to make a higher order out of gifts given to his monks than to the involuntarily poor. 'It is one thing', he reassured the archbishop, 'to fill the belly of the hungry, and another to have a zeal for poverty. The one is the service of nature the other the service of grace.' Further on, Bernard endorses the saying: 'Let your offerings grow warm in your hand until you find a just man to whom you may give them.'[73]

Bernard's diatribes against the superfluous beauties and comforts of Cluny are classic statements of monastic criticism.[74] Nothing he said of Cluniac buildings, however, would have been inappropriate for Cistercian buildings of the late twelfth century and of the thirteenth. Something, indeed, of Bernard's own calculated exaggeration and stinging polemic is reflected in Peter the Chanter's critique of Cistercian building:

In order to show off their wealth, even their granges are often fortified like castles . . . and in the wish of showing off the riches of their granges and fields, they have permitted dormitories and refectories to be constructed for them by robbers and usurers, as an eternal monument and symbol of their own greed.[75]

But again, one need not go to the end of the twelfth century to find the beginning of Cistercian decay. The Cistercians used money and hired labourers for pay from as early as the time of Bernard.[76] At Clairvaux itself in 1136 the brothers in charge of the day-to-day operations of the monastery decided to put before the abbot their dissatisfaction with the present complex of buildings and their plan for a new monastery on a vastly preferable site, a few miles away. In order to get across the message, according to Arnold of Bonnevaux, 'they strove to bring down for a while to the level of earthly things the man of God whose conversation was in heaven.' That was not easy; Bernard had just returned from negotiating papal-imperial-communal politics in Milan.[77]

Bernard at first resisted, arguing that people would get the impression that they were rich, which he reminded them they surely were not, or else would think them fastidious. But Bernard was won over by the argument that the removal was necessary to accommodate the steady influx of novices. And so a splendid new Clairvaux, not an expansion of the old one, was built on the River Aube, amidst plentiful meadows, vineyard, arable, and forest. Count Thibaut of Champagne and several other wealthy people supplied all that was necessary for the new monastery, which was built of stone. Clairvaux, even if poor, had rich friends. 'The waters of the river,' boasted Arnold of Bonnevaux, 'were diverted to run into every place where they would be useful, and then sent back into their original course.'[78] Here indeed was a splendid feat of engineering, similar to the one that had caught the eye of Peter Damian when visiting Cluny.

The New Monastery and her daughters eventually (and quite unintentionally) showed more than superficial resemblances to the monasteries of the old order. They had initially sought to avoid as much as possible contact with urban society; also, they had sought to avoid the elaborate and sumptuous religiosity of the black monks. They did not slip casually into the profit economy, as had the black monks before them; instead—even if for the most part unintentionally—they plunged headlong into it. Their staying so far away from towns and their brilliant economic success together indicate how thoroughly the profit economy had permeated the countryside.

The Carthusians and the Premonstratensians, as well as the Cistercians, flourished in the twelfth century. In trying to stay far from the turbulence of town life, these orders, like the eremitic movement of which they were an elaboration, all displayed a sensitivity to the problems raised by the new economic and social circumstances. But they also all made their contribution to the historic phenomenon of internal colonization. By showing far greater concern for the issue of geographical and sociological setting than for the matter of involvement in monetary, profit-making operations, they did not so much offer solutions as they helped their own adherents avoid these problems. Bernard typified them well; a man without answers, he at least asked the right questions: 'Who will grant, before I die,' he inquired, 'to see the Church of God as in the days of old, when the Apostles let down their nets for a draught, not of gold or of silver, but of souls?'[79]

PART III

Confronting the Crisis:
Canons, Laymen and Friars

7

The regular canons

The religious responses to the profit economy included—in addition to those of the hermits and monks, who turned away from cities—movements firmly planted within urban society itself. The first direct religious confrontation with this society came in the reform programme of the regular canons, a programme intended to render the secular clergy, many of whom lived *more laicorum*, 'in the manner of lay people', clearly distinct from the laity. The key to this reform of the priesthood was individual poverty and the common life together with an active apostolate. A second confrontation was mounted by various groups of laymen who sought deeper spiritual meaning outside the established forms of the religious life. What many of these had in common was a rejection of the new, specifically monetary, materialism, particularly as found in ecclesiastical institutions. Whether they tried to co-operate with the clerical hierarchy, to challenge it directly, or merely to avoid it, these groups all encountered official resistance and hostility. Moreover, their making explicit so much of the dualism implicit in Christian theology led many of them over the fine line separating orthodoxy from heresy, thus further endangering their already precarious situations. In a third confrontation, there was the movement of the friars. The achievements of the most important of these, the Dominicans and Franciscans, resulted in part from a synthesis of the canonical reform and the new lay spirituality. Dominic was a regular canon and Francis was a layman. More significantly, the orders they founded combined the clerical discipline of the canons with the apostolic ideals of some of the leading lay groups. Yet the programme of the friars transcended these earlier reforms, for besides giving expression to a new spiritual life for themselves, they went on to formulate a meaningful spiritual programme for the urban laity.

As cathedral churches were, by definition, urban, escape from city life was not a realistic alternative for members of the cathedral clergy. All the priests named on the official list (*matricula* or *canon*) of a large church were known as canons; together they constituted the *ordo canonicus*. As early as the fourth century, certain bishops had their priests share in some form of common life, such as a common refectory, a common dormitory, and a common treasury. The formula chosen was not everywhere the same. St Augustine, even before being made bishop, instituted a 'monastery of clerics within the episcopal household', prescribing for them a full common life. From the following centuries, one can find many instances of a bishop and his *familia* living a common life together; in some cases, where they followed a rule, they called themselves monks.[1]

In the middle of the eighth century, Bishop Chrodegang of Metz drew up a *Regula canonicorum* for the household of canons he established at his cathedral. In this work, he distinguished between two types of canon: those who lived a cloistered, common life, and those who lived outside the cloister, in town (*foras claustra, in civitate*).[2] For the first of these types, a full common life was suggested as the most suitable, but was rejected as being impracticable. As a compromise, these canons were to convey their property to the church but to retain control over any income it produced. The cloister did not have to have a common dormitory. Canons of the second type maintained their separate incomes and residences but were supposed to be present at the cathedral cloister for meals as well as for major services of worship. In both cases, canons were allowed to eat meat, to wear linens, and to keep their own possessions about them.[3]

At the Council of Aix-la-Chapelle (or Aachen) in 816, in a meeting similar to the one of the following year in which Benedict of Aniane guided through Louis the Pious' legislation making the Rule of St Benedict the standard rule for all monasteries, an *Institutio canonicorum* was drawn up, perhaps by Amalarius of Metz, and most of Chrodegang's rule was incorporated into it, along with a large collection of supporting texts from patristic and conciliar sources.[4] The Rule of Aix was well suited to the economic and social structures of the first feudal age. Cathedral churches were endowed almost exclusively with landed estates, and the canons' collective share of this endowment was divided into prebends, each of these fragments of a church's worldly resources coming under the direct supervision of an individual canon. This canon was considered the lord of that particular parcel of territory: he administered the land with his own officials and servants (that is, his own personally loyal retainers), and he protected the land, with arms if necessary, against encroachment by outsiders. The pressing need for direct supervision kept the canon close to the estate he controlled. Personal loyalty was best sustained by the personal presence of the lord; having absentee canons was less risky than having absentee landlords.[5]

The same system was admirably suited to a society dominated by a military and rural aristocracy. The opportunity given individual canons to live in their own houses greatly facilitated the entry into cathedral chapters of sons of the great families of the diocese. These younger sons secured the benefits of collective prayer for their relatives, while at the same time continuing to live pretty much as lords and knights, hunters and soldiers, besides being able to contribute significantly to the family fortune. In the tenth century, the practice of clerical marriage tended both to encourage and to be encouraged by the general disregard for the common life. Prebends, like secular fiefs, tended to stay with families through several generations. A prebend, that is, tended to become another fixed portion of a family's landed endowment, a portion that provided special ties with the sacred sphere of a cathedral church. The way to characterize a community of canons no longer observing the Rule of Aix was to say that they lived in a secular way (*seculcriter*) or, in the phrase cited above, in the manner of laymen (*more laicorum*). A curious confusion had therefore arisen between the *ordo canonicus* and the *ordo laicus*.[6]

The reform movement of the mid eleventh century, well known for trying to free the church from lay control and for advocating clerical celibacy, pursued the related goal of getting canons to return to the common life. In the view of Pope Leo IX (1048–54), the way to accomplish this was to revive the Rule of Aix; indeed he criticized strongly those who advocated a reform that went any further.[7] One of the latter was Peter Damian, who in the late 1050s addressed a tract, *On the Common Life of Canons*, to the clergy of the cathedral of Fano.[8] Some of the priests at Fano at that time already led a common life, but the others Peter criticized severely for retaining private possessions.[9] In this tract, as in another one of about 1065 against regular priests who have property, Peter announced a radically new perception of the proper life for canons: he rejected the Rule of Aix entirely, calling it a deviation from the apostolic life, and he argued that no priest whatever should hold private possessions.

The question was raised officially at the Roman synod of 1059, held under Pope Nicholas II (1059–61). Damian's associate in the reform movement, Hildebrand, then a sub-deacon of the Roman Church, delivered an attack against the regime of Aix. Many canons, he stated, had chosen to live in complete poverty with their fellow canons, according to the example of the primitive church. But others were urging on them the provisions of the Council of Aix as a precedent for maintaining private property. These provisions Hildebrand regarded as not sufficiently austere and as violations of the proper tradition of the Apostles. He called on the synod to revoke these Carolingian intrusions.[10] Besides Hildebrand's remarks, only the official decisions of the synod of 1059 remain. The fourth of these appears to be a compromise between the position of such reformers as Damian and Hildebrand and proponents of the Rule of Aix. The decree took the form of an exhortation that priests live an 'apostolic common life', but did not formally condemn those who still adhered to the old rule.[11] The same moderate stance was taken by the Roman synod of 1063.[12]

In the actual instances of reform, which had started well before these Roman synods, the essential choice was between a full reinstatement of the Rule of Aix and a modified one, in which chapter 115 was so altered as to forbid the holding of private possessions. One of the most important of the early foundations was that of Saint-Ruf, established at Avignon in 1039.[13] The cathedral chapter itself was not reformed, but a group of four clerics, with their bishop's permission, went just outside the town to the little church of Saint-Ruf, which at the time lay in ruins. The bishop granted them a charter saying they could live there *religiose*. In Italy the earliest reformed communities were at or near Turin, Siena, Florence, Velleti, Rome, Milan, and Lucca.[14] Alexander II (1061–73) instituted the regular life among the canons at Saint-John Lateran.[15] In France some of the earliest houses were at or near Paris, Senlis, Fréjus, and Apt.[16] The first section of Spain to be touched by the reform movement was the County of Barcelona.[17] Canonical reform reached Germany only at the end of the eleventh century[18] and England not until the early part of the twelfth.[19]

An alternative to returning to the Rule of Aix, integrally or not, was offered by the so-called 'Rule of St Augustine'. The first known specific mention of this rule occurs in connection with the reform at Rheims in 1067, though vague references for Milan and Senlis from a few years earlier might have alluded to the same rule. Mention of this rule appeared again in 1076 at Soissons and Senlis, at Saint-Ruf in 1084, and then suddenly in many places in France, Italy, Spain, and Germany in the final decade and a half of the eleventh century. This type of reform was eventually to be the predominant one, indeed the exclusive one, as gradually something very much like a monastic order grew up: the order of the regular canons of St Augustine.[20]

The Rule of St Augustine was an enigma in the eleventh century and still raises complex historical issues. This rule meant many different things to the various people who spoke and wrote of it. There are usually three main elements. The first is an actual letter of Augustine, his Epistle 211 to his sister, who had requested advice on the orderly conduct of the community of nuns to which she belonged; it is sometimes called the *Regula sororum*.[21] This rule does not provide a complete guide to the religious life and is not known ever to have served as the exclusive rule for a religious community.

The *Regula secunda*, or *Ordo monasterii*, is a 400-word document setting out a programme for the religious life, with a listing of daily offices and regulations about such matters as discipline, manual labour, and reading.[22] The *Regula tertia* is an adaptation of Epistle 211 for a male community.[23] These latter two 'rules' usually appeared together in manuscripts and carried the title *Regula Sancti Augustini*. The earliest extant manuscript with this combined rule dates from the late sixth century. The composition of the *Regula secunda* and the juxtaposing of the two are said by historians to have taken place in Italy in the late fifth century.[24] There is little evidence that this combined rule was much used after the sixth century, and although it was known, and indeed was included in Benedict of Aniane's *Concordance of Rules*, it remained out of use until the eleventh-century revival.

The historical memory of the common life fostered by Augustine at Hippo, especially as described in the biography of Augustine by Possidius, was never lost.[25] But in the eleventh century it gained a new currency as the regular canons sought greater precedent and authority—precedent was indeed a form of authority—in the history of the church. There developed from this search a fully articulated view of the history of the canons. This view, the work mainly of canonists, particularly Anselm of Lucca, became part of papal policy, or at least of the rationalization of papal policy, in the time of Urban II.[26] Pope Urban, a former canon as well as a former Cluniac prior, in giving approbation to the regular life of the canons of Rottenbuch in Bavaria, attested to the venerable tradition of the canons, placing them on the same footing as the monks with respect both to their antiquity and to their spiritual worth.[27] He did not deny that the canonical tradition had suffered a lengthy decline and fundamental corruption; but he saw equal merit in reviving the canonical life and in maintaining that of the monks. The pope first recalled how the church, from its beginning, had instituted two fundamentally different ways of living. One was the lesser way for laymen, who use earthly things; the other was a higher way for those who would both despise and renounce such earthly things. The critical part of the pope's letter came at that point:

But those who by divine favour abandon the things of the world are in their turn divided into two groups the religious purpose of which is almost identical, that of the canons and that of the monks. The latter way of life greatly aided by the divine mercy flourishes in the entire universe; the former, on the contrary, because the fervour of the faithful grows cool, has declined almost everywhere. Yet this is the way of life that was instituted by Pope Urban the Martyr, that Augustine organized by his rules, that Jerome moulded by his letters, that Gregory commissioned Augustine, the Bishop of the English, to institute. Thus it should not seem any less praiseworthy to revive this earliest life of the church with the inspiration and help of the Spirit of the Lord than to maintain the prosperous religion of the monks through continuing steadfastly in the same spirit.[28]

The reference to Pope Urban the Martyr is particularly revealing.

Virtually nothing of that pope is known; even the dates of his reign can at best be placed approximately in the third decade of the third century. Five centuries and more after his death, however, decrees concerning the life of canons were attributed to him, so that within reforming circles in the late eleventh century, Urban I was seen as a principal founder of the regular life for canons. Thus when Odo of Ostia, a long-time associate of Hildebrand and Anselm of Lucca, was elected to the papacy in 1088, he quite possibly chose the name Urban for particular reasons of policy.[29] Portions of his letter to the canons of Rottenbuch became a standard part of the apologetic literature of the regular canons.

An influential repetition of this historical view emanated from Saint-Ruf.[30] That house had received two bulls from Urban II stressing the apostolic and traditional character of the common life. In the years around and shortly after Urban's pontificate, Saint-Ruf came to inspire reform in Provence, Languedoc, Lombardy, Catalonia, and Burgundy. A secular priest named Lethbert joined the house in 1096, and became abbot in 1100, serving in that position until his death about eleven years later. Lethbert is credited with drawing up a new customary for the house, a customary that was then widely sought after as a model of reform. His classic restatement of the history of the canonical order reads as follows:

This our order, as I have said, first blossomed forth with Christ and the Apostles in the primitive church. But as love grew cold and persecution threatened, it later dwindled away. Pope Urban the Martyr began to revive it with his decrees, the blessed Augustine to regulate it by his holy decrees, holy Jerome to extol it in his letters, as also various other holy men whom it is tedious to recall. Thus encouraged, already many servants of God in many lands are returning to the former regime of this our Saviour's order.[31]

The canons' quest for legitimacy thus produced both a rule and a history. This success in turn added greatly to the size and influence of the reform movement. One result of the canons' success, particularly their acquisition of a rule, was that some new groups—clearly more monastic than priestly—adopted the Rule of St Augustine. This was the case with St Norbert's Premonstratensians. During the twelfth century and shortly beyond, the rule was also adopted by such groups as the Order of Grandmont, the Victorines, the scholars who withdrew to Val-des-Ecoliers, and the Order of Preachers. Communities of regular canons were set up in many types of non-episcopal churches, some even in the countryside, and many of these had as a chief function the chanting of the divine office. In function, then, some canonical communities differed little from Benedictine monasteries.

Not only was there not a uniform interpretation of the apostolate among all adherents to the Rule of St Augustine, there continued to be disagreement over what constituted the rule itself. Amidst a wide variety of possible views, one essential distinction that emerged was determined by the place accorded the *Regula secunda*, or *Ordo monasterii*. This document imposed an especially rigorous religious life, with long fasts, an absolute prohibition of meat, coarse woollen habits instead of linen, and stern restrictions against talking. Those houses that embraced this rule came to be regarded as the *ordo novus*. The *ordo antiquus* consisted of those houses that ignored the *Regula secunda*; they probably followed a modified version of the Rule of Aix (that is, without private property), and were also guided by the *Regula tertia*.[32] The most notable adherents to the *ordo novus* were the Premonstratensians and the canons at Springiersbach, near Trèves.[33] The internal difficulties of the *ordo novus* and the modifications enacted attest to the unusual austerity of the *Regula secunda*. Saint-Ruf is typical of the more easy-going communities, which had nothing whatever to do with the *Regula secunda*.[34]

The canonical reform movement made its appearance in all parts of Europe, but an important distinction is to be made between those areas where cathedral chapters were reformed and those where, instead, new communities of regular canons were founded. The studies made so far suggest that reforms of existing communities were common in those areas where nobles lived in towns and had relatively liquid fortunes. These areas included central and northern Italy, the Alpine provinces, Provence, Aquitaine, and Spain. But in England, northern and central France, the Rhineland, and western Germany, where the nobility had an interest in retaining the old, landed prebends, the old canonical life changed little or not at all, and canonical reform had to enter via newly established communities. Those who participated in the setting up of new communities were people whose lives were caught up in the mobile sphere of commerce, industry, and finance.[35]

In the case of Mâcon, the canons of the cathedral of Saint-Vincent were sons of knights provided with prebends contiguous with their family allods; the canons tended to treat these prebends as annexes to or extensions of their allods. There was little hope of instituting the common life in such a church. Meanwhile the common life was instituted and practised at the collegiate church of St Peter, a parish in one of the new sections of the city. This church was patronized by merchants and artisans. They donated alms in cash, and in return they asked for certain spiritual benefits, including the solace of burial in the canons' church.[36]

At Toulouse, reform initiative is largely credited to Bishop Izarn, who instituted the full common life in the cathedral chapter during the mid 1070s.[37] The cathedral churches at Nîmes and Carcassonne also led the way in canonical reform for their respective areas, as did cathedral churches generally in Italy.[38] Reform was neither automatic nor easy. A bishop needed considerable influence to impose reform on an unwilling chapter. Often a bishop could win over only some of the canons, and thus he, and probably his successor, had to wait for the deaths of refractory canons before they could integrate their prebends into the common treasury. This was the case at both Lucca and Narbonne. At Parma the process of reform was spread over a half century.[39]

The English cathedral chapters, already predominantly monastic, did not switch over to become houses of regular canons.[40] At Rheims, not the cathedral church of Notre Dame but the basilica of Saint-Denis set up a community of Augustinian canons.[41] The fervent and articulate canonical reformer Ivo of Chartres, some of whose views appear in the following pages, was able to get regular canons installed in Saint-André at Chartres but not in his own cathedral church there.[42] In Limoges, the canons of the cathedral of Saint-Etienne continued to hold private as well as common possessions; meanwhile the new Order of Grandmont and other eremitic groups were absorbing much of the region's reform fervour.[43] At Tournai, reform came about not at the prosperous cathedral church of Notre Dame but at the little suburban church of Saint-Martin revived by Odo, a canon of Tournai. About ten of those people who joined Odo had been canons of the cathedral chapter.[44] In Germany, also, canonical reform was usually better sought in some church other than an established cathedral. Gerhoh of Reichersberg tried to effect a reform at Augsburg cathedral but failed; the secular canons already in place, whom Gerhoh called *pseudocanonici*, were just not 'expellable' (*inexpugnabiles*), he lamented.[45] St Norbert's career demonstrates the same point: setting up a community of regular canons in the forest of Prémontré, however difficult, was much easier than getting his canons at Magdeburg to surrender their prebends. After narrowly escaping at least three assassination attempts, Bishop Norbert had to settle for reforming the nearby collegiate church of St Mary.[46] On the eastern frontiers, which were relatively free of firmly entrenched interests, the bishoprics newly established or recently resurrected often had regular canons.[47]

The reformed styles of the canonical life carried no single interpretation of the apostolate. They all involved to some extent a common liturgical life, a point on which the canonical spirituality was clearly derivative of the monastic.[48] Competition between monks and canons often became lively; their polemics centred on such issues as relative antiquity, the active life versus the contemplative, and the association of one or the other group with such venerable figures as

Mary and Martha, Michael and Peter, or Augustine and Gregory. One writer respectfully placed the canons below the monks on the basis of the relative status of their patrons: 'We do not scorn the blessed bishop Augustine, but we confidently place before him Martin, bishop and monk, and even more Gregory, apostle [i.e., pope] and monk.'[49] The supposed mid-twelfth-century dialogue between a Cluniac and a Cistercian asserted with reference to the Rule of St Augustine that canons are monks: 'Whether they like it or not, all who have professed that rule are monks.'[50] Yet in spite of their similarities, canons and monks were fundamentally different, and the key to this difference is found in their attitudes toward the apostolate.[51]

'The incontrovertible verdict of the Fathers of the church decides solemnly that the order of canons should be by every right placed above all others. This is not astonishing, since it carries on the work of Christ and the Apostles in preaching, baptizing, and administering the other sacraments of the church.'[52] Such was the claim advanced in the customary of Saint-Ruf. Of course the historical view presented there was controversial, but so, too, was the functional definition. There were some regular canons who themselves believed the proper functions of canons to be contemplative, or liturgical, or both. St Géraud of Sales (died 1120) quit his life in a community of contemplative regular canons in order to join up with Robert of Arbrissel as a preacher. The report of Géraud's biographer says: 'He was glowing in the cloister but not beaming forth his light to a world in peril because he was not properly situated for that. He could see the abundant harvest but also the scarcity of workers and the richness of the reward.' And so Géraud left the quiet of the canons' cloister for the activity of itinerant preaching.[53]

There were critics who felt that the canons should restrict themselves to non-social, inner-directed activities, which would keep them aloof from contemporary problems and from inquiring into the sources of their support. One of the reasons for this feeling was probably a form of professional jealousy. Canons of the old style did not like the preaching of the regular canons; the mention even, by the latter, of apostolic poverty carried an implicit criticism of the former. Neither did the canons of the old style like to see the faithful patronizing the churches of the regular canons. The friars were later on the objects, and victims, of a similar jealousy.

The question of whether regular canons should assume pastoral responsibilities arose within the diocese of Orléans and was submitted to Ivo of Chartres (c. 1040–1115) for an opinion. Ivo replied in a letter to the Bishop of Orléans, arguing first on historical grounds that, in the primitive church, no one was given the care of souls except someone living the common life. The argument was that one person could not take on the responsibility for another's life unless he had his own life under control. If the common life was not everywhere found at the present time, that was to be explained by the intrusions of greed and selfishness, and a general disintegration of values. Having established such a historical base, Ivo came to the heart of his argument.

We firmly maintain those should not be listened to who say that regular canons ought to be barred from the care of souls because they have renounced the world. On the contrary, I say they are all the more suited to assume it because they have rejected the pleasures and pretensions of the world. For the business of the world does not consist in reclaiming souls from vice and stimulating them to the excellency of virtues. These things are more properly taught by those who carry out in deed that which they preach, instead of by those who are teachers but not doers of the law.[54]

The connection between deeds and words had been essential also for Peter Damian in establishing the tie between poverty and preaching. His argument was that if the function of a priest is to preach, and that a preacher has to be poor, then all priests worthy of the designation should be poor. Damian reminded his readers both that the programme of the canons was modelled after the kind of life lived by the Apostles and that that life was one where no one called anything his own and everything was common among them. Damian then asked whether the prerogative of having property should be accorded to clerics when Christ did not permit it to his Apostles.[55]

Ivo of Chartres likewise tended to think that all priests should lead regular lives. He expressed such a view when he heard that the Bishop of Limoges proclaimed that the regular canons of his diocese could neither take charge of parishes nor hear confessions. Ivo commented sourly on the bishop's action: 'He would have done better to invite all priests to undertake the regular life, instead of wholly removing those who already live by a rule from caring for the Lord's flocks.'[56]

Anselm of Havelberg (died 1158) later on echoed both these general views and some of Ivo's exact wording. In writing to a Benedictine abbot, he also explicitly raised the problem of jealousy.

Word has reached me that you have not feared to put in the ears of some and not blushed from saying to others that regular canons ought not to have charge of parishes nor exercise the care of souls among the people. Now if this is true, I wonder very seriously about your judgment; because anyone who strives to assert this ... is clearly doing it more out of jealousy of the canonical order than out of love for the truth. One who understood the situation correctly would rather invite all priests to undertake the regular life, instead of wholly removing those who already live by a rule from caring for the Lord's flocks.... It is apparent that the usual practice in the entire church is that just as no monk is appointed archdeacon or archpriest or to any parish, so no regular canon is removed by ecclesiastical enactments or cases in synod from having the care of souls or from any ecclesiastical office or dignity whatever. For indeed he is sought out, chosen, and accepted by plain people and, like a lantern lighting a dark place, teaching by word and example, he is loved and honoured. And so anyone who, desiring to vent his ill will, has sought to detract from the canonical order in this way, does not know what he is talking about, why he talks as he does, or against whom he talks. Like someone utterly unskilled in scripture he boils over with malice merely from jealousy of good.[57]

The tensions created by this radical wing of the canonical reform are apparent in the career of Arnold of Brescia (c. 1100–55), who was in charge of a house of canons in his native city. At the time of the communal revolt in Brescia, when there was an episcopal schism (between the bishop expelled by the commune and the one imposed by the pope), Arnold preached and organized resistance to both episcopal claimants, expanding on the ideals of the canonical reform to argue that no monk or priest or bishop who owned property could be saved. When the papal party secured its triumph in 1139, Arnold was expelled from Italy. He next appeared, the following spring, as an advocate for Abelard at the Council of Sens. 'The bee who was in France', explained Bernard of Clairvaux, 'gave a buzz to the bee in Italy, and they have joined forces against the Lord and against His Anointed One.'[58]

Following the condemnation of Abelard's writings, Arnold went to Paris where he lectured on the scriptures in the church of St Hilary, a church run by regular canons and which had once sheltered Abelard. His appeal was largely to poor students 'who publicly begged their bread from door to door to support themselves and their master'. Such was Arnold's audience, according to this report by John of Salisbury, because

he said things that were entirely consistent with the law accepted by Christian people, but not at all with the life they led. To the bishops he was merciless on account of their avarice and filthy lucre; most of all because of the stains on their personal lives, and their striving to build the church of God in blood. He denounced the abbot [St Bernard], whose name is renowned above all others for his many virtues, as a seeker after vainglory, envious of all who won distinction in learning or religion unless they were his own disciples.[59]

Word reached Bernard, and he responded by getting Louis VII to expel Arnold from the kingdom. When Bernard learned that Arnold had gone to Bavaria, he wrote to the papal legate there a letter of warning, which began in this way: 'Arnold of Brescia, whose religious life may be honey but whose doctrine is poison, who has the head of a dove and the tail of a scorpion, whom Brescia has vomited, Rome cast out, France rejected, Germany despises, and Italy will not receive, is reported to be with you.'[60]

Arnold was called to Rome in about 1147 to be reconciled with the pope, at the time when a communal revolt against the pope's secular rule of Rome had been under way already for four years. Walter Map said that when Arnold first saw the papal court he was shocked by 'the tables of the cardinals loaded with gold and silver plate, and their luxury in feasting. He reproved them in modest terms before the lord pope.' And it may be precisely because, as Walter went on to say, the cardinals took this criticism very badly and threw him out, that Arnold joined the communal revolt and 'began to teach indefatigably'.[61] He frequently addressed public gatherings on the Capitol and elsewhere, on such themes as the scribes and pharisees of the present-day Christian Church, or the College of Cardinals as a marketplace or a den of thieves. As for Arnold's view of the pope:

The pope himself was not what he professed to be—an apostolic man and a shepherd of souls—but a man of blood who maintained his authority by fire and sword, a tormentor of churches and oppressor of the innocent, who did nothing in the world save gratify his lust and empty other men's coffers to fill his own. He was so far from apostolic that he imitated neither the life nor the doctrine of the Apostles, wherefore neither obedience nor reverence was due to him.[62]

Arnold became a leader of the commune, which called itself the Roman Republic and created a senatorial order; in fact it was only with the intervention of the emperor that the republic was crushed and the papacy's authority restored. Arnold had pursued the canonical (or indeed the Gregorian) reform to its logical end: by advocating a church that was entirely free of material or political involvements, he was advocating at the same time a secular authority completely independent of any ecclesiastical tie. The combining of secular power with ecclesiastical dignity in the first place, either in the papacy or in the episcopacy (as at Brescia, for example), had prefigured and in a sense foreordained the uniting of communal politics with apostolic spirituality. Eventually Arnold was captured and turned over to Frederick Barbarossa. He was tried, condemned, and hanged; then the corpse was burned. Frederick's uncle, the imperial (and Cistercian) historian, Otto of Freising, recorded Arnold's death: 'After his corpse had been reduced to ashes in the fire, these were scattered on the Tiber, lest his remains be held in veneration by the mad populace.'[63]

Like Peter Damian, Ivo of Chartres, Anselm of Havelburg, and Arnold of Brescia, Gerhoh of Reichersberg (1093–1169) also tried to expand the scope of the canonical reform. Unsuccessful at introducing the reform into the old-style chapter to which he belonged at Augsburg, Gerhoh became a regular canon at Rottenbuch and then for over 35 years was provost of the Augustinian monastery of Reichersberg.[64]

In his earliest work, *Book Concerning the House of God* (1128–9), Gerhoh formulated a comprehensive notion of the apostolic life, a notion of living by an apostolic rule. He wrote: 'Every order and absolutely every profession, in the Catholic faith and according to apostolic teaching, has a rule adapted to its character; and under this rule it is possible by striving properly to achieve the crown of glory.' For monks the authentic apostolic rule was the one formulated by St Benedict; for priests, that formulated by St Augustine.[65] 'And therefore,' asserted Gerhoh, 'just as among all Catholics there is one faith only, so among the servants of God ought there to be one rule only, namely the apostolic rule.'[66] The basis of this rule was the common life, and those who adhered to it were the *pauperes Christi*. Clerics who held property were by definition violators of the clerical order and accordingly, if not actually excommunicated, ought to be removed from their posts and set back among the laity, where they belong.[67] Those persons were saintly who, for the sake of God, possessed nothing.[68] Voluntary poverty, in other words, was the key to the holy life. Later he tried to work out a moderate position on the question of propertied clerics: he suggested that they be permitted neither to celebrate the eucharist nor to preach, and that they be admitted only to the lower orders of the clergy, but this suggestion also went unheeded.[69]

The canonical reform had been under way for more than a century when Gerhoh perceived it as a historical entity both with an internal structure and consistency and in relation to other historical periods and phenomena. He expressed this view in one of his last works, *On the Fourth Nightwatch*, written in the summer of 1167.[70] The figure of a vigil or nightwatch came from the evangelical text (Matt. 14:22–3) in which Christ walks on the sea. He did that during the fourth watch of the night, when the disciples' boat had been tossed about by an unfavourable wind.

Gerhoh related the four watches of the night to four major periods of Christian history. The first of these periods lasted from Christ to Constantine; the second from Constantine to Gregory I; the third from Gregory I to Gregory VII; and the fourth from Gregory VII to the present. Each period had known an unfavourable wind and these were, in order: the persecutions, the heresies, the corruption of morals, and avarice. In like manner, each age received help from God through those who kept a vigil. In the past, these had been the martyrs, then the confessors, and then the holy Fathers; in the present age, they were the disciples of Christ, whom he defined as those people who renounced all their possessions.[71]

Thus, in the view of Gerhoh of Reichersberg, a new historical period had started back in the middle of the eleventh century and it continued to flourish at the time he was writing, more than one hundred years later. The biggest challenge, or problem, of this period was avarice, and the most effective antidote to avarice was voluntary poverty. The same period also marked the great age of clerical reform, a movement spurred on not only by the writings and examples of well known clerical reformers but also by the rising expectations of an increasingly pious and conscientious laity.

8

The Humiliati, Waldensians, Beguines and Cathars

During the second feudal age, lay people became far more deeply involved in the Christian religion than in previous centuries. Some of them formulated programmes of religious values and practices, often with the aid of clerics, and some in turn lent their support to ecclesiastical reform movements. Four lay groups are here singled out on account of their sensitive responses to the profit economy and because of their widespread impact on Latin Christian society: the Humiliati, the Waldensians, the Beguines, and the Cathars. The Humiliati originated in Milan and soon spread to other cities of Lombardy. The Waldensians, followers of a wealthy Lyonnais merchant who had a religious conversion, spread throughout southern France, northern Italy, the Rhineland, and southern Germany. The Beguines were a movement of pious women active in the cities of the Low Countries, the Rhineland, and northern France. The Cathars were particularly strong in south-western France but also numerous in the Rhineland and in northern Italy. What follows is a highly selective account of these groups, which stand out prominently from the mass of Christian lay people. The geographical pattern they form corresponds to the map of Europe's most advanced commercial and industrial areas.

1. HUMILIATI

In the half century between 1170 and 1220, the Humiliati (or Humble Ones) evolved from an informal grouping of lay people into an officially sanctioned order of the church, with three variant forms of life—canonical, monastic, and lay—for both men and women. The beginnings of the Humiliati date back probably to the early 1170s or before, but documents yield proof only that the Humiliati were well established by 1178. The anonymous chronicler of Laon mentions in his entry for that year that there were people calling themselves Humiliati living in various cities of Lombardy.[1] A document of the same year records an exemption gained by the people of religion living at the Casa di Brera, on the edge of Milan.[2]

The Humiliati of those early days were mostly laymen, some married who continued to live at home with their families, or else unmarried or formerly married who chose to live a common life in the religious manner. There were some priests in the movement as well. The Humiliati were noted for wearing simple, undyed clothing as a symbol of the humility they professed. They neither withdrew completely into cloisters nor engaged fully in the social life about them, for (in the words of the chronicler of Laon) 'they refrained from lies, oaths, and law suits'. The connection of lies with oaths and law suits was not explained but their being grouped together suggests that the Humiliati saw some necessary connection between urban political and juridical life and perjury.[3]

Since the document of 1178 states that there were people of religion living at the Brera, the purpose of holding property and a house was probably to have a place of residence where unmarried members could live in common. But the house most likely also served as a headquarters and as a meeting place, because the pope shortly afterwards forbade the Humiliati to continue to hold secret meetings.[4]

This speculation on the uses of Humiliati property and houses suggests the dual nature of their spiritual programme, for in addition to the personal reformation of their inner lives, the Humiliati sought to reach out into society to oppose actively the enemies of the Christian faith. The Humiliati not only claimed to follow the model of apostolic simplicity in their own lives, but with uncommon audacity engaged in the apostolic act of preaching the Christian faith publicly.[5]

On this latter point, the Humiliati sought the approval of Pope Alexander III (1159–81) in 1179. That was the year of the Third Lateran Council, but the pope apparently handled the case of the Humiliati by himself. A professor of canon law by training, Alexander had served in the papal curia since 1150, had been a close personal adviser to Hadrian IV, and had himself already been pope for twenty years. He had lived through the days of the Roman Commune and of Arnold of Brescia, and he had observed the advance of the Catharist heresy in more recent years. His reaction to the Humiliati was straightforward. While commending their honesty and humility, he expressly forbade them to hold any more secret meetings and warned them severely against ever again presuming to preach in public.[6]

The Humiliati took the risk, and then had to answer for it to Alexander's successor, Lucius III (1181–5). A Cistercian monk in his early days and then a cardinal for 40 years before becoming pope, Lucius had lived through the same troubled decades of Roman history as Alexander, and more. In addition, he had been the close associate and adviser of Alexander, so the question of the Humiliati hardly came to him as something unfamiliar. The pope assembled a council at Verona in 1184, with the Emperor Frederick I in attendance. After many years of regarding Frederick as an enemy, and then serving as the architect of Alexander's peace negotiations and peace treaty with Frederick, Lucius now managed to elicit an imperial vow to go on crusade and an imperial pledge to help stamp out heresy. To facilitate this latter point of policy, the pope understandably identified and condemned each group then perceived by Rome as schismatic or heretical. Along with Cathars and Arnoldists and other heretics who had started 'to breed in many parts of the world in modern times', Lucius placed under perpetual anathema those schismatics calling themselves Humiliati.[7]

Considering the seriousness of the charge, remarkably little information about the Humiliati during the next fifteen years has survived. On the basis of their size and importance at the end of that time, one can surmise that the intervening period was marked by significant expansion.[8] For the Roman Church, the same period witnessed the continued mounting of major problems, but little in the way of constructive solutions. The election of Celestine III (1191–8) brought an 85-year-old Roman aristocrat to the papal throne. He, too, had witnessed the mid-century upheavals in Rome from the viewpoint of the papal court. The advent of Innocent III (1198–1216) at last brought a redirection of policy. The Humiliati sent a delegation, including men from Como and Lodi, to see the new pope in either 1198 or the following year. They brought him a description of their manner of living for his approval. The text of this *propositum* is not extant, but its contents can be fairly accurately pieced together out of documents later emanating from the papal court. Innocent handed over the *propositum* to a committee made up of the Bishop of Vercelli and two Cistercian abbots, from Vercelli and Lodi, so that they and subsequently a committee of cardinals could study it and make recommendations to him.[9]

The results of this particular investigation and the ensuing papal decision were not announced until June 1201, but Innocent revealed his basic stance on such issues as early as December 1199 in a letter to the Bishop of Verona.[10] Innocent reminded the bishop of the delicate problem of weeding out tares from the wheat and of removing cutworms from vines without doing harm to the harvest of grain and grapes. The task of rooting out heretics from among the faithful was similarly delicate. He had learned of some wholesale excommunications of heretics in the diocese of Verona, and he was writing precisely to demand that the distinction between orthodox and heterodox be maintained by applying a test of orthodoxy in particular cases. By no means should all people who call themselves or who are called Humiliati be excommunicated. If Humiliati are found who uphold the faith correctly and who exercise humility of heart and of body, then clearly they should not be cut off from the community of the faithful.

Such was the conciliatory mood prevailing at the Roman court when the Humiliati *propositum* was under investigation there. The policy that Innocent enunciated in June of 1201 made of the Humiliati an official religious order, in turn divided into three distinct orders. The first was to be priestly, made up of canons and canonesses; the second order was to be monastic, made up of continent laymen living in adjoining but separate convents for men and women; the third order was to consist of married laymen continuing to lead their secular, familial lives.

There was to be one rule for the first and second orders, consisting of an amalgam of the Benedictine and Augustinian rules. It stressed the common life and the lack of personal possessions held by individual members. The order itself was not to own any land that its members did not work by hand.[11] In the letter announcing his approval, Innocent exempted the first order from paying tithes and made them revise their strong stand against all oaths, citing many biblical instances of oath-taking and urging them to swear their loyalty to the Lord. He added, significantly, that they should never swear to anything that was not true.[12] The pope's concern about the Humiliati position on oaths formed a major part also of the letters of approbation for the second and third orders.[13] The address on the letter to the second order singled out the houses at Milan, Monza, Pavia, Bergamo, and Brescia. The houses of the second order were held responsible for paying tithes.[14]

As for the third order, the main problem was to find a meaningful form of religious life—which for several centuries had been defined as a common life—for people who, because of conjugal and familial commitments, could not adopt the common life. There being no rule for this third order, the pope's letter serves as the fullest official statement of their spiritual plan. The head of each local group was called a 'minister', and the pope's letter went to the ministers at Milan, Monza, Como, Pavia, Brescia, Bergamo, Piacenza, Lodi, and Cremona, and 'to the other ministers of the same order'. The letter reads in part like an omnibus sermon. He urged them, among other things, to enter by the narrow gate, to be penitent, to maintain peaceful relations with everyone, to return anything gained by usury or any other improper means, to make satisfactory amends for any wrong done to anyone, not to possess tithes, not to lay up treasures on earth, not to love the world, and not to dissolve one's marriage except on grounds of fornication.[15]

The particular piety of these laymen consisted in their fasting two days a week, saying the Lord's Prayer before and after dinner, and reciting the seven- canonical hours. They were to wear simple clothing, and should any of their number become ill or face some other kind of hardship, the others were to come to his aid; in case of death, to the aid of the departed person's soul and family.[16]

The most radical innovation in this spiritual life came in the pope's approval of Humiliati lay preaching. He acknowledged and approved their practice of gathering every Sunday to hear preaching by one or more of their brothers known to be strong in faith, knowledgeable in religion, gifted in speech, and consistent in behaviour and speech. The key to this extraordinary acceptance of preaching by lay Christians rested in the pope's distinction between preaching doctrine and giving witness to faith and morals. The latter, built of exhortations to observe decent moral behaviour and to engage in works of piety, was wholly acceptable; the former, involving discussion of theological issues and of the sacraments of the church, was judged outside their competence and expressly forbidden.[17]

The constitutional relationships among the three orders were not specified at this time. Only in 1246, during the reign of Innocent IV, did all the Humiliati come under the leadership of a single master-general.[18]

The texts relating to the internal structure and legal status of the order reveal little about who the Humiliati were and what they did. A fifteenth-century chronicler mentioned that the mission to Rome in 1199 was undertaken by Guy of Eastgate 'and certain other nobles of the city of Milan', but this is hardly compelling evidence that the Humiliati were all nobles.[19] Far more deserving of attention is the observation of that astute reporter James of Vitry, namely, that even the lay Humiliati recited the canonical hours, 'for they are almost all literate'. He just as clearly went on to say that those who were not literate recited the Lord's Prayer a certain number of times daily instead. Elsewhere in the same account, James told of the public preaching by Humiliati priests and literate laymen, and mentioned that they had converted many noble and powerful citizens to their movement.[20] Some have argued that the Humiliati insistence on avoiding elaborate clothing could have had meaning only for people previously accustomed to elaborate clothing.[21] But such regulations are characteristic of socially heterogeneous groups, where they serve the function of minimizing the social differences among the members. The provision for the return of ill-gotten gains, especially from usury, suggests the presence of merchants and moneylenders among the Humiliati.[22]

The members of the third order were not required to surrender all or even most of their possessions. They were supposed to live simple, humble lives, and to dress accordingly. They were supposed to do manual labour and to engage in works of charity. As they did not move out of their houses, they could presumably have maintained relatively comfortable surroundings. But if all Humiliati lived in this style, there would have been little need for the mutual-aid provision of the *propositum*. The implication of that provision is that many of the Humiliati were living on the margins of society, and that only the charity and solidarity of the Christian lay brotherhood to which they belonged kept them from slipping into a critical state of involuntary poverty.

The limits of Humiliati charity stretched beyond the order itself to embrace all the poor and downtrodden. They fed and clothed the poor and cared for the sick, giving special attention to lepers. The consciousness of their attempt to follow scriptural precepts seems assured by their constant readiness to hear readings from scripture and to listen to sermons, as well as by their requirement that a lay preacher be someone whose activity was consistent with what he preached.[23]

'These people live by the work of their own hands after the manner of the primitive church,' Humbert of Romans wrote of the Humiliati in the mid thirteenth century.[24] The work they engaged in most frequently was cloth-making, particularly woollen cloth of inferior quality and fustian, a cheap, coarse cloth of cotton or of cotton and flax. The poor grade of Italian wool gave a cloth that could not stand the competition of Flemish and French cloth, especially as that competition grew sharper in the course of the twelfth century. Had it yielded far better results, one could well imagine the Italians giving over more and more land to sheep-raising and buying more of their food at greater distances. But the reverse happened. The Po Valley was more profitably used for raising food than sheep. The need for inexpensive cloth became increasingly urgent meanwhile, as the population continued to expand and as the local woollen industry declined. The purchase of woollen cloth manufactured in northern Europe was beyond the means of most people. The eventual solution was to import cotton and make cheap cotton cloth. The cotton was of two types: the longer, more flexible type, which came from Egypt and Syria and was imported through Venice; and a second type from Calabria, Apulia, Sicily, Malta, and North Africa was imported through Genoa. The industry was located in a few central Italian cities such as Todi, in many more Tuscan cities, and in nearly every northern Italian city.[25]

The fustian industry had a unique organization, for it remained almost exclusively in the hands of merchants. The importer of the new material could own and control the entire operation right through production. The fustian workers themselves never became organized, as they did in the woollen cloth industry. Given these peculiar circumstances, the workers were completely at the mercy of the merchants. The poorest, and hence most vulnerable, workers hired themselves out to the fustian merchants; the alternative to taking such work was unemployment. It was among these workers that the Humiliati were sometimes found. In lieu of a guild, that religious brotherhood offered them some measure of economic and social security. The individual, defenceless fustian worker was prey to the usurer as well as to unemployment. The merchant-entrepreneur sometimes came to him as or through a usurer, who offered him an advance to cover the cost of food against so much labour. Officially notarized documents refer to one such usurer as 'John of Dolchera, known as "the pig" '.[26]

Our knowledge of fustian-making tells something of the motive for joining the Humiliati as well as something of the work done by the Humiliati, whatever their individual origins. They are, of course, better known for their work in woollen cloth, and they took for their symbol the Lamb of God, which conveniently combined the signs of their humility and of their trade.[27] Humiliati cloth came to be specified by name on the market. Eventually, in the course of the thirteenth century, they themselves became entrepreneurs and grew rich.

How widespread was the Humiliati movement? James of Vitry said in 1216 that there were 150 convents or congregations of them in the diocese of Milan;[28] in 1278 Bonvicinus of Ripa said there were 220 convents of the second order and seven canonical houses of the first order in the city and region of Milan.[29] One of the two fifteenth-century chronicles of Humiliati history contains a list, which is supposed to date from 1298, of various cities and of the number of Humiliati houses in each.[30] According to this list, Brescia had fifteen houses, Lodi eleven, Pavia six, and Bergamo twenty-one among Lombard cities, while there were just five houses in Tuscany, one each in Padua, Venice, and Rome, and a grand total of 389. These were mostly houses of the second order; the few canonical houses were singled out, while the number of families adhering to the third order remains beyond calculation. It seem reasonable to conclude that there were communities of Humiliati in virtually every cloth-producing town of northern and central Italy. One can only guess at the strength and security this movement was able to provide for its individual members. In the history of the Christian apostolate, the Humiliati as a group hold a prominent place. One cannot assert that the second feudal age created economic problems that in turn led to the formation of the Humiliati, with the prime function of solving those economic problems. The second feudal age instead provoked a social and spiritual crisis to which the Humiliati were a response, for they articulated a new interpretation of the Christian Gospel, yielding a new style of life, especially for lay people, that gave meaning to their existence in Christian Europe's first commercial age.

2. WALDENSIANS

Lyons was not nearly the size of Milan. Yet this dynamic port city at the confluence of the Rhône and the Saône, with its population of perhaps 10,000–15,000 people, witnessed the passage of pilgrims, crusaders, and merchants along one of Europe's busiest north-south routes. From early in the eleventh century, Lyons was part of the new commercial-industrial society. The city's economy was built on cloth-making as well as on trade and hospitality. Money was available from both Christian and Jewish moneylenders. Construction of a bridge over the Saône started in about 1050; between 1183 and 1190 a second bridge, twice as long as the first, was made to span the Rhône. In the period between 1165 and 1180, construction began on a vast, new cathedral, incorporating the current style that later detractors would call 'gothic'.[31]

Lyons and its environs were under the political control of the local archbishop. The archbishop in turn shared some of his ecclesiastical and political authority with the canons of the cathedral chapter. This chapter was an immensely wealthy corporation, with a membership of between 28 and 48 men. They all came from the feudal nobility and they all benefited materially from being canons; in the twelfth century it was they who elected the archbishops. The church of Lyons had undergone a reform in the eleventh century upon the initiative of Emperor Henry III. Lay investiture and clerical marriage were effectively eliminated, and the church of Lyons became a leading centre of the Gregorian reform movement. At Lyons, however, this movement did not include the canonical reform. As at Mâcon and several other places cited earlier, the canonical reform movement had little chance of success at a cathedral church run by nobles with extensive landed wealth. The first community of the new style of canons in Lyons was a priory of the Order of Saint-Ruf organized in about 1080, and that was in a new section of the city. The cathedral canons, meanwhile, went on living in individual houses grouped about the episcopal palace. Their wills provided legacies to parents, other relatives, friends, servants, and sometimes their physicians; these legacies included land, houses, vineyards, money, weapons, horses, furs, jewelry, books, and cooking utensils of iron or copper. The canons enhanced their fortunes by advancing money to impoverished nobles, receiving as surety lands, villages, and châteaux, which they administered for profit. It is not surprising that, by the chapter's own regulation, a canon was to be properly dressed, properly escorted, and mounted on horseback whenever he went out.[32]

In 1176, the Lyonnais region suffered a severe famine along with other communities throughout the eastern parts of France and the western parts of Germany.[33] The contrasts of wealth and poverty at Lyons under such conditions were striking. There had of course been an overall increase of wealth in the community during recent decades, but the ostentatious spending of the thriving upper classes was what made the contrast especially evident. It was made even more evident by way of contrast with the urban poor, with the dockers and the dyers' assistants who could not afford to buy food, which was scarce and expensive. Wealth and ostentation were probably most evident, in people's minds, and the contrast most vivid, where the wealth concerned was in the hands of churchmen.

Lyons at this time was the home of a wealthy merchant named Waldes. He lived there with his wife and two daughters. He bought and sold cloth; he probably invested money in the manufacture of cloth; and, as the early merchants so often did, he practised rudimentary forms of banking, including moneylending for interest. The list of his principal possessions attests to a formidably successful career. In addition to his house in the city, Waldes owned pastures, arable fields, woods, ponds and streams, vineyards, ovens, and mills. He drew income from most of these and from various properties and buildings in Lyons, and he owned fine clothes and furniture as well. In terms of wealth, Waldes was one of the great men of Lyons, though from a social standpoint, he was only newly rich.[34]

At some time in the early or middle 1170s, Waldes experienced a religious conversion. One source specifically relates this conversion to the period of famine, though it places the famine in 1173 instead of the more reliably attested year of 1176.[35] The immediate inspiration for the particular form of conversion was the story of St Alexis. Waldes stood on the edge of a crowd and heard a minstrel reciting that popular French poem about the wealthy Roman who abandoned family and fortune to live a life of Christian perfection as a mendicant. The story apparently made a deep impression, for the next day Waldes went to seek the advice of a master of theology. They discussed various ways of achieving salvation, and then Waldes asked which was the surest and best way of all. The master's answer was taken from scripture (Matt. 19:21): 'If you wish to go the whole way, then go and sell everything you have, and give to the poor.'[36]

Waldes first went to his wife, confided to her about his intentions, and then gave her a choice of keeping either his real property or his movable goods; she chose the former. With the income from selling the movable goods, he reimbursed several people from whom he felt he had taken profit unjustly, and provided for his daughters at the monastery of Fontevrault. The greatest part of it, however, he gave to the poor. For several months in that difficult period of famine, he regularly spent three days per week distributing food to needy people. He reminded those about him that 'No servant can be a slave to two masters; you cannot serve God and money' (Matt. 6:24).[37]

However familiar that biblical phrase, the sight of a great burgher dispensing his fortune freely in the streets of Lyons was unique and startling. Waldes alluded to this reaction and turned it to advantage the first time he addressed a large group of his fellow townsmen in the open. 'I am really not insane, as you think, but I have gained revenge over my enemies who made me their slave, in such a way that I was always more concerned about money than about God, and I was serving the creature more than the Creator.' Waldes was not talking to an audience of complete strangers, and his words and actions must have scandalized some of his erstwhile friends. He could not have made such a radical transformation and remained in his native city without drawing sharp criticism. He showed his sensitivity to criticism when he concluded in this way: 'I know that many disapprove of my having done this in public view. But I did it both for myself and for you: for myself, so that those who henceforth see me in possession of money can declare me insane; but in part also for you, so that you may learn to place your hope in God and not to trust in riches.'[38]

The Dominican author Stephen of Bourbon wrote an interesting account of the conversion of Waldes. Though he actually put it in writing as late as 1250, he had received his information several decades before from people who had been personal acquaintances of Waldes. Stephen reported that Waldes, who of course was not sufficiently well educated to understand the Gospels when read out in Latin, desired to learn to his own satisfaction just what they really said. He engaged two priests, one to translate the Gospels and other books of the Bible into the local vernacular tongue, and the other to write down these translations as the first one dictated. They did the same with many selected passages from patristic literature. Waldes studied these texts, committing whole passages to memory.[39]

He began to preach the Gospel as well as to live it; indeed preaching it was a requisite part of living it. His audience was responsive, and many came forward not only to reform their own lives but also to join him in his evangelical enterprise.[40] The evidence shows that people from almost all social levels were represented among his followers.[41] Waldes vowed never again to possess any gold or silver, and never again to give a thought to the next day. He proposed to his followers that they observe poverty and evangelical perfection as had the Apostles.[42] They accepted the challenge and emulated him in each detail. 'Those who followed his example, having given away everything to the poor, became propagators of voluntary poverty' (*professores paupertatis spontanee*).[43] The women among them preached as well as the men. The uneducated and the unintelligent among them preached. People of even the most lowly occupations, reported Stephen of Bourbon with a slight tone of scandal, went out to preach. These early Waldensians preached in towns and villages, in homes, in public squares, and even in churches.[44]

In March 1179 Waldes went to Rome where, in the words of the chronicler of Laon, 'the pope embraced Waldes, approving the vow of voluntary poverty he had taken, but ordering that neither he nor his associates take on the office of preaching except at the request of the local clergy.'[45] In the account of this visit to Rome given by Walter Map, who headed a papal investigation into their orthodoxy, the Waldensians appeared ridiculous in their theological ignorance. Still, Walter admitted that they were trying to follow the example of the Apostles. 'They have no permanent homes; they go travelling two by two, barefoot, dressed in woollen cloth, possessing nothing and having everything in common like the Apostles, naked, following the naked Christ.'[46]

Back at Lyons almost two years later, Waldes had to go before a synod convened by Archbishop Guichard and presided over by a cardinal named Henry of Marcy. Guichard was a former abbot of Pontigny, Cîteaux's second daughter house, and Henry a former abbot of Clairvaux.[47] It was Henry who had responded to an appeal for help against heretics from Count Raymond V of Toulouse by leading a mission there in 1178. He was now on his way to Toulouse again as a papal legate. Also present at Lyons was Geoffrey of Auxerre, abbot of the Cistercian house of Hautecombe and a companion of St Bernard on his trip to Toulouse back in 1145.[48] Thus the Cistercian establishment was out in full force at the synod of Lyons and obviously well versed in matters of heresy. In the view of Geoffrey of Auxerre, the point of the synod was to deal with allegations that Waldensians had continued to preach and that they had been making unduly inflammatory remarks about the clergy.[49]

Henry of Marcy made Waldes abjure all doctrinal error and affirm his beliefs by subscribing to a document known as a profession of faith. This document was rediscovered in 1946 and has been the subject of minute scholarly examination ever since.[50] Its main source was a fifth-century formula that was put before bishops-elect to test whether their faith was tainted by Arian heretical beliefs, and that was later adapted to fit cases where suspicions of heresy arose. A recent set of additions was intended to drive as sharp a wedge as possible between orthodox doctrine and the beliefs current among dualist heretics. There were also additions inserted purposely to deal with specific Waldensian beliefs and practices. At the end came a critical passage on the meaning of Waldensian poverty, a passage in which

Waldes affirmed both their own resolve to remain poor and their belief that others need not do the same in order to be saved. 'We renounced the world, and whatever we had we have given to the poor, as the Lord advised, and we have decided to be poor in such a way that we shall not give any attention to the next day, and we shall not accept from anyone either gold or silver or anything like that beyond food and clothing for the day.' Waldes was thus able to combine evangelical literalism with a life free from calculation. He confirmed the point that those people who remained in the world and kept their material possessions and obeyed the commandments of the Lord could still, by giving alms and doing other good works, be saved. In return for agreeing to this statement Waldes got from Henry of Marcy official approbation for his band of evangelical cohorts.[51]

Perhaps the Waldensians violated this agreement; in any case they remained under official suspicion. Geoffrey of Auxerre said that Waldes went right back to his own vomit and that he continued to attract adherents, and to send them out to propagate his views.[52] In 1182 the new Archbishop of Lyons, John Bellesmains, summoned Waldes to reply to these charges, and Waldes, taking on himself the role of Peter, spoke to the archbishop as Peter had spoken to the chief priests: 'It is better for us to obey God than men.' The reply of John Bellesmains, former Bishop of Poitiers and colleague of Henry of Marcy on his first expedition against heretics in 1178, was firm; he excommunicated Waldes and his companions, expelled them from the archdiocese, and denounced them to the pope.[53]

At the Council of Verona in 1184, the Poor Men of Lyons (*Pauperes de Lugduno*), as Waldes and his followers had come to be called, were placed under anathema by Lucius III and thus, along with the Humiliati, were now officially regarded as schismatics. The distinction between their orthodox, indeed commendable, religious life and their continued defiance of ecclesiastical authority was maintained. Thus they were declared schismatics, while the Cathars and others were being denounced as heretics.[54]

The spread of the Poor Men of Lyons is documented by the various edicts and laws promulgated in which they were condemned and ordered expelled.[55] In the mid 1180s, the new Archbishop of Narbonne, Bernard Gaucelin, an appointee of the legate Henry of Marcy, assembled a local synod to condemn the Waldensians who were then active in that region.[56] In 1190 he arranged for a formal debate to take place between Waldensians and those calling themselves 'true Catholics'. The judge's final assessment was wholly favourable to the Catholics.[57] An edict of Alfonse II, King of Aragon, dated 1192, ordered the Poor Men of Lyons to stay out of his territories, which included Provence. Anyone found aiding these people, giving them food or shelter or otherwise promoting their efforts, was to have his belongings seized by the crown. A stronger version of the same edict was promulgated in 1197 by Alfonse's successor, Peter II.[58]

To the north, there was evidence of the Waldensian presence already by 1192, according to the statute passed by a synod at Toul in that year, a statute advising anyone who came upon a follower of Waldes to bring him before the bishop.[59] Caesar of Heisterbach told of some Waldensians from Montpellier who came to Metz in about 1199.[60] By two letters of 12 July 1199, Innocent III gave evidence both of the reality of the Waldensian settlement at Metz and of the apprehension it raised in official circles.[61] The sources of apprehension were mainly three: unauthorized biblical translations, unauthorized preaching, and secret meetings. Innocent moved cautiously in these matters, just as he did where the Humiliati were concerned. He asked three Cistercian abbots to investigate the problem on his behalf; they reported the presence of several genuine Waldensians, and ordered their translations to be burned.[62]

In addition to the Rhône valley, Languedoc, north-eastern Spain, and Lorraine, the Poor Men of Lyons carried their message to Lombardy, where Milan became their headquarters. Their establishment in that city was called a 'school' (*schola*), probably a gathering-place for preaching and the public reading of scripture.[63]

The Italian Waldensians were like their French forebears at the start, but by 1205 serious differences of belief and practice forced them to sever their connections. These differences touched fundamental matters such as work, property, marriage, mendicancy, and priestly authority. The positions taken by the Italian Waldensians on these subjects turned out to be much more like those of the Humiliati than those of the French Waldensians. The *schola* in Milan, for example, bears a resemblance to the Humiliati Casa di Brera, whereas the French Waldensians had nothing comparable because they owned no property.

When the rift of 1205 occurred, the Italian Waldensians consisted of the original Italian Waldensians plus some unreinstated Humiliati. This formal separation of the French and Italian groups left the French with the original name of Poor Men of Lyons; the Italians then called themselves the Poor, or the Poor in Spirit, or the Italian Brethren, but they were generally known as the Poor Men of Lombardy, or Poor Lombards (*Pauperes Lombardi*). Waldes remained leader of the Poor Men of Lyons, while a man from Piacenza named John of Ronca was the leader of the Lombards. The Lombards did not reject manual labour, as had the Waldensians. Instead, they formed workers' collectives or cooperatives (*congregationes laborantium*). They continued to maintain private possessions, houses, and real property, as well as the institutions of marriage and the family.[64] The Humiliati influence is obvious, even if we do not know when it was first exerted. Negotiators for the French and Italian factions met at Bergamo in 1218 but failed to reconcile their disagreements.[65]

The final branch of the Waldensian movement was an off-shoot from northern Italy: from there the message of Waldes was carried to communities in southern Germany. A list of heretical groups given by an inquisitor in the diocese of Passau in 1260 included the Runcarii; these were Waldensians established by missionaries from Lombardy who acknowledged John of Ronca as their leader. A lengthy report of the Bergamo conference of 1218 was written by the leaders of the Poor Lombards and sent to their 'beloved brothers and sisters' in Germany.[66]

The Poor Men of Lyons neither sought nor accepted the designation 'heretic'. They defended themselves staunchly in the name of orthodoxy, and indeed they devoted much skill and energy to opposing those people whom they and officials of the hierarchy agreed were heretics: the Cathars. They preached, engaged in disputations, and wrote tracts against these sponsors of a new dualism.

The earliest known Waldensian writing against the Cathars is the *Book Against Heresy* (*Liber antiheresis*) by Durand of Huesca.[67] It was rediscovered in the same manuscript as Waldes' profession of faith of 1180, so it also has been known to modern scholars only since 1946. Durand's book dates from the early 1190s, a period when, on the one hand, the Waldensians debated with and were condemned by Catholics, and when, on the other, they engaged Catharist heretics in disputations. While professing loyalty to all ranks of the church's hierarchy, Durand stressed that the Waldensians thought of Jesus Christ as their bishop, and he reiterated the critical Waldensian argument that, in case of conflict, it is better to obey God than man. Still, despite blistering criticism of corrupt and incompetent clerics, he upheld the intrinsic value of the duly ordained, properly sacerdotal ministry. The wealth and ostentation and greed of heretics was denounced no less than that of orthodox clerics. The New Testament, he reminded his readers, nowhere shows the Apostles to be merchants, busily engaged in making real estate deals and in accumulating money. Durand made clear that poverty was not a prerequisite for salvation, but that ill-gotten money was surely an impediment to salvation. The positive foundation of Waldensian poverty was the imitation of Christ and the Apostles: 'Our faith and our works are justified by the Gospels. If you ask why we are poor, we say it is because we have read that our Saviour and his Apostles were poor.' The conclusion resounded with an affirmation of loyalty to the Roman Church, Durand promising to maintain and to defend even unto death the faith of God and the sacraments of the church. To the end, the *Liber antiheresis* defended a middle position against enemies on two fronts.[68]

In 1207, Durand took part in a meeting between Waldensians and Catholics at Pamiers, a town in the foothills of the Pyrenees, about 30 miles south of Toulouse.[69] The Catholic party was headed by some abbots as well as Bishop Fulk of Toulouse, Bishop Navarre of Couseran, and Bishop Diego of Osma, the spiritual master and companion of St Dominic. Durand emerged from this meeting determined to remain a Catholic and to refrain from further defending the Waldensians. He formed a group of evangelical, anti-heretical preachers under the title of 'Poor Catholics' (*Pauperes catholici*).[70] They approached Pope Innocent in December 1208 to make a profession of faith and to request papal approval for their proposed manner of living. This was granted, and the profession, modelled after the one taken by Waldes in 1180, was included in the papal letter announcing the approval. A notable innovation in this profession of faith was the recognition of a need for proper episcopal authority for any preaching on the church's behalf.[71] The pope registered official approval of the organization of the Poor Catholics on 13 May 1210, Durand of Huesca having been elected by the brothers as prior.[72] In a similar way, Bernard Prim led a contingent of Poor Lombards to Rome in the spring of 1210 to request formal reintegration into the Roman Church. Again there was a profession of faith and joined to it a refutation of all previous 'errors', plus their plan for an evangelical, anti-heretical group. Innocent gave them his approval in a bull of 14 June 1210; they were known as the 'Reconciled Poor' (*Pauperes reconciliati*).[73] They differed from the Poor Catholics in that they were more an organization of simple laymen who engaged in manual labour, though their goal was to oppose the church's enemies, in part by preaching. This preaching was limited to penitential exhortation.[74]

The discoveries of the profession of faith taken by Waldes in 1180 and of the *Liber antiheresis* written by Durand of Huesca have made possible a modern reassessment of the Waldensians. Without these documents, scholars had made the understandable assumption that people who were at one time regarded as heretics had been heretics all along. But it is now clear that the early Waldensians did not have a peculiar theology. The conversion of Waldes and his attracting several people to join him had nothing to do with doctrine. None the less, the Waldensians posed a serious challenge to the purpose, the utility, and the prerogatives of the clergy. As laymen, they led lives of Christian perfection—they had faith and they engaged in good works—and they were doing so apparently without clerical help. Pushed to a logical extreme, as it was by some, this suggested that Christian society could get along without priests. They also offered a formidable challenge to those regular clerics, like the Cistercians, who held to the monastic vocation as the truly apostolic life. Without making formal declarations, the Waldensians constituted a living advocacy of voluntary poverty for the entire clergy. The anonymous inquisitor of Passau saw the matter in such a way, for he said clearly that the Runcarii, meaning the German Waldensians, hoped to reduce the clergy to the condition of apostolic poverty (*clerum reducere ad statum paupertatis apostolorum*).[75] At Lyons, where the cathedral clergy constituted the keystone of the economic, social, and political organization of both the city and its surrounding countryside, the Waldensians could hardly have failed to be seen as a threat to the existing order. Such was the perception of Walter Map, who gave a candid explanation for clerical apprehension about the Poor Men of Lyons: 'They are starting off now very humbly only because they can't get a foot in; but as soon as we let them in,' warned Walter, 'we shall be driven out.'[76]

3. BEGUINES

Early in October 1216, James of Vitry waited on a ship in the port of Genoa for departure to the Holy Land and his new post there as Bishop of Acre. On the way to Genoa, he had stopped in Perugia to be consecrated by the pope, and while there, he advised the pope about a developing religious movement in the region around Liège. This was a movement of pious women called Beguines, who chose to live together and give one another encouragement to lead simple, actively charitable, religious lives. The pope, Honorius III, gave his approval to this form of life, as known and practised in the diocese of Liège and in nearby parts of France and the Empire.[77] This papal consent as reported by James of Vitry constitutes the original Beguine charter, although a more formal statement is contained in a bull issued by Gregory IX in 1233.[78]

Before reaching Perugia, James had stopped to preach in Milan, which he found to be a 'cesspool of heretics', but also where he gained first-hand knowledge of the Humiliati, on whose life he reported most favourably.[79] And before that, while crossing the Alps, James had been rescued from dangerous adventures by the intervention of Mary of Oignies, of whom he carried a relic in his baggage.[80] This renowned, recently deceased Beguine from Oignies (a town in the diocese of Liège), had originally inspired James to surrender the prebends from which he lived and to become a regular canon. Now he carried one of her relics and later on he wrote her biography.[81] One of the great preachers and propagandists of the early thirteenth century, James actively spread the reputation of Mary of Oignies and of the Beguine movement.

Yet the start of this movement cannot be located precisely in a formal act of foundation or in the spiritual conversion of some individual, for it is inextricably woven into the fabric of lay piety in twelfth-century northern Europe. A standard feature of the spiritual history of that century was the increasing absorption of facets of the religious life into the lives of laymen. Lay people from various levels on the social scale engaged regularly in religious devotions and scriptural reading, trying in such ways to incorporate into their lives something of the spirituality hitherto restricted to the technically 'religious' people of society. When the setting up of a Beguine community did take place in a formal way, reference was usually made to an earlier, informal stage in which a few pious women had lived quasi-religious lives together. Of the important figures in early Beguine history, some were men who helped give formal organization to groups already assembled; no one person can properly be labelled a founder. The first known of these male organizers was Lambert, surnamed le Bègue (probably signifying 'the stammerer' and unrelated to the name of the religious movement), a parish priest in the diocese of Liège. The son of a smith, Lambert wrote without shame of his humble origins. While little is known of his formal education, and some referred to him as unlettered, he became a gifted preacher and he translated portions of the Bible for laymen to read.[82] He had several times to face charges of heresy, but in fact he seem to have upset people mainly because of his insistent demands for the observance of Christian principles and for adherence to existing canon law. He preached an urgent message of clerical reform, denouncing priests who take money for administering sacraments and priests who are dominated by women and the desire to amass personal fortunes.[83] At his church in Liège, he brought together a group of holy women (*mulieres sanctae*) and guided the formation of what came to be thought of as the first beguinage. His express purpose in doing this was the preservation of their chastity. Unfortunately, no detailed record of Lambert's community is known to remain. We have only glimpses of his reputation, as in the observation of Alberic of Trois-Fontaines that Lambert was 'a most fervent preacher of the new religion that was sweeping Liège and the surrounding lands'.[84]

Another important inspirer and organizer of Beguines was John of Nivelles. Apparently a native of the town that Mary of Oignies claimed as her birthplace, John had studied and preached in Paris and became a canon of Saint-Jean in Liège. Then as deacon of Saint-Lambert, the cathedral church of Liège, he ministered to groups of holy women who chose, often under his influence, to embrace the common life. He won renown for protecting the chastity of these women, particularly when Liège was under attack in the spring of

1212. In addition, he was an active promoter of Cistercian nunneries and of crusading expeditions. In the second decade of the thirteenth century, he underwent a deepening spiritual conversion and became an Augustinian canon at Oignies, thus making a complete, personal commitment to evangelical poverty.[85]

The efforts of Lambert le Bègue, John of Nivelles, James of Vitry, and doubtless other organizers of the Beguine life of whom we know little or nothing, yielded a variety of forms. One way of grouping and analysing these forms is to place them, as the Flemish historian Philippen did, in a chronological framework. At first there were individual women living in towns, perhaps by themselves or else in the homes of their parents, abiding by evangelical principles as best they knew how and were able. They were neither organized nor even necessarily aware of other like-minded persons. The less wealthy of them worked to support themselves and most of them made donations of money or service to the poor and the sick. At this stage they were known as Beguines individually remaining in the world (*beguinae singulariter in saeculo manentes*). They reached a second stage in the final decades of the twelfth century and in the beginning of the thirteenth century when, as we have seen, they were gathered into semi-religious associations of disciplined Beguines (*congregationes beguinarum disciplinatarum*). These associations followed some of the practices of nunneries, and the obedience of the members was given to a head mistress. At the same time, many of the members continued to support themselves by working outside the community. A formal community marked the third phase, that of the cloistered Beguines (*beguinae clausae*). This kind of nearly monastic organization, which even had a rule, got the express support of Gregory IX in his bull of 1233. As wealthier women contributed to the endowment of such communities, poorer women were able to join them and be assured of steady support from the communities themselves. Finally, in a fourth stage of development, some of these communities were separated from the parishes where they were located and were themselves reconstituted as autonomous parishes, with their own clerics in residence.[86]

The earlier types of Beguine life did not disappear when subsequent types came into existence. And yet as the better organized Beguine communities became more numerous and available, responsible officials looked less and less favourably upon individual attempts at the Beguine life. Robert of Thourote, Bishop of Liège from 1240 to 1246, made his preference clear by stating that there was going to be no support from him for woman calling themselves Beguines but who, no matter how pious and modest, did not live in a beguinage. He argued that just as with merchants, cloth manufacturers, bakers, brewers, fullers, weavers, and other kinds of craftsmen, any group of three Beguines or more should live together in a house and be obedient to a mistress.[87] The craft-guild model might not have been very relevant, but the bishop's distrust of unorganized, individualistic, pious women could not be misunderstood.

Robert's successor, Henry of Liège, set about to organize the Beguines of Aachen in 1262. Until that time, many girls and women lived their pious, chaste lives in private homes scattered about the various parts of the city. Not only did he arrange to have them all settle at a single place, with a pastor of their own, outside the walls of Aachen, and thus to constitute there a separate parish, but he specifically threatened any self-styled Beguine who refused to join this community with a loss of spiritual privileges.[88]

The varieties of Beguine experience can be sorted out geographically as well as chronologically. Indeed the two methods really go together because the chronological scheme here outlined most nearly conforms to the development that took place in the Netherlands. There only was the final stage reached, the stage in which the beguinage became so large that, like some maturing offspring, it broke off from its parent parish and gained independent parochial status.[89] The Flemish or Walloon beguinage, at its height of prosperity an enclosed complex of buildings capable of housing 100, 200 or even 300 women, was a village within a town; a fine example can still be seen in Bruges. Of the many strategies by which people fought off the undesirable complexities of urban life, and built homogeneous communities on a personal, human scale, one of the most interesting and successful was the building of the Netherlandish beguinages.

In the Rhineland cities, on the other hand, the development barely got through the second phase. The records show that, while in any given city there were perhaps several hundred Beguines, these Beguines tended mostly to live either alone or in small groups. The number of Beguine houses in Cologne reached 99, in Frankfurt 57, in Basel 36, in Nuremberg 22, and in Strasbourg 85.[90] The number of women in these houses varied in Cologne from 3 to 67 (the latter being an exceptionally high figure); in Frankfurt from 2 to 15; and in Strasbourg from 3 to 26. The development of the Beguine movement was relatively slow in the Rhineland, where its history began in Cologne in 1223 and reached Frankfurt only in 1242, Mainz in 1259, Koblenz in 1271, Marburg in 1277, and Bonn in 1299–1300.[91]

The situation of the Beguines in France bore the clear mark of royal influence. In the 1260s, Louis IX (1226–70) set up a beguinage in the parish of Saint-Paul in Paris. The property was purchased from a Benedictine monastery for a large sum, and one observer estimated, perhaps rather freely, that this beguinage could accommodate 400 women. Moreover the king provided an endowment for the continued support of the many poor women who came there. Louis is also credited with founding the beguinage at Rouen and with making several donations to other beguinages.[92] According to Louis' biographer, Joinville, what pleased the king most about the beguinages was the preservation of chastity that they made possible for so many women.[93]

Even with these variations in time and geographical-sociological setting, the Beguines shared certain fundamental beliefs and practices. Beguines everywhere and always were committed to the preservation of chastity. For the most part, however, this chastity was seen largely as protection against illicit sex, because the Beguines took no vow not to marry. Anyone was free to leave in order to get married and apparently this was done commonly. There were no formal vows at all, in the sense of monastic vows, but a Beguine was expected to obey the mistress of her house, as well as her pastor and the bishop. Moreover she was to observe geographical stability while she belonged to a community.[94]

The attitude of the Beguines towards poverty was generally mild; many of them were rich and, as Beguines, lived comfortably. They retained their possessions and property for, once again, they made no vow to abandon such things. Wealthy new members paid their own way and made substantial contributions in addition. Those whose fortunes were diminished or lost while they were in the beguinage were guaranteed, just as were the poorer members, support by the community. Many of the Beguines worked, either by earning wages in the textile industry to help support themselves and their community, or by offering their services in an institution that catered for the sick and old in need of care, or the young in need of instruction. The beguinage was thus very much like a monastery, coming closest perhaps to the Premonstratensian nunnery, whose members lived in or near secular society and served many vital functions therein. Clearly the Beguines represented something of a middle way between regular and secular lives. As late as the 1270s, Gilbert of Tournai, who was preparing a treatise on church problems for the forthcoming Second Council of Lyons, wrote of the Beguines and admitted freely that he could not figure out whether to call them 'nuns' or 'seculars'.[95]

The social origins of the Beguines are easier to determine than their religious status. At least there is widespread agreement that they represented a full range of social classes. The women in Lambert le Bègue's group at Liège included daughters of barons, knights, nobles, and burghers.[96] In Cologne, with the largest Beguine population of any city in Europe, an overwhelming 88 per cent of all Beguines can be identified as either patrician or middle class, that is, from groups in between the landed nobility and the working class. This suggests that wealthier persons were more conspicuous because of the sizeable donations they were able to make.[97] Most nunneries of the time were open only to women of wealth, so the Beguines served a peculiar need in being open to all. And still in 1321, according to a letter of Pope John XXII, these numerous ladies spanned the social range from distinguished (*clari*), to noble (*nobilis*), to middling (*mediocris*), to lowly (*humilis*).[98]

The argument that because the Beguines came from a wide range of social backgrounds, theirs could not have been a social movement, is as weak in this case as in others.[99] The Beguines flourished in northern commercial and industrial cities starting in the latter half of the twelfth century. As with the poor who joined the Humiliati, the poor women of Netherlandish towns could find economic security, social stability, and a deep sense of spiritual fulfilment in the urban religious confraternity or consorority of the Beguines.

For the wealthy women, however, the problem was rather one of distaste for the family fortune and the distractions common to a life of ease. There were many discreet and devout girls, according to James of Vitry, who did not find it suitable to remain in their parents' homes among secular-minded and shameless persons. Some were able to avoid these problems by joining monasteries. Those that took up the disciplined life of a Beguine got instruction in manners and letters, in vigils and prayers, in fasts and other torments, in manual work and poverty, in self-effacement and humility. Many of these girls scorned their parents' riches and rejected the noble and wealthy husbands offered them, preferring to live in poverty, having nothing except what they got by spinning and working with their hands, and being content with shabby clothes and simple food.[100] Mary of Oignies distributed her belongings before devoting herself to the care of the sick, though she was restrained from becoming a mendicant.[101] Indeed, Mary may well have felt disgust with her family's fortune, for John of Nivelles claimed to have been told by Mary that her mother had made money from usury and dishonest trade.[102] Not only did wealthy ladies surrender their own fortunes but they were highly influential in converting other wealthy people, such as the rich merchant converted by Mary of Oignies,[103] and they helped to attract a formidable response in the form of donations, sometimes in wills, from other wealthy people.[104] The Beguine life was thus more than an expression of evangelical piety for those people who actively embraced it; that life also nourished, even if vicariously, the spiritual lives of its benefactors.

The spiritual possibilities of this kind of life were realized to their fullest by Mary of Oignies, not only for herself or even for all Beguines, but for all people who came to know about her. Towards the end of her life, she went far beyond her exemplary, Christ-like poverty, far beyond her exemplary charity towards others, and far beyond her exemplary mystical piety. In the midst of an ecstatic vision, she saw a seraph standing by her side and then she felt the pain of the five wounds of Christ in her body. James of Vitry said that she inflicted the wounds herself during the vision. At the time of her death, the holy women who washed the corpse were startled to find evidence of the stigmata.[105]

There was a Cistercian monk who had heard some terrible things said about the Beguines and who could not make up his own mind about their spiritual worth. He presented his puzzlement in the form of a question to God in prayer, and the reassuring answer came back that their faith was solid and their behaviour worthy.[106] Meanwhile Caesar of Heisterbach judged for himself that many Beguines surpassed in charity those who lived in cloisters, for in the midst of worldly people they were spiritual, in the midst of pleasure-seekers they were pure, and in the midst of noise and confusion, they led serene, eremitic lives.[107] He did not mean that to be a Beguine was to be an urban recluse. He meant that the Beguines had shown a way of making the Christian life attainable by the laity, by women, by city-dwellers both rich and poor.

4. CATHARS

The 'Pure Ones', or Cathars, constituted a loose amalgamation of sects, established in various parts of Europe in the twelfth and thirteenth centuries, with the heaviest concentrations in southern France, the Low Countries, the Rhine valley, and northern Italy. The most important factor common to these various individuals and groups was doctrinal—their belief in the existence of two primary forces in the universe, one the founder and patron of all that is spiritual, and thus good, the other the founder and patron of all that is material, and thus evil. The principal manifestation of this belief was a rejection of the physical world, including the abandonment of material possessions and abstinence both from sex and from the food of animals born of coition. The differences among various types of Cathars on even these fundamental points, though, were numerous and significant. Indeed, in some of the groups to be mentioned here, the name 'Cathar' was not at all used and only the barest traces of dualism were discernible.[108]

Traditional Catholic historians have seen the Cathars always as heretics, as enemies of, or at least outsiders to, the true faith. Protestant historians for long sought to prove that the Cathars were in some respects forerunners of the Protestant Reformation.[109] The Cathars have also been seen as forerunners of socialism, as contributors to the gradual progress of liberty, and as the first sustained voices of dissent in Western Europe.[110] Historians generally have accepted the designation of 'heretic' for the Cathars, resorting to the arbitrary but convenient device of calling heretical anyone whom the Roman pope regarded as heretical at any given time. The question even of whether or not the Cathars were Christians has been raised and seriously discussed.[111] Yet, as Delaruelle argued, all heretics are reformers; by definition, they work within the system.[112] And Chenu, in a related argument, observed that heresy occurs within the faith; complete outsiders may be infidels or apostates, but not heretics.[113] As for the Cathars, there is no denying that they thought of themselves as Christians. They referred, as we shall see, to the same texts, the same historical realities, and the same myths as did the Roman Church, claiming that they, and only they, were the true interpreters, in their own time, of the early Christian tradition. It is not for us to question whether the Cathars were really Christian. We can only note that in the twelfth century there existed, side-by-side, conflicting claims to a monopoly on Christian orthodoxy.

The dualist doctrines can be very revealing about the thought and life and feelings of the Cathars, giving insight into their perceptions of the world and their reactions to it. But these doctrines, even if regarded by most as heretical and by some as non-Christian, do not prevent our including the Cathars in this discussion about Christian lay people in the spiritual crisis of twelfth-century society. In point of fact, all the other lay groups thus far discussed, groups that probably no one would want omitted from such a discussion, were at one time or another considered 'heretical'. In order to demonstrate the unique character of each of these groups, one could concentrate on the doctrinal differences separating them, particularly on those separating the Cathars from the others, or on the quite different fates ultimately suffered by these groups. Such differences—and they are indisputably real—are essential both in the history of doctrine and in the history of the church, particularly when considered from the viewpoint of certain modern teachings and institutions and of how they originated. But from the viewpoint of trying to understand the new lay spirituality that grew up in the second feudal age, such differences, however real, are just not very important.

In the first half of the eleventh century, there took place a few, scattered incidents in which the name 'Manichean' was invoked and applied to the people in question, though not all of them appear to have been dualists.[114] Adhémar of Chabannes, writing of the period just before 1020, said that 'Manicheans appeared throughout Aquitaine leading the people astray. They denied baptism and the cross and every sound doctrine. Abstaining from food, they seemed like monks and they pretended to be chaste, but among themselves they indulged in every debauchery.'[115] At Orléans in 1022, ten canons of the church of the Holy Cross were found to be Manicheans and were accordingly executed by burning. They had apparently fallen under the influence of a certain rustic from Périgord, being led by him into devil worship and forms of behaviour referred to tantalizingly by monastic authors as too shameful to mention. Adhémar said that at about this time Manicheans were discovered and put to death at Toulouse.[116]

A synod at Arras in 1025 brought to light a group of people whose faith had been perverted, it was said, by certain men who had come there from Italy (northern Italian merchants, in all probability). These people of Arras claimed to live exclusively by the precepts of the Gospels and of the Apostles. They abstained from sex, earned their food by doing manual labour, and showed loving kindness to all who shared their evangelical zeal. What troubled the authorities was that these people denied the validity of all established religious institutions and practices. In the end, they were peacefully reunited with the church and so there took place no executions at Arras.[117]

Many people were sent to their deaths, however, at Milan in 1028. These were country people, noble landlords as well as peasants, from Monforte outside of Turin. They refrained from sex and from eating meat. They rejected the authority of the church. They held all their goods in common, in imitation of the Apostles, and they centred their spiritual devotion about prayer and the reading of scripture. Here, as at Arras, an alien influence was held to blame. Landulf the chronicler said that wicked persons had come secretly into Italy from unknown parts of the world to implant in the local population false principles based on distortions of scripture. A few of the people from Monforte abjured and were saved; the rest went into the fire to their deaths.[118]

In the 1040s, Bishop Roger of Châlons-sur-Marne noted the presence in his diocese of 'certain rustics' whom he identified as Manicheans, and he wrote to Wazo, Bishop of Liège (1043–8) for advice on what to do about them. Wazo's reply was a model of restraint and patience; basically he argued that there be no killing of these heretics because of the chance that they might come to realize their error.[119] The fate of these rustics is not known, but some 'Manicheans' said to be similar to those of Châlons were hanged at Goslar in 1051.[120]

Despite the mention of alien influences in a few of these cases, no clear connection among the various incidents has been established. No one case is very fully known or understood. Taken together, these incidents may represent some kind of dissatisfaction, for they share a rejection of clerical authority. But the similarity of these incidents seems to lie not so much in their reality as in the perception of that reality by contemporaries who had no way of coping with diverse

views in their communities. They saw all proponents of such views as
heretics, and all heretics as Manicheans. They knew, or were at least
vaguely familiar with, patristic writings against the Manicheans. In his
letter of advice to Roger of Châlons, Bishop Wazo acknowledged these
writings at the outset in this way: 'Concerning those of whom you
wrote, their error is surely obvious, for it was long ago exposed by the
holy Fathers and confuted by their brilliant arguments.'[121] Wazo cited
Gregory the Great, and he relied on the parable of the tares as
Augustine and others had done before him.

In 1114 attention fell on a group of people at Soissons who opposed
infant baptism, marriage, any propagation by intercourse, and the
eating of food produced by sexual generation. Historians of heresy
have pointed out that this view was not very different from the one
expressed some fifteen years later by a Bishop of Soissons.[122] The
bishop railed against sexual intercourse and even against marriage.
Sexual pleasure he defined as a punishment resulting from original
sin, and everything conceived as a result of intercourse he said was
conceived in sin. Guibert of Nogent told of these Soissons people,
adding the usual embellishments about their underground meetings
and their licentious behaviour. Guibert also fell into the usual pattern
of trying to comprehend this startling phenomenon in terms of the
intellectual equipment already at hand. 'If you will study over the
various accounts of heresies made by St Augustine,' observed Guibert,
'you will find that this one resembles that of the Manicheans more
than any others.'[123]

Guibert said that these people claimed to revere especially the Acts
of the Apostles and to lead the apostolic life. In addition to this
implied criticism of the contemporary clergy, they—again, according
to Guibert—equated the mouths of priests with the mouth of hell. For
these various crimes, the heretics of Soissons were arrested and
brought to trial. An ordeal was conducted. And finally, while the
ecclesiastical authorities were trying to decide how to dispose of the
heretics, 'the faithful people, fearing clerical leniency, rushed to the
prison, seized them, built a fire outside the city, and burned them to
ashes in it. The people of God were righteously stirred up against
them,' commented Guibert, 'because of the danger that their cancer
would spread.'[124] This kind of popular violence was probably not
unconnected with agitation for a commune, because the first
communal charter for Soissons was signed within about a year of the
time when the heretics were burned there.[125]

In 1143, a Premonstratensian prior named Eberwin of Steinfeld
wrote to Bernard of Clairvaux to tell him about some heretics at
Cologne and to elicit from him a commentary on the problem: 'We
therefore beg you, father, to analyse all aspects of the heresy of those
people that have come to your notice, set against them the arguments

and authoritative statements of our faith, and thus destroy them.'[126] And in reply Bernard did not intervene, but instead in 1144 devoted one of the sermon-commentaries he was writing on the Song of Songs to the situation that had arisen at Cologne and elsewhere.[127]

According to Eberwin, the heretics at Cologne renounced the material world in order to lead unusually ascetic lives. They were opposed to marriage and they refused to eat any food that derived from sexual generation. When they ate, they consecrated their food by saying the Lord's Prayer, and they believed this consecrated food to be the body and blood of Christ. They had their own version of baptism as well as of the eucharist. This they did by the imposition of hands, a method justified by John the Baptist's prediction that Christ would not baptize by water but with the Holy Spirit, and also by the example of Paul's baptism by Ananias at Christ's command, the account of which (Acts 9:17) mentions the imposition of hands but no water. By the ceremony of baptism one passed from the status of hearer (*auditor*) to that of believer. A believer was entitled to attend the prayers and to qualify eventually for the highest status, that of an elect. Again by the imposition of hands, a believer might become an elect; as such, he would then have the power to baptize others and to consecrate the body and blood of Christ at his table.[128]

This group had some organizational superstructure also, as we see from the confrontation with authority at Cologne, where they were represented by a bishop and his assistant. Moreover, they claimed to be in touch with other, similar communities elsewhere in the world and even to have a pope of their own. Their sense of history was highly developed, for their group could trace its ancestry back to the age of the Christian martyrs, adding that their forebears had kept up the tradition, mainly in Greece.[129]

They alone, according to this historical interpretation, followed truly in the footsteps of Christ. They were the *pauperes Christi*, the true imitators of the apostolic life, because they did not possess houses or land or anything whatever of their own, just as they believed that Christ owned nothing and demanded that his disciples not own anything either. 'You, however,' and here Eberwin quoted the heretics' critique of the Catholic Christians, 'add house to house, field to field, and seek the things that are of this world; it is thus even with those among you thought to be most perfect, such as monks and regular canons who, although owning nothing of their own and holding everything in common, none the less possess all these things.'[130] Their complaint was directed not against corrupt clerics but against the most high-minded sector of the clergy, arguing that their high-mindedness was not good enough, that individual poverty practised within a wealthy corporation was no poverty at all.

Then Eberwin moved on to quote what the heretics had to say about themselves:

We, the poor of Christ, who have no home and flee from city to city like sheep amidst wolves, are persecuted as were the Apostles and the martyrs. This happens even though we lead a holy and most strict life, persevering day and night in fasts and abstinence, in prayers and in work from which we seek only the necessities of life. We undergo this because we are not of this world. But you, lovers of the world, have peace with the world because you are of the world. False apostles, who pollute the word of Christ, who are concerned only about their own interests, have led you and your fathers astray. We and our fathers, of apostolic descent, have continued in the grace of Christ and shall remain so until the end of time. To distinguish between us and you, Christ said [Matt. 7:16], 'By their fruits you shall know them.' Our fruits are seen in our following of Christ's footsteps.[131]

While a few of these self-styled *pauperes Christi* returned to the church, their own theologians and their own bishop and his assistant defended their position in an assembly presided over by the Archbishop of Cologne. Neither side showed any sign of yielding to the other; for the heretics the choice was between recanting and dying. Finally, in a scene reminiscent of Soissons in 1114, the heretics were seized by a mob, 'who were moved by rather too great zeal,' said Eberwin, and thrown into a raging fire to die.[132]

Bernard's sermon of 1144, directed against heretics in general and not just those Eberwin had described, insistently attacked the secretiveness of heretics, who, unlike the ancient heretics who spoke out openly, 'prefer to slink about' (*serpere*). The reason for this, suggested Bernard, was that these fox-like heretics really knew the shameful nature of their faith. Furthermore, 'they are said to engage secretly in execrable and obscene practices, since indeed foxes' behinds have an evil smell.' The Apostles, too, Bernard continued, spoke their minds openly: 'Where is the apostolic model and life of which you boast? They cry aloud, you whisper.'[133]

But if these foxy heretics were hard to find, the evidence of their malicious enterprise was everywhere found. 'Women, leaving their husbands, and also men, dismissing their wives, are flocking to those people [the heretics]. Clerics and priests, young and old, are leaving their congregations and churches and are commonly found among them in the company of weavers of both sexes. Is that not serious damage? Is that not the work of foxes?' These men and women thereupon lived and worked together, and Bernard was not going to believe their claim that they remained chaste. 'To be always with a woman and not to have intercourse with her, is not this more than to raise the dead? You cannot do the lesser of these, so why am I to believe that you can do the greater? Daily you sit beside a maiden at the table, your bed is next to hers in the bedroom, your eyes meet hers in conversation, your hands touch hers in work, and still you wish to be thought continent?' In this way Bernard sought to expose 'the foxes' and thus destroy them. Once in the open, they would be easy prey. 'These people are truly crude and rustic, unlettered and utterly lacking in fighting qualities; indeed they are foxes, and rather puny ones at that.'[134]

Some of these people, apparently, were textile workers. To say that they were unlettered falls short of the whole truth because they had theologians to put their case before the Archbishop of Cologne. As for their lack of fighting qualities, which could have been Bernard's way of saying they were not of the fighting class (as he was), the observation appears accurate in the light of Eberwin's description of how they died. Their illegal seizure and precipitous deaths were astounding enough; but 'what is yet more marvellous, they met and bore the agony of the fire not only with patience but even with joy.' This gave evidence, thought Eberwin, of a constancy on the part of the heretics in their own heresy as could hardly be found even in those who are most devoted to the faith of Christ.[135]

An urgent letter of about 1145 from Liège to Pope Lucius II told of widespread heresy at Liège and in neighbouring parts of France. The descriptions given match closely those set down by Eberwin of Steinfeld for Cologne. The church of Liège was sounding a clear warning to the pope that the matter was most serious, that an entire rival church existed and was growing rapidly. They told the pope: 'according to what we have learned from those whom we apprehended, all the communities of the Gallic realm and of our own have been in large measure infected with the poison of this error.'[136] The point was corroborated by the letter written in the later 1140s by a monk of Périgueux who warned of the wave of heretics—'people who claim to follow the apostolic life' (*qui se dicunt apostolicam vitam ducere*)—that was sweeping over the neighbourhood of his city.[137]

Certain of the warnings about heretics and appeals for help were perhaps exaggerated and alarmist, but by the middle of the twelfth century there was indeed taking shape in western Europe a large-scale, organized, heretical movement. This movement spread quickly to most of Europe, the near uniformity of its terminology and practice testifying to a unity of inspiration and organization. The designation *Cathari* was first applied to a group of dualist heretics at Cologne in 1163 and within a few years it had gained general currency. Finally, evidence came to light that missionaries of the dualist sect of Bogomils were leaving Constantinople and the Balkans to proselytize actively in the West, and had perhaps been doing so for some time already.

A major encounter between Catholics and heretics took place in

1165 at Lombers, near Albi. The heretical views were fully aired and each side was able to get a general assessment of the other's resources.[138] At about this time a missionary named Nicetas arrived in northern Italy from Constantinople. He was reputed to be bishop of the heretics in that city, and in Lombardy he set about organizing bishoprics among the Italian dualists. There was fierce competition among factions, Nicetas being of a more radical dualist persuasion that many of the Italians he met, but the Italian heretics emerged more unified and better organized than before.[139] Their doctrinal unity was never very stable, however, for by 1190 they were divided into six sects.

Nicetas then travelled to France, where the heretics reassembled after the colloquy of Lombers at Saint-Félix-de-Caraman, a village near Toulouse. Here again Nicetas was successful both in persuading his audience to embrace a more radical dualism than they previously held to and in getting them to organize themselves into bishoprics.[140] By 1170, a solidly organized and doctrinally coherent anti-church existed within Latin Christendom, with its greatest concentrations of strength in the Low Countries, the Rhineland, southern France, and northern Italy, and with some adherents in most other sections of western Europe.

Organized opposition to this anti-church grew gradually within the Catholic Church during the latter half of the twelfth century. A large and distinguished mission of prelates went to Toulouse in 1178. And there followed in 1204 the Cistercian missions sent upon the initiative of Innocent III. Church councils were now steadily preoccupied with the matter of heresy. Theologians, for example Alan of Lille, devoted their energies directly and specifically to the refutation of heretical teachings.[141] And finally, early in the thirteenth century, the machinery of the crusade and of the inquisition was brought into action against the heretics. Preaching, councils, theological tracts, armies, and adjudication were all pressed into service to meet the western church's gravest crisis to date.

On the side of the Cathars, informative sources are rare and problematic. The surviving Catharist writings include *A Manichean Treatise, The Book of the Two Principles, A Vindication of the Church of God, A Gloss on the Lord's Prayer*, two descriptions of Catharist ritual, of which one is in Latin and the other in Provençal, and two works taken over from the Bogomils and translated into Latin: *The Vision of Isaiah* and *The Secret Supper*.

The so-called *Manichean Treatise* was an Albigensian work of about 1220 excerpted and refuted by Durand of Huesca in his *Liber contra manicheos*, and it was he who supplied the work's title. Moreover, Durand called the Albigensians 'modern Manicheans' (*Manichei moderni*).[142] The treatise put forth a lucid exposition of dualism, marshalling scriptural texts carefully and avoiding polemical diatribes altogether. *The Book of the Two Principles* is of mid-thirteenth-century Italian origin; it is both more complete and more contentious than the Albigensian treatise. The opening sections flatly assert the existence of two principles, good and evil, and of two wholly separate creations. The argument is directed in part against orthodox Catholics but also against moderate dualists. The author assigns to his friends such designations as 'wise men' and 'true Christians', while his opponents are 'unlearned', 'unenlightened', and 'ignorant'.[143]

The *Vindication of the Church of God* is a Provençal text of the mid thirteenth century in which the holy church is defined as an 'assembly of the faithful and of holy men in which Jesus Christ is and will be until the end of the world'. Unlike the holy church, the Roman Church is not persecuted on account of its goodness or justice; on the contrary, it persecutes and kills those who refuse to condone its sinful activity. It does not have to flee from city to city; instead it rules over cities and towns and provinces and is feared by kings and emperors. It is not like sheep among wolves, but rather like wolves among sheep. Most notably it tries to persecute and kill the holy church of Christ. This polarization of the two churches seems both to reflect the dialectic of dualist theology and to reveal something of the dynamics behind that theology.[144]

The formal ceremonies of the Catharist Church, well known from both friendly and hostile sources, were markedly simple, being oriented about a view of what the early church must have been like.[145] The novice was like a catechumen; he underwent a probationary period of at least a year of discipline and instruction. He became a full-fledged Christian believer and member of the Christian Church when, by a simple ceremony, he took up the privilege and responsibility of saying the Lord's Prayer. This prayer was the central act of Catharist formal worship, and the initiation ceremony included a phrase-by-phrase explication of it. The *Gloss on the Lord's Prayer* is an entire work devoted to such an interpretation.[146] In the most important of Catharist ceremonies, the consolamentum, a ceremony of spiritual baptism, the believer gained forgiveness for all his sins, and the perfected ones, those who had been through the same ceremony, administered baptism to the believer by placing their right hands upon him. They did so as 'true Christians, instructed by the primitive church'.[147] In one of the surviving descriptions of this ritual, the reader is urged not to look down upon his earlier baptism in the Roman Church, but to receive his Catharist baptism ('the holy consecration of Christ') as a supplement to that which was insufficient for his salvation.[148] An abbreviated and simplified form of the consolamentum was made available for the sick and dying.[149] The consolamentum was a ceremony that could not be repeated, yet a perfected one who sinned had to confess and pray for forgiveness.[150] The regular worship of the Cathars, called simply a 'service', was held monthly and consisted of the acknowledging of sins and penitential requests for pardon.[151]

The emphasis in both the theology and the ritual of the Cathars on Christian thought and models of Christian ceremony is plainly evident. The use of scripture is impressive both in quantity and quality. The *Manichean Treatise* has 189 biblical references; the *Vindication of the Church of God* over 100; and the *Gloss on the Lord's Prayer*, 232. The scholars who have worked on these texts attest that the biblical usage is consistently accurate.[152] The Cathars considered themselves Christians. Without any intrusion of 'foreign' or Bogomil ideas, they could have inherited many of their basic ideals and practices from Catholic Christianity, witness the strictures against sex and against eating meat, both of which had a long history in monastic spirituality, and similarly the strictures against accumulating material possessions, that had both a solid evangelical base and a long history. All of these themes and many others like them were embodied in the fervent revival then going on of the apostolic life as the leading model of the ideal Christian existence, a model that stressed scriptural literalism, simplicity, and poverty.

But apart from theological tracts and descriptions of ritual, what can be said of the Cathars' actual behaviour? Virtually nothing about this survives from Catharist sources, and for the most part only distorted views survive in unfriendly sources. The practice of *endura*, for example, suicide by starvation, was a supposed form of exaggerated asceticism practised by the Cathars. But there is no solid proof that this ever happened, let alone that it was an established pattern of behaviour.[153] Some Cathars died soon after receiving the consolamentum, perhaps even without eating in the meantime. The reason, though, is not that, as perfected ones, they chose to die rather than eat, but rather that they chose to receive the consolamentum as they lay dying. This was similar to a standard Christian practice of the time, which was to seek entry into a monastery *ad succurrendum*, that is, seeking help in the face of grave illness; conversion to the religious life was considered a second baptism that could save a person from damnation no matter what kind of life he had led nor how late the conversion.[154] Another charge against the Cathars is that they favoured usury. This charge may be accurate although it has not been substantiated. One thirteenth-century Dominican inquisitor and former Cathar, it is true, wrote of the Cathars 'that almost all of them are very avaricious and grasping', but that says little about usury.[155] The importance of the charge about Catharist usury is as a projection of forbidden activity by orthodox Christians on to a marginal social group, similar to the charges of aberrant sexual behaviour also made against the Cathars. It is noteworthy that one knowledgeable Franciscan, James Capelli, writing in about 1240, strove to put down such rumours about the Cathars. Without apology he condemned their misguided quest for the purity of virginity and chastity, a quest that looked upon all sexual intercourse as shameful, base, odious, and thus damnable. 'Although spiritually they are prostituted and they corrupt the word of God, physically they are very pure.'[156] He then described the heavy penalties for any Cathars who violated this code, and proceeded to deflate the stories that were told of them:

Certainly the rumour of the fornication that is said to flourish among them is most false. It is quite true that once a month, either in the day or at night, so as to head off popular gossip, both men and women gather together, not to fornicate as some falsely suggest, but that they may hear preaching and make confession of sins to their leader [*prelato*], as if by his prayer forgiveness for their sins would follow. They are unjustly torn apart in common talk with false charges of blasphemy, being accused of countless shameful and horrid acts of which they are innocent.[157]

Capelli was not preaching tolerance, but just a greater realization of the true situation; even the virtuous behaviour of the Catharists he took as a sign of their diabolical character. With respect to the special *consolamentum* for the ill, he wrote:

They administer to believers of their sect who are ill this same imposition of hands in the manner already described. From this has arisen the popular rumour that they strangle these people to death, so as to make martyrs or confessors of them. From experience we assert that this is untrue and we urge that no one believe they perpetrate such a shameful act. For we know that they consider what they do to be good and indeed many things that they do are in the nature of good works; in fasts, in frequent prayer, in vigils, in sparseness of food and clothing, and—as I must truly confess—in austerity of abstinence, they surpass virtually all other religious. Whence in them is truly realized the saying of the Apostle [2 Cor. 11:13]: 'Such men are false apostles, crooked in all their practices, masquerading as apostles of Christ.'[158]

The Cathars were not true apostles of Christ, according to James Capelli, but they gave a convincing performance in that role.

There were peasants, industrial workers, craftsmen, merchants, and nobles represented anong the Cathars. One Italian account mentions successively a notary, a grave-digger, a weaver, and a smith.[159] For the poor there seemed to be a chance for security by trading in their corrupting and distressing involuntary poverty for a morally and spiritually sanctioned voluntary poverty. For women, whether miserable prostitutes or titled ladies, the Cathars offered a genuine sense of equality, in a way that the patriarchal and priestly Roman Church never could.[160] For burghers there was the comfort of an ultimate, spiritual security. There is no single reason why various people became Cathars, any more than there is to explain why people became hermits or Cistercians or Humiliati. In a few cases, such as Soissons in 1114 and Cambrai in 1135, there seems to have been some connection between communal revolution and religious heterodoxy. At Toulouse, economic instability and resulting social friction have been put forth as the main factors contributing to the high incidence of religious heterodoxy there. The more successful participants in the new commercial society, big businessmen and usurers, tended to remain faithful to the church in a traditional manner. But the patricians whose very fortunes were threatened by the newcomers, and the unorganized and unprotected poor together flocked to the new anti-church of the Cathars.[161]

The significance of the consolamentum for the Cathars has been compared with the significance of baptism in the early church. In the same way Caesar of Heisterbach observed that the charges of outrage and scandal made against the Cathars were to be compared with like charges against the early Christians.[162] The stoic manner in which condemned heretics went to their deaths was compared by some Catholic observers to the manner of early Christian martyrs. This helps explain how that Franciscan writer James Capelli, an undoubted enemy of the Cathars, was able to say sincerely of them that 'they believe themselves to be successors to the Apostles'.[163]

The clergy's monopoly on the religious life faced repeated challenges, in various localities and under various forms, during the decades surrounding the year 1200. Lay people, not content with pressing for a more spiritually responsive clergy, claimed for themselves a share of participation in Christian spirituality. It was in about 1218 that James of Vitry gave this knowledgeable evaluation of lay piety: 'Not only those who renounce the world and go into religion are *regulares*, but so are all the faithful of Christ who serve the Lord under the Gospel's rule and live by the orders of the single greatest Abbot or Father of all.'[164] It was at this time also that two new religious orders were taking shape, orders that incorporated the cutting edges of lay and clerical reform movements alike.

9

The Franciscans and Dominicans

The Order of Friars Minor, founded by St Francis of Assisi (c. 1182–1226), and the Order of Preachers, founded by St Dominic (c. 1172–1221), brought to fulfilment the quest for a spirituality based upon voluntary poverty. That quest had begun with the Italian hermits and had been partially realized in one way or another by certain religious figures and groups of the eleventh and twelfth centuries. The friars in a sense combined the successful ways of their forerunners into a coherent and workable spiritual programme. Other mendicant orders appeared in the thirteenth century, but the Franciscans and Dominicans far surpassed them in size and influence.

1. FRANCISCANS

The beginnings of the Franciscan Order are inextricably woven into the intense personal crisis of one individual. Francis Bernardone was the son of a wealthy cloth merchant of Assisi. At the very time Waldes of Lyons was experiencing his conversion, Francis of Assisi was an infant. He grew to be an attractive and vivacious young man, the natural leader of his companions. The sources make no mention of a bookish education, so apparently his family did not intend that he pursue a professional career. Instead, he started to work with his father in the business of buying and selling cloth.[1] Presumably, he was brought up to perpetuate and pass on the Bernardone family and fortune just as they were being passed on to him. But then, at about age twenty-five, he was derailed from this clearly outlined path of normality.

Francis sank into a period of doubt and confusion, marked by recurring illness and disturbing dreams and visions. One night, for example, he had a startling dream, in which he saw his house filled with the paraphernalia of war. Each room was stocked with swords, shields, saddles, and other knightly equipment. He marvelled at these artifacts, which for the moment replaced the bolts of cloth he was accustomed to seeing in the house every day. He interpreted this dream as a sign that he should join a military expedition of the kind then often formed in connection with the hostilities between the popes and the Hohenstaufen. He prepared himself with all the necessary finery for such an expedition and then set out, but only to be stopped shortly by another vision, in which he was told to return to Assisi where a spiritual vocation awaited him. His religious conversion was under way.[2]

Francis now spent much of his time in prayer, meanwhile preferring not to confide in even his closest friends about what was happening to him. Long sessions spent in prayer became the setting for the working out of his agony. Sometimes he would take a friend with him near to where he prayed in a cave, leaving the friend outside on the pretext that he had to make further explorations of a large treasure he had found. 'Thousands of contrary thoughts,' said his biographer, Thomas of Celano, 'would flood his mind and thus aggravate his confusion and suffering.' One can appreciate Thomas' comment that when Francis returned to his companion waiting outside the cave, 'he was worn out from the effort'.[3]

Later on, when his spiritual vocation was coming into steadily clearer focus, Francis one day harnessed his horse, loaded up a cargo of expensive cloth, and went off to the market at Foligno, about ten miles from Assisi. He sold the cloth and also his horse, then returned on foot to Assisi. On the outskirts of town, he stopped at the little church of S. Damiano, where he begged the priest to take the money and to let him stay awhile. The priest refused the money but agreed to let Francis stay. Francis threw the money out of a window as if it were so much trash, and he announced that he was there seeking 'to possess wisdom, which is worth more than gold, and to acquire understanding, which is more precious than silver'.[4]

Peter Bernardone, Francis' father, searched everywhere, 'like a diligent spy', for that son of his, but Francis was warned and went into hiding for an entire month. When he reappeared, the people he encountered started to insult him abusively, to call him crazy, and to throw mud and stones at him. 'Seeing him so transformed from his former ways and so worn out by austerity, they attributed his behaviour to exhaustion and madness.'[5] He withstood this humiliation calmly. When Peter Bernardone heard what was going on, he ran to the spot, his face wild with rage and his eyes bursting from his head; like a wolf pouncing on a lamb, he lunged at his son and beat him and then led him home to lock him in chains. Eventually both parents came to understand that they could not dissuade him from his chosen way, so they released him while making two requests. They asked Francis to return the money from the cloth he had taken and sold. Francis found it on the ground outside S. Damiano where he had thrown it and he gave it to his father. The other request was that Francis go with his father before the Bishop of Assisi to renounce formally all claims to an inheritance.[6]

Peter Bernardone was an active and decisive man, and we see him in far better control of himself now that he had seized the initiative from his son. He had his money back and he was going to get a final settlement on his obligations to this son-gone-mad. When they met with the Bishop of Assisi, Francis suddenly once again seized the initiative. Before any word was spoken he stripped off all his clothes until he stood completely naked before his father, the bishop, and a crowd of retainers and passers-by. The gesture was as sincere and meaningful as it was theatrical. He threw off all the symbols of his social status. He threw off his old vanities. He put aside fine clothes forever. He rejected any material form of patrimony. He turned away from his natural father and took refuge with a new spiritual father, the Bishop of Assisi, who threw his cloak about the naked young man. Francis had definitively thrown off the old Francis.[7]

Thus emancipated, Francis built up his inner resolve by a number of humiliating experiences. He submitted to a beating by robbers; he served without compensation in a monastic refectory; he took care of lepers; and he helped poor people in any way he could. He gave his services in helping to rebuild the church of S. Damiano, which was in a dilapidated condition. On his own initiative he then worked on the nearby little church of the Portiuncula, which was in a state of almost total collapse, and had been completely abandoned. Francis stayed on at the Portiuncula, making it usable again, enough for the cult to be reestablished there. More than two years had passed since the start of his conversion.[8]

One day at the Portiuncula, Francis listened carefully as the evangelical text on the sending out of the disciples to preach was read. He felt that text speaking directly to him as never before, and so, immediately after the mass was completed, he went to discuss this text with the priest. In a sort of double exposure we can at the same time picture that other unschooled layman, Waldes, consulting a priest for elucidation of a passage from the Gospel. In the present case the priest gave Francis a point-by-point commentary, and Thomas of Celano left us a report of the effect this biblical lesson had.

When St Francis heard that the disciples of Christ were to possess neither gold nor silver nor any money, that they were to take with them on the road neither purse nor bag nor bread nor staff, that they were to have neither shoes nor a second tunic, but that they were to preach the kingdom of God and penance, he was carried away with joy in the Holy Spirit: 'This is what I want,' he cried; 'this is what I have been looking for, what, from the bottom of my heart, I burn with desire to accomplish.'[9]

Francis lost no time in putting into practice what he had just heard and newly understood. He removed his shoes, threw away his staff, kept only one tunic, and replaced his belt with a piece of rope. Then he started to preach. To any who would listen he preached penance. He spoke in a simple language that resonated deeply with his listeners. Not any longer just poor and humble, Frances was now consciously poor and consciously humble and even consciously dressed on the apostolic model. His new vocation was yet closer to starting when, in addition, he had begun to preach the Gospel. But such preaching was not for any one man to do alone; with the conversion of a few other persons to his way of life and the formation of a small band of poor, evangelizing preachers, Francis arrived at a full stage of preparedness for his new calling.[10] The moratorium was over. All doubt and confusion were left behind. Talent, ambition, psychological drive, physical energy, historical perspective, dreams, ideals, thought, and speech had all been brought into a harmonious coordination. Like some perfectly conditioned athlete, a new, mature Francis had emerged, fully prepared for the arduous decade and a half in which he was to capture the imagination of Latin Christian society as no individual had done before.

He had hated money and wealth, and these were now replaced in his life by evangelical poverty. He had hated vanity and self-indulgence and social pretentiousness, and these were now replaced by evangelical humility. He had hated expensively finished cloth, the source of his father's fortune, and this was now replaced for him by a single, coarse woollen tunic. He hated his father, though that is not the whole truth; he hated and he loved his father. He believed in the Gospel text (Luke 14:26), quoting it in the rule he wrote in 1221, which said that one who wanted to be a disciple of Christ would have to hate his father and his mother, his spouse, his sons, his brothers and sisters, and his very own life. For the father towards whom he felt so ambivalent, Francis substituted an adopted family of brothers; in such a way the new man established himself within the structure of a new family. Thomas of Celano, who wrote this comprehending account of a religious conversion, said of Francis when he started to preach: 'He seemed to be a completely different man from the one he had formerly been.'[11]

'The Lord gave me brothers,' wrote Francis toward the end of his life, truthfully but with understatement.[12] The very first ones to commit themselves were some of his friends who lived in Assisi. We should not be surprised that the new Francis was as much a leader as the old, that he was as magnetic and persuasive as ever, for basic traits of personality are not lost in the process of exchanging one cultural identity for another. When the group numbered eight, Francis divided them into four sets of two, that they might separate and go out in the manner of the Apostles to preach a message of peace and penance. When they attained the apostolic number of twelve, Francis composed a brief rule consisting mainly of passages from the Gospels. The Bishop of Assisi helped sponsor Francis at the papal court, and the approval of Innocent III for his new group came through without difficulty or delay. The world had changed markedly in 30 years, since Waldes had been expelled from Lyons by his bishop and had gone to the papal court with a proposal similar to that of Francis, only to be warned by the pope and made fun of by the courtiers. But Innocent III was not Alexander III; he had given his approval to the Humiliati in 1201 and to the Poor Catholics in 1208. In 1210 he granted approval to the Reconciled Poor, led by Bernard Prim, and to the Lesser Brothers, led by Francis of Assisi.[13]

Francis now launched into an intense period of preaching, attracting many recruits to the order and holding his large audiences spellbound. This magic worked on the future St Clare in 1212; Francis was then 30 years old and Clare, a noble girl of Assisi, was eighteen. She abandoned the world and all she had in it to be his devoted follower. Clare became the nucleus of a community of religious women living in strict poverty in S. Damiano, a community that in turn became the nucleus of the Order of the Sisters of St Francis.[14]

The brothers preached but also spent most of their days either working with their hands or serving in leproseries or otherwise earning a little food. At first the members stayed generally close to Assisi and then in periods of good weather went off to other parts of the Italian peninsula to preach. Gradually these periods away from Assisi lengthened, so that ultimately the brothers were scattered throughout Italy and only occasionally reunited in Assisi. All of this took place prior to the development of a formal geo-political structure within the order. As they already lived by an approved rule, they encountered no difficulty with the Lateran Council's provision against new rules and new orders in 1215.[15]

James of Vitry, in that same letter of 1216, which is so informative about the Humiliati and the Beguines, gave also his estimate of the Franciscans he met in Italy at that time. He introduced them at a point in the letter where he was lamenting the worldliness of the papal court.

In the midst of all this I none the less found one consolation, namely many rich and worldly people, both men and women, giving up everything to flee the world for Christ; these people are called Lesser Brothers *(Fratres Minores)* and Lesser Sisters *(Sorores Minores)*. They are held in high esteem by the lord pope and the cardinals; they have no concern whatever for worldly matters; but with fervent desire and vehement striving they work every single day to draw souls that are in peril away from the vanities of the world and to bring these along with themselves. Already by God's grace they have had great success and made many conquests, in such a way 'that one who hears the call in turn calls others' [Rev. 22:17], and one audience draws in another audience. They live by the model of the primitive church, of which it is written: 'the whole community of believers was united in heart and soul' [Acts 4:32].

James described how these people lived on the edges or outskirts of towns, the women engaging in manual labour to support themselves and the men going into town during the day to preach and to minister to the needy. The women, he said, were especially disturbed by the fact that they were honoured far more than they desired by clerics and laymen alike.

The men of this religious order gather once a year in a chosen place, to their great benefit, that they might dine together and rejoice in the Lord. They get the advice of worthy men and they decide on and then promote and get papal approval for holy projects. After this they disperse for the whole year, to go throughout Lombardy and Tuscany and Apulia and Sicily.... I am convinced that the Lord, out of disgust with prelates who are 'like muted dogs who don't have it in them to bark' [Isa. 56:10; i.e., prelates who do not preach], wishes before this world comes to an end to save many souls through these simple and poor men.[16]

At the general chapter in the spring of 1217, the assembled friars made the critical decision to send out parties to various far-off places to establish outposts of their growing fraternity.[17] This move evolved naturally enough from what they had already been doing. The difference was one of degree: they were now going outside Italy and would have to set up homes far away from Assisi. The same general chapter provided for the administrative division of the order into provinces: six in Italy, two in France, and one each in Germany, Spain and the Holy Land. In Italy the friars had already been active in such places as Bologna, Florence, Pisa, Milan, Rome, Naples, as well as many communities closer to home in Umbria. One group was organized to go to Paris and another to go to the towns of Languedoc sometime between 1217 and 1219. The Franciscans had certainly reached the Holy Land by 1219.[18] For Germany and England, the first expeditions were carefully recorded by historians. The Franciscans were successfully established in Germany in 1221 and in England three years later.[19]

For such a growing international organization, the original rule of 1210 (*regula primitiva*) was thought inadequate; a group of friars thus prevailed upon Francis to compose another rule (*regula secunda*) in 1221. The latter, with a number of significant modifications, was accepted by Pope Honorius III in 1223 as the order's definitive rule (*regula bullata*). By that time, there were Franciscans all over Europe, and Francis was withdrawing into a private, mystical world, communicating only with a circle of immediate companions. The order had passed into the hands of capable administrators, who in turn worked in close co-operation with the papacy. The continued growth of the order, although not unopposed, went on with a confident determination fed by success. By the year 1316, there existed in the towns of Latin Christendom over 1,400 Franciscan convents.[20]

2. DOMINICANS

The beginnings of the Dominican Order are found not in a personal crisis but in a protracted institutional struggle in which Dominic happened to be peripheral participant. The growing anti-church of the Cathars in Languedoc put officials of the Roman Church to a severe test. The special missions of 1145 and 1178 as well as the continuing missions of papal legates to that region carried the responsibility of eliminating heresy and restoring the exclusive control there of Catholic Christianity. Heretics were only part of the problem. In May 1203 the pope pleaded with Berengar, absentee Archbishop of Narbonne, to visit his archdiocese and minister to the faithful placed under his charge, to serve, as befitted his pastoral office, 'the little people begging for bread'.[21] The pope chose two Cistercian abbots, Peter of Castelnau and Ralph of Fontfroide, to go on mission to Narbonne, though still in January 1204 he was trying to get Berengar to co-operate. The full papal commission was appointed in May 1204, and it included Arnold Amaury, the Abbot of Cîteaux. The pope advised his agents not to say or do anything that would compromise their task, urging them to let their modesty keep the impudence of ignorant men silent, and to give the heretics no opportunity to criticize their words or deeds. No direct report on the first phase of this mission has survived, but we can surmise a lack of positive results from the letter Innocent III wrote to Peter of Castelnau the following winter. The pope lectured Peter and his colleagues on the superior merits of the active life and on the need to sacrifice some of the joys of contemplation in order to carry out an evangelical task.[22] Such was the scene in south-western France in which Dominic became involved.

Born in a Spanish sheep-raising village named Caleruega, south-east of Burgos, Dominic studied at Palencia and then became a priest and regular canon in the cathedral church of his diocese at Osma. Bishop Diego, who in the days before Dominic joined was instrumental in introducing the canonical reform, including the Rule of St Augustine, into the cathedral chapter of Osma, had Dominic join his entourage on a diplomatic mission in the summer of 1203. They were going to Scandinavia to arrange the marriage of a Castilian prince to a Danish princess. When they passed through Toulouse, Diego and his colleague Dominic stayed in the home of a Cathar. Through the night, we are told, host and guests stayed up to dicusss their theological differences until finally, at daybreak, the Cathar host had been brought back to the orthodox fold. The Spanish churchmen continued on with their mission but the experience in Toulouse left them both with a resolve to return.[23]

The marriage alliance necessitated a second expedition, this one in the summer of 1205, and its final resolution required a trip to Rome, where Diego and Dominic prolonged their stay through the following winter and spring. Diego confided to the pope his intense desire to become a missionary among pagans beyond the frontiers of Christendom. He accordingly offered to resign his episcopal chair, claiming insufficient ability to carry out his responsibilites. But Innocent would have none of this and ordered Diego to return to Osma.[24] On the way they made a detour to Cîteaux and then went to Montpellier where the pope's Cistercian emissaries were conferring. Diego soon entered into their deliberations.

A Cistercian historian, Peter of Vaux-de-Cernay, wrote a contemporary account of the meeting at Montpellier. He acknowledged the Cistercians' frustration about their failure in regaining heretics to the Catholic faith and their frank appeal to Diego for advice. Peter did not mention the trip to Cîteaux, saying rather that Diego had gone directly from Rome to Montpellier.

There he found the venerable man Arnold, Abbot of Cîteaux, and Brother Peter of Castelnau and Brother Ralph, Cistercian monks, legates of the Apostolic See. Out of discouragement they were wanting to abandon the mission confided to them, for they had been able to gain nothing or practically nothing by their preaching to the heretics. Whenever they wished to preach to these heretics, the heretics brought up the scandalous behaviour of the clergy; were they to choose to correct the lives of the clerics, they would have to take time away from their preaching. In the face of such a dilemma, the famous bishop gave some helpful advice. He counselled and urged that, putting everything else aside, they throw themselves even more fervently into their preaching. Moreover, so as to clamp shut the mouths of the evil, they should follow and teach the example of the Pious Master, proceeding in all humility, going on foot, with neither gold nor silver, imitating in everything they did the apostolic way. But the legates, not wishing on their own to latch on to these ways, which they saw as quite innovative, did state that if some duly authorized person wished to go ahead of them and show the way, they would follow him most willingly.[25]

Diego's suggestion does not seem very original. The idea must go back at least as far as Peter Damian and we have seen it proposed and practised by such men as Gerhoh of Reichersberg, Arnold of Brescia, and Waldes. Yet such an awareness of history should not blind us to the genuine sense of novelty and hence strangeness felt by those Cistercian legates. They apparently thought they were doing their job properly, all the while accepting without question that they maintain their large entourage, their horses, their fine clothing, and their high expenditures.[26] They complained to Diego that their mission was being frustrated by the bad behaviour of the clergy; thus the blame fell on others. Diego, also, had his horses and retainers, but his perception of what was wrong with the papal mission was different.

Peter of Vaux-de-Cernay's only comment at this point in the story is:

What more was there to say? This godly man offered to do it himself. Right away he sent his entourage and his equipment back to his city of Osma, content to have one companion stay with him. Then he left Montpellier with the two monk-legates, Peter and Ralph.[27]

At this time the Abbot of Cîteaux had to return home for a general chapter meeting. Other sources inform us that Dominic was the companion who stayed with Diego. The little group of three or four—Peter does not include Dominic—travelled about from town to town for over a year engaging in disputations with the heretics. They were not alone all that time. The Abbot of Cîteaux returned in the following spring with twelve fellow abbots, who showed a willingness to follow Diego's example.[28] Under the bishop's leadership, wrote Jordan of Saxony, 'in voluntary poverty they began to proclaim the faith' (*in voluntaria paupertate fidem annuntiare ceperunt*).[29]

On 17 November 1206 Innocent wrote to Ralph of Fontfroide. The pope's letter ordered an expansion of the apostolic mission, without specifying any figures, but specifying very clearly that any candidate chosen by Ralph must, besides being qualified for the work involved, be ready to imitate the poverty of Christ the pauper. He must be prepared to approach the heretics wearing wretched clothes but with a fervent spirit, so that, by the example of his deeds and the teaching of his words, the heretics might be recalled from their error.[30]

Diego's activities in the summer of 1206 and Innocent's letter of the following autumn together mark a critical moment in the history of voluntary poverty in Latin Christian society. Full credit for establishing in the Western Church itinerant preachers living in absolute and voluntary poverty, in conscious imitation of Christ and the Apostles, cannot be assigned exclusively to either of these men. The pope had had his experience with the Humiliati and the Waldensians, but so also had Diego had experience with the Cathars and the Waldensians. The two men had met in Rome in the winter of 1205–6, and each of them was to play a critical role in implementing the apostolic ideal in the year 1206.[31]

The new form of mission scored some isolated successes, for example, with the Cathars in Montreal in 1207 and with the Waldensians—recall Durand of Huesca's conversion—at Pamiers in the same year.[32] But then Ralph of Fontfroide died in September 1207, and later in the autumn Diego returned to Osma to tend to his duties there, though with the firm intention of returning to the anti-Cathar mission and of bolstering it with some of the resources of his diocese. The mission instead suffered a series of setbacks. Diego died at home on 30 December 1207. Two weeks later Peter of Castelnau was assassinated and Rome reacted by putting in motion the machinery of a crusade. The organization of Peter of Vaux-de-Cernay's *Hystoria Albigensis* tells the story in brief. Part I describes the heretics and their beliefs. Part II concerns preaching, that is, essentially the Cistercian mission and its revitalization by Diego of Osma. That section ends with the return to France (*ad partes Gallie*) of most of the missionaries, having been able to accomplish virtually nothing by their preaching and debating because, explained Peter, of the obstinance of the heretics in their evil errors.[33] Part III is devoted to the Albigensian Crusade, including a full year-by-year account of the war.

The story would perhaps have ended thus in open warfare were it not for the persistent labours of Durand of Huesca, whose group of *Pauperes catholici* gained papal approval in 1208, and for the continuing spiritual presence of Diego in Cathar territory in the person and activities of his loyal follower Dominic. While the sources continue to be almost totally silent on Dominic, his activities came to be centred in an institution that did leave traces. In 1206, the missionaries established at Prouille, a tiny fortified locality close to Fanjeaux, west of Carcassonne and south-east of Toulouse, a religious house for females converted from Catharism. Bishop Fulk of Toulouse made the principal donation. In the spring of 1207 Berengar of Narbonne gave to Notre-Dame of Prouille the proprietary rights over a church at nearby Limoux. These were the first of several donations of property and privileges that would make of Prouille a religious house endowed in the old-fashioned way. Simon of Montfort, for example, after taking Carcassonne and settling at Fanjeaux, became a generous benefactor of Notre-Dame of Prouille. This community became an adjunct to the preaching mission after the manner of Catharist way-stations, run usually by women, where *perfecti* would retire to restore their health or merely to rest from the rigours of itinerant preaching and to prepare for the next round. Though the Catholic missionaries continued to beg for food, at Prouille they had guaranteed to them a certain measure of security.[34]

Further evidence of Cathar influence on the Catholic missionaries, in addition to the poverty of the preachers and the haven for preachers at Prouille, is contained in a letter written by Dominic in about 1208. This is one of three surviving letters, all strictly formal and thus not at all revealing of the author's individuality, three letters that together represent all that remains extant from Dominic's pen. The letter in question prescribes the religious behaviour for an erstwhile Cathar seeking to be reinstated as a Catholic Christian. The convert was to attend mass every day, and vespers as well on feast days. He was to recite ten Our Fathers seven times a day and twenty in the middle of the night. He was to remain chaste. He was to abstain at all times from meat, eggs and cheese, indeed all food originating in animals born of carnal intercourse. On Christmas, Easter, and Pentecost, however, he was supposed to eat precisely such kinds of food as a sign of renunciation of his former errors. The extremely fine line separating this programme from ordinary Catharist spirituality is strikingly apparent.[35]

Of the period 1208–14 in Dominic's career we know practically nothing, except that Notre-Dame of Prouille continued to receive donations and that both purchases and sales of land were made on its behalf. Anything received by Dominic or his fellow preachers, who remain unknown, went in turn to Prouille. For the period between the death of Diego and the Fourth Lateran Council, Jordan of Saxony says that Dominic remained virtually alone with just a few followers in that region, continuing as best they could in time of war their apostolic mission.[36]

In the year of the council, 1215, Bishop Fulk of Toulouse gave Dominic the special charge of organizing and leading a group of diocesan preachers. This charge was meant to fulfil an order from the pope to all bishops to sponsor more and better preaching in their dioceses. In his bull of 10 March 1208, which prepared the way for the Albigensian Crusade, Innocent had recalled to bishops their obligation to preach; that is, while preparing the short-range and emergency policy of a crusade, he put partial blame for the present crisis on the bishops who had hitherto failed to fulfil their responsibilities and he set down the lines for a new, or renewed, long-term policy of episcopal preaching.[37] The first canon of the Council of Avignon, 1209, restated the charge to bishops but added that they should also engage other preachers, capable and discreet, who by their words and examples could restore and strengthen the faith.[38] The same points were to be restated at the Fourth Lateran Council, in its canon ten, which acknowledged the problems of bishops who were extremely busy, or occasionally ill, or who had numerous heretics in their lands, or who had exceptionally large and diffuse dioceses. The preaching now called for was not limited to opposing heretics but embraced the full range of preaching the Gospel to the faithful.[39]

Fulk engaged 'Brother Dominic and his associates' for the task of preaching in his diocese by a charter dated sometime in 1215. The significant point at which it went well beyond the emerging papal policy was in specifying that the men would go about on foot, preaching the work of the true Gospel, in evangelical poverty (*in paupertate evangelica*). Yet they were not to be beggars, for the charter went on to explain that these evangelical brothers must be nourished, and that to such an end he, the bishop, with the consent of his cathedral chapter and diocesan clergy, was devoting one-sixth of the tithes from parish churches in the diocese to the support of these new preachers. One-sixth meant one-half of one-third, which was the portion normally reserved for the poor. The bishop here explained that particular point, adding that he was obviously bound to assign a part of this portion to those who, for Christ, had chosen evangelical poverty.[40]

Fulk and Dominic went to Rome at the time of the council, 12–13 November. They apparently sought approval of the charter and recognition of a new, even if only local, religious order. There was to be no question of allowing them to set up a new order, for the forces opposed to the century-old proliferation of orders prevailed at the council, as expressed in canon thirteen:

Lest the extreme diversity of religious orders lead to confusion in the Church of God, we firmly prohibit anyone else to found a new religious order. But whoever wishes to enter the religious life, let him join an order already established. Similarly with anyone wanting to set up a new religious house, let him choose a rule and form of life from among the approved religious orders.[41]

The pope advised Fulk and Dominic to return home and to consult with the other preachers. The group met and they chose the Rule of St Augustine; moreover they adopted a set of ascetic practices drawn largely from the customs of Prémontré. While they decided not to accept or hold landed property other than that on which their houses and churches might stand, they allowed themselves the security of receiving revenues. Then Bishop Fulk and his chapter gave the preachers three churches, one of which, Saint-Romain, was in the city of Toulouse. Here Dominic and his companions—they numbered sixteen altogether—set themselves up with a cloister and with individual cells for sleeping and studying.[42]

Dominic sought approval for his new organization and received it from the new pope, Honorius III, in a bull dated 22 December 1216.[43] Doubt remains about just what the group was called at this time. In his bull Honorius addressed them as the canonical order established at Saint-Romain; but in the following month he addressed them as the prior and brothers of Saint-Romain, preachers (or preaching) in the Toulouse region.[44] At the latest by February 1218 he was calling them the brothers of the Order of Preachers.[45] But that takes us beyond 15

August 1217, the most revolutionary moment in the history of the order.

On that day Dominic astonished his brothers with the announcement that they were going to leave Toulouse, that they would never again all live there together. They were going to split up and go out into the world.[46] Dominic's decision was most likely prompted by the deteriorating military situation. His patron and protector, Simon of Montfort, was losing his grip on Toulouse during the summer of 1217, and indeed he lost it entirely in September.[47] The way chosen by Dominic at this particular juncture was characteristically eclectic. For twenty years he had been a regular canon living by the Rule of St Augustine, first at Osma, then for a long time as a preacher on special mission in heretic territory, and most recently as the founder of a group of canons, living in the manner of Premonstratensians, in and near Toulouse. He moved from the first to the second of these stages under the influence of the Bishop of Osma, and from the second to the third under the influence of the Bishop of Toulouse. Now, faced with the threat of expulsion from Toulouse, Dominic adopted the course laid out by the Franciscans three months earlier at their general chapter meeting.

Seven of Dominic's associates went straightway to Paris. Dominic and a few others went to Rome, possibly via Bologna, and the remaining few went to Madrid. The settlement at Bologna dates either from the autumn of 1217, or at the latest, from the following spring, and a convent for women was established at Madrid, with Dominic himself present, in 1218.[48] The search for recruits, especially in university towns, yielded success rapidly. Soon there were convents at Barcelona, Palencia, Limoges, Poitiers, Orléans, Rheims, Metz, Verona, Brescia, Asti, and Faenza. By 1221, the year of Dominic's death, the Order of Preachers had developed a constitution of its own and been placed on a firm institutional foundation. By the close of the thirteenth century, Europe and the Holy Land had over 500 Dominican convents. By their administration of the Inquisition as well as the high quality of their studies in theology and of their practice of rhetoric, the Dominicans held a forward position in the defence of the church in the thirteenth century.[49]

3. THE SPIRITUALITY OF THE FRIARS

Despite the essentially different sets of circumstances out of which they originated, and although they always maintained their separate identities, the Franciscan and Dominican Orders shared both a unity of purpose and many of the approaches to achieving that purpose. Histories that treat the two orders separately do so at the cost of ignoring their mutual influences as well as the rivalry between them. Thus while their respective origins have to be discussed separately, any discussion of their geographic spread, social composition, forms of ministry, or style of life should concern itself with both the orders.

A map showing the spread of either of them should not be interpreted in the same manner as one showing the implantation of Cluniacs, or of Cistercians. A friars' convent was not a place where several persons settled for the rest of their lives, taking vows not to leave, but instead it was a temporary base from which a group of friars might carry out an active apostolate. The earliest settlements of friars are difficult to perceive precisely because they were not real 'settlements'. The Franciscans tended to stay in caves and huts, or just wherever they could find temporary shelter. Often they were invited under someone else's roof. From all such cases there obviously remains no documentary proof of property rights secured or of convents constructed. The particular members of local groups frequently came and went, as the needs of the order at large shifted. Francis urged his brothers to live in the world as pilgrims and strangers, in part so that they would not become too attached to any one place.[50] The friars avoided utterly the Benedictine notion of stability of place, having absorbed into their notion of the apostolate something of the extensive travel engaged in by the original Apostles. The contrast between monastic stability and the friars' mobility is succinctly stated in Robert Brentano's comparison of two thirteenth-century historians, the Benedictine Matthew Paris and the Franciscan Salimbene. While he depicts Matthew as 'gathering things behind his walls', he characterizes Salimbene as 'out chasing the world'.[51]

The spectacular rapidity and success of the friars' institutional expansion should not be allowed to obscure either the problems involved or the occasional setbacks and outright failures. The Franciscans were indeed successful in Germany in 1221, but only after experiencing a disastrous failure two years before. In that earlier expedition, 60 brothers, not one of whom knew how to speak German, set out in the apparent hope that they would be able to communicate with their audience by some miraculous means. Not only did they fail to communicate their message, but they were mistaken for 'heretical Lombards', a point itself worth noting. In France, too, some of the earliest Franciscans were confused with Albigensians.[52]

Lack of careful preparation threatened to cancel the effect of the friars' infectious enthusiasm. James of Vitry, who in 1216 had depicted the Franciscans as a providential counterweight to the worldliness of the hierarchy, became aware by 1220 of serious weaknesses in the movement. He made reference to the Friars Minor, which religious order is expanding rapidly throughout the whole world, because they expressly imitate the form of the primitive church and the life of the Apostles. This religious order, however, seems to us especially dangerous, because they send out into the world by two's not only mature religious (*perfecti*) but also young people without training, who ought to be tested and for some time kept under the discipline of a convent.[53]

In the same letter James described admiringly the trip made by Francis to the Holy Land and to Egypt, where he preached before the sultan late in the summer of 1219. As Francis continued his spontaneous and audaciously unstructured apostolate, men less free and less daring were organizing the religious fraternity he had founded. When he returned to Italy, he was greatly disturbed by developments in the order, especially the purchase of a house at Bologna. It was increasingly the case that he did little more than register his displeasure.[54]

The apparent weakness of the Dominicans at the start of their expansion—namely, their small numbers—was perhaps instead a source of strength. In 1217 they still numbered fewer than twenty men. For them there could have been no thought of lavishing 60 ill-prepared brothers on one potential province. Therefore they were cautious—James of Vitry did not criticize them for undisciplined enthusiasm—and when they went to Paris and Bologna they took a firm hold and then concentrated on recruiting suitable candidates for their order. Early in 1217 when Francis was a figure known through much of Italy and would soon be known through much of Europe, Dominic's fame was limited to one diocese, a limitation that the pope tried to help redress in February 1218 with a letter of commendation to all prelates.[55] Whereas the Franciscans seemed to scatter their shots widely and then look to see what they hit, the Dominicans by contrast were forced to choose narrow and specific targets, and then take care not to miss them. With no set plan Francis preached to elderly people, soldiers, birds, merchants, and princes; but Dominic, and his successor Jordan of Saxony, adhered to carefully arranged schedules that kept them constantly engaged in the business of the order. For Jordan this task consisted principally in travelling from university to university in search of recruits. He kept a record of his successes and he commented candidly on the social and intellectual qualities of those he won over.[56]

Who joined these orders? As with most of the other groups under study, we are better informed about leaders than ordinary members. The original members of both orders included some substantially wealthy people, and James of Vitry, as noted, was impressed to see many rich persons joining the Franciscans. In Germany, the social origins of 168 individual friars (about 6 per cent of the estimated total number of German friars) have been ascertained and analysed. This sample almost certainly represents the leadership circles of the orders rather than the rank-and-file membership. There were no peasants or lower-class workers of any kind, although one must expect such people to be less noticeable in the sources. Besides a large group of nobles (disproportionately in evidence in the sources), the largest groups were made up of ministerials, knights, patricians, and burghers. These were groups that commanded vast material resources but lacked commensurate social prestige and political power.[57] More studies of this kind are needed for other regions, and these should include a mosaic of individual cases. Salimbene, for example, at the age of seventeen had to struggle against his father, a well-known and well-connected knight and crusader from Parma, in order to become a Franciscan. The father, upset about losing his heir, went so far as to get Frederick II to intervene on his behalf with Brother Elias, the minister general. Elias, of course, protected the young candidate, who, by persisting in his desire, offended his father for life.[58]

Similarly painful—and more forcibly resisted—was the departure of young Thomas Aquinas for the life of a Dominican. Inheritance was not at stake, and neither was the loss of a son to the religious life. The fourth son of a solidly established noble family, the boy Thomas was offered to the Benedictine monastery of Monte Cassino at the age of six. His parents perhaps had in mind for him a high ecclesiastical post. When later he studied in Naples and came under the influence of Dominican teachers, however, he upset their plans by seeking to become a Dominican himself. His older brothers captured him and held him prisoner for nearly two years but this merely strengthened his resolve, with a result well known to the world.[59] St Francis displayed a deep sensitivity to such problems. In the case of one rich young nobleman who came to him weeping, wanting to join the order, Francis expressed doubt about the young man's sincerity. Suddenly they heard the approach of horses and the young man looked out anxiously only to see his parents, who had come to seize him and take him home. The young man got up to leave and Francis made no move to stop him.[60] On the other hand, a certain peasant who wanted to join the order convinced Francis of his complete sincerity. Here again the family was extremely upset, but probably for urgent, material reasons. Francis, whom we think of—correctly—as emaciated from his extensive fasts and his diet of weeds and stale crumbs, suggested they prepare a big meal and promised to make them happy. Everyone joined in the feast and had a good time (*et commederunt omnes cum multa letitia*). The family was thus reassured and Francis went away with his new brother.[61]

Such family traumas were to be expected when sons decided to become friars. For many of the sons themselves, the inner turmoil provoked by such a decision and by such a family reaction must have been difficult to bear. But the burden, however difficult, was easier to bear because of what Francis of Assisi had gone through. When a sensitive person like Francis penetrates the unknown on his own, with no guide or model to follow, he undergoes severe torments of doubt and uncertainty, as we have seen. Such a painful individual crisis can then serve the needs of others who need not suffer again the same agonies. The precise model was given by those whom Francis himself converted. These listened to him, made a firm resolve, and then took all their possessions, sold them, and distributed the money to poor people—not to their own families, and not to the new family of friars they were about to join. This was the pattern set by Francis' friend Bernard of Quintavalle, a pattern that Thomas of Celano identified as the model for so many of the conversions that came after.[62] The lack of such a charismatic model in the Dominican tradition probably helps to explain the modest size of the Order of Preachers in relation to the Friars Minor. A few stories out of the vast stock of those concerning Francis did get taken over into the standard lives of Dominic, although there was no possibility of making him into as powerfully attractive a figure as Francis.[63]

Mutual borrowing was more efficacious when it came to matters such as preaching or poverty or obedience. Preaching was obviously fundamental to Dominic and his cohorts from the earliest days of the mission they served with Diego of Osma. For Francis in the early days, preaching was at most one important aspect of the evangelical life. In 1210 Innocent III gave him and his group the same limited licence to preach *(licentia exhortandi)* he had given the Humiliati and the Poor Catholics, and would give shortly afterwards to the Reconciled Poor.[64] As the Franciscans became increasingly a priestly order, in part through the recruitment of many men already ordained, more and more of the members were thus able to engage in the preaching of doctrine *(articuli fidei et sacramenta)*. While we lack strong evidence about Dominic as an impressive or successful preacher, stories abound of the unsophisticated yet highly efficacious preaching of St Francis. One particularly candid description of Francis the preacher, from a non-Franciscan source, occurs merely in passing in a chronicle by a Dalmatian cleric named Thomas of Spalato, who had seen and heard Francis in 1222. Thomas described how on 15 August of that year, when he was a student at Bologna,

I saw Francis preaching in the square in front of the public palace, where practically the entire city had gathered.... He spoke so well and sensibly that this preaching of an unlettered man stirred the very enthusiastic admiration of even the especially erudite people who were there. He did not, however, hold to the classical manner of preaching but just shouted out practically whatever came to mind. ... His clothing was filthy, his whole appearance contemptible, and his face unattractive. But God put such force in his words that many factions of nobles, among whom the wild fury of old hatreds had caused much bloodshed, were in fact peacefully reconciled. So great was the respect and devotion of this audience that men and women crowded in on him, seeking to touch his hem or to carry off a piece of his ragged clothing.[65]

This manner of going before an audience wearing rags and with a beard and dirty, unkempt hair recalls those scraggy and unwashed hermit-preachers of twelfth-century western France. His mockery of and contempt for the pretentious refinement of his listeners apparently did not offend them, but instead lent authority to his already persuasive speech. This way of preaching was so spontaneous and unmethodical that Francis could not really train anyone else to imitate him, though in the rule of 1221 he urged his followers not to take pleasure in words and in that of 1223 he urged them, when preaching, to be brief.[66]

A parallel development in the history of these two orders involved the role of intellectuals. Again, the role of studies was always paramount for the Dominicans, but, at least initially, only secondary for the Franciscans. Dominican life generally was built around the preparations for and practice of preaching. The ideal Franciscan apostolate was more spontaneous. But this emphasis also shifted, mainly through the adhesion of intellectuals to the order, for the Franciscans as well as the Dominicans found the universities to be their most fertile recruiting grounds. In 1225 alone, four doctors of the University of Paris put on the Franciscan habit.[67] In a letter said to be by St Francis, but of questionable authenticity, the study of theology is approved as long as it does not interfere with the students' spirit of holy prayer and devotion. In any case, the rule of 1223 places the same limitation on any work engaged in by the brothers.[68] In the prologue to the Dominican constitution, on the other hand, discretionary power was already granted for putting aside all unusual obligations should any of these get in the way of studying or preaching.[69] The intellectual renown of the Dominicans was from their early days great and fully merited; that of the Franciscans, however, had to be built up from a more humble starting point. But by the middle of the thirteenth century the Franciscans were second to none as scholars, and St Bonaventure was able to turn to great advantage this path taken by his order. 'Before God I confess,' he wrote to a friend who had doubts about the seriousness of the Franciscan intellectual tradition, 'that what attracted me especially to the Franciscan life was that it is similar both in origins and in mature development to the church, which was made up at the start of simple fishermen and afterwards went on to include the most famous and talented scholars.'[70]

Concerning the critical notion of poverty, we have seen its fundamental importance for Francis, its efficaciousness in the views of Innocent and Diego, and its occasional and limited utility for Dominic. The preachers of Toulouse at one time accepted all kinds of properties and revenues. In 1216 they gave up the rights to properties away from where they lived, but retained rents.[71] Then in 1220 at Bologna they decided not to retain rents either. The chapter of 1220 also stipulated that no brother could ask for, or intrigue to get, a benefice for any of his relatives.[72] The Dominicans were always able to own their own priories, a point that gave them greater institutional stability at the start of their expansion than the Franciscans had in theirs. Such a prudent programme would not have satisfied Francis' commitment to poverty. But neither did the compromises made by his own followers receive his approval.

The Franciscans were divided on the issue of whether to keep the house purchased at Bologna in 1219. This dispute was settled by Hugolino, then cardinal-protector of the order, who stepped in to relieve them of the onus of owning property by publicly declaring that the house in question was his private possession.[73] In this way a wedge was driven between the use and ownership of goods, a device that was used frequently through the rest of the century. On the question of work, the Dominicans always preferred that the preacher spend his time either preaching or preparing to do so, and hence that he be supported from some source other than his own labour. According to one later text, Dominic even tried, although unsuccessfully, to get the order to take in lay brothers (conversi), as the Vallombrosians, Carthusians and Cistercians had done, to care for all of the brothers' domestic and material needs.[74] The Franciscans, though, maintained the ideal at least that a friar should either work or beg for his food. As for money, the Dominicans at their chapter of 1220 decided that the brothers should never handle money nor receive alms in the form of cash.[75] But the Franciscans had a more deep-seated hatred of money, which originated with Francis himself and was then projected by him to a remarkable degree on to the order as a whole. The stories told about Francis and money show an almost pathological fear of touching what to him was filthy and disgusting. In one story he reprimanded a brother for picking up a sack of money and just then the money turned into a snake. And once, to punish a brother who had picked up a coin left as an offering (only to throw it away, we might add), Francis had the brother pick up the coin with his teeth and place it in a dung-heap.[76] While such attitudes were passed on in the stories about St Francis, there was also strict legislation in the rules of 1221 and 1223 forbidding the brothers so much as to touch a coin. Money accidentally found was to be esteemed no more highly than the dirt that the friars trampled upon in their travels.[77]

As the Franciscans became more solidly established in the world, measures were introduced to allow the order to become wealthy while protecting the friars, just as the Cathar *perfecti* had been protected, from direct contact with money. The rule of 1221 provided that a sick friar could be cared for, if absolutely necessary, by someone other than a friar, designated as a 'faithful person' (*fidelis persona*).[78] The principle was extended in 1223 to a money agent, the 'spiritual friend' (*amicus spiritualis*), who was able to receive and spend money on behalf of sick friars, and also to provide clothing for any of the friars.[79] By 1230 Hugolino, now Gregory IX, extended the range of the spiritual friend to cover all 'imminent necessities', at the same time setting up a new official, an 'agent' or 'middle man' (*nuntius*), whose job was to receive money for the order but always under the fiction that he was acting as the agent of the almsgiver. By 1245 the distinctions between the original jobs of these officials had broken down, as had virtually all the barriers concerning their capacity to transact financial matters for the friars.[80] The story of poverty in the two orders is too often seen as a simple shift by the Preachers in 1220 to the position of the Friars Minor, but the shift was neither that simple nor without reciprocal influences.

Both orders fostered conceptions of obedience that set them apart from the monastic orders of the past. Both also, of course, held to a strict obedience towards the ecclesiastical hierarchy; that was the condition of their being acceptable reform movements within the church and that was what differentiated them from certain revolutionary lay groups of the twelfth century. But within the mendicant orders something new was taking place. The rule of the black monks had been and was still thought of as the Holy Rule, and indeed this document was revered by them as a sacred text. Any violation of it by a monk constituted a sin, a fault that weighed on the conscience. A notable change in attitude had already been heralded by Stephen of Muret, who, we should recall, rejected all monastic rules in favour of letting the Gospel be his only binding guide. Rules of operation developed at Grandmont, but these were to be regarded as nothing more than the customs of the house. A similar distinction was taken over by Francis. His primitive 'rule' had apparently been little more than a collection of evangelical excerpts, and in the two extant 'rules' written by him, he insistently reiterated his view that the Gospel was to be the only real rule of the friars.[81] When in 1222 a group of friars persuaded Hugolino to discuss with Francis the possibility of the order's adopting one of the standard rules long in use, Francis led Hugolino before the brothers then assembled in general chapter and gave this reply:

My brothers, my brothers, God has called me by the way of simplicity and of humility, and He has pointed out this way as being the true way, both for me and for those who wish to believe me and imitate me. So don't talk to me about some rule or other, either that of St Benedict nor of St Augustine nor of St Bernard, nor about any life or way of living other than that which the Lord has mercifully shown and given to me.[82]

The rule of 1221, moreover, said that a brother who perceived an order given him by a superior to be contrary either to this same rule or to his conscience must not obey, for obedience is not enjoined when it involves committing a fault or a sin.[83]

The Dominicans, on the other hand, lived by one of the venerable, established rules, that of St Augustine, but at the general chapter of 1220, according to an account written about three decades later by Humbert of Romans, Dominic insisted on the principle that his order's rules did not oblige in conscience and that violation of them entailed not a sin but merely a matter to be corrected. And then, still according to Humbert, Dominic said that if anyone thought otherwise he would himself travel about from one convent of the order to another, scraping out the regulations with his own knife.[84]

This combination of an old rule with a new conception of obedience typifies the general situation of the friars; to a contemporary observer like James of Vitry, both this newness and this continuity with the past were evident. In the *Histories of the East and of the West*, written in the early 1220s, he devoted a chapter to the Dominicans at Bologna, although never calling them by their official name. He saw them as a house of canons, observing the canonical hours and otherwise living in conformity with the Rule of St Augustine. At the same time he was fully aware of their exceptional qualities. Completely willing to follow naked the naked Christ, they treated all material things and all worldly matters as so much excrement; they accepted alms, he said, but for the present day only, never giving any thought to the future. They taught and studied at the university and on feast days they preached, in accordance with a special commission given by the Roman pontiff. 'They have fused an order of preachers to an order of canons. This felicitous mixture of good elements attracts, stimulates, and fires up a great many people to follow them; each day this holy and distinguished congregation of Christ's students both grows in number and expands in charity.'[85]

The Franciscans clearly struck James of Vitry as being more novel, and—at least in that letter of 1220—as perhaps too novel and too hastily expansive. But in the *Histories* he said that they constituted 'an order of the poor men of the One who was crucified and an order of preachers'.[86] Three religious orders had existed previously, he explained in the same work: those of the hermits, the monks, and the canons; and to these the Lord had recently added a fourth, that of the Friars Minor. These friars had a rule of their own, but when one thought of it in connection with the way of living practised in the primitive church, it seemed not a new rule at all but a very ancient and effectively dead one, brought back to life 'in this twilight of a world headed into decline'. They strive with great care to reproduce in themselves the religious life, the poverty, and the humility of the primitive church, imitating as exactly as they are able the apostolic life. They possess nothing whatever, and can truly be called 'poor men of Christ'. Within a very short period they have spread everywhere. There is no province in Christendom where they cannot be found; the world is their 'spacious cloister' (*spaciosum claustrum*).[87]

The Dominican writer Stephen of Salagnac emphasized the specially close ties linking his order with the Humiliati. He claimed that the Rule of St Augustine was the best of all rules, for it was truly 'apostolic' and it was also much older than 'modern rules' (*modernae regulae*), even older than that of St Benedict. He listed the various groups who had lived by the Augustinian rule, including the Humiliati, who live by an approved rule 'more or less excerpted from those of St Augustine and St Benedict'. There were many thousands of these people in Lombardy, he said, and they tended both to respect and to be respected by the members of his own Order of Preachers.[88] Humbert of Romans also placed the Order of Preachers in a favourable perspective in claiming that from the start it was specially concerned with preaching and saving souls: 'in this it surpasses all other orders, since these others were established for the salvation of their own members only.'[89]

The most comprehensive view extant of the friars' organic development is the one expressed by Burchard of Ursperg, who was writing close in time to what he saw, a fact that may account for his accuracy but makes all the more remarkable his broad historical vision. Burchard was the provost of a house of Premonstratensian canons at Ursperg, in the diocese of Augsburg. He had been to Rome twice; first in 1198, the year of Innocent III's accession, and then in 1210, the year of Francis of Assisi's and of Bernard Prim's appearances before the pope. He entered the office of prior in 1215 and about fifteen years later, shortly before his death, he wrote a chronicle. For the period including the Fourth Lateran Council, he wrote:

At that time, with the world already growing old, two religious orders arose in the church—whose youth is renewed like the eagle's—and were confirmed by the Apostolic See, namely the Friars Minor and the Preachers. These were perhaps approved on this occasion [the council] because two sects, which had previously arisen in Italy, were still around, one called the Humiliati and the other the Poor of Lyons.[90]

Burchard described having seen Bernard Prim and his followers in Rome in 1210; but the views he then ascribed to them would have better suited a group of 'unreconciled' Poor Lombards or Waldensians. He leaves the reader with the incorrect, or at least incomplete, impression that Innocent rejected their proposal. In any case, he continued as follows:

In place of these the lord pope approved certain others then on the rise who called themselves the 'Lesser Poor' (*Pauperes minores*). These rejected the above mentioned superstitions and scandalous practices [of the Waldensians], but, to be brief, walked barefoot both summer and winter and accepted neither money nor anything else except food, and sometimes a needed garment that someone might offer them on his own, for they requested nothing from anybody.

After a while these people decided that their name might seem arrogant and boastful, so they changed it from Lesser Poor to Lesser Brothers (*Minores fratres*).

The others, namely the Preachers, Burchard believed to have taken the place of the Humiliati:

These Humiliati, without having any authority or permission from prelates, thrust their sickle into the harvest of others; they preached to the people and busied themselves most of the time at trying to run other people's lives, to hear confessions, and to denigrate the ministry of the priests. The lord pope, wishing to correct this situation, established and confirmed the Order of Preachers.[91]

As the Humiliati were simple, illiterate people, they had to work with their hands as well as preach. But the Preachers instead spent their effort in the study of sacred scripture, copying out texts and hearing them expounded by their masters. This was how they prepared themselves to go into the world to defend the church. Burchard did not get the story of the friars in quite the way we have it, but he had what seems a correct sense of the overall evolution taking place throughout the church in his time.

The Dominicans and Franciscans did more than simply replace the Humiliati and Waldensians. They summed up and synthesized the canonical reform and the new lay spirituality. The Franciscans inherited the eremitical tradition as well; for while St Bernard had fostered the notion of incorporating the hermitage into the cloister, and even into the individual cloistered monk, St Francis experienced and propagated a mobile, or itinerant, hermitage.[92] In spite of—but also because of—these many traditional roots, the friars arrived at a revolutionary programme of mendicant preaching, albeit in two somewhat different versions and via two markedly different paths.

They arrived there under the watchful guidance of Innocent III and Cardinal Hugolino. The revolutionary programme of mendicant preaching, a deadly threat to so many established interests, was turned into a form of orderly internal church reform by the skill of these astute administrators. The apostolic life, for several generations outside or on the remote edges of the church, was cautiously guided back into the fold; it was recovered from marginality.

The price exacted by the hierarchy for this recovery or accommodation was that the radical drift of the religious life now come to a halt, that no groups more radical than the friars be founded or tolerated. The history of the Spiritual wing of the Franciscan Order, a faction that decried the accommodation worked out between the order and the hierarchy, shows where the limit between tolerable and intolerable—the new margin—was placed. The Spirituals were denounced, hounded out of the order, some out of the church even, and, in 1318, four of their leaders were put to death.

Since this is neither a social history of the period 1000–1300 nor a history of the theme of voluntary poverty, but a study of the confluence of the two, it would be inappropriate to continue with a narrative history of the Franciscan or Dominican Orders. We will instead investigate the social role assumed and played by the friars, who of all the more radical poverty movements had the broadest support and were therefore the best suited to influence society. The task remaining is to see how, during the thirteenth century, they used the opportunities available to them.

PART IV

The Formation of an Urban Spirituality

10

Scholastic social thought

The unique achievement of the friars was their creation of new forms of religious expression specifically for the urban sector of society and those people dominant within it. These new forms included an ethical justification for urban society itself as well as for the characteristic activities of its more influential members; they also included new forms of worship, new devotional practices, new structures for lay participation in organized charity, and, above all, an enhanced sense of spiritual worth.

The avenues by which they arrived at this achievement were both intellectual and pastoral. First, they brought about a harmonious integration of the latest intellectual developments with the front rank of the religious life. Scholasticism and the spirituality of the friars were thoroughly intertwined during the middle two quarters of the thirteenth century. Second, the intellectual achievements of the friars and their contemporaries were brought to a large audience beyond the universities by means of new techniques of pastoral communication, techniques in many cases not invented by the friars but nevertheless skillfully exploited by them. These chapters on the intellectual and pastoral accomplishments of the friars will in turn be followed by a look at the religious life of thirteenth-century city people in an attempt to assess the impact of the friars on their society.

The city schools, or universities as they came to be called in the thirteenth century, provided the setting for the friars' intellectual activity. These schools had broken the monopoly of high culture and education long held by the Benedictine monasteries, and naturally they drew criticism from the old-style Benedictines as well as from those reformed Benedictines, the Cistercians, in the course of the twelfth century. Masters and students alike, whatever their social backgrounds, became participants in the busy pattern of urban life, having to confront such problems as material support, lodgings away from home, fees, and salaries. The students usually attended the schools to get the requisite training for a career, such as priest, teacher, notary, lawyer, or administrator. An expanding secular clergy and the newly developing professional bureaucracies of urban, episcopal, royal, and, most notably, papal governments were absorbing this élite of specially trained people. Unlike the Benedictines, who had schools within their monasteries, which they ran themselves for their own purposes, the Dominicans and Franciscans, both as teachers and as students, entered the pre-existing structure of the city schools.

The monasteries and the schools were as antithetical in the methods they used as they were in their social settings and spiritual aims. The monastic novice had to be schooled for a life of contemplation and liturgical intercession. He studied the sacred texts of the Bible and the virtually sacred texts of the Fathers by intensive reading and repetition, in effect by memorization. In such a way he sought to absorb as much of this tradition as he could, to incorporate into his mind and being an entire spiritual vocabulary and literature, which in turn would supply the idiom for his specifically religious vocation.[1] His thought and language both were to remain free of discord.[2] How different from this monastic ideal was the programme of the urban school, based as it was on disputation. Urban scholars, while retaining their respect for the received tradition and drawing strength from it, sought to expose its weaknesses and contradictions in order to build upon it, in order to reach higher and to see further.[3] This notion of progress became a goal that nourished several generations of school masters, while at the same time it dismayed and outraged leading monastic intellectuals.[4] Undaunted by the attacks of their monastic critics, the schoolmasters sharpened their dialectical tools and cut into the toughest of legal and theological problems. Would-be lawyers and theologians absorbed much of the old literature just as monastic novices did, but for the purpose of gaining support in the main task they were learning to perform: the marshalling of persuasive arguments.

The curriculum of the schools consisted principally of the liberal arts and then, at more advanced levels, of theology and law. The application of what one learned in the arts course to the study of God held the key to the dramatic changes in theology, for where students had once concentrated on the sacred text itself, with the tools of analysis newly at their disposal they could now focus their attention on problems that arose out of the text. In a different but analogous way, law developed from a traditional craft, whose secrets one absorbed over a long apprenticeship, into an object of academic scrutiny, subject to the methods of analysis being developed in the schools. Jurisprudence, like theology, was becoming a science.[5]

Law and theology met at the critical juncture of human behaviour, and in the latter half of the twelfth century collaborated to form the sub-discipline of moral theology. In the pre-commercial society, both law and theology had been relatively mechanical and superficial with respect to crime and sin. External acts were what mattered both in the wrong-doing itself and in the amends that had to be made for it. But as the new sciences of law and theology evolved, scholars pushed below the surface of mere action to get at the complexities of intention, motivation, peculiar circumstances, rules of evidence, and the psychology of contrition. Abelard was the first great figure in that triumph of the twelfth-century school that Chenu called 'the awakening of the conscience'. The resulting development of moral theology—the term seems to have been used first by Alan of Lille in the 1160s—led scholars to the systematic investigation of concrete cases. Principle and experience were joined on the level of casuistry.[6]

The first real school of moral theology ('school' in the informal sense of the term) was centred at Paris in the closing decades of the twelfth century, where a coterie of notable intellectuals gathered about Master Peter the Chanter. This was just the time when the accelerating needs of business and government for a credit system were coming into conflict with the rigid anti-commercial morality. Peter the Chanter was one of the moralists who exposed and denounced the legal fiction by which Christian moneylenders could be considered Jews and thus evade the usury prohibition.[7] Those who studied with Peter included a future cardinal, Robert of Courçon, a future archbishop of Canterbury, Stephen Langton, and the famous preachers Fulk of Neuilly and James of Vitry. These men discussed, for example, the legitimacy of the activities of judges, notaries, merchants, teachers, and physicians. And although they repeated some of the old clichés so hostile to commercial activity, they none the less began the painstaking investigation, point by point, of the many particular activities engaged in by merchants and urban professionals. In the end they did not by any means approve all such activities, but they prepared the way for the spiritual justification of merchants and professionals that the thirteenth-century theologians were going to develop.[8] Thus the educational scene on which the friars arrived shortly before 1220 was dominated by the urban school, an institution where grammar and logic had been brought to bear on theology and law, and where theologians and lawyers were devoting much of their effort to investigating and resolving contemporary social problems.

The Dominicans, as we have seen, headed directly for the leading centres of learning in 1217, and although the Franciscans were less certain about their destination in the dispersal of their own order in that same year, they were very soon as thoroughly involved in university life as their Dominican confrères.[9] By going to the universities, by recruiting in the universities, by establishing programmes of study there for their members, and by taking up teaching posts in the universities, the friars put the new religious movement on a firm—and very particular—educational footing. No other group with a distinctive spirituality since the Benedictines had had a distinctive educational policy as well. The Benedictine school had been an integral part of the monastic life; it had had the proper means, an agreed-upon method and a clear purpose. But this integration of education with the religious life only occasionally carried over into the various religious groups that appeared in the eleventh and twelfth centuries, for example, for about one generation at Saint-Victor.[10] This lack of integration afflicted even the Cistercians, with their many important intellectual figures. But the religious and intellectual spheres were to be reintegrated by the friars in the early thirteenth century. While the antecedents of the friars' spirituality can be traced in such groups as the hermits, the regular canons, the Waldensians, and the Humiliati, the same groups do not seem to have bequeathed to the friars any particular intellectual legacy. The friars' intellectual inheritance came instead from the twelfth-century schools, and in particular from such scholars as Peter the Chanter and his associates. These scholars, one should note in turn, were of no particular originality when it came to the spiritual life.[11] The friars perhaps served certain scholars well by offering them a meaningful way to live free from any concern about material support. But the friars were not invented to serve the needs of the schools any more than the schools, in supplying an intellectual programme to the friars, were created to serve them. The urban schools and the urban apostles, after a lengthy period of independent development, formed a powerful coalition late in the first quarter of the thirteenth century. The main problems taken up by the friar intellectuals included private property, the just price, money, professional fees, commercial profits, business partnerships, and moneylending.[12]

Private property existed in fact in feudal society but the intellectual problem of its legitimacy lay dormant through the long period between the Church Fathers and the middle of the twelfth century.[13] Those who finally did take up the problem at first restated the patristic arguments, which said that private property had no place in the ideal, divine society, but that in the far-from-ideal society of sinful man, private property was necessary to satisfy human greed and to maintain public order. Then with the aid of newly translated texts of Aristotle, thirteenth-century moralists revised this position so fundamentally as to emerge with an appreciation of private property as sometimes both natural and good. In the view of the Dominican, Albert the Great, rational reflection favours private property as being for 'the convenience and utility of man'.[14] And for Albert's student, Aquinas, quoting and agreeing with Aristotle, private property is a necessary instrument of the good life and of an orderly society.[15] The pattern of this evolution in attitudes toward private property conforms with that in notions of the state, from the grudging approval by the Church Fathers of the state as a necessary evil, to the full scholastic acceptance of the naturalness and goodness of the state.[16]

When property changed hands not by the patronizing grant of a lord to a vassal but by cash sale between two persons whose social status was irrelevant to the transaction, moralists felt compelled to establish a way of determining fair prices. The civil lawyers and the canonists after them took up the old Roman legal principle of a market in which all parties would be able to bargain freely.[17] The only controls were those intended to protect such freedom in bargaining, that is, to prevent fraud and to prevent severe harm (*laesio enormis*) from being done. A fraudulent price implies the existence of a just price, and it was to the determining of the just price that Albert the Great, Thomas, and other scholars devoted much attention. They invoked Aristotle to argue that human need—demand—was the chief determinant, but they added also the available supply as a factor and, subsumed in supply, the value of labour. The result was a clear definition of the just price as the going market price, with the limitation that a manipulated market price, for example due to monopoly or hoarding or speculation, could not qualify as just. Not every price higher than the just price had technically to be considered illegal and immoral, but one that was 50 per cent higher than the just price was manifestly unjust. In cases of dispute, the current market price would be determined in the streets by a group of upstanding citizens (*boni viri*).[18]

The professional fees gathered by lawyers and teachers had originally been called into question, as we observed earlier, because of the old maxim that knowledge is a gift of God and therefore cannot be sold. Once the teachers and jurists got to work on this problem, they did not, of course, find their own professions illegitimate; instead they found that they were selling their effort and their advice and their time, but not knowledge, which they consistently recognized was not theirs to sell.[19] One of the critical elements here was the new appreciation of the value of time, an appreciation that emerged from the need to calculate so characteristic of the new forms of commercial and industrial activity.[20] This theoretical solution did not necessarily satisfy everybody, for example those teachers who, for whatever reason, did not want to be bothered by having to look after their own material welfare. An argument has been made, at least, that the reason so many intellectuals, particularly teachers, rushed to join the mendicant orders was that they were able thereby to remove themselves from the 'scramble for benefices'; one might add that they thus avoided the risks attendant both in failing to earn a professional income and in succeeding.[21]

Money has been the subject of much of this investigation: the love of money, the excessive desire for money, the corrupting influence of money, the equation of money with excrement and hence the feelings of disgust that money can arouse—in short, an ambivalence built of a fatal attraction and a moral revulsion. These attitudes share a notable irrationality, whereas the change that came about in the thirteenth century was precisely that moral theologians began to think of money in straightforward, rational terms as a convenient tool. Aquinas joined in this de-mythologizing of money, which he defined as a measure of the price of things and as a medium of exchange.[22]

The profit made by a merchant had long been considered unjust because he did not seem to do anything other than buy goods at one price to sell at a higher. The ideals of Christian society as formulated in earlier centuries had come to include high regard for creative work, and so the problem of the legitimacy of the merchant's activities generally, as well as of the profit he made, turned largely on the question of whether what he did could properly be considered creative work.[23] The clichés of earlier centuries, so hostile towards, or at the very least suspicious of, merchants received new life in the twelfth century once the problem had again arisen but before anyone had thought very deeply about it. Towards the close of the twelfth century, this problem drew the attention of Peter the Chanter and his colleagues, and even they, as we have said, repeated some of those venerable clichés.[24] Yet one of their number, Thomas of Chobham, wrote approvingly of the benefits of commerce, for example of the way it can make up for deficiencies in one place by bringing in the surplus from some other place.[25] The schoolmen, in particular Alexander of Hales, further demolished the old theology in a manner very unusual for them, by reviving a little-exploited argument of St Augustine, who had written that a merchant performs beneficial services and deserves compensation for his labour. Augustine had, moreover, distinguished trade from the trader: where fraud and cheating were involved, the dishonest merchant was personally at fault but not the profession he practised.[26] A more predictable source of support for these new social attitudes was Aristotle, who supplied the schoolmen with a whole theory of social utility. With this theory, Albert the Great and Thomas brought about the emancipation of Christian merchants. Other writers, such as Hugh of Saint-Cher and a follower of the Franciscan theologian and prelate Eudes Rigaud, had established the crucial distinction between honest and deceitful merchants.[27] The honest merchant, for all these writers, was a man deserving of the profit he made, for they considered it as payment for his labour (*quasi stipendium laboris*).[28] Besides honesty, however, the merchant had to have a proper purpose. The schoolmen's emphasis on intention was essential to this aspect of their social theory, for they would not justify a merchant, however honest, whose purpose was to accumulate riches; such a person they would judge guilty of avarice. But they approved of the honest merchant who sought only a modest profit in order to serve his immediate needs and those of his family. The Dominican canonist William of Rennes would argue thus in his commentary, towards the middle of the thirteenth century, on the summa by his fellow Dominican, Raymond of Peñafort.[29]

The other principal legitimate purpose for gaining a profit was to make charitable donations to the needy. In such a way merchants were to be useful not only in distributing goods but in re-distributing wealth as well. The scholastic approval of a person who, in a case of urgent and extreme necessity, takes what he needs from someone else, has to be seen in this context; it is not a blanket approval of the poor stealing from the rich. In the words of Aquinas, 'he who suffers from extreme need can take what he needs from another's goods if no one will give them to him'.[30] This is hardly a programme for social revolution; it is more a reminder of the continuing responsibliity of those who have to share with those who have not. In such ways did the scholastic theorists of the thirteenth century determine that an honest, modest, charitable merchant was indeed able to lead a good, Christian life.

Merchants did not have to operate solely as individuals. Already at the end of the eleventh century Ivo of Chartres mentioned the partnership (*societas*) as a legitimate form of contract, though the matter was very little discussed before the thirteenth century. Even then the concept of partnership was not in question, but the central point to emerge from the discussion was that a proper partner, a person who invested money in an enterprise and claimed part of the profit, had also to share in the risks of a failure of that enterprise; otherwise he was thought to be engaging in usury.[31]

Let us recall briefly the strictures against usury that had been elaborated by the end of the twelfth century, for here indeed was the central ethical problem of the new economy. Any return on a loan over the amount originally lent was usury; so too was a credit price that was higher than the usual cash price. Usury was a sin, according to certain passages from the Old Testament (Exod. 22:25, Lev. 25:35–38, Deut. 23:19–21), and the many writers who had commented on them in the meantime. The demands of justice required that one who had accepted usury restore the full amount to the person who had paid it. We might also recall at this point how the prevailing behaviour of the twelfth century differed dramatically from this ethical ideal.

In the closing years of that twelfth century, intellectuals began to think and write and argue about usury. They and their followers were no less opposed to usury than those who had gone before; indeed they set out to bolster the condemnation with arguments intellectually more up-to-date. Pope Urban III (1185–7) brought into the arsenal of arguments the key role of intention when he cited, presumably for the first time in this context, the Gospel text (Luke 6:35) in which Christ said: 'Lend without expecting any return.' Intention alone could thus constitute usury; this view was held to by writers through the next three centuries, who consistently cited this evangelical injunction and the pope's use of it.[32] An influential theologian at Paris, William of Auxerre, began the consideration of usury in terms of natural law. Albert the Great later introduced Aristotle into the discussion. A canon lawyer, Sinibaldo Fieschi, the future Innocent IV (1243–54), maintained that usury is prohibited because of the evil consequences it produces; in social terms it produces poverty, and in personal, moral terms, it presents grave dangers for the soul, for usury is in fact the sin of avarice. By about 1270, Aquinas had developed a fully elaborated natural law argument against usury. Reduced to a few simple terms, this argument maintains that when a lender sells both the substance of money and the use of money (use having already been defined as inseparable from the thing itself), he in fact either sells something that does not exist or sells the same thing twice. Such a transaction, whichever way it is described, is manifestly contrary to natural justice.[33] Thus usury was soundly condemned, and in ever more sophisticated ways, by the scholastics.[34]

The scholastic approach to moneylending was not limited, however, to a refinement and up-dating of the case against usury, for it simultaneously undertook to justify certain forms of interest payment. There had always existed in Roman law a concept of interest that provided for a penalty to be paid by a borrower who was delinquent in repaying his loan. Interest was not part of the loan agreement, or a price for the loan, but something related only accidentally or extrinsically to the loan. It referred to the penalty, which was to correspond to the difference between, or the amount that came in between (*quod inter est*), the present financial position of the lender and the position he would have been in if he had not made the loan in the first place. The substantive term 'interest' (*interesse*) is thought to have been used first by the Bolognese civil lawyer Azo, writing in the first two decades of the thirteenth century. The lawyers had to consider whether claims to interest were legitimate by taking particular cases. Out of such casuistry there took shape a list of types of claims, or titles, which, because they remained always as exceptions to the prohibition against moneylending for profit, and thus remained outside of, or not integral to, moneylending, were called 'extrinsic titles'. In the case of a defaulted repayment of a loan, the extrinsic title to interest went by the name of 'standard punishment' (*poena conventionalis*).[35]

Again the originality of the Parisian masters of the 1190s can be seen, this time in the fact that Robert of Courçon, who we would do well to recall was exceptionally sensitive to and disturbed by what he saw as the omnipresence of usury, was the first theologian to engage in a searching discussion of the validity of extrinsic titles to interest. One section of his summa was entitled *De usura*.[36] He gave a reserved approval to *poena conventionalis*, stipulating that the penalty not be paid to the original lender but be distributed instead to the poor. He also considered 'profit ceasing' (*lucrum cessans*), which referred to the profit the lender was not making because he could not benefit from the money he had loaned out. He rejected this title, just as Peter the Chanter would consider but reject the similar title of 'loss occurring' (*damnum emergens*), which referred to the damages suffered by the lender.[37] But the way was open; the crucial questions were being asked. Raymond of Peñafort was eventually sympathetic to interest being paid for a delay in repayment on a loan, and the Franciscan masters John of La Rochelle and Alexander of Hales both agreed. Later on in the thirteenth century Aquinas was cautiously ready to accept *lucrum cessans* and *damnum emergens* as legitimate forms of compensation to a lender, on the basis of the utility of money and the just price of its value. Others would follow, such as the canon lawyer Hostiensis with his full approval of *lucrum cessans* in 1270, and still others with approval of other titles.[38]

The time had not yet arrived for a coherent theory of credit operations, but the net effect of the various extrinsic titles to interest, that is to say of a collection of exceptional cases, was to justify the trade of moneylending at least within the confines of a competitive money market. The friars, and a few of their contemporaries who were not friars, by building on intellectual developments already under way in the schools of the late twelfth century, began to consider the problems of private property, fair prices, money, professional fees, commercial profits, business partnerships, and moneylending. In each case they came up with generally favourable, approving views, in sharp contrast to the attitudes that had prevailed for six or seven centuries right up to the previous generation.

Work done by students of the most famous professors gives an indication of how the ideas of these masters were received, understood, and passed along. Giles of Lessines (c. 1235–1304), to cite a Dominican example, studied under Albert the Great at Cologne and later under Thomas Aquinas at Paris. Giles wrote a *Tractatus de usuris* in reply to a severe criticism of the friars and their teachings by Henry of Ghent, a Parisian master; written in about 1280, it is notable as the first theological tract devoted entirely to the problems surrounding the handling of money.[39]

Without the complexity, subtlety, or originality of his teachers,

Giles gave a comprehensive survey of what he had learned from them on the subject. He pointed out that scholars in his time were debating not only natural philosophy but morals, a matter wherein differences of opinion can be dangerous, and especially in that aspect of morals having to do with what Aristotle called 'retail trade', and even more particularly, with that part of retail trade that involves the vice of usury.[40] He used, as Aquinas had done, a natural-law argument against usury, saying that while exchange itself is legitimate, danger creeps in as soon as anyone loans something to someone else. Particularly noteworthy in this tract is the wide range of specific credit situations that Giles proposed and treated sympathetically.[41] In all such cases, interest would be tolerable as compensation for loss but not as sought-after profit.[42] Giles also included a justification for the profession of the moneychangers.[43] Their work stemmed from the nature of money itself and was both useful and convenient. While some people had taken to condemning moneychangers on the basis of Christ's driving them from the temple, Giles explained that the trouble in that particular situation lay not with the profession itself of those who were expelled but with the fact that they were practicing their worldly trade in a place reserved exclusively for spiritual matters. Giles devoted his concluding chapters to the rationale and regulations for having usurers make restitution payments.

A Franciscan counterpart to Giles, Alexander Lombard, was a theologian from Alessandria who studied and taught in Paris at the end of the thirteenth century. When Alexander refused to sign the appeal of Philip IV against Boniface VIII in 1303, he went to Rome and shortly became a master of theology at the Lateran Palace. He subsequently taught at Genoa, engaged in disputation at Paris in 1307–8, and then returned to Genoa. As the crisis over poverty in the Franciscan Order mounted during the next few years, Alexander emerged as leader of the Conventual wing of the order. In June 1313 they elected him minister-general but he died only four months later.[44]

Among his writings, which included commentaries on some of Aristotle's work, Alexander wrote a *Tractatus de usuris*.[45] This tract was apparently composed for oral presentation in a disputation at Genoa in 1307[46]. He cited no texts from the ancient philosophers, the Bible, or the Church Fathers that had not previously been cited, though he was less eclectic when it came to canon law. He gave the standard natural-law case against usury and also made use of Luke 6:35.[47] Even more than Giles of Lessines, Alexander Lombard concentrated on the application of principle to cases, and it was here that he was able to appear relatively original. He discussed twelve major types of cases in which to accept something in return over the original amount paid out was legitimate.[48] Then he went on to a series of cases where there was doubt. He was particularly interesting on the subject of the *census*, which is an obligation to pay an annual return from a property. A person in need of money sells the *census*; the purchaser is a lender and the seller a borrower. Each year the purchaser is entitled to receive income from the seller's property. While some writers, such as Henry of Ghent, called this transaction a usurious loan, Alexander saw it as the sale of a right to money; therefore this transaction was subject to the provisions of the just price but not to the prohibition against usury. From this transaction only a short distance remained to arrive at the sale of a state *census* on taxes (virtually a government bond, thought to have been utilized for the first time at Genoa late in the thirteenth century), and the sale of debts by a creditor to a third party at a discount.[49] Here again Alexander maintained that money was not being sold but the right to money; and because there remained always some doubt about whether such money could be collected, an interest payment could legitimately be demanded. As with Giles of Lessines, moneychangers also found professional justification with this influential Franciscan writer.[50]

The rationality of the school masters when confronted with the monetary, profit-oriented economy stands in sharp contrast to the puzzlement and confusion of those who sought uniquely religious solutions. The friars had the advantage of being able to integrate this work by their scholarly predecessors into their radically new spirituality. From Peter the Chanter and his circle to the third-generation Franciscans and Dominicans who simplified and propagated the teachings of the great masters of the mid thirteenth century, the evolution of social thought was rapid and far-reaching. Scholastic teachings were oriented towards the careful examination of social problems, were tolerant of new social realities, and were concerned with giving guidance for living amidst—rather then away from—those social realities. Conveying these teachings from the universities to the Christian laity entailed a major spiritual and organizational effort.

11

A reformed apostolate

The new integration of the intellectual with the religious life meant, on a more specific level, that theological studies became geared to an active ministry. As Hugh of Saint-Cher, the Dominican biblical scholar, put it: 'First the bow is bent in study, then the arrow is released in preaching.'[1] Peter the Chanter anticipated the friars not only in the theological questions he asked but also in his inclusion of preaching within the definition of scriptural study, as its ultimate stage and goal:

The study of sacred scripture consists in three operations: in explication, disputation, and preaching.... Explication is a sort of foundation or base for what follows, because upon it other uses of the text rest. Disputation is a sort of structural siding in this exercise, this building, because nothing is fully understood or faithfully preached unless first analysed by disputation. Preaching, however, which the previous ones support, is a sort of roof protecting the faithful from the raging storms of vice.[2]

Humbert of Romans, in writing *On the Utility of Studies in Our Order*, enumerated the benefits of study for the individual student but went on to list its benefits for others. Only if study flourished in their order would the Dominicans be able to preach or give counsel or hear confession. In an apparent allusion to one of the early Franciscan ideals, Humbert observed that 'Holy simplicity' (*Sancta simplicitas*) profits only oneself, whereas learned justice serves not just oneself but others also.[3] His views were tersely summarized in this question about the study of sacred scripture: 'But if this study has not preaching for its end, of what use is it?'[4]

Early reports on the friars indicated that they had been attempting to fulfil this ideal of integrated study and preaching. James of Vitry, for example, said of the Dominicans he observed at Bologna: 'Each day they attend lectures on the Holy Scriptures given by one of their own. That which they have diligently heard they then on feast days present to the Christian faithful through the ministry of preaching.'[5] Thomas of Eccleston told of those first English Franciscans who were so ardent in their study of theology that they would go off to study every day—still barefoot in the worst weather—so that, with the help of the Holy Spirit, they might eventually be advanced to the high office of preaching. And of those Franciscans at Oxford during the early 1230s when Robert Grosseteste was their teacher, Thomas wrote: 'Within a short time they made incalculable progress both in scholastic discussions and in the subtle moralities suitable for preaching.'[6]

The Dominicans set up three categories of preacher, based upon their amount of schooling: a friar who had been through a priory's school could preach within that priory to his own brothers; the preacher-in-ordinary, who had to be 25 years old and had to have studied theology for one year, could preach within the territory of his own priory with the permission of his prior; the preacher-general, whose territory was an entire province and whose authority came from the provincial chapter meeting, had to have studied theology for three years.[7]

In the juridical distinction made by Innocent III for both the Humiliati and the first Franciscans, a distinction between merely giving testimony to one's faith and actually expounding on the church's sacred teaching, the pope was of course trying to preserve the integrity of a priestly function, a function that had been usurped by laymen with increasing frequency in the preceding years.[8] But there was more to Innocent's position than the legal defence of a hierarchical corporation and its privileges. Underlying the juridical distinction was a practical distinction that had to do with schooling. The increasing sophistication of the church's faithful members as well as of its enemies had created the compelling need for erudite preaching, and as schooling remained largely a clerical preserve, tying preaching to the clergy was in effect tying it to learning. Measures had to be taken both to provide the requisite schooling for preachers and to discourage preaching by the unschooled. Thus being a member of one of the new, specifically evangelical, religious orders was not in itself a sufficient qualification for the office of preaching.

In addition to schooling, the personal moral and psychological preparedness of the preacher was a matter of concern. Bonaventure demanded perfection equally in the life of a preacher and in his teaching, for the Lord, he explained, speaks to souls not only through preaching itself but also through the witness given by the preacher's life.[9] Humbert of Romans, in his treatise *On the Education of Preachers* (*De eruditione praedicatorum*), opened with a definition of the office of preaching and immediately launched into a discussion of the requisite personal qualities of the preacher.[10] Hugh of Saint-Cher emphasized strongly a preacher's enthusiasm, because a preacher who is not ardent, he wrote, could not arouse a congregation.[11] Thus learning, irreproachable morals, and enthusiasm were all thought to serve as adjuncts to preaching, along with the preacher's personal poverty.

The thirteenth century became one of the great ages in the history of preaching, and here, just as in many other fields, the friars played an overwhelmingly dominant role. Among the most popular of the well-known preachers were Anthony of Padua and Berthold of Regensburg. St Anthony (1195–1231), a native of Lisbon, was a learned young canon at Coimbra who was moved to join the Friars Minor when he learned about the five Franciscan missionaries who had been martyred in Morocco.[12] He set off on an expedition to Morocco to preach, became ill, and on the return trip was thrown so far off course that he landed in Sicily. He made his way north to Assisi, where he attended the general chapter meeting of 1221. For a decade Anthony preached in northern Italy and southern France; at times he taught theology as well.[13] Stories are told of immense crowds that assembled for his sermons, of the many who came several hours early to be sure of getting good places, and of the need for protecting him from souvenir-seekers. His greatest triumph came during the Lenten season of 1231, with his preaching campaigns against civil strife, against usury, and in favour of including the lower classes in the processes of communal politics. Erudition and preaching were neatly balanced in this popular figure whom Gregory IX saw fit to make a saint within less than a year of his death.

Bavaria, after Portugal, produced one of the Franciscan Order's most famous preachers. Berthold (c.1210-72), who was born and died at Regensburg, studied at the convent in Magdeburg and then became a preacher at the convent in Regensburg in about 1240. Throughout Bavaria and in Switzerland and other parts of Germany as well, he preached steadily throughout the year, attracting large crowds and building a reputation as the finest German-language preacher that there had ever been.[14] Berthold would often preach in open places, his crowds were so large. A wooden tower for him to preach from would be set up beforehand, and to the top of it would be attached a pennant that listeners could watch for an indication of wind direction and hence of the best side of the tower on which to stand. His voice was said to carry to the farthest reaches of his audiences and he regularly held the attention of his listeners to the very end. In 1262 he undertook a preaching tour through Hungary and Czechoslovakia. In 1263 he received a special commission from Urban IV to preach against heresy, and again he went off through much of Germany and Switzerland, extending his tour also into France as far as Paris, where he met Louis IX.

The successful popular preachers, while manifestly intelligent and well-educated, managed to express themselves in an idiom that was accessible to large audiences of uneducated people. Bonaventure reminded preachers of their obligation not to seek ornate words or deep arguments, but to use with constancy and fervour the pure and simple truth of faith.[15] Humbert of Romans was more explicitly critical of some of his contemporaries. Many preachers, he complained, had a predilection for words; they repeated parts of their sermons, endlessly cited their authorities, and used several words that meant essentially the same thing. In preaching just as in the liturgy, brevity fosters devotion. One test of a good preacher was the ability to perceive, during a sermon, that he had prepared too much material and to cut it accordingly as he went along.[16] On a less theoretical level, a synod held at Lambeth in 1281 listed the subjects on which priests were to instruct their parishioners, specifying that they do so 'in the vernacular language and without any fantastic web of subtle distinctions' (*vulgariter absque cuiuslibet subtilitatis textura fantastica*).[17]

The friars' keen awareness of their audience is apparent in the agreements concluded between and within the orders about the division of preaching territories.[18] Moreover, their leaders formulated justifications for the choice of an urban apostolate. Bonaventure posed the specific question of why the friars preach more often in towns than in the country. He replied that as the potential audience was large and the friars few, these should go where large audiences could be more easily assembled. Also, where there was not a sufficiently large pool of resources, the friars would not be able to eat. He added that those who supplied his order most with temporal alms deserved the most from it in spiritual ministrations.[19] In answer to the same question, Humbert of Romans stressed the greater density of urban population and the more sinful behaviour of urban dwellers. Besides, he observed, the countryside emulates the town, so that if one had to choose between preaching in town or in the country, it would be better to opt for a town on the chance that some part of the message would be diffused into the surrounding rural area.[20] Humbert's observation is borne out by the description of people coming into Padua from surrounding towns and villages to hear St Anthony.[21]

The rhetorical goal of the preacher was always to produce a certain reaction in his audience, but specific rhetorical goals varied with the changing needs of different historical circumstances. Over the centuries, Christian preaching had been directed toward such goals as converting Roman pagans, Germanic pagans and Jews to Christianity, keeping the faithful free from heresy, and inspiring Christians to go on crusades. A recently established goal was that of moving the individual Christian believer to do penance. Humbert made a list of the ten fruits of good preaching and at the head of the list following the conversion of infidels to the faith he put the penitence of sinners.[22] The friars became centrally involved in major new developments in both the theory and practice of the sacrament of penance.

The old system based on penitentials, or handbooks of penance, with their lists of specific wrong-doings each accompanied by a specific penalty, was no longer adequate. The main challenge to the penitentials came from Abelard, in whose remarkable book on *Ethics*, subtitled *Know Thyself*, appears the new emphasis on intention referred to earlier. As intention is the key moral factor in the behaviour of the individual who acts, so contrition is the key moral factor in his subsequent reflection. Sin is neither the act nor the inclination to perform the act but the giving of consent to the inclination.

The time when we consent to what is unlawful is in fact when we in no way draw back from its accomplishment and are inwardly ready, if given the chance, to do it. Anyone who is found in this disposition incurs the fullness of guilt; the addition of the performance of the deed adds nothing to increase the sin.[23]

Consenting to the inclination to act badly is nothing less than contempt of God; sighs and feelings of contrition that proceed from love of God rather than from fear of punishment are accordingly regarded as truly fruitful repentance.

With this sigh and contrition of heart, which we call true repentance, sin, that is, the contempt of God, or consent to evil, does not remain, because the charity of God, which inspires this sigh, does not put up with fault. In this sigh we are instantly reconciled to God and we gain pardon for the preceding sin.[24]

Reconciliation had been a major public ceremony in the early church; in the Celtic church it came about with the carrying out of a penance. The view that it came at the time of the priestly absolution and in anticipation of the penance had developed gradually and gained general currency by the eleventh century.[25] Abelard was now placing reconciliation still further back, to the moment of the contrite sigh. He did not argue against maintaining confession, though he did indicate cases where he thought it unnecessary;[26] but because of his arguments the priest's function had been greatly reduced in importance, and absolution, as Chenu has said, had been 'downgraded to a mere parting word'.[27]

There were those who gave support to some of Abelard's basic views, such as Peter Lombard (who helped fix the place of penance as one of the seven sacraments), as well as those who reacted strongly against them, such as Hugh of Saint-Victor.[28] A major theological problem had been formulated, but for the next few generations scholars would tend either to support or oppose Abelard's formulation of it rather than try to resolve it. Meanwhile change occurred more readily on a relatively practical level. The *Liber poenitentialis* written by Alan of Lille late in the twelfth century broke clearly with the earlier works of its type. The tariffs had virtually disappeared; the determination of appropriate penances was left entirely to the discretion of confessors.[29] Alan's work was followed shortly afterwards by that of Robert of Flamborough, an Englishman who served as penitencer at Saint-Victor in the early years of the thirteenth century. His penitential book, written between 1208 and 1213, contained an opening section on the relationship between confessor and penitent, a section where the confessor could find advice on recognizing the types of cases before him.[30] On a still more practical level, the Fourth Lateran Council decreed that every Christian must faithfully confess all his sins to his own priest at least once a year. Confession was necessary; so, also, was sacramental absolution. And the priest's obligation to maintain the secrecy of the confessional was backed up by severe sanctions.[31]

Francis of Assisi instructed his followers to preach penance. For the Dominicans, the administration of penance was always one of the duties of a preacher; the order's general chapters usually bracketed the functions of preaching and penance in formulating regulations. The earliest Dominican general chapters commissioned special works on penance for the instruction and use of preachers.[32] Outsiders also saw the friars as having these different functions. In 1227 a Polish bishop whose diocese included Danzig issued a charter authorizing the Dominicans of Danzig to fulfil the office of preaching throughout his diocese, as well as to hear confessions, to enjoin penances, and to reconcile with the church people who had been previously excommunicated.[33] In a bull of recommendation Gregory IX advised using the friars as both preachers and confessors.[34] And in 1238 Robert Grosseteste reported to Gregory, concerning the friars, that 'people run to hear the word of life from them, for confession, and for instruction in daily life'.[35] Matthew Paris took an altogether different view of the same situation, reporting sourly on the Dominicans that they strove to be 'not only Preachers but also confessors, usurping to themselves the functions of the clergy'.[36]

Preaching, by the nature of the medium, is more efficient than hearing confession; Humbert of Romans was fully aware of this simple point.[37] Yet preaching is supposed to move people to confess, so the preacher, Humbert insisted, has no right to turn away those who are so moved.[38] One who might serve as a model of the successful and at the same time conscientious preacher is Haymo of Faversham, a Franciscan who once preached at Saint-Denis so fervently that it then took him three full days to hear the confessions of his listeners.[39] Anthony of Padua was another preacher who inspired penitent feelings; he moved 'such a multitude of men and women' to confess their sins that the several friars and other priests who accompanied him were often not numerous enough to hear all the confessions.[40]

The friars' resolution of the theoretical problem concerning penance that they had inherited was integral to their whole religious programme. They were sympathetic to the new emphasis on piety, on an internalized morality, and on the understanding and forgiving nature of God. On the other hand, they were emphatically sacerdotal—as solid supporters of both the sacramental system and of priestly authority. Thus they could not tolerate penance becoming solely a matter of the sinner's contrite prayer to God. The answer to this dilemma came out of the combined efforts of several leading friar intellectuals, principally Alexander of Hales, Bonaventure, Albert the Great, and Aquinas. They sought to achieve a new equilibrium between contrition and absolution, between grace and sacramental activity, between the penitent sinner and the priestly confessor. Using Aristotelian distinctions, they integrated the acts of the penitent (matter) with the absolution of the priest (form) into the single, and necessary, sacrament of penance.[41] The ministry of the friars consisted of an indissoluble whole of preaching and penance. At the beginning, the friars had found the theory and practice regarding both preaching and penance in a condition of uncertainty and fluctuation. But they brought all of these elements together into an organic spirituality; such accordingly was the figure employed by Humbert when he wrote: 'As the seed is planted in preaching, the fruit is harvested in confession.'[42]

The teaching and learning of the friars was thus consciously directed towards a ministry consisting principally of preaching and penance, and within that ministry, there was a progressive connection between preaching to an audience and administering penance to individuals. Guides to the new forms of ministry were prepared by scholars in various forms: in preaching manuals, in concordances, in books of *exempla*, and in handbooks of penance. Some of these works, as well as certain scriptural and patristic texts, appeared also in vernacular translations.

The art of preaching (*ars praedicandi*) was the name assigned to a genre of written tract giving instruction about preaching which appeared roughly between 1200 and 1500. Over 200 works in this genre and from this period are known to exist; they remain for the most part only in manuscript, unedited. The friars had a near monopoly of this genre, although they did not invent it and they did have a few non-friar contemporaries who used it.[43] The long-range background of the art of preaching can be traced to classical treatises on rhetoric and such intervening works as Gregory the Great's *Book of Pastoral Care*.[44] The friars' immediate predecessor in writing about the art of preaching was Alan of Lille, who wrote a *Summa de arte praedicatoria*.[45] In the preface to this work he placed a ladder of perfection that gave a newly important position (the seventh and highest step) to preaching. Robert Grosseteste, never a friar but a friend and protector of the Franciscans as well as their teacher, designated eight classes of audiences in his work on preaching: soldiers, judges, princes, nuns, priests, married people, widows and virgins. For each group he indicated those scriptural injunctions that he thought particularly applicable. He left behind a large collection of sermons. Ninety-two have been confidently ascribed to him and another 75 are thought most likely to be by him.[46]

In addition to his work on the education of preachers, Humbert of Romans wrote a book on how to prepare promptly sermons for all types of persons and occasions.[47] He presented outlines and materials for 100 sermons directed to particular groups or classes of society, and the same for 100 sermons which were addressed to particular circumstances. Gilbert of Tournai, a Franciscan, left a collection of some 35 of these sermons addressed to special groups.[48] Other friars who wrote on the art of preaching in the thirteenth century included Arnold of Podio, a Dominican, and John of La Rochelle, a Franciscan. The latter also delivered sermons to groups of secular priests in which he stressed the importance of their responsibilities to preach and to hear confessions.[49]

Treatises on preaching thus sometimes stood alone and sometimes contained or were accompanied by model sermons. One exceptionally well integrated work was the sermon collection of a Dominican named Guy of Evreux, completed in 1293. It contains 74 sermons, fully written out and relatively lengthy for the time. The author stated clearly his intention to aid preachers, including those who might be fairly ignorant of theology, by giving them sermons to suit all possible occasions. To facilitate the use of his book, Guy prepared for the reader an alphabetical index of the key terms dealt with in the sermons. He also gave the preacher advice on how best to use these sermons. Guy's work was important enough for its reproduction and cost to be regulated by the University of Paris in 1304; its text could be rented by copyists for five shillings.[50]

The *artes praedicandi* gave instruction about preaching, and collections of sermons gave models. But preachers needed tools that would help them remain always fresh in their work and force them to be more original than they would be if they always relied on someone else's models. One such tool was the biblical concordance. Under the direction of Hugh of Saint-Cher a group of Dominicans working at the Convent of Saint-Jacques in Paris during the 1230s produced a verbal concordance of the entire Bible. The resulting *Concordance of Saint-Jacques* listed words and beside them gave references to all the biblical passages where they could be found. The work made use of the recently devised division of biblical books into chapters. A second version followed, and by 1286 a third version of the concordance was available for purchase from university stationers in Paris. Eighty extant manuscripts from the period between the 1280s and 1330 remain as testimony of its widespread reproduction and acceptance.[51]

A standard part of the thematic sermon was the example (exemplum), an anecdote introduced to illustrate the point being made. Collections of exempla constitute another of the genres developed in the thirteenth and fourteenth centuries especially for the assistance of preachers. Among the early preachers and writers to make extensive use of exempla were James of Vitry, Caesar of Heisterbach, and Odo of Cheriton.[52] The first proper collection of exempla was the work of a Dominican, Stephen of Bourbon, who assembled his *Tract on Various Preachable Materials* between 1250 and his death in 1261.[53] The unfinished collection as it stands contains just under 2,900 exempla. Humbert of Romans wrote a book sometime between his resignation as master-general of the Dominican Order and his death in 1277 that gives instruction and a rationale for the use of exempla; he based his outline on the first part of Stephen's book, and presented 228 exempla, four-fifths of which were taken directly from Stephen's collection.[54] Another Dominican whose work derived directly from Stephen of Bourbon's is Martin of Troppeau, 'the Pole', who wrote between 1261 and 1279.[55] During the same period, Nicholas of Hanapes, a Dominican who became patriarch of Jerusalem and eventually died in the siege of Acre in 1291, compiled a book of biblical examples,[56] whereas a collection of over 600 exempla using non-scriptural sources almost exclusively was put together by John of Wales, a Franciscan writing near the end of the thirteenth century.[57]

Books of exempla, like concordances, were books of reference, so innovations in form and arrangement had their own significance alongside that of changes in substance. An English Franciscan took the decisive step during the later 1270s of arranging his exempla collection in alphabetical order.[58] A French contemporary, also a Franciscan, entitled a similar though somewhat larger work: *Tabula exemplorum secundum ordinem alphabeti*.[59] It contains 300 exempla grouped under 151 subjects, from *accidia* (sloth, torpor) to *Xristi ascensio* (the ascension of Christ).

Just as ministers had guides to preaching and collections of sermons and of exempla available to assist them in their role as preachers, they also had at their disposal a kind of handbook that served them in their related role as administrators of penance. Handbooks of penance usually included an exposition of the theology of penance, a guide to the relationship between priest and penitent, principles for hearing confession and imposing penances, and, finally, a number of specific cases—penitential exempla.[60] With the maturing of the sciences of jurisprudence and theology, as well as with the new independence of moral theology, scholars developed the genre of the summa of penance or the summa for confessors. Certain of these summas were purposely and unmistakably academic; they indicated their sources throughout and they were technical both in their form and language. Others, however, lacked such scholarly apparatus. They were intended to serve as handbooks for those charged with administering penance; these indeed were the modern counterparts (or descendants) of the old penitentials.[61]

Works in the new vein were already appearing by 1200. Mention has been made of Alan of Lille's book on penance, with its advice for priests about hearing confessions, and of the canonist Robert of Flamborough's summa, a work that contains a large collection of cases of conscience. Around the time of the Fourth Lateran Council and the formation of the orders of friars, Thomas of Chobham wrote a comprehensive summa for confessors. He tells the reader he will not deal with theoretical questions; in fact the book is based on experience as well as formal learning.[62]

He cautions the priest against abruptly asking the person who has come to confess to spill out a list of sins, advising him instead to instruct the person and ask him questions so that ultimately the confession will be fuller and more devout. He shows an up-to-date knowledge of the moral problems relating to prostitution and to moneylending.[63] Still, in any form, Thomas' summa is a very large book (the text runs for 572 pages in its modern, printed edition) whose organization and style are hardly free of scholastic formality.[64]

A handier book is the summa of penitence compiled in 1220-21 by Paul of Hungary.[65] Paul was a Bolognese jurist who had become prior of the Dominican Convent of St Nicholas at Bologna. The designation 'of Hungary' refers not to his origins but to the last stage of his life, when he went out from the general chapter meeting held at Bologna in May of 1221 with a commission to establish a Dominican province in Hungary. Paul had apparently written the summa between the general chapters of May 1220 and May 1221 or, in a broader perspective, between the Fourth Lateran Council, whose canon 21, on penitence, he cited and referred to as the new dispensation (*nova constitutio*), and the Dominican dispersal that followed the general chapter of 1221.[66] His 'brief treatise', as he called it, dealt with the essentials of confession, and these were listed under headings in such a way that the reader could easily find what he was looking for. He specified the proper time for confession, the necessary preparation for confession, and the manner in which the priest should carry out his interrogation. He raised the issue of whether the circumstances could make any sin more or less serious and of whether the priest should take these into account when imposing a penance. The last two of his 24 chapters dealt with the principal vices and virtues.

Another noted jurist who left Bologna at about the time Paul went to Hungary was Raymond of Peñafort. Between joining the Order of Preachers at Barcelona in 1221 and assuming his legateship to Spain for Gregory IX in 1229, Raymond wrote a summa of penitence, or of cases of conscience.[67] For all his claims to have written a practical guide, Raymond's book remains an uncompromisingly academic treatise. It has been judged 'strikingly different' and as having 'overwhelming authority'.[68] Above all it transferred to moral theology the lawyers' taste for, and use of, casuistry, which he intended to be used for instructing the faithful.[69] Like Paul of Hungary and many others, Raymond listed sins under the general headings of the vices and, perhaps under the direct influence of Paul, he closed with an analysis of four obstacles to confession (fear, shame, presumption, and despair), as well as of the means for combating these obstacles.[70] Raymond's work was not only reproduced and used widely; it formed the basis of later commentaries and simplified versions. Among these were the gloss done in the 1240s by his fellow friar, William of Rennes; a didactic poem called the 'Little Summa of the Poor', composed at mid century by a Cistercian named Adam of Aldersbach; and a summa of canon law arranged alphabetically by key words written in the 1270s by a Franciscan named Monald of Capo d'Istria.[71]

Towards the end of Aquinas' life, portions of his work appeared in popularizations by a fellow Dominican, James of Genoa. A decade later, the master-general of the order commissioned Galienus Ozto to prepare a short version of that part of the *Summa theologiae*, the *Secunda secundae*, which contains most of Thomas' moral theology. In the final years of the thirteenth century, another Dominican scholar combined the legal and theological strands in two works on penance: one scholarly, the *Summa confessorum*, and the other popular, the *Confessionale*. The author, John of Freiburg (died 1314), who had certainly known Albert the Great and had perhaps studied under Thomas Aquinas, began lecturing at the Dominican convent at Freiburg-im-Breisgau in 1280.[72] The summa he subsequently wrote followed exactly the plan of Raymond's summa; but John included material from later jurists such as Innocent IV and Hostiensis, integrated much of Aquinas' moral thought with the juridical reflections of these canonists, assembled an exceptionally rich collection of cases, and rendered his own work more readily usuable by compiling an alphabetical index. In his preface, John advised that all his references to Thomas' summa, unless specified, were to the *Secunda secundae*. The *Confessionale* was directed expressly to those readers with less education and less learning; on a few difficult points he referred the reader to his summa or else to a competent confrère. The first section includes the sins, arranged under the capital vices (avarice is exceptionally inflated), while the second part includes fourteen groups of people, designated by status. John of Freiburg also issued a set of additions to Raymond's summa and he put together a small collection of clear, uncomplicated cases, 'especially for clerics who know nothing about all this'.[73]

Around 1320, a Dominican writer named Guy published excerpts from the *Summa confessorum* by John of Freiburg.[74] This fact alone contains no surprise, for the influence of John's work is attested to by many extant manuscripts and by the influence it had on others, for example on Franciscan theologians like Durand of Champagne, or Astenasus of Asti, whose scholarship also embraced the recent contributions of Alexander Lombard.[75] But the portions of John's summa excerpted by Guy—the fact is worth noting—were those dealing with the just price and usury. And more notable yet is the title Guy selected for this work: *Regula mercatorum* (*Rule for Merchants*). This is a clever play on *Regula monachorum*, but it represents far more than a pun. This work is a handbook devoted exclusively to the moral concerns of merchants; it does not condemn them outright, but condemns only certain of the activities in which they are liable to become involved. It gives a simplified version of the moral theology relating to commerce of Thomas Aquinas, as refracted through two generations or more of Dominican students and writers. The book's very existence announces flatly that there is such a thing as a Christian morality for merchants, indeed that there is a religious life for merchants. There had been a time when *vita religiosa* was a technical term, referring to a level of spiritual worthiness reserved exclusively to those who vowed to live according to a rule, the *Rule for Monks*.

We have traced the evolution of this notion from that lone, dominant rule, through various revised, reinvigorated and new rules, even to the attacks against there being any rule at all apart from the Gospel. What we find at the end is not that we have traced a thread of institutional or constitutional history from the monks to the friars, or indeed the history of a genre, the religious rule, interesting for its own antiquarian sake, but we have arrived at a point where we see that those who claimed to live by the Gospel and who had their new conceptions of rules and of obedience were sponsoring a spiritual programme that accorded the status of *religiosi* to a group of laymen, and that granted them accordingly a *regula religiosa*. We have been witnessing nothing less than the progressive spread through Christian society of the term 'religious life', from the monks, who once had a nearly exclusive hold on it, to merchants.

The formulation of a new moral theology was thus accompanied by significant developments in the mechanics of transmitting ideas. These parallel developments appeared again in the age of printing and the century of Reformation and Counter-Reformation. Indeed, just as the history of the Reformation is inseparable from the early history of printing, in a similar way the history of the evangelical awakening of the twelfth century, with its fulfilment during the following century in the friars, cannot be understood apart from the new types of pastoral literature that the friars, among others, developed.[76] The various handbooks designed originally for use by preachers and confessors were the direct forerunners of the spiritual guides that became available to the secular clergy and that came to be so widely used by laymen in the fourteenth and fifteenth centuries. The friars, then, played a central role both in the cultivation of lay piety itself and in the elaboration of the technical means that fostered lay piety.

12

Urban religious life

The social significance of the friars' programme emerges from an analysis of its message, or content, which included discussion of property, interest, credit, insurance, and moneylending. That same social significance is further clarified by an analysis of the medium used to transmit the friars' message. Preaching and the administration of penance were the principal means of expression used; but why, it must now be asked, were these means considered appropriate and therefore selected?

The dominant members of the urban sector of society were merchants, bankers, lawyers, notaries, school masters, and certain of the landlords who organized production on their lands for the market. They did not make their living by praying, or by fighting, or by 'working', not, at least, by working with their hands. They talked; they argued; they negotiated; they wrote; they entertained; above all, they tried to persuade other people. Such were the defining or characteristic activities of those who prospered in the urban environment.

In order to see how a spirituality, both in its message and in the means used to propagate that message, can be related to the activities of the dominant class of a society, one can refer back to the first feudal age, where society was dominated by those who fought and the leading form of spirituality was that of the black monks. Their characteristic medium of expression was praying, the *opus Dei*. Praying had been part of the Benedictine programme from as far back as the sixth century, but it had changed significantly, coming to occupy a much larger proportion of the monks' waking hours, and developing into an intensely aggressive war carried on by the monks against the devil, a war in which the souls of the Christian faithful were at stake. Further examination of this war has shown that the monks themselves came from the class of fighters and also that their outside support came from that same group. The special virtue cultivated by the monks was patience, which was one of the main forms of humility, in turn defined as poverty, meaning poverty in spirit. The monks had to be able to bear affliction but at the same time inflict no harm upon anyone else. The ideal they sought to impose upon the laity was of the Christian knight who was strong, who protected the poor (including, among others, the monks themselves), but who, at the same time, did not shed blood. This ideal became a concrete programme in the Peace Movement, where armed strength found its justification in the maintenance of a peaceful order, and ultimately in the crusades. Such was the message of monastic spirituality. The medium of this spirituality was a symbolic war, ritual aggression in the form of liturgy, fought figuratively by spiritual soldiers.

The medium was a form of the very activity against which the monastic message was directed. The medium was fighting (a point noted by their enemies), but not reckless, physically violent fighting in which people got injured and killed; instead it was a kind of aggression that was carefully controlled and made predictable by ritual. The monks in this way confronted the great social problem of their day, namely violence. In the first instance they renounced it utterly for themselves as individuals; secondly they engaged in the same activity but transformed it so as to remove from it the harmful, objectionable elements; and thirdly they elaborated an ethic for the dominant members of society that permitted them to continue in their usual activities but in limited, unharmful, spiritually constructive ways. The connection between monastic spirituality and feudal society is explicable; both the monastic ideal, however traditional, and the monastic means of expression (again, no matter how traditional) were shaped by feudal society, and they in turn had a profound impact (for the very reason that they had been so responsive) upon that same society.[1]

The Benedictines meanwhile did not cultivate talk. While they did not live under a strict rule of silence, they discouraged conversation and set prescribed periods for silence, including those reserved for spiritual reading; after all, they had brought about a major alteration of human behaviour in the West with their invention of silent reading.[2] Neither did the Benedictines cultivate contentiousness; indeed the rule specifically admonishes against it.[3] Nor did they cultivate entertainment; a good sense of humour can be found at nearly every turn in their history, but the rule frowns on levity.[4] Nor did the monks specialize in persuasive discourse. They gave witness by their form of life to a truth they considered established. When they got drawn into the apostolate to the Germanic peoples they accomplished the task by their witness and by miraculous demonstration. Persuasive discourse would have been just as inappropriate for them to use as it would have been unsuited to their audience.

Urban audiences, on the other hand, wanted to hear speakers; they relished amusement and spectacle; they sought to be convinced and they demanded explanations. We must not exaggerate the new urban literacy, but neither can we deny or ignore its existence as a reality and as a factor in the changing abilities and desires of the laity. Urban society fostered a need for a spirituality that would express itself in speech. Yet at the same time the moral problems being raised in connection with the various urban professions focused upon this very means of expression. The masters, merchants, and lawyers all talked. While the masters lectured and disputed, the merchants hawked. Alan of Lille's model sermon directed to lawyers is entitled *Ad oratores, seu advocatos*; here the *oratores* are not the monks, not 'those who pray', but the lawyers who plead in court.[5] Who could be sure that these people who lived by talking were right or were telling the truth? Who can be sure of the truth when scholars are capable of arguing both sides of a question, when lawyers strive for justice in proportion to the amounts of money they are paid, and when prices that are said to be as low as possible one day are cut by one-third the next? Naturally enough people felt anxious about being manipulated by others. We should not be surprised by the exemplum in which a crafty lawyer gets his tongue pulled out,[6] or the one that tells of a merchant who plies prospective customers with drinks.[7] Less vivid (but more real) is the regulation of the town of Saint-Omer forbidding sellers in a certain market to attract the attention of potential buyers by coughing or sneezing.[8]

But while the arts of persuasion lay under a cloud of doubt, the friars entered upon the scene talking: talking, preaching, or, as Thomas of Spalato said about Francis, 'shouting'.[9] Francis engaged in a sort of street-corner or public-square hawking, a legacy from his pre-conversion days. Everywhere the friars went they talked, and where they encountered opposition they argued. They disputed the arguments of those they saw as heretics, especially in southern France and northern Italy, as well as the arguments of those clerics who saw the advent of the friars as an encroachment. The friars came forward with a new approach to confession and penance; they willingly entered into negotiation with the confessee to determine, through a series of questions and responses, the relative seriousness of the fault and hence the appropriate harshness of the penance. Federigo Visconti, the Archbishop of Pisa, described such an encounter as a battle of wits and words:

O what a great battle takes place between the friar confessor and the penitent sinner. The sinner says, for instance, 'I will do everything that you wish, but I can in no way whatever give up such a one as my lover, or usury, or hatred, or the grudge I have against so-and-so.' Whence it is fitting that, as one knight fights another powerful, rebellious knight, the friar struggle and do battle with the spears of reason and persuasion against the sinner, that he may conquer him spiritually.[10]

The disciplined contentiousness of the schools served the friars in administering penance as well as in preaching.

The friars were not staid in their public appearances. Francis himself willingly lived in the image of a jongleur,[11] and the friars' use of the exempla was an open attempt to give sermons an immediacy, a recognizable quality, and a humour capable of holding an audience. There was nothing necessarily wrong with the work of the jongleur. How, indeed, had Waldes of Lyons been converted? But shouting and entertaining was not all there was to preaching; it was, as we have seen, a carefully developed art designed to gain a certain effect in listeners. The friars thus indulged in those very activities that were most characteristic of the new urban society, especially the urban élite—those very activities which, by the same token, were the nub of the argument of moral corruption in the new urban professions.

The friars further reflected the society they entered by their frequent use of a marketplace vocabulary, a practice that gained authority and impetus from that one-time cloth merchant, Francis of Assisi.[12] Starting around 1240, the biographies of St Dominic included a parody of legal practice and commercial language in the mention of a will he was purported to have made out to his followers: 'Have charity,' he is supposed to have told them, 'keep humility, and possess voluntary poverty.'[13] There is an early Franciscan allegorical work on poverty entitled *The Holy Commerce* (*Sacrum Commercium*), or, as a fourteenth-century writer once called it, *The Business of Poverty* (*Commercium Paupertatis*).[14] The sermons of Anthony of Padua were laced with references to the types and places of work familiar to his hearers: pharmacists, shops in the square, usurers, mercenaries, metalworkers, and merchants.[15] St Bonaventure, too, occasionally used a commercial vocabulary, as when he argued for the usefulness of the friars, characterizing them as trustees for the Christian people, who are like debtors, and whose debt the friars try to pay off, or at least reduce.[16]

In justifying the itinerancy of the preaching friars, Humbert of Romans cited the example of the Apostles but by passing first via a mercantile image. Worldly trade offered the example of those who, because they were eager to amass fortunes, never ceased to travel about in the world seeking profits. 'And the Apostles also did thus, travelling through various provinces making a fortune in souls.'[17] Humbert still again used a variant of this same image where, in a long string of metaphors, he called preaching 'a business that increases a householder's goods'.[18] Humbert proposed for preaching the standards usually applied to coinage:

In money, one takes into account the metal, the stamp, and the weight.... The doctrine is the metal, the example of the Fathers that the preacher follows is the stamp, and humility is the weight. Whoever turns aside from duty is no longer precious metal, but only a worthless piece of clay; where formerly he had the sound of pure metal, now he produces no sound at all.[19]

Another Dominican writer explained the system of indulgences, which came into more frequent use around 1230, as transactions with the church's Treasury of Merits. For a cash payment the penitent person could get credit against his penitential debt from the store of supplemental merit and good works on deposit there from the lives of Christ, Mary, and the saints.[20] From such examples we can see that the friars employed an idiom that was unmistakably urban, just as their behaviour reflected, in a formal sense, the behaviour of the urban professions.

The friars would not have seen or described what they were doing as buying and selling and pleading and negotiating, but the point did not altogether elude their critics. Matthew Paris reported without comment some of the epithets applied to the friars in the university battle of the 1250s, such as 'hypocrites', 'false preachers', and 'vagabonds'.[21] Matthew was less restrained in observing how, at the time when the Dominicans were building a comfortable home for themselves at Dunstable (1259), everyone was amazed to see these poor brothers, who professed voluntary poverty, spending so much money.[22] Matthew was at his sharpest when he likened the friars' traffic in indulgences to the sale of sheep on the wool market.[23] The cult of St Francis grew in the thirteenth century, and it seemed to stimulate a proportionate growth of opposition. In 1289 a priest at Dieppe drew a sharp rebuke from the pope for something he had said and done during a sermon. The priest had apparently been preaching angrily against St Francis; then from the pulpit he gestured irreverently at a representation of the saint in a window and denounced Francis as an avaricious merchant.[24] And finally there was William of Saint-Amour, the friars' chief antagonist at Paris, who gave special emphasis to their facility of speech and their ability to seduce by means of swindling, double-dealing talk.[25]

Like the Cluniacs who had once been insultingly called soldiers and described in military dress with their swords and lances and helmets, the Franciscans and Dominicans were correspondingly denounced for their avarice, their wealth, their merchandizing, their bargaining—in short, for their similarity to merchants. In a way that recalls the tie between the monks and feudal society, we have seen how the friars confronted the chief problem of the new society, namely money-making. In the first place, they rejected money-making for themselves, turning instead to the recently matured ideal of voluntary poverty. Secondly, however, they persisted in the linguistic and formal mode of the money-makers, while avoiding the spiritually harmful aspects of such people's work. And thirdly, having themselves demonstrated part of the way, they provided for the leaders of urban society a revised moral theology that approved of money-making in certain, carefully defined circumstances. The friars' spirituality was both determined by, and a determining factor within, the new urban society.

The case of the Benedictine monks and that of the Franciscan and Dominican friars are not merely two random cases chosen from two different historical periods. They are consecutive cases; one leads into the other. The experience of the monks was present as a factor during the formative period of the friars; the development of the friars' spirituality inevitably contained a more or less conscious reaction against that of the monks. Humbert of Romans, always an exceptionally astute and self-conscious observer, pictured the spirituality of preaching not only as a positive good (for numerous reasons, some of which have been cited above) but also as something better than a spirituality of liturgical intercession:

Others consecrate themselves to the praises of God following assiduously in church the Divine Office, but the laity do not usually comprehend the words that are recited in the Office, whereas they do understand the language and instructions of the preacher. By preaching, too, God is extolled more manifestly and clearly than by these Offices ... [26]

Humbert's central criterion, we should note, is how well the message gets through to the laity. He emphasized that the sacraments are of no benefit to people who are not sufficiently informed and properly disposed to receive them; yet preaching can supply the information needed and can foster the right disposition. Since knowledge and good will can be obtained without the aid of the sacraments through preaching alone, preaching is to be thought preferable to the sacraments.[27]

In a related argument, Humbert goes beyond the usual practice of citing apostolic authority for preaching to specify that that authority stands behind preaching more solidly than it does behind liturgy.

The second reason that should lead us to prefer preaching is found in certain examples that recommend it. Jesus Christ, in the whole time He spent upon earth, celebrated mass but once, at the Last Supper; moreover, it is not said that He heard one confession. He administered the sacraments rarely and to a small number. He never devoted himself to the recitation of the canonical Office, and one can make the same observation about all the rest, except for preaching and prayer. It is also worthy of note that when He began to preach He spent more time in that than in prayer.[28]

Humbert cites the example of St Paul to the same effect, and then widens the focus.

Did the other Apostles and disciples of the Lord, throughout the world, devote themselves to any other task more than they did to preaching? 'They went forth', says St Mark, 'and preached everywhere' [Mark 16:20]. And so for our instruction there is the example of Our Lord, of St Paul, and of all the Apostles and disciples of Jesus Christ.[29]

A new, comprehensive approach to the spiritual life was being worked out by Humbert and Bonaventure and other leading friars in the middle of the thirteenth century. Many of the particular points of newness had made an appearance decades before, but when that had happened they had been unacceptable because they were perceived as too radically upsetting and threatening. By 1250, such changes could be looked at calmly, evaluated, accepted, justified, and—on the part of the friars and their most enthusiastic backers among the laity—truly assimilated.

Townspeople responded to the friars with material support. St Francis had warned his followers, in the *Testament*, against having recourse to regular, wealthy patrons.[30] The steady support that such patrons could supply would compromise the friars' vow of poverty and their self-imposed material instability. Still, Bonaventure figured that the margin of urban wealth in general was sufficient to support the friars, and he was apparently right.[31] In other words, the sociological fact was that just by staying in cities the friars were fairly well assured of support. Stephen of Bourbon taught that while all alike shared an obligation to support the poor, this obligation fell particularly upon the rich.[32] Moral considerations aside, Stephen was probably also right; the same point, moreover, confirms the aptness of the warning given by St Francis.

The friars' material support did indeed come from the rich, much of it from the royal and aristocratic rich who had supported the monks all along. The exception among European monarchs in this regard was the Emperor Frederick II.[33] While he chided clerics about their wealth and their involvement in secular affairs, holding up to them an ideal in fact very similar to that of the friars, he looked upon the friars, understandably, as agents of his political enemy, the pope.[34] For James I of Aragon and Catalonia, though, as well as for Ferdinand III of Castile and Leon, the friars served as advisers, confessors, and crusade (*reconquista*) preachers.[35] They also played a role in the occupation of newly conquered Valencia. Two Franciscans, John of Perugia and Peter of Sassoferrato, had gone to preach in Valencia while it was still under Moslem control; they were publicly executed there in 1228.[36] During the siege of Valencia (1236–8), there were friars in the entourage of King James; and before the city fell, he granted them sites for their convents.[37] With the king as a witness, the sister of one of the great barons of Aragon willed 100 shillings to the house of the Friars Minor that was to be established after the Christian victory.[38] The queen later willed 100 shillings to each of eight Franciscan convents in the kingdom, and King James bore the posthumous reputation of having laid with his own hands the cornerstones of all of the mendicants' convents in his kingdom.[39] Both orders had representatives in the cortes of Aragon as early as 1236, and when the same body assembled in 1262 to consider the king's drive for higher crusade taxes, the meeting was held in the Dominican church of Zaragoza, with both the Franciscans and the Dominicans supporting the king.[40] The relatively thorough records for England show that Henry III made 300 grants to the Franciscans, three-fourths of which were gifts in kind: wood for fuel, timber for construction, clothing, and food. He made similar grants to the Dominicans. Henry supported the provincial chapter meetings for both orders in 1240 and 1241, and was the principal benefactor of the Franciscan convents at Norwich and Shrewsbury.[41]

King Louis IX was founder and chief patron of the Dominican convents at Rouen, Compiègne, Mâcon, and Carcassonne, as well as of the Franciscan convents at Jaffa and at Paris. He visited and made gifts to the friars of both orders wherever he travelled, and brought gifts to the Parisian friars when he returned home. He paid the expenses of those who travelled with him and willed large payments to both orders and to several individual convents.[42] One of his biographers summed up this munificence by observing: 'In brief, Louis bore the largest part of the expenses of the Franciscans and Dominicans in Paris and in other nearby places.'[43]

Louis' wife founded a convent of Poor Clares outside of Paris, and retired there following his death.[44] The king's brother, Alphonse of Poitiers, with his exceptionally well-organized fiscal administration, left records that show him a steady and generous supporter of the friars, even in years when his resources were strained and he cut his other charitable donations.[45] When the Franciscans came to Mâcon in 1245, they were set up in the palatial town house of the De Feurs family, wealthy bourgeois of Lyons who had become landlords close by Mâcon.[46] The Franciscans were showered with benefactions by various relatives of the Count of Savoy and of the Count of Forez, as well as by many lesser nobles. The Dominicans arrived on the scene in about 1255 and were installed by Louis IX in what had once been the château of the Count of Mâcon, the king having purchased the county in 1239. Their benefactors included a chamberlain of Lyons and a bishop in addition to many of the nobles of the Mâconnais. Virtually every English bishop patronized the friars.[47] In the same way, hardly a will among those that survive from thirteenth-century Valencia does not include a legacy for the friars; moreover, such legacies usually included equal amounts for the Franciscans and

Dominicans. Wealthy cathedral canons and the greater knights of King James' victorious crusading army (one bequeathed his body plus 1,000 shillings) alike remembered the friars in their wills. Bishop Raymond of Valencia left the Dominicans of his diocese the princely sum of 6,000 shillings and endowed the support of one Dominican student at Paris.[48]

The largely new element in benefactions to the friars came from newly rich city dwellers. A case study of the financial support given the friars in Mâcon reveals an overall trend in which the local nobles dominated in benefactions to the friars at first but were gradually supplanted during the later thirteenth century by the bourgeoisie.[49] A register of estimates drawn up to include all properties in the city in 1386 lists the financial obligations attached to every property and building, with beneficiaries and precise amounts included. Nearly every building carried a commitment to yield annually a certain amount of money or percentage of its income to some charitable enterprise; in two-thirds of the cases these were ecclesiastical institutions. Of the some 920 properties in town (held by 720 separate owners), 59 carried obligations to supply an annuity to either the Franciscans or the Dominicans. The arrangement in each case was some form of the *census*, a form of financial transaction that had been denounced and argued against, for example by Henry of Ghent, as usurious, but which, significantly, had found legitimacy in the work of canonists like Hostiensis and theologians like Alexander Lombard in the late thirteenth century. The friars thus did more than give gratuitous support to a social group in search of moral justification; they benefited directly from the very type of transaction that they had been helping to legitimize.

In London the burgesses provided land for the Franciscans and paid for the construction of their convent as well;[50] in Germany there are cases where the friars were brought in at the invitation of town governments and subsequently given help by them.[51] In Valencia, we read that Peter Oller, a draper, gave the Franciscans 100 shillings and the Dominicans 50 shillings in 1249, while William of Jaca, a notary, left the Franciscans 100 shillings and the Dominicans 150 shillings in his will of 1263.[52] Analogous donations could be found in towns throughout Europe. Beyond the reach of detailed, written records are the small, miscellaneous, often-repeated donations given the friars as they went about to beg. No evidence, and no logic either, would suggest that the urban poor, themselves so badly off that they sometimes had to beg, gave alms to the friars.[53] St Francis' warning against sustained reliance on wealthy patrons offers a clearer insight into the source of the friars' support; so, too, does the complaint of the Augustinian canons at Cambridge: 'The friars with honeyed words have procured for themselves the burials, legacies, and alms of rich citizens, which before their arrival had benefited our community.'[54]

Perhaps the most conspicuous use to which the friars put their income was construction. Like the monks of the past and the bishops of their own time, the friars became great builders.[55] They do not hold one of the key places in the history of style, but in order to meet the needs of effective preaching, they specialized in developing large, uncluttered halls with good acoustics.[56] Their competitors and critics found an easy target in the monumental materiality of church buildings erected by the proponents of poverty. St Bonaventure showed his sensitivity to criticisms by explaining why the friars had large convents and sumptuous churches.[57] There were two main factors: the high price of urban land and the danger of fire. On account of high land prices, it was necessary to use ground space as efficiently as possible, and hence to build high. On that account in turn, and also because of the danger of fire, it was necessary to build in stone. Obviously one could not erect a tall, sound, relatively fire-proof building in a city at low cost. So long as the question did not centre on why friars should have any buildings at all, this was a straightforward answer. It was an earthy, materially sound, coolly analytical answer; it reveals with startling clarity how the world had changed in a century, since Abbot Suger had formulated a mystical theology of light, flighty and ethereal, to justify his building a soaring new church, with vast expanses of glass wall, at the Abbey of Saint-Denis.[58]

The patronage of religious establishments by princes and nobles was not new in the thirteenth century. The friars seem merely to have stepped in as new beneficiaries to an ancient, solidly established tradition. The old-fashioned ways lived on in some benefactions to the friars, complete even to the details of the anniversary banquets, including maundys for the poor, provided by some Aragonese nobles.[59] But, as we have seen, the new element in patronage, not without its twelfth-century antecedents to be sure, lay in the participation of the prospering and influential people of urban society.

These people displayed an eager desire to participate in the religious life. They were able to do so by going to the friars' churches to listen to sermons, to make their confessions, and perhaps ultimately to be buried. Giving alms was also an important means of participating in the friars' spirituality. But for a still closer tie with the friars, short of the total commitment involved in giving up everything and joining one of their orders, the appropriate way was to join one of their lay confraternities.[60]

St Francis, from the early days of his ministry, moved some of his listeners to reform their lives, and he sought to prescribe for people so moved ways of life appropriate to their respective social conditions.[61] His letter to all the faithful, written in about 1214, shows how he expanded the conception of the religious life to include lay people, even those who were married and who continued to work at their worldly jobs.[62] In 1221 Francis, perhaps with the aid or even at the instigation of Cardinal Hugolino, drew up a rule for groups of lay people. This rule is not extant, but a revised version of it is found in the one promulgated by Nicholas IV in 1289.[63] The principal theme preached by Francis was penance, and those lay people who entered into some sort of formal association with the Franciscans were known as brothers or sisters of penance. There is a papal letter of commendation and privilege from as early as 1221 that refers to such groups at Faenza 'and certain other nearby cities and places'.[64] In 1224 Honorius III granted that exceptions be made in case of an interdict for those many people throughout Italy known as 'Brothers of Penance' (*Fratres de Poenitentia*).[65] The need for papal protection for these groups arose particularly because the men who joined them were not to bear arms or swear oaths, a point that brought them into conflict with municipal authorities. Membership lists were thus drawn up. The list for Bologna in 1252 bears the names of 57 adherents, sometimes with their professions, for example notary, scribe, baker, barber, wood-supplier, and stationer.[66] In the city of Valencia the guilds of shoemakers, tailors, leatherworkers, and potmakers placed themselves under the spiritual guidance of the Franciscan Order.[67]

The Franciscan 'Congregation of Penance' at Brescia, dating from the late thirteenth century, gives some indication of the religious practices of such groups. They were to attend mass together on one Sunday of each month at the Franciscans' church; they were to go to confess their sins at least two times a year (twice the minimum number required of all lay people by Lateran IV); they were to observe the same fasts as the friars themselves observed; and they were to carry out cooperative works of charity.[68]

Since Thomas of Celano referred already in 1229 to what appear to be the three orders founded by St Francis, the notion of a 'third order' seems to date from the early days of Franciscan history.[69] The Third Order of Brothers and Sisters of Penance of St Dominic, based somewhat on the model of the Franciscan Third Order, received papal approbation only in 1406, but it had forerunners during the preceding century and three-quarters.[70] Peter of Verona, the first Dominican martyr, organized a Confraternity of the Faith (or the Faithful) at Milan in 1232.[71] Whereas one of the main interests of St Francis lay in establishing peace among warring civic factions, an interest reflected in the Franciscan confraternities, that of Peter Martyr lay especially in the eradication of heresy. The group he formed was made up of militant Catholics committed to support his work as inquisitor. Still, these are differences only of emphasis; members of the Confraternity of the Faith attended mass together at the church of the Dominicans on the third Sunday of each month, joined in many of the Dominicans' religious observances, and joined together in works of charity.[72] Other confraternities associated with the Order of Preachers were named in honour of the Holy Virgin; others went by the name Militia of Christ (for which there is a rule dating from 1285); and still others, following that bloody scene on the road between Como and Milan in 1253, under the name of St Peter Martyr.[73]

Of particular interest is the Congregation of St Dominic organized at Bologna within the decade following Dominic's canonization. Its statutes are known from a letter of approval directed to the congregation in June 1244 by John of Wildeshausen, at that time the Dominican master-general.[74] Membership in this group, according to these statutes, was open to anyone except a person known or suspected to be in error concerning the faith (*nisi fuerit infamatus aut suspectus de errore fidei*). The members were to attend mass on the final Sunday of each month at the Preachers' church; each person was to donate one *denarius* at that monthly mass (or send it by another person if unable to attend). Similarly they were to attend mass on the Feast of St Dominic and to offer, according to their respective means, a candle in his honour. The leadership was to be put in the hands not of one person but of four, one from each of the city's quarters, precisely as was then being done in some communal governments. Each member was to say the Lord's Prayer seven times a day, and also when one of his confrères or one of the friars in the convent at Bologna died. All were to attend the funeral of a confrère; the congregation was to keep two great candles for use at such funerals and it was to pay the expenses of the funeral and burial of its poorer members. The statutes close with an explicit and concise statement of the friars' new conception of obedience: the confrères were not to be bound in conscience by these rules nor punished for transgressing any of them, a position based on the notion that God prefers a service freely rendered to a servile carrying-out of orders. All of these points appear again in the rule written by a Dominican, Pinamonte Brembate, for the Misericordia of Bergamo, a lay confraternity established jointly by Dominicans and Franciscans in 1265.[75] The first headquarters of the Misericordia was in a vast twelfth-century basilica built and maintained by the communal government and which literally overshadowed the cathedral church of the time. In Valencia, the hide dealers and belt makers became associated with the Order of Preachers by (or before) 1252; a brotherhood in honour of St Peter Martyr was formed by 1269; and by the end of the century there was a social and benevolent confraternity in honour of God, the Virgin,

Peter Martyr, and the Order of Preachers.[76] In the Rhineland there appeared another Order of Penitents, this one established for reformed prostitutes (and hence also known as the Order of Magdalenes); it came to have branches in France, Italy, Spain, and Portugal, and in 1286 it came under the direction of the Dominicans.[77]

The lay fraternities with ties to the mendicant orders do not form, at least for the thirteenth century, a clear historical picture. Nothing would be more misleading than to project on to that period the highly organized, uniformly structured third orders of later times. There had been lay fraternities before the friars, for example, those established by the Benedictines in the eleventh century or by the Premonstratensians in the twelfth.[78] The guilds had long had a religious aspect (group worship, mutual aid, collective charity) which appears to have anticipated the programme of the friars' lay counterparts. The initiative for forming a lay confraternity did not have to come from a convent of friars, for there are cases in which an existing lay confraternity of penance in a given city welcomed and assisted in the establishment there of a convent of friars.[79] Such laymen were thus able, like so many initial investing partners, to become the first and thus crucial patrons of the friars. At Florence, moreover, the Fraternity of Penance owned and administered all goods donated to the Dominicans throughout the thirteenth century, serving a worldly, financial role similar to that of the 'spiritual friends' of the Franciscans.[80]

The most exact and in every way most revealing predecessor of the friars' lay fraternities was the 'third order' of the Humiliati. Here perhaps is the origin of the very terminology of first, second, and third orders, even though the friars used the terms differently from the Humiliati.[81] It may be, then, that the most significant thread of historical continuity to be traced here leads from the Humiliati to the confraternities of penance of the thirteenth century. Another possible source is suggested by developments going on at just this time in the Sūfi orders of Islam. These were brotherhoods of mendicants led by holy men of strong personality and great spiritual authority. In the twelfth and thirteenth centuries they spread over the entire Islamic world. Membership was of two kinds: a higher class of initiates and disciples occupied with religious duties in the monasteries, and a large body of lay members attached to the orders and meeting on stated occasions but otherwise carrying on their secular occupations in village or town.[82]

In the period following the establishment of the mendicant orders, from the later thirteenth century until the Reformation, the significant area of development in the religious life was found not in the formally patented religious orders but in the various group manifestations of lay piety. The fourteenth and fifteenth centuries constituted, as Marc Bloch said, 'the golden age of the small lay associations of piety'.[83] The prediction of Joachim of Flora that a new, spiritual age was about to àppear, with the friars as its harbingers, an age in which the priesthood would be superfluous, was far from senseless, even if it proved incorrect. St Francis himself, in his enthusiasm for the laity and his ambivalence about a formal religious order, seemed to show an awareness that the main development of the future rested with the laity and that the friars were to be the agents of this development. In this connection, there is weighty meaning as well as gentle humour in the comment of Berthold of Regensburg on the order of married people:

God has sanctified marriage more than any other order in the world, more than the bare-footed friars, the preaching friars, or the grey monks, who upon one point cannot match holy matrimony; namely, society could not do without the latter. God therefore commanded it, whereas the others he merely counselled.[84]

The intensified religious engagement of lay people is clear in the case of Florence, precocious both in its commercial-industrial development and in its socio-political development.[85] The population in 1278 had reached 73,000 after a three-fold increase in just a century. The people in control of this populace, moreover, were mostly 'men of recent origins'. The power of the old feudal nobility had been drastically reduced, to be taken up by a new, urban nobility, whose fortunes were founded in business. 'If there is any single generalization concerning upper-class bourgeois behaviour in the thirteenth century,' writes Marvin Becker, 'it would treat the alacrity with which the *popolani grassi* sought to participate in religious life.'[86] They controlled one-third of the city's churches; they had long since helped reforming clerics chase out simoniacs; and they were among the first to welcome the friars. The Franciscans were given the hospital of S. Gallo in 1218; the Poor Clares were accommodated in 1221, the same year in which the Dominicans received the church of S. Maria Novella from the cathedral chapter. In 1228 the Franciscans moved to S. Croce, where a modern visitor becomes aware of the 'high rate of religious investment that Florentine burghers made when given an unrivalled opportunity to enter the sacred portals and bury their dead'.[87]

The old religion of the monks, with its daily rounds of prayers and psalm recitations, was partially absorbed into lay spirituality, as the familiar books of hours (for princely patrons) testify. But there were new elements in the ritual observances of the laity; reference has been made already to their multiple recitations of the Lord's Prayer. To these they joined multiple recitations of the angelic praises of the Virgin, the 'Hail Mary'. A formal pattern combining the *Pater Noster* and the *Ave Maria* was worked out in the thirteenth century to form the Rosary. While the belief that the Rosary was started by St Dominic upon a direct commission from the Virgin is now regarded as a fifteenth-century invention, the Dominicans were mainly responsible for the refinements in length and arrangement of the Rosary as well as for its propagation as a form of worship.[88] Multiple recitations required, some sort of counting device, and in the thirteenth century the string of beads, a standard Indic device for keeping track of the number of times a prayer was said, made its appearance in the Latin West. Another Indic spiritual practice, that of holding the hands together in front of oneself when praying, appeared in the West at about this time, eventually replacing the posture in which a person prayed with outstretched arms. Both the counting device and the new gesture for praying might have come, along with the idea of multiple recitations of the Lord's Prayer, via the Cathars.[89]

The new spirituality also inherited and exploited the religious procession, which the friars staged in the squares that were being opened up in front of their convents in the latter half of the thirteenth century. These convents, usually placed strategically by the main city gates, together with their adjoining squares became new poles of attraction for urban activity in addition to, and in certain cases in careful coordination with, the cathedral square and the seat of municipal government. The integration of open urban spaces with the mendicants' churches served particularly well the ostentatious corporate worship of the confraternities, better able to display their numbers and their colours by the light of day. Thus outdoors as well as in, the friars created a dramatic setting for their apostolate.[90]

Usury went right on being one of the leading concerns of this apostolate; attacks against it remained a principal theme of Franciscan and Dominican preaching.[91] The condemning tone of the Third Lateran Council (1179) did not fade in the thirteenth century; it reappeared with greater intensity at the Second Council of Lyons (1274). The former council decreed (canon 25) 'that notorious usurers are not to be admitted to the communion of the altar, nor, if they die in that sin, to receive Christian burial'.[92] The latter council in turn decreed (canon 26) 'that the canon of the Lateran Council against usurers be inviolably observed under threat of divine malediction'. Stern punishments were promised to any who cooperated with non-local usurers, for example by renting offices or houses to them. Whole territories in which foreign usurers were tolerated ran the risk of an ecclesiastical interdict. The succeeding canon of the Second Council of Lyons affirmed:

Even though notorious usurers have made definite or general provision in their wills regarding restitution in the matter of illegally charged interest, church burial shall nevertheless be denied them until full satisfaction has been made to those to whom it is due, if they are available; in case of absence, to those who are authorized to act for them [often local clerics].[93]

The usurer could thus be put under some spiritual sanction and obliged to make payment of restitution, either directly to those from whom he had taken usury, or, in their absence, to some church official. In addition he faced the possibility that secular authorities might bring him to court for his activities.[94]

The combination of the moralists' constant harping on the theme of usury with the sanctions that secular and ecclesiastical governments could impose suggests an unhealthy climate for business. Yet the economic history of the thirteenth century suggests otherwise; in fact the taking of interest for *damnum emergens* was being explicitly written into ledgers and notarial acts from the middle of the century on.[95] What was once deviant behaviour, which by definition is marginal, was here becoming standard practice and thus simultaneously, from an official point of view, increasingly difficult to define as deviant, particularly as more and more of those in positions of authority had mercantile backgrounds.[96] This is self-evident in the case of the urban patriciate, but it was also true of the ecclesiastical hierarchy.[97] Even the strong language of the conciliar decrees specified only the 'manifest' or 'notorious' usurers (*usurarii manifesti*). In 1208 Pope Innocent III wrote to the Bishop of Arras urging him to be moderate in applying the decrees of the Third Lateran Council.[98] And Thomas Aquinas, too, spoke warmly of moderation in the same area:

Human laws leave certain sins unpunished because of the imperfection of men; many useful things would disappear, in fact, if all improper operations were rigorously forbidden. This is why civil legislation has at times tolerated usury, not because usury is thought to be just but so as not to hinder the advantages that so many derive from it.[99]

Civil authorities in the thirteenth century were indeed licensing moneylenders, just as Thomas had said.[100] Some ecclesiastical authorities, too, readily accepted offerings from moneylenders and made no further mention of usury. In one case the Bishop of Metz was accused by priests of his own diocese of retaining restitution payments for his own use.[101] More than once were Franciscans accused of absolving wealthy usurers without requiring them to make restitution to the victims of their malpractice; they were also accused, like the Bishop of Metz, of benefiting improperly from usurers' payments made in lieu of proper restitution.[102] Such complaints indicate a significant shift in the behaviour of the wealthy from restitution to philanthropy. Analysis of the wills of wealthy Italian merchants and bankers shows a sharp decline in restitution in the early fourteenth century.[103] Businessmen wanted their work to be seen in the most favourable light possible and so preferred to be honoured for spontaneous generosity than to be forced to make amends for immoral behaviour. Consistent with general scholastic theory on the efficacy of good works, philanthropy thus held one of the keys to the justification of profit-making. The small-scale, local pawnbroker continued to be harassed by officials, but the merchant-bankers were well on their way to assuming their role as patrons of charity. The proliferation of various types of hospital is one of the leading manifestations of the new style of philanthropy.[104]

Beyond a favourable moral ethic, new forms of worship, and the encouragement of charitable donations, the friars supplied city people with what may justly be called an urban ideology. They enhanced the setting of the new philanthropy and spirituality with honourable associations, biblical and historical.[105] Around the year 1260, Albert the Great preached a cycle of seven sermons at Augsburg during a week-long festival in honour of St Augustine.[106] He opened and closed the cycle in the Dominican church, preaching elsewhere during the interval, for example to the Dominican sisters and to the cathedral canons. To the canons he spoke in Latin, to his other audiences in German. The text for the entire cycle came from Matthew 5:14, 'A city upon a hill cannot be hidden.' He set out to ask why the Fathers of the church can be compared with a city, especially a city upon a hill, and why it cannot remain hidden. Albert observed that the sacred doctors share the qualities of a city that, following Plato's definition, is well ordered: security, urbanity, unity, and liberty. He discussed in turn the roles played in maintaining the social order by the monarch, by the aristocracy, and by the wealthy. The aristocrats were in a sense extensions of the monarch; they gave him advice and they rendered justice in his courts. 'These will have to be men of such virtue that in no way whatever could they be corrupted by money or made to abandon justice for fear, hatred, or favour.'[107] But no matter how powerful a king or how virtuous and wise an aristocracy a city had, it would be nothing without riches. Thus a stable city must have rich people; it should have a government (*thimocratia*) in which magistrates are chosen on the basis of the property they own. In a time of emergency, these rich people would be the ones who would keep the city going, supplying arms if necessary but especially food to the shoemakers and the menders and the day labourers, who otherwise could not survive.[108] 'We see this in many cities, that some who are very powerful and rich are able to maintain a thousand men in time of war.' This was true, he said by way of example, in Rome and Milan and in other cities.[109]

Albert reminded his audience that not every way of acquiring riches was acceptable, condemning those who lie, commit fraud, use false weights and measures, and cheat 'in a thousand other ways'.[110] This message would seem to have fallen harder on the petty, local merchant than on the big-time, cosmopolitan merchant. But the city itself with its wealth and its wealthy was glorified by Albert for its light, its beauty, its erudite culture, and its dense population.[111] Above all in these remarks it is the friendly and favourable tone employed by Albert that reveals the significant change taking place, a change of sensitivity and of attitude, essential elements both in a change of spirituality.

In 1288 a Milanese Franciscan named Bonvicinus of Ripa wrote a pamphlet *On the Marvels of the City of Milan*.[112] It includes descriptions of the streets, buildings, houses, churches, shops, and convents of Milan as well as the various trades (300 bakers, 440 butchers, 150 hostelries that gave 'hospitality to strangers for profit') and professions (1,500 notaries) of the Milanese. Literary conventions notwithstanding, Bonvicinus clearly loved the city: 'How could the people not thrive where it is so glorious to live?' His tone throughout is positive, even exuberant. And no one understood better than this Franciscan the enduring rule of big-city life: 'After what has been said, it is evident that in our city, life is wonderful for those who have enough money.'[113]

The crown of any spirituality is made up of its saints. Saints Francis, Dominic, Peter Martyr, Raymond of Peñafort, Anthony of Padua, Bonaventure, Albert the Great, and Thomas Aquinas give sparkling testimony to the successful establishment of the mendicant orders, their steadfast opposition of heresy, and their spectacular achievements in law, preaching, and theology. The great Dominican collector of saints' lives, James of Voragine, was himself venerated as a saint in Genoa and its environs, both for his patronage of the poor and for his role as a peace-maker.[114] All of these friar-saints though, have something traditional about them, namely that they took up religion full-time as a profession. While their particular style of religious life was new, the religious life as such was not new; and thus the test of newness comes with those saints who emerged from the new professions.

Reference in this context is sometimes made to Godric of Finchale, a man from Lincolnshire whose life spanned the first three-quarters of the twelfth century.[115] Drawn away from his peasant background by the attractions of a pedlar's life, already as a young man he was well versed in making profit from buying and selling. After four years of making the rounds of markets and villages in Lincolnshire, he expanded his operations northward into Scotland and southward to the Continent, eventually reaching as far as Rome. He rose to become a major figure in the commerce among the countries bordering the North Sea. His travels often took him to Lindisfarne and there, under the impact of that holy place and the still vivid presence of St Cuthbert, he began to yearn for solitude and to feel discontent with his highly successful career as merchant. He sought spiritual solace in making pilgrimages and being so well-to-do was able to visit the greatest sites of all, Rome, Jerusalem, and Saint-James of Compostella. When at last he resolved his spiritual crisis, he sold all his possessions and distributed the resulting income among poor people. He then became a hermit in the forest near Durham, where one Reginald served as his confessor and also wrote for posterity his biography. The problem with this life is that Godric does not at all appear to qualify as a merchant saint; on the contrary his sanctity derives, just as that of St Francis, from his having ceased to be a merchant.

The case of Omobono of Cremona was different.[116] Omobono was a second-generation merchant active during the latter half of the twelfth century. He married but never had any children of his own. He was intensely devout, attending mass daily and reciting the divine office in the manner of a monk. Furthermore, his home served as a centre for dispensing charitable aid. He took care of abandoned children, fed poor people, and otherwise offered help to those who did not know where else to turn. But despite this piety and charity, Omobono never ceased to be a merchant. He worked, he made a profit, and he used this profit to support himself, his wife, and his life of religious devotion and service. Omobono maintained a strong and highly favourable reputation, so that shortly after he died, his story was brought to the new pope, Innocent III, by the Bishop of Cremona, along with a request for canonization. Pope Innocent replied early in 1199 with a formal declaration of Omobono's sainthood. The new saint in turn became the patron of Cremona, and in the early fourteenth century a full-sized statue of him was placed next to a statue of the Virgin and Child above the main entrance to the cathedral church.

Omobono qualified as a merchant saint. Cremona yielded an artisan saint as well. Facio of Cremona was born in about 1200 at Verona.[117] He became a leading gold- and silversmith in his native city, but was driven out by political troubles in the late 1220s. He settled at Cremona and continued his work there, at the same time maintaining a rigorously pious life. The claim of his biographer is that Facio made eighteen pilgrimages to Rome and eighteen to Compostella. He gained admittance to the Society of the Holy Spirit, a confraternity whose members included all the nobles and merchants of Cremona (*in quo consortio erant omnes nobiles Cremonenses et mercatores*).[118] He subsequently took leave of this group, very likely because of its aristocratic character and pro-imperial leanings; shortly afterwards he was to organize, with papal approval and support, his own Order of the Holy Spirit, a lay fraternity that became successfully established in Cremona and in several other cities of Lombardy. At his own home Facio made a hostel for poor pilgrims. He carried on with his work, using proceeds from it to help poor people. He also made pious donations of his handiwork, such as the silver cross in the cathedral treasury, at the base of which stands a representation of St Omobono. His charity included a special concern for poor people who were ashamed to beg, a category difficult to identify, referring perhaps to people once well off who had lost their fortunes and social positions.[119]

In Brittany there appeared a lawyer saint, Ivo Hélory (1253–1303), who studied theology at Paris—apparently under some disciples of Bonaventure—and law at Orléans.[120] He became a priest, and therefore did not earn his living by practising law as such, but specialized in organizing legal aid for those poor who could not pay lawyers' fees. He preached, he enlisted lawyers in his scheme, and he set up lay confraternities. While St Ivo was far more priest than lawyer, his later designation as patron of lawyers suggests that his reputation stressed the novel aspect of his career.

The friars did not ordinarily press for the canonization of those who did not belong to their respective orders. One exception was King Louis IX, whom they tried to associate as closely as possible with themselves.[121] Their main effort, however, went into the canonizing of their own confrères, and especially into the continual re-defining and re-writing of the saintly spiritualities of Francis and Dominic.

The appearance of urban saints in addition to the beginnings of an urban ideology marked the coming of age of Europe's commercial economy. The leading practitioners of voluntary poverty, themselves city-dwellers, formulated an ethic that justified the principal activities of the dominant groups in urban society. The need for scapegoats subsided, and accordingly the English and French kings replaced 'their Jews' with Christian bankers. Edward I expelled the Jews from England in 1290 and Philip IV did the same in France sixteen years later. Even with this maturation of Christian Europe's profit-oriented commercial economy, gift-economy behaviour, as we observed at the outset, did not altogether vanish. On the contrary, the very ones who had been most concerned about profit-making and most successful at it poured huge sums of money into religious movements and institutions; their reversion to the gift-giving mode became notably intense as they awaited the approach of death.[122]

That the *pauperes Christi* should have served the profit economy in such direct and elemental ways remains a paradox, and a paradox that has not been perceived exclusively by modern eyes. We would not have thought to call Francis of Assisi, as urban a saint as any, a merchant saint. And yet, during the 1260s, the Archbishop of Pisa presented a quite different view when preaching at the Franciscans' church in his city on the feast of St Francis.[123] Preaching in the vernacular because his audience included lay devotees of the saint,[124] Federigo Visconti told them how, through God's grace, he had stood some four decades earlier in a crowded square in Bologna and seen and even touched the blessed Francis himself.[125] Federigo generally made a point of denouncing usurers and those who traffic in arms with the Moslems, for they drag down the reputation of the Pisan merchants, known throughout the world as good Christian men.[126] Consistently he praised these merchants, just as he usually reminded the congregation that Francis had been a wealthy merchant.[127] Then, in one of these annual sermons, the archbishop exclaimed: 'How pleasing it must be for merchants to know that one of their cohorts, St Francis, was a merchant and was also made a saint in our time. Oh, how much good hope there must be for merchants, who have such a merchant intermediary with God.'[128] Pisa, 1261: St Francis of Assisi had become the patron and protector of merchants.

Conclusion

'You are the light of the world,' wrote Pope Urban II to the Cluniacs in 1097; it seemed only natural, as observed earlier, that he should do so.[1] How misguided we would be to dismiss this remark as a literary commonplace, devoid of historical significance. For the individual Benedictine monk, the world was perhaps only as big as his own monastery and its surrounding lands. A cloister lay at the centre of this world and prefigured the paradise of the next.[2] In the higher levels of Cluniac administration, however, an inter-monastery structure had been built, and its administrators had had to develop in the mind's eye a corresponding vision broad enough to comprehend most of western Europe. The same vision, perhaps still broader and sharper, was shared by the Roman papacy, newly self-conscious about its importance, its powers, and its sphere of influence.

Within Latin Christendom at the end of the eleventh century, the Cluniacs built the largest, most expensive, most elegant church ever built in the West. They had a major voice in some of the leading political issues of the time, such as the Peace Movement and the *reconquista*. They offered what was unquestionably the chief model of the religious life, and they played a crucial role in the economic transformation of Burgundy. Urban II, himself a former Cluniac prior, gave recognition to a concrete reality of the eleventh century when he called the Cluniacs the 'light of the world'.

Then the world changed. The internal transformations of Latin Christian society that we have been studying were accompanied by the advances of western soldiers, missionaries, and colonists into eastern Europe, Spain, and Scandinavia. Islamic and Byzantine control of the Mediterranean was rolled back so that Latin Christians now came into regular contact with the Near East. Italian merchants and missionaries made their way as far as China, and Portuguese ships would soon venture out to the Azores and the Canaries. Meanwhile the Benedictines of the twelfth and thirteenth centuries stayed at home, minding their properties, while their pre-eminent place in the religious life passed to the friars. In fact, the missionaries who were going to North Africa, to the Holy Land, to the Mongols, and beyond were friars. Little wonder that Matthew Paris—a unique writer but a representative Benedictine[3]—would say of the Franciscans that they were spread throughout the world and of the Dominicans that: 'The whole earth is their cell and the ocean is their cloister.'[4]

Matthew was no friend of the friars, but his testimony on the length and breadth of their ministry was accurate. As for the depth of that ministry, at home in Latin Christendom, one does better to hear the judgment of Pierre Dubois, one of the French king's lawyers and advisers. 'In our times,' wrote Pierre in the year 1300, 'the Dominicans and Franciscans are better informed than anyone else on the current state of society.'[5]

European society in the late thirteenth century was not run by merchants and professionals, nor was the landscape of that time dominated by cities. The countryside, its inhabitants, its produce, its imagery, and its rhythms determined the overall appearance and direction of life. And yet the cities, with their inhabitants and their products and their particular modes had come to assume a role in contemporary affairs of great importance in proportion to their modest size. The dominant sectors within urban society had in turn become disproportionately influential, and it was their particular kind of holy man, the friar, who had fallen heir to the leading role in the religious life once held by the monk. The metaphor of paradise invoked by Albert the Great in his Augsburg sermons did not apply to the monastic cloister but to the city square.[6]

When Federigo Visconti visited the Franciscans and Dominicans of Pisa, he sometimes preached to them on the text, 'You are the light of the world'.[7] He was paying them a compliment, to be sure, but we should not dismiss his remarks as mere cliché and hyperbole, for just as when Urban II wrote to the Cluniacs, Federigo when preaching to the friars nearly two centuries later was acknowledging a contemporary, even if controversial, reality.

Notes

Abbreviations

AF	*Analecta Franciscana*, 10 vols. (Quaracchi, 1885–1926).
AASS	*Acta Sanctorum* (Antwerp and Brussels, 1643–).
CEH	*The Cambridge Economic History of Europe*, ed. M. M. Postan *et al.*, I, 2nd ed. (Cambridge, 1966); II and III (Cambridge, 1952, 1963).
CJC	*Corpus Juris Canonici*, ed. E. Friedberg, 2 vols. (Leipzig, 1879–81).
COD	*Conciliorum Oecumenicorum Decreta*, ed. G. Aberigo *et al.* (Basel, 1962).
CSEL	*Corpus Scriptorum Ecclesiasticorum Latinorum* (Vienna and Prague, 1886–).
DHGE	*Dictionnaire d'histoire et de géographie ecclésiastiques* (Paris, 1912–).
DTC	*Dictionnaire de théologie catholique*, 15 vols. (Paris, 1903–50).
EcHR	*Economic History Review*, 2nd series.
FEH	*The Fontana Economic History of Europe*, ed. C. Cipolla, I (London, 1972).
HF	*Recueil des historiens des Gaules et de la France*, 24 vols. (Paris, 1738–1904).
HO	*The Historia Occidentalis of Jacques de Vitry*, ed. J. F. Hinnebusch, Spicilegium Friburgense, XVII (Fribourg, 1972).
LJV	*Lettres de Jacques de Vitry (1160/70–1240)*, ed. R. B. C. Huygens (Leiden, 1960).
LPV	*The Letters of Peter the Venerable*, ed. G. Constable, 2 vols., Harvard Historical Studies, LXXVIII (Cambridge, Mass., 1967).
Mansi	J. D. Mansi, ed., *Sacrorum conciliorum nova et amplissima collectio*, 31 vols. (Florence and Venice, 1759–98).
MGH	*Monumenta Germaniae historica*; *MGH, SS Scriptores*, 32 vols. (Hanover, 1826–1934).
MOPH	*Monumenta Ordinis Fratrum Praedicatorum historica* (Louvain, Paris, and Rome, 1896–).
MP	Matthew Paris *Chronica Majora*, ed. H. R. Luard, 7 vols., *RS*, LVII (London, 1872–84).
NCE	*New Catholic Encyclopedia*, 15 vols. (New York, 1967).
PL	*Patrologia Latina*, ed. J.-P. Migne, 221 vols. (Paris, 1844–64).
RS	*Rolls Series*, 99 vols. (London, 1858–96).
SBO	*Sancti Bernardi Opera*, ed. J. Leclercq *et al.* (Rome, 1957–).
TRHS	*Transactions of the Royal Historical Society*, 5th series.

Introduction

1. M. Bloch, *Feudal Society*, tr. L. A. Manyon (Chicago, 1964), p. 60 (translation altered).
2. ibid., pp. 60–1.

3. ibid., pp. 65–9.
4. ibid., pp. 69–71.
5. See R. S. Lopez in *CEH*, II, 289–93, and the same author's book, *The Commercial Revolution of the Middle Ages* (Englewood Cliffs, 1971). For further historiographical discussion and references, see L. K. Little, 'Pride Goes before Avarice: Social Change and the Vices in Latin Christendom', *American Historical Review*, LXXVI (1971), 27–9.
6. Note these titles: *Hérésies et sociétés dans l'Europe pré-industrielle, 11e–18e siècles*, ed. J. Le Goff, Civilisations et Sociétés, X (Paris, 1968); C. M. Cipolla, *Before the Industrial Revolution: European Society and Economy, 1000–1700* (New York, 1976).
7. F. Braudel, *Civilisation matérielle et capitalisme, XVe–XVIIIe siècle*, I (Paris, 1967).
8. For this problem as several critics have seen it in connection with Braudel's *La Méditerranée*, see J. H. Hexter, 'Fernand Braudel and the *Monde Braudellien* ...', *Journal of Modern History*, XLIV (1972), pp. 531–2.
9. G. Duby, 'L'histoire des systèmes de valeurs', *History and Theory*, XI (1972), 15–25.
10. ibid., p. 23, '... l'objectif majeur que doit, à mon sens, se fixer la recherche actuelle en histoire sociale est précisément d'éclairer la manière dont s'articulent les mouvements discordants qui animent l'évolution des infrastructures et celles des superstructures, et dont ces mouvements retentissent l'un sur l'autre.'

Chapter I: From gift economy to profit economy

1. Paul the Deacon *Historia Langobardorum* iii.34, ed. L. Bethmann and G. Waitz, *MGH, Scriptores rerum Langobardicarum et Italicarum, saec. VI–IX* (Hanover, 1878), pp. 112–13.
2. Ralph Glaber *Les cinq livres de ses histoires* ii.5, ed. M. Prou (Paris, 1886), pp. 35–6.
3. M. Mauss, *The Gift: Forms and Functions of Exchange in Archaic Societies*, tr. I. Cunnison (New York, 1967), first appeared in 1924. On the application of Mauss' theories to early European history, see P. Grierson, 'Commerce in the Dark Ages: A Critique of the Evidence', *TRHS*, IX (1959), 123–40, especially 130–9. Cf. G. Duby, *The Early Growth of the European Economy: Warriors and Peasants from the Seventh to the Twelfth Century*, tr. H. B. Clarke (Ithaca, 1974), pp. 48–72.
4. Mauss, *The Gift*, pp. 1–16; C. Lévi-Strauss, *The Elementary Structures of Kinship*, tr. J. Bell and J. von Sturner (London, 1969), pp. 52–63.
5. B. Malinowski, *Argonauts of the Western Pacific* (London, 1922), pp. 510–11.
6. Mauss, *The Gift*, pp. 31–7; H. Codere, *Fighting with Property*, American Ethnological Society, Monograph XVIII (New York, 1950).
7. Tacitus *Germania* xv, ed. E. Koestermann (Leipzig, 1957), p. 14.
8. Jordanes *Getica* 146, ed. T. Mommsen, *MGH, Auctores Antiquissimi*, V (Berlin, 1882), 96.
9. *Beowulf, The Oldest English Epic*, l. 351, tr. C. W. Kennedy (New York, 1940), p. 14.
10. *Beowulf*, ll. 121, 159, 712, 2198–710 (ibid., pp. 6, 8, 25, 71–87). Prof. John M. Hill of the U.S. Naval Academy kindly discussed with me material relevant to this point from his forthcoming publications on *Beowulf*.
11. *Beowulf*, ll. 69–71 (ibid., p. 5).
12. *Beowulf*, ll. 34–48 (ibid., p. 4); C. Green, *Sutton Hoo: The Excavation of a Royal Ship-Burial* (New York, 1963).
13. Jordanes *Getica* 158 (ed. Mommsen, p. 99). The Huns did the same in 453 at the burial of Attila: see Jordanes *Getica* 258 (ibid., pp. 124–5).
14. For examples of capitularies outlawing pagan practices, see *MGH, Leges*, II, *Capitularia regum francorum*, I, ed. A. Boretius (Hanover, 1883), 25, 45, and 69.

15. Gregory of Tours *Historia Francorum* ii.37, ed. W. Arndt, *MGH, Scriptores rerum Merovingicarum*, I (Hanover, 1885), 101–2.
16. Paul the Deacon *Historia Langobardorum* vi.58 (ed. Bethmann and Waitz, p. 185).
17. *Die Briefe des Heiligen Bonifatius und Lullus*, no. 105, ed. M. Tangl (Berlin, 1916), p. 230; the translation is by E. Emerton, *The Letters of Saint Boniface*, no. 85 (New York, 1940), p. 179.
18. Duby, *Warriors and Peasants*, pp. 54–5.
19. C. Violante, *La società milanese nell'età precomunale*, 2nd ed. (Bari, 1974), pp. 3–26.
20. Duby, *Warriors and Peasants*, pp. 105, 125–9; Grierson, 'Commerce in the Dark Ages', pp. 131–3.
21. Duby, *Warriors and Peasants*, pp. 128–9.
22. *Decretum*, IIa pars, C.23, q.7, c.2 (*CJC*, I, 951).
23. G. Luzzatto, *An Economic History of Italy from the Fall of the Roman Empire to the beginning of the Sixteenth Century*, tr. P. Jones (London, 1961), pp. 47–53, 58–60; A. O. Citarella, 'The Relations of Amalfi with the Arab World before the Crusades', *Speculum*, XLII (1967), 299–312; for the Milanese canal system, see P. Jones, *CEH*, I, 359–60.
24. R. Lopez, 'Aux origines du capitalisme génois', *Annales d'histoire économique et sociale*, IX (1937), 429–54; D. Herlihy, *Pisa in the Early Renaissance: A Study of Urban Growth*, Yale Historical Publications, Miscellany, LXVIII (New Haven, 1958), pp. 162–75; A. Dupont, *Les relations commerciales entre les cités maritimes de Languedoc et les cités méditerranéennes d'Espagne et d'Italie du Xème au XIIIème siècle* (Nîmes, 1942), pp. 68–77, 126; A. Germain, *Histoire du commerce de Montpellier*, 2 vols. (Montpellier, 1861), II, 1–53; R. Lopez, *CEH*, II, 302.
25. *A History of the Crusades*, ed. K. M. Setton, II (Philadelphia, 1962), 160–7, 492–4, 511–12.
26. M. Postan, *CEH*, II, 119–256.
27. ibid., pp. 183–4, 121–2.
28. Salimbene de Adam *Cronica*, ed. G. Scalia, 2 vols., *Scrittori d'Italia*, CCXXXII–CCXXXIII (Bari, 1966), 313: 'Non enim seminant nec metunt nec in orrea congregant homines terre illius, sed mittunt vinum Parisius, quia flumen habent iuxta, quod Parisius vadit, et ibi nobiliter vendunt, et inde habent totum victum suum et vestimenta quibus teguntur.'
29. Postan, *CEH*, II, 123; R. Dion, 'Introduction à l'histoire de la viticulture française', in *Eventail de l'histoire vivante: Hommage à Lucien Febvre offert par l'amitié d'Historiens, Linguistes, Géographes, Economistes, Sociologues, Ethnologues*, 2 vols. (Paris, 1953), I, 111–20. On the quality of wine at the time, see H. Enjalbert, 'Comment naissent les grands crus: Bordeaux, Porto, Cognac', *Annales E. S. C.*, VIII (1953), 319–20.
30. O. Verlinden, *CEH*, III, 126, 134.
31. ibid., pp. 126–37; G. Duby and R. Mandrou, *A History of French Civilisation*, tr. J. B. Atkinson (London, 1965), pp. 115–16; R. Bautier, 'Les foires de Champagne: Recherches sur une évolution historique', in *La Foire, Recueils de la Société Jean Bodin*, V (Brussels, 1953), 97–147.
32. J. A. Van Houtte, 'The Rise and Decline of the Market of Bruges', *EcHR*, XIX (1966), 29–47; de Roover, *CEH*, III, 43; Verlinden, ibid., pp. 138–42.
33. Chrétien de Troyes *Le Conte du Graal (Perceval)* ll. 5711–12, ed. F. Lecoy, *Les Romans de Chrétien de Troyes*, V1 (Paris, 1972), 178: 'Bien poïst an et dire et croire qu'an la vile eüst toz jorz foire.'
34. Verlinden, *CEH*, III, 128–9. R. Doehaerd, *Les relations commerciales entre Gênes, la Belgique et l'Outremont d'après les archives notariales génoises aux XIIIe et XIVe siècles*, 3 vols. (Brussels, 1941), I, 89–90.
35. ibid., I, 153–64. Cf. R. L. Reynolds, 'The Market for Northern Textiles in Genoa, 1179–1200', *Revue belge de philologie et d'histoire*, VIII (1929), 831–51; idem,

'Merchants of Arras and the Overland Trade with Genoa: Twelfth Century', ibid., IX (1930), 495–533.

36. R. W. Emery, 'Flemish Cloth and Flemish Merchants in Perpignan in the Thirteenth Century', in *Essays in Medieval Life and Thought in Honor of Austin Patterson Evans*, ed. J. H. Mundy, R. W. Emery, and B. N. Nelson (New York, 1955), pp. 153–65; E. Delaruelle, 'Toulouse et la route des Deux-Mers', *Annales du Midi*, LXII (1950), 215–28.

37. Y. Renouard, 'Les Cahorsins, hommes d'affaires français du XIIIe siècle', *TRHS*, XI (1961), 43–67.

38. E.-R. Labande, 'Recherches sur les pèlerins dans l'Europe des XIe et XIIe siècles', *Cahiers de civilisation médiévale*, I (1958), 159–69, 339–47.

39. G. Duby, *Rural Economy and Country Life in the Medieval West*, tr. C. Postan (London, 1968), pp. 131–4; Verlinden, *CEH*, III, 122–5.

40. E. Carus-Wilson, *CEH*, II, 355–428.

41. A. van de Vyver and C. Verlinden, 'L'auteur et la portée du *Conflictus ovis et lini*', *Revue belge de philologie et d'histoire*, XII (1933), 59–81.

42. E. Carus-Wilson, 'The English Cloth Industry in the Late Twelfth and Early Thirteenth Centuries', in her *Medieval Merchant Venturers: Collected Studies* (London, 1967), pp. 211–38.

43. Luzzatto, *Economic History of Italy*, pp. 104–5.

44. Postan, *CEH*, II, 126–7.

45. L. White, jr., 'Medieval Borrowings from Further Asia', *Medieval and Renaissance Studies*, V (1971), 8–9.

46. Carus-Wilson, *CEH*, II, 376–9.

47. J. Gimpel, *Les bâtisseurs de cathédrales* (Paris, 1958). G. P. Jones, *CEH*, II, 493–518.

48. Ralph Glaber *Les cinq livres de ses histoires* iii.4 (ed. Prou, p. 62).

49. J. U. Nef, *CEH*, II, 429–92; R. Sprandel, *Das Eisengewerbe im Mittelalter* (Stuttgart, 1968), pp. 93–220.

50. D. Herlihy, 'Treasure Hoards in the Italian Economy, 960–1139', *EcHR*, X (1957), 1–14.

51. E. Fournial, *Histoire monétaire de l'occident médiéval* (Paris, 1970); M. Bloch, *Esquisse d'une histoire monétaire de l'Europe*, Cahiers des Annales, IX (Paris, 1954); C. M. Cipolla, *Money, Prices, and Civilization in the Mediterranean World* (Princeton, 1956).

52. M. Bloch, 'Le problème de l'or au moyen âge', *Annales d'histoire économique et sociale*, V (1933), 1–34; Cipolla, *Money, Prices, and Civilization*, pp. 42–3; P. Spufford, *CEH*, III, 597–602.

53. R. S. Lopez, 'Back to Gold, 1252', *EcHR*, IX (1956), 219–40; A. M. Watson, 'Back to Gold—and Silver', ibid., XX (1967), 1–34. For the great advances registered in the second half of the twelfth century in German mining, see A. Suhle, *Deutsche Münz- und Geldgeschichte von den Anfängen bis zum 15. Jahrhundert* (Berlin, 1964), maps I–IV; Fournial, *Histoire monétaire*, p. 80.

54. Duby, *Warriors and Peasants*, p. 148.

55. de Roover, *CEH*, III, 44, 49–57, 66–7, 97; Luzzatto, *Economic History of Italy*, p. 133.

56. ibid., p. 135; de Roover, *CEH*, III, 70–8.

57. Duby, *Warriors and Peasants*, pp. 260–4.

58. R. de Roover, 'The Development of Accounting Prior to Luca Pacioli according to the Account-Books of Medieval Merchants', in *Studies in the History of Accounting*, ed. A. C. Littleton and B. S. Yamey (Homewood, 1956), pp. 114–74.

59. R. de Roover, *L'évolution de la Lettre de Change, XIVe–XVIIIe siècles* (Paris, 1953), pp. 23–42.

60. Luzzatto, *Economic History of Italy*, p. 132; E. V. Morgan, *A History of Money* (Harmondsworth, 1965), pp. 22–3.

Chapter 2: *Adapting to the profit economy*

1. Duby, *Rural Economy*, pp. 3–58.
2. ibid., pp. 5–6, 56, 76; Jones, *CEH*, I, 380–81. In modern Israel, kibbutz theory holds that a kibbutz should have no more than a few hundred members to ensure that each of its inhabitants is an integral member of the group. In 1964, the average kibbutz population was 320. B. Bettelheim, *Children of the Dream* (London, 1969), pp. 12, 15.
3. J. H. Lynch, *Simoniacal Entry into Religious Life from 1000 to 1260: A Social, Economic, and Legal Study* (Columbus, 1976), pp. 25–6.
4. *Regula monachorum* liii, ed. R. Hanslik, *CSEL*, LXXV (Vienna, 1960), 123–6; lxi (ibid., pp. 141–3).
5. For further discussion of community size and references to relevant anthropological studies, see L. K. Little, 'The Size and Government of Medieval Communities', *Studia Gratiana*, XV (1972), 377–97.
6. L. White, jr., *Medieval Technology and Social Change* (Oxford, 1962), pp. 39–78. For an argument that makes population growth the single critical factor in the developments of these centuries, see D. C. North and R. P. Thomas, *The Rise of the Western World: A New Economic History* (Cambridge, 1973), p. 26. For a case study attributing the urban renaissance of eleventh-century Barcelona to an 'agricultural rather than a technological revolution', see J. E. Ruiz Domenec, 'The Urban Origins of Barcelona: Agricultural Revolution or Commercial Development', *Speculum*, LII (1977), 265–86.
7. Duby, *FEH*, p. 196.
8. Duby, *Rural Economy*, pp. 5–6, 11–15, 128–9; N. J. G. Pounds, *An Historical Geography of Europe, 450 B.C.–A.D. 1330* (Cambridge, 1973), pp. 253–8, 363–5; J. C. Russell, *FEH*, p. 30; idem, *Late Ancient and Medieval Population*, Transactions of the American Philosophical Society, XLIII, 3 (Philadelphia, 1958), p. 95.
9. B. H. Slicher Van Bath, *The Agrarian History of Western Europe, A.D. 500–1850*, tr. O. Ordish (London, 1963), pp. 73–4.
10. P. Toubert, *Les structures du Latium médiéval: le Latium méridional et la Sabine du IXe à la fin du XIIe siècle*, 2 vols., Bibliothèque des Ecoles françaises d'Athènes et de Rome, CCXXI (Rome, 1973), I, 290–549.
11. J. C. Russell, *British Medieval Population* (Albuquerque, 1948), pp. 246–60, 263, 280.
12. Duby, *FEH*, pp. 198–9.
13. J. H. Mundy, *Liberty and Political Power in Toulouse, 1050–1230* (New York, 1954), pp. 3–8.
14. P. Lavedan, *Histoire de l'urbanisme*, I (Paris, 1926), 227–444.
15. Luzzatto, *Economic History of Italy*, p. 80; Lopez, *CEH*, II, 303; Russell, *Late Ancient and Medieval Population*, pp. 110–11; H. van Werveke, *CEH*, III, 38–9; Pounds, *Historical Geography*, pp. 350–1.
16. van Werveke, *CEH*, III, 39; Pounds, *Historical Geography*, pp. 329, 350.
17. van Werveke, *CEH*, III, 39; Pounds, *Historical Geography*, p. 350; Russell, *Late Ancient and Medieval Population*, pp. 102–5, 111–12; J. B. Freed, *The Friars and German Society in the Thirteenth Century*, The Mediaeval Academy of America, Publication No. 86 (Cambridge, Mass., 1977), p. 53.
18. Russell, *Late Ancient and Medieval Population*, pp. 106–7, 101.
19. ibid., pp. 55–9, 105–11; Pounds, *Historical Geography*, pp. 326–31; R. S. Lopez and H. A. Miskimin, 'The Economic Depression of the Renaissance', *EcHR*, XIV (1962), 414–16: M. Beresford, *New Towns of the Middle Ages* (London, 1968) notes the settlement of 400 new communities in England alone between 1066 and 1349.
20. Luzzatto, *Economic History of Italy*, pp. 81, 92; M. Bloch, *French Rural History: An*

Essay on its basic Characteristics, tr. J. Sondheimer (Berkeley and Los Angeles, 1966), pp. 92–3.

21. Pounds, *Historical Geography*, p. 354; Duby, *Rural Economy*, p. 129.

22. J. Le Goff, 'Ordres mendiants et urbanisation dans la France médiévale', *Annales E. S. C.*, XXV (1970), 924–6, 937–41. For sectors, although economists and economic historians do not agree on the definitions, see M. Wolfe, 'The Concept of Economic Sectors', *Quarterly Journal of Economics*, LXIX (1955), 402–20.

23. On the social history of notaries, see Toubert, *Les structures du Latium*, I, 95–134.

24. Pounds, *Historical Geography*, pp. 351–2, 355.

25. T. R. Anderson, 'City: Comparative Urban Structure', *International Encyclopedia of the Social Sciences*, II, 466. Mols sets the figure at 4,000, see R. Mols, *Introduction à la démographie historique des villes d'Europe du XIVe au XVIIIe siècle*, 3 vols. (Louvain, 1954), I, xxii.

26. Cited by Le Goff, 'Ordres mendiants', p. 941, n. 2.

27. ibid., p. 930.

28. R. L. Reynolds, *Europe Emerges: Transition Toward an Industrial World-Wide Society, 600–1750* (Madison, 1961), p. 397.

29. Pounds, *Historical Geography*, pp. 339–40; Russell, *FEH*, p. 66.

30. E. Coornaert, 'Les ghildes médiévales (Ve–XIVe siècles)', *Revue historique*, CXCIX (1948), 22–55, 208–43; for a more narrowly economic interpretation, see G. Mickwitz, *Die Kartellfunctionen und ihre Bedeutung bei der Entstehung des Zunftwesens* (Helsingfor, 1936), p. 8.

31. For examples of urban crime, see *The London Eyre of 1241*, ed. H. M. Chew and M. Weinbaum (London, 1970).

32. Older works: W. W. Sanger, *The History of Prostitution: Its Extent, Causes, and Effects Throughout the World* (New York, 1858); P. Lacroix, *History of Prostitution*, written in French in 1851, tr. S. Putnam, 3 vols. (New York, 1926); M. Rabitaux, *De la prostitution en Europe depuis l'antiquité jusqu'à la fin du XVIe siècle* (Paris, 1865). See V. L. Bullough, *The History of Prostitution* (New Hyde Park, 1964), pp. 107–16; L. Le Pilear, *La prostitution du XIIIe au XVIIe siècle, Documents* (Paris, 1908), pp. 1–3.

33. Richard of Devizes, *The Chronicle of Richard of Devizes of the Time of Richard the First*, ed. and tr. J. T. Appleby (London, 1963), p. 65.

34. R. Brentano, *Rome Before Avignon: A Social History of Thirteenth-Century Rome* (New York, 1974), pp. 53–6, 85, 134–5, 286.

35. J. Leclercq, *The Love of Learning and the Desire for God: A Study of Monastic Culture*, tr. C. Marsh (New York, 1961), pp. 233–86; M.-D. Chenu, *Nature, Man, and Society in the Twelfth Century: Essays on New Theological Perspectives in the Latin West*, tr. J. Taylor and L. K. Little (Chicago, 1968), pp. 300–309.

36. William fitz Stephen *Vita Sancti Thomae prologus* xiii, ed. J. C. Robertson in *Materials for the Life of Thomas Becket*, 7 vols., RS, LXVII (London, 1875–85), III, 9. William's description of London is extensively quoted in C. N. L. Brooke and G. Keir, *London, 800–1216: The Shaping of a City* (Berkeley and Los Angeles, 1975), pp. 112–21.

37. See the illuminating discussion of the problem in seventeenth-century Massachusetts by B. Bailyn, *Education in the Forming of American Society* (Chapel Hill, 1960).

38. Chenu, *Nature, Man, and Society*, pp. 270–3.

39. Abelard *Historia Calamitatum; Texte critique avec une introduction*, ed. J. Monfrin (Paris, 1959), p. 94.

40. *Historia Occidentalis* vii (*HO*, p. 91).

41. Joinville *Histoire de Saint Louis*, ed. N. de Wailly (Paris, 1874), p. 395.

42. William fitz Stephen *Vita Sancti Thomae prologus* xii (ed. Robertson, p. 8); W. E. Jackson, *London's Fire Brigades* (London, 1967).

43. J. H. Mundy, 'Hospitals and Leproseries in Twelfth- and Early Thirteenth-

Century Toulouse', in *Essays in Medieval Life and Thought*, pp. 181–205.

44. E. L. Sabine, 'City Cleaning in Medieval London', *Speculum*, XII (1937), 19–43.

45. *Etudes sur l'histoire de la pauvreté (Moyen Age-XVIe siècle)*, ed. M. Mollat, 2 vols., Publications de la Sorbonne, Série 'Etudes', VIII (Paris, 1974); note particularly the editor's essay, 'Les problèmes de la pauvreté', I, 11–30, and that of J.-M. Bienvenu, 'Fondations charitables laïques au XIIe siècle: l'exemple de l'Anjou', II, 563–9. For Richard of Devizes, see above, n. 33.

46. J. Plesner, *L'émigration de la campagne à la ville libre de Florence au XIIIe siècle*, tr. F. Gleizal (Copenhagen, 1934); G. Luzzatto, 'L'inurbamento delle popolazioni rurali in Italia nei sec. XII–XIII', in *Studi di storia e diritto in onore di Enrico Besta*, 4 vols. (Milan, 1939), II, 183–203; Lopez, *CEH*, II, 298.

47. Russell, *FEH*, pp. 57–66; Pounds, *Historical Geography*, pp. 339–40; Plesner, *L'émigration*; D. Herlihy, 'The Tuscan Town in the Quattrocento: A Demographic Profile', *Medievalia et Humanistica*, n.s., I (1970), 81–109; F. Rörig, *The Medieval Town*, tr. D. Bryant (London, 1967), p. 115.

48. J. O. Prestwick, 'War and Finance in the Anglo-Norman State', *TRHS*, IV (1954), 453–87; H. G. Richardson and G. O. Sayles, *The Governance of Medieval England* (Edinburgh, 1963), pp. 46–7, 70–83. Cf. J. R. Strayer, 'The Two Levels of Feudalism', in *Life and Thought in the Early Middle Ages*, ed. R. S. Hoyt (Minneapolis, 1967), pp. 52–3.

49. B. D. Lyon, *From Fief to Indenture: The Transition from Feudal to Non-Feudal Contract in Western Europe*, Harvard Historical Studies, LXVIII (Cambridge, Mass., 1957), 23–40.

50. *Layettes du trésor des chartes*, II, ed. A. Teulet (Paris, 1886), 400.

51. S. Runciman, *The Sicilian Vespers* (Cambridge, 1958), pp. 53–77.

52. Bloch, *Feudal Society*, pp. 421–37.

53. J. R. Strayer, *Les gens de justice du Languedoc sous Philippe le Bel*, Cahiers de l'Association Marc Bloch de Toulouse, Etudes d'histoire méridionales, V (Toulouse, 1970).

54. R. W. Southern, *Western Society and the Church in the Middle Ages* (Harmondsworth, 1970), pp. 105–25; H.-W. Klewitz, 'Cancellaria: Ein Beitrag zur Geschichte des geistlichen Hofdienstes', *Deutsches Archiv für Erforschung des Mittelalters*, I (1937), 44–79; W. E. Lunt, *Papal Revenues in the Middle Ages*, 2 vols. (New York, 1934); D. B. Zema, 'Economic Reorganization of the Roman See during the Gregorian Reform', *Studi Gregoriani*, I (1947), 137–68; D. Waley, *The Papal State in the Thirteenth Century* (London, 1961); P. Herde, *Beiträge zum päpstlichen Kanzlei- und Urkundenwesen im dreizehnten Jahrhundert*, Münchener historische Studien, Abteilung Geschichtliche Hilfswissenschaften, I, 2nd ed. (Kallmünz, 1967).

55. R. Brentano, *Two Churches: England and Italy in the Thirteenth Century* (Princeton, 1968), p. 10.

56. Herde, *Beiträge*, pp. 80–100.

57. Lynch, *Simoniacal Entry*, pp. 61–75.

58. *MGH1*, SS, XXX2, 1473; R. W. Southern, *The Making of the Middle Ages* (London, 1961), pp. 128–30.

59. L. Bourgain, *La chaire française au 12e siècle* (Paris, 1879), p. 283.

60. Guibert de Nogent *De vita sua* i.11 (*PL*, CLVI, 853):'Bonus, ait, esset Rememsis archiepiscopatus, si non missas inde cantari oporteret.'

61. *COD*, pp. 197, 265.

62. Paris (1212), canon VIII (Mansi, XXII, 821); Rouen (1214), canon IX (ibid., 901).

63. V. and H. Hell, *Die grosse Wallfahrt des Mittelalters; Kunst an den romanischen Pilgerstrassen durch Frankreich und Spanien nach Santiago de Compostela* (Tübingen, 1964); Y. Bottineau, *Les chemins de Saint-Jacques* (Paris, 1966).

64. C. N. L. Brooke, *The Structure of Medieval Society* (London, 1971), fig. 97; O. Morisani, *Gli affreschi di S. Angelo in Formis* (Naples, 1962), fig. 52. The cycle of

frescoes is discussed in A. Grabar and C. Nordenfalk, *Romanesque Painting from the Eleventh to the Thirteenth Century*, tr. S. Gilbert (Lausanne, 1958), pp. 33–7.

65. R. Graham, 'An Appeal about 1175 for the Building Fund of St Paul's Cathedral Church', *Journal of the British Archaeological Association*, 3rd series, X (1945–7), 73–6.
66. C. R. Cheney, 'Church-Building in the Middle Ages', *Bulletin of the John Rylands Library*, XXXIV (1951), 20–36.
67. C. E. Woodruff, 'The Financial Aspect of the Cult of St Thomas of Canterbury', *Archaeologica Cantiana*, XLIV (1932), 13–32.
68. R. G. Witt, 'The Landlord and the Economic Revival of the Middle Ages in Northern Europe, 1000–1250', *American Historical Review*, LXXVI (1971), 965–88.
69. Duby, *Rural Economy*, pp. 52–3, 91, 180–1, 205–6, 208, 217–18.
70. Carus-Wilson, *CEH*, II, 381. See chart 3, dealing with specialization of jobs in the textile industry, in the exhaustive study of G. Espinas, *La draperie dans la Flandre française au moyen-âge*, 2 vols. (Paris, 1923). For an appreciation of the complexity of the textile industry, see G. de Poerck, *La draperie médiévale en Flandre et en Artois: Technique et terminologie*, 3 vols. (Bruges, 1951).
71. G. Post 'Masters' Salaries and Student-Fees in the Medieval Universities', *Speculum*, VII (1932), 181–98. Some references are found in H. Rashdall, *The Universities of Europe in the Middle Ages*, rev. ed. F. M. Powicke and A. B. Emden, 3 vols. (Oxford, 1936), I, 208–9, 229, 240–1, 439, 487–8; III, 163.
72. P. Kirbe, *Scholarly Privileges in the Middle Ages* (Cambridge, Mass., 1962).
73. G. Paré, A. Brunet, and P. Tremblay, *La renaissance du XIIe siècle: Les écoles et l'enseignement*, Publications de l'Institut d'Etudes médiévales d'Ottowa, III (Paris, 1933), 75–84.
74. *Metalogicon* i.4 (*PL*, CXCIX, 831).
75. For notaries, see above, n. 23.
76. M. Weber, 'Religious Rejections of the World and Their Directions', in *From Max Weber: Essays in Sociology*, ed. and tr. H. H. Gerth and C. W. Mills (New York, 1958), p. 331. Cf. *The Sociology of Georg Simmel*, ed. and tr. K. R. Wolff (Glencoe, 1950), pp. 335, 411–15.
77. J. A. Yunck, *The Lineage of Lady Meed: The Development of Mediaeval Venality Satire*, University of Notre Dame, Publications in Mediaeval Studies, XVII (Notre Dame, 1963), 105.
78. G. Owst, *Literature and Pulpit in Medieval England* (Cambridge, 1933), p. 280.
79. K. Strecker, ed., *Moralisch-satirische Gedichte Walters von Chatillon* (Heidelberg, 1929), p. 6.
80. *Opusculum* XXX (*PL*, CXLV, 523).
81. *Narratio de Alberico presbytero et ejus sceleribus*, in E. Martène and U. Durand, *Veterum Scriptorum et Monumentorum amplissima Collectio*, I (Paris, 1724), 253–5.
82. MS, London, BL, Add. 29253, f. 410v. Reproduced in Little, 'Pride Goes before Avarice', fig. 10.
83. MS, London, BL, Add. 29253, f. 41v. Reproduced in Little, 'Pride Goes before Avarice', fig. 11.
84. MS, Oxford, Bodleian, Douce 6, f. 157v.
85. A. Boinet, *La miniature carolingienne, ses origines, son développement* (Paris, 1913), pl. 41; A. Boeckler, *Das goldener Evangelienbuch Heinrichs III.* (Berlin, 1933), pls. 8, 9. For this observation and the references I am grateful to Professor Carl Nordenfalk.
86. S. Freud, *The Interpretation of Dreams*, The Standard Edition, ed. J. Strachey *et al.*, IV (London, 1953), 200; T. Reik, 'Gold und Kot', *Internationale Zeitschrift für ärztliche Psychoanalyse*, III (1915), 183. Cf. J. Harnik, 'Kulturgeschichtliche Studien zum Thema: Geldkomplex und Analerotik', ibid., V (1919), 121–2. R. G. D'Andrade, 'Anthropological Studies of Dreams', in *Psychological Anthropology: Approaches to Culture and Personality*, ed. F. L. K. Hsu (Homewood, 1961), pp.

296–332. Cf. C. G. Seligman, 'Anthropology and Psychology', *Journal of the Royal Anthropological Institute*, LIV (1924), 13–46; and 'Anthropological Perspective and Psychological Theory', ibid., LXII (1932), 193–228; J. S. Lincoln, *The Dream in Primitive Cultures* (London, 1935); W. H. Desmonde, *Magic, Myth, and Money: the Origin of Money in Religious Ritual* (New York, 1962). On the scatological symbolism of gold, see P. de Carvalho-Neto, *Folklore and Psychology*, tr. J. Wilson (Coral Gables, 1972), pp. 100–10.

87. E. Durkheim, *The Division of Labor in Society*, tr. G. Simpson (Glencoe, 1947), pp. 130–1; I am deeply indebted to Professor Charles M. Radding of Loyola University of Chicago for his helpful criticism, in particular on this point concerning social complexity and morality.

88. Gervase of Tilbury *Otia Imperialia ad Ottonem IV. Imperatorem* xix, ed. G. W. Leibnitz, *Scriptores rerum Brunswicensium*, 4 vols. (Hanover, 1707), I, 898; cf. J. Le Goff, *FEH*, p. 72.

89. Little, 'Pride Goes before Avarice', p. 20.

90. *Ep.* i.15 (*PL*, CXLIV, 234).

91. *Ep.* iii.2 (ibid., 289).

92. *Op.* xii.4 (*PL*, CXLV, 255).

93. *Polycraticus* viii.4, ed. C. C. J. Webb, *Policraticus, sive de nugis curialium et vestigiis philosophorum libri VIII*, 2 vols. (Oxford, 1909), II, 241.

94. *PL*, CXCI, 1059.

95. *PL*, CLXXXIV, 1266.

96. *PL*, CCX, 465.

97. *De miseria humane conditionis* 2.14, ed. M. Maccarrone (Lucca, 1955), pp. 49–50. For avarice with an open mouth, see Little, 'Pride Goes before Avarice', fig. 7; with closed mouth, ibid., fig. 6; at Chartres, ibid., fig. 3; and at Parma, ibid., fig. 9. Avarice as a fat monster is at Journay-en-Bray; one avarice in the guise of a distinguished-looking person is at Chanteuges and another in the Museum of Fine Arts, Boston.

98. For examples, see Little, 'Pride Goes before Avarice', figs. 4, 8.

99. M. Schapiro, 'The Romanesque Sculpture of Moissac', *The Art Bulletin*, XIII (1931), 249–350, 464–531, especially pp. 496–511.

100. *Tractatus Garsiae or The Translation of the Relics of SS. Gold and Silver*, ed. and tr. R. M. Thomson, Textus Minores, XLVI (Leiden, 1973).

101. For the *Gospel According to the Mark of Silver*, see P. Lehmann, *Die Parodie im Mittelalter*, 2nd ed. (Stuttgart, 1963), pp. 39–40, 183–8. For the satirical acclamation, see *Moralisch-satirische Gedichte* (ed. Strecker, pp. 110–112). Cf. Alan of Lille in *PL*, CCX, 464: 'Nummus vincit, nummus mundum regit, nummus imperat universis.' Concerning the *Christus vincit* triad, see E. H. Kantorowicz, *Laudes Regiae: A Study in Liturgical Acclamations and Medieval Ruler Worship*, University of California Publications in History, XXXIII (Berkeley and Los Angeles, 1946), 21–31. While probably an amalgam of the triumphal cheers of Roman and Frankish warriors, the phrase had become a central element of the royal litany. This liturgical phrase reverted to soldiers when the crusaders took it up as a battle cry.

102. Mansi, VI, 404.

103. *Decretum* de pen., dist. 5, c.2 (*CJC*, I, 1240): 'quia difficile est inter ementis vendentisque commercium non intervenire peccatum.'

104. *Decretum*, Ia pars, dist. 88, c.11 (ibid., I, 308): 'Mercator vix aut nunquam potest Deo placere.'

105. *Decretum* C.12, q.1, c.7 (ibid., I, 678). See the discussion of this text by L. Prosdocimi, 'Chierici e laici nella società occidentale del sec. XII: A proposito di Decr. Grat. C. XII, q. 1, c. 7: "Duo sunt genera Christianorum"', *Annali della Facoltà di Giurisprudenza dell'Università di Genova*, III (1964), 241–62.

106. de Roover, *CEH*, III, 47.
107. G. Le Bras, ibid., 560.
108. *Vita sancti Guidonis* (*AASS*, September, IV, 42).
109. Honorius of Autun *Elucidarium* ii.18, 'De variis laicorum statibus', ed., Y. Lefèvre, *L'Elucidarium et les lucidaires: Contribution à l'histoire des croyances religieuses en France au moyen âge* (Paris, 1954), pp. 428–9.
110. *Sententiarum* iv.16.2 (*PL*, CXCII, 878).
111. J. Mabillon, *Annales ordinis sancti Benedicti* (Lucca, 1739–45), IV, 357.
112. *COD*, p. 223.
113. *Historia pontificalis* xlii, ed. M. Chibnall (Edinburgh, 1961), p. 85.
114. Peter the Chanter *Verbum abbreviatum* (*PL*, CCV, 158); see below, at the conclusion of chapter 3.
115. J. T. Noonan, *The Scholastic Analysis of Usury* (Cambridge, Mass., 1957), pp. 42–4.
116. ibid., pp. 41–2.
117. G. Post, K. Giocarinis, and R. Kay, 'The Medieval Heritage of a Humanistic Ideal: "Scientia donum dei est, unde vendi non potest"', *Traditio*, XI (1955), 195–234; J. Le Goff, 'Métiers licites et métiers illicites dans l'Occident médiéval', *Etudes historiques, Annales de l'Ecole des Hautes Etudes de Gand*, V (1963), 41–57; and 'Métier et profession d'après les manuels de confesseur au moyen âge', in *Beiträge zum Berufsbewusstsein des mittelalterlichen Menschen*, ed. P. Wilpert, Miscellanea Mediaevalia, III (Berlin, 1964), 44–60.
118. For the *cambiatores*, see Toubert, *Les structures du Latium*, p. 677.
119. Roger of Wendover *Flores Historiarum*, ed. H. G. Hewlett, 3 vols., RS, LXXXIV (London, 1886–89), II, 28–9. Ellen S. Karnofsky kindly brought this text as well as the two that follow to my attention.
120. Roger of Wendover *Flores Historiarum* (ibid., I, 247).
121. Ordericus Vitalis *Historiae ecclesiasticae libri tredecim* viii.17, ed. A. Le Prevost, 5 vols., *Société de l'Histoire de France* (Paris, 1838–55), III, 373–4.
122. MS, London, BL, Yates Thompson, 13, f. 143.
123. *La vie de saint Alexis*, ed. C. Storey, *Blackwell's French Texts* (Oxford, 1968); A. Gieysztor, 'La légende de saint Alexis en occident: un idéal de pauvreté', in *Etudes sur l'histoire de la pauvreté*, ed. Mollat, I, 124–39.

Chapter 3 : The Jews in Christian Europe

1. B. Blumenkranz, *Juifs et chrétiens dans le monde occidental, 430–1096* (Paris, 1960), part 1.
2. Cited by Duby, *Warriors and Peasants*, p. 134.
3. S. W. Baron, *A Social and Religious History of the Jews*, 2nd ed., 13 vols. (New York, 1952–67), IV, 164; Blumenkranz, *Juifs et chrétiens*, p. 20.
4. *Regesten zur Geschichte der Juden im fränkischen und deutschen Reiche bis zum Jahre 1273*, ed. J. Aronius (Berlin, 1902), no. 168.
5. M. Güdemann, *Geschichte des Erziehungswesens und der Cultur der abendländischen Juden während des Mittelalters und der neureren Zeit*, 3 vols. (Vienna, 1880–88), I, 92–106.
6. *COD*, p. 266.
7. Y. Baer, *A History of the Jews in Christian Spain*, tr. L. Schoffman, 2 vols. (Philadelphia, 1961–6), I, 39–110; I. Loeb, 'Le nombre des Juifs de Castille et d'Espagne au moyen âge,' *Revue des études juives*, XIV (1887), 183; L. Poliakov, *De Mahomet aux Marranes* (Paris, 1961), p. 127; Baron, *History*, IV, 34. Cf. G. Jackson, *The Making of Medieval Spain* (New York, 1972), pp. 99–110; and J. L. Schneidman, *The Rise of the Aragonese-Catalon Empire, 1200–1350*, 2 vols. (New York, 1970), II, 419–20.

8. *PL*, CXLV, 41.
9. C. Roth, *The History of the Jews in Italy* (Philadelphia, 1946), pp. 74, 83; and 'Genoese Jews in the 13th Century', *Speculum*, XXV (1950), 190–1. Cf. Baron, *History*, IV, 24–6.
10. G. Caro, *Sozial- und Wirtschaftsgeschichte der Juden im Mittelalter und der Neuzeit*, 2 vols. (Leipzig, 1908, 1920), I, 171–4; J. Stengers, *Les juifs dans les Pays-bas au Moyen Age* (Brussels, 1950), pp. 9–16.
11. B. Blumenkranz, 'Géographie historique d'un thème de l'iconographie religieuse: les représentations de *Synagoga* en France', in *Mélanges offerts à René Crozet*, ed. P. Gallais and Y.-J. Riou, 2 vols. (Poitiers, 1966), pp. 1141, 1143. R. Chazan, *Medieval Jewry in Northern France: A Political and Social History*, The Johns Hopkins University Studies in History and Political Science, 91st series (Baltimore, 1973), pp. 207–220.
12. Guibert of Nogent *De vita sua* ii.5 (*PL*, CLVI, 903).
13. N. Golb, 'New Light on the Persecution of French Jews at the Time of the First Crusade', *Proceedings of the American Academy for Jewish Research*, XXXIV (1966), 12; I. Loeb, 'Les négociants juifs à Marseilles au milieu du XIIIe siècle', *Revue des études juives*, XVI (1888), 73–83; J. Regné, 'Etude sur la condition des juifs de Narbonne au Ve au XIVe siècle', ibid., LVIII (1909), 75–105, 200–25; R. W. Emery, *The Jews of Perpignan in the Thirteenth Century: An Economic Study Based on Notarial Records* (New York, 1959), pp. 11–13, 16–25. For Manosque, in Provence, see J. Shatzmiller, *Recherches sur la communauté juive de Manosque au moyen age, 1241–1329*, Etudes juives, XV (Paris, 1973), p. 139. A study of the royal inquests in the middle of the thirteenth century shows that three-fourths of all complaints against Jews had to do with loans; see G. Nahon, 'Le crédit et les Juifs dans la France du XIIIe siècle,' *Annales E. S. C.*, XXIV (1969), 1121–48.
14. H. G. Richardson, *The English Jewry Under Angevin Kings* (London, 1960), pp 63, 93–4, 121, 161–75; P. Elman, 'Jewish Trade in Thirteenth Century England', *Historia Judaica*, I (1938), 91–104; 'The Economic Causes of the Expulsion of the Jews in 1290', *Economic History Review*, VII (1937), 145–54; W. E. Rhodes, 'The Italian Bankers in England and their Loans to Edward I and Edward II', chap. 5 of *Historical Essays*, ed. T. F. Tout and J. Tait (Manchester, 1907), pp. 137–68; R. W. Kaeuper, *Bankers to the Crown: The Riccardi of Lucca and Edward I* (Princeton, 1973).
15. Hermannus quondam Judaeus *Opusculum de conversione sua* ii (*MGH, Quellen zur Geistesgeschichte*, IV, 72): 'Siquidem omnes Iudei negotiationi inserviunt.'
16. Baron, *History*, IV, 184–5; Caro, *Sozial- und Wirtschaftsgeschichte*, I, 434.
17. J. W. Parkes, *The Jew in the Medieval Community: A Study of his Political and Economic Situation* (London, 1938), pp. 37–9; Adhémar of Chabannes *Historiarum libri III* iii.47 (*MGH, SS*, IV, 136–7).
18. Alpertus *De diversitate temporum* i.7 (ibid., 704).
19. Adhémar of Chabannes *Historiarum libri III* iii.52 (ibid., 139); Parkes, *Jew in the Medieval Community*, pp. 43–4; Blumenkranz, *Juifs et chrétiens*, pp. 55–6.
20. Baron, *History*, IX, 35.
21. *PL*, CLXVI, 1386–7.
22. L. Poliakov, *The History of Anti-Semitism*, I, tr., R. Howard (New York, 1965), pp. 43–6; Baron, *History*, IV, 94–106.
23. Guibert of Nogent *De vita sua* ii.5 (*PL*, CLVI, 903).
24. Poliakov, *Anti-Semitism*, p. 42; Golb, 'New Light'; cf. Richard of Poitiers in *HF*, XII, 411. Chazan, *Medieval Jewry*, p. 28, stresses that 1171 was a more decisive moment for the northern French Jewry than 1095–6.
25. Otto of Freising *Gesta Frederici imperatoris* i.37–9, ed. G. Waitz, 3rd ed. (Hanover and Leipzig, 1912), pp. 58–9.
26. Otto of Freising *Gesta* i.40 (ibid., pp. 59, 61–3).

27. H. Bloch, 'The Schism of Anacletus II and the Glanfeuil Forgeries of Peter the Deacon of Monte Cassino', *Traditio*, VIII (1952), 159–264.
28. Baron, *History*, IV, 124–6.
29. Rigord *Gesta Philippi Augusti* xii-xiv, ed. H.-F. Delaborde (Paris, 1882), pp. 24–7.
30. B. Blumenkranz, *Les auteurs chrétiens latins du moyen age sur les juifs et le judaisme* (Paris, 1963); A. Williams, *Adversus Judaeos: A Bird's-Eye View of Christian Apologiae Until the Renaissance* (Cambridge, 1935), pp. 366–74, 400–7.
31. *PL*, CLXXXIX, 507–650.
32. M. Schlauch, 'The Allegory of Church and Synagogue', *Speculum*, XIV (1939), 448–50.
33. G. K. Anderson, *The Legend of the Wandering Jew* (Providence, 1965), pp. 18–22; MP, V, 341–2.
34. L. Canet, 'La prière "Pro judaeis" de la liturgie catholique romaine', *Revue des études juives*, LXI (1911), 213–21; and R. Fawtier, 'The Jews in the "Use of York" ', *Bulletin of the John Rylands Library*, V (1918–20), 381–5.
35. B. Blumenkranz, *Le juif médiéval au miroir de l'art chrétien* (Paris, 1966), pp. 85, 105–109; W. S. Seiferth, *Synagogue and Church in the Middle Ages: Two Symbols in Art and Literature*, tr. L. Chadeayne and P. Gottwald (New York, 1970), pls. 1–65; I. Shachar, *The 'Judensau': A Medieval Anti-Jewish Motif and Its History*, Warburg Institute Surveys, V (London, 1974).
36 S. Grayzel, *The Church and the Jews in the XIIIth Century*, rev. ed. (New York, 1966), pp. 76–8, 92–5.
37. Baer, *Jews in Christian Spain*, I, 44–5, 85, 88–90.
38. G. I. Langmuir, ' "Judei nostri" and the Beginning of Capetian Legislation', *Traditio*, XVI (1960), 203–30; F. Pollock and F. W. Maitland, *The History of English Law*, 2nd ed., 2 vols. (Cambridge, 1905), I, 468; Poliakov, *Anti-Semitism*, p. 76; G. Kisch, *The Jews in Medieval Germany: A Study of Their Legal and Social Status* (Chicago, 1949), p. 133.
39. *Tractatus contra Judaeorum inveteratam duritiem* iii (*PL*, CLXXXIX, 551).
40. G. I. Langmuir, 'The Knight's Tale of Young Hugh of Lincoln', *Speculum*, XLVII (1972), 459–82.
41. Thomas of Cantimpré *Bonum universale de Apibus* ii.29.17, ed. G. Colverenius (Douai, 1627), p. 145.
42. J. Tractenberg, *The Devil and the Jews: The Medieval Conception of the Jew and its Relation to Modern Antisemitism* (New Haven, 1943), pp. 124–39; Poliakov, *Anti-Semitism*, pp. 56–64.
43. Langmuir, 'The Knight's Tale', pp. 464–9.
44. Tractenberg, *Devil and the Jews*, p. 114; Baron, *History*, XI, 164–70.
45. K. Young, *The Drama of the Medieval Church*, 2 vols. (Oxford, 1933), I, 492–539; E. K. Chambers, *The Medieval Stage*, 2 vols. (Oxford, 1903), II, 133; V. A. Kolve, *The Play Called Corpus Christi* (Stanford, 1966), pp. 33–56; F. E. Barnes, 'The Background and Sources of the Croxton Play of the Sacrament', The University of Chicago, Ph.D. dissertation, 1926; and D. Devlin, '*Corpus Christi*: A Study in Medieval Eucharistic Theory, Devotion, and Practice', The University of Chicago, Ph.D. dissertation, 1975.
46. G. I. Langmuir, 'From Xenophobia to Prejudice: The Emergence of Anti-Semitism in the Thirteenth Century', paper delivered at the annual meeting of the American Historical Association, Toronto, 29 December 1967.
47. Baron, *History*, XI, 158–64; Tractenberg, *Devil and the Jews*, pp. 97–108.
48. Letter 130 (*LPV*, I, 327–30).
49. *HF*, XII, 215; cf. Rigord, cited above, n. 29.
50. MP, V, 114–15.
51. Poliakov, *Anti-Semitism*, p. 124.

52. Güdemann, *Geschichte des Erziehungswesens*, I, 145; Stengers, *Juifs dans les Pays-bas*, pp. 55–6.
53. Tractenberg, *Devil and the Jews*, p. 48.
54. Blumenkranz, *Le juif médiéval*, p. 45.
55. Pseudo-Gilbert Crispin *Disputatio ecclesiae et synagogae*, ed. E. Marténe and U. Durand, *Thesaurus novus Anecdotorum*, 5 vols. (Paris, 1717), V, 1497–1506.
56. Thomas of Froidmont [Bernard] *Liber de modo bene vivendi* xlv (*PL*, CLXXXIV, 1266).
57. MP, III, 163.
58. On the tympanum at Conques Judas hanged has a moneybag suspended from his neck in the manner of avarice personified. For an example of Judas dressed as a typical Jew, see Little, 'Pride Goes before Avarice', fig. 5.
59. Young, *Drama of the Medieval Church*, I, 101–2.
60. P. F. Baum, 'The Medieval Legend of Judas Iscariot', *Publications of the Modern Language Association of America*, XXXI (1916), 481–632; on p. 497 Baum discussed the manuscript known as Lc, from the late twelfth or early thirteenth century, which was almost certainly in the possession of Bury St Edmunds. Cf. W. Creizenach, *Judas Ischarioth in Legende und Sage des Mittelalters* (Halle, 1875).
61. Othlon de Saint-Emmeran *Liber de cursu spirituali* vii (*PL*, CXLVI, 160): '... quae de Iuda traditore sunt dicta, congruunt iudacio populo....' Cf. Geoffrey of Vendôme *Opuscula* vii (*PL*, CLVII, 222).
62. Cited by B. Monod, 'Juifs sorciers et hérétiques au moyen age', *Revue des études juives*, XLVI (1903), 237–45.
63. Golb, 'New Light', p. 18; Parkes, *Jew in the Medieval Community*, pp. 64, 371.
64. ibid., pp. 367–82.
    de Cluny entre 1080 et 1155', *Annales E. S. C.*, VII (1952), 169–70; L. Voss, *Heinrich von Blois, Bischof von Winchester (1129–71)*, Historische Studien, CCX (Berlin, 1932), pp. 114–15.
66. Letter 130 (*LPV*, I, 327–30).
67. *Ep.* ccclxiii (*PL*, CLXXXII, 567): 'Taceo quod sicubi desunt, pejus judaizare dolemus Christianos, feneratores, si tamen Christianos, et non magis baptizatos Judaeos convenit appellari.'
68. DuCange, *Glossarium mediae et infimae latinitatis* (Niort, 1887), IV, 437.
69. I found the following instances of scholars working towards a similar interpretation: O. Fenichel, 'Elements of a Psychoanalytic Theory of Anti-Semitism', in *Anti-Semitism, A Social Disease*, ed. E. Simmel (New York, 1946), p. 29; R. M. Loewenstein, *Christians and Jews: A Psychoanalytic Study*, tr. V. Damman (New York, 1951), p. 84; F. G. Friedman and K. Rahner, 'Unbefangenheit und Anspruch: ein Briefwechsel zum jüdisch-christlichen Gespräch', *Stimmen der Zeit*, CLXXVIII (1966), 81–97, especially p. 85 where Friedman is writing; and G. Langmuir, 'Anti-Judaism as the Necessary Preparation for Anti-Semitism', *Viator*, II (1971), 388.
70. Rupert of Deutz *Commentaria in duodecim prophetas minores: in Habacuc prophetam* ii (*PL*, CLXVIII, 616): 'Quisnam ille est, qui congregat, vel congregavit avaritiam malam domui suae, magis quam populus Judaicus ...?'
71. See the complaint by Peter the Chanter *Verbum abbreviatum* (*PL*, CCV, 158); discussed by J. W. Baldwin, *Masters, Princes, and Merchants: the Social Views of Peter the Chanter and his Circle*, 2 vols. (Princeton, 1970), I, 298–300.

Chapter 4: The old order

1. P. Guilhiermoz, *Essai sur l'origine de la noblesse en France au moyen âge* (Paris, 1902), pp. 370–3; J. Le Goff, 'Note sur société tripartie, idéologie monarchique et

renouveau économique dans la chrétienté du IXe au XIIe siècle', in *L'Europe aux IXe–XIe siècles: Aux origines des états nationaux*, ed. T. Manteuffel and A. Gieysztor (Warsaw, 1968), pp. 63–71.

2. C. de Lasteyrie, *L'Abbaye de Saint-Martial de Limoges* (Paris, 1901), p. 422; H. E. J. Cowdrey, 'Unions and Confraternity with Cluny', *Journal of Ecclesiastical History*, XVI (1965), 152–62.

3. J. Hourlier, 'Cluny et la notion de l'ordre religieux', in *A Cluny: Congrès scientifique de Cluny 9–11 juillet 1949 en l'honneur des Saints Abbés Odon et Odilon* (Dijon, 1950), pp. 219–26; J. Evans, *The Romanesque Architecture of the Order of Cluny* (Cambridge, 1938), p. 7; D. Knowles, *From Pachomius to Ignatius: A Study in the Constitutional History of the Religious Orders* (Oxford, 1966), pp. 10–15.

4. G. de Valous, 'Les monastères et la pénétration française en Espagne du XIe au XIIIe siècle', *Revue Mabillon*, XXX (1940), 89. H. E. J. Cowdrey, *The Cluniacs and the Gregorian Reform* (Oxford, 1970), pp. 214–19.

5. H. Jakobs, *Die Hirsauer. Ihre Ausbreitung und Rechtstellung im Zeitalter des Investiturstreites*, Kölner historische Abhandlungen, IV (Köln-Graz, 1961); cf. E. Werner, 'Bemerkungen zur Hirsauer Bewegung', *Wissenschaftliche Zeitschrift der Karl-Marx-Universität Leipzig, Gesellschafts- und Sprachwissenschaftliche Reihe*, II (1952–3), 13.

6. K. Hallinger, *Gorze-Kluny: Studien zu den monastischen Lebensformen und Gegensätzen im Hochmittelalter*, 2 vols., Studia Anselmiana, XXII–XXV (Rome, 1950–51), pp. 49–317.

7. D. Knowles and R. Hadcock, *Medieval Religious Houses: England and Wales* (London, 1953), pp. 359–60.

8. B. Hamilton, 'The Monastery of S. Alessio and the Religious and Intellectual Renaissance in Tenth-Century Rome', *Studies in Medieval and Renaissance History*, II (1965), 263–310; idem, 'The Monastic Revival in Tenth Century Rome', *Studia Monastica*, IV (1962), 35–68.

9. *The Monastic Agreement of the Monks and Nuns of the English Nation*, ed. and tr. T. Symons (London, 1953).

10. de Valous, 'Les monastères,' pp. 77–97; Cowdrey, *The Cluniacs*, p. 216.

11. G. Chenesseau, *L'abbaye de Fleury à Saint-Benoît-sur-Loire* (Paris, 1931), pp. 21–3; cf. F. Lot and R. Fawtier, *Histoire des institutions françaises au moyen âge*, III, 'Institutions ecclésiastiques' (Paris, 1962), 49–77.

12. The fullest general account remains that of G. de Valous, *Le monachisme clunisien des origines au XVe siècle: vie intérieure des monastères et organisation de l'ordre*, 2 vols., Archives de la France monastique, XXXIX–XL (Paris, 1935); also the same author's article in *DHGE*, XIII, 35–174.

13. *Bibliotheca Cluniacensis*, ed. M. Marrier and A. Duchesne (Paris, 1614), cols. 9–12.

14. ibid., c. 11: 'Et certe pauperior est possessione et numerosa fraternitate.'

15. Hamilton, 'Monastic Revival', pp. 46–60.

16. Hamilton, 'Monastery of S. Alessio', p. 279.

17. Hallinger, *Gorze-Kluny*, p. 55.

18. *The Monastic Constitutions of Lanfranc*, ed. and tr. D. Knowles (London, 1951), p. viii.

19. A study of Cluny's social connections is found in J. Fechter, *Cluny, Adel und Volk: Studien über das Verhältnis des Klosters zu den Ständen (910–1156)* (Stuttgart, 1966).

20. H.-E. Mager, 'Studien über das Verhältnis der Cluniacenser zum Eigenkirchenwesen', in *Neue Forschungen über Cluny und die Cluniacenser*, ed. G. Tellenbach (Freiburg-im-Breisgau, 1959), pp. 167–217. Cf. M. Dillay, 'Le régime de l'église privée du XIe au XIIIe s. dans l'Anjou, le Maine et la Touraine', *Revue historique de droit français et étranger*, 4th ser., IV (1925), 253–94; and O. Gautier, 'Recherches sur les possessions et les prieurés de l'Abbaye de Marmoutier du Xe au XIIIe siècle', *Revue Mabillon*, LIV (1964), 125–33; G. Constable, *Monastic Tithes from their Origins to the Twelfth Century* (Cambridge, 1964), pp. 57–83.

21. D. Duby, *La société aux XIe et XIIe siècles dans la région mâconnaise* (Paris, 1971), p. 267.
22. D. Knowles, *The Monastic Order in England*, 2nd ed. (Cambridge, 1963), p. 712.
23. Duby, *La société*, pp. 145–8.
24. M. Salmi, *L'Abbazia di Pomposa* (Rome, 1936).
25. Hamilton, 'Monastic Revival', pp. 35–68; Toubert, *Les structures du Latium*, I, 93–4; B. Bligny, 'Monachisme et pauvretè au XIIe siècle', in *La povertà del secolo XII e Francesco d'Assisi* (Assisi, 1975), pp. 99–147.
26. *Bibliotheca Cluniacensis*, c. 520.
27. Duby, *Warriors and Peasants*, p. 165.
28. H. C. Kreuger, 'The Italian Cities and the Arabs before 1095', Chap. II, sect. B in *A History of the Crusades*, ed. K. M. Setton, I (Philadelphia, 1955), 52.
29. C. J. Bishko, 'Liturgical Intercessions for the King-Emperors of Leon', *Studia Monastica*, III (1961), 53–76. Texts in *Recueil des chartes de l'abbaye de Cluny*, ed. A Bernard and A. Bruel, 6 vols. (Paris, 1876–1903), no. 3441 (IV, 551–3), no. 3509 (IV, 627–9).
30. *Recueil des chartes*, no. 3638 (IV, 809–10).
31. *Recueil des chartes*, no. 3789 (V, 135), no. 3790 (V, 136), no. 4132 (V, 475–82), no. 4143 (V, 490–505). These were used by G. de Valous, *Le temporel et la situation financière des établissements de l'Ordre de Cluny du XIIe au XIVe siècle, particulièrement dans les provinces françaises*, Archives de la France monastique, XLI (Paris, 1935); and far more satisfactorily by G. Duby, 'Economie domaniale et économie monétaire: Le budget de l'abbaye de Cluny entre 1080 et 1155', *Annales E. S. C.*, VII (1952), 155–71.
32. J. Sydow, 'Cluny und die Anfänge der apostolischen Kammer', *Studien und Mitteilungen zur Geschichte des Benediktinerordens und seiner Zweige*, LXIII (1951), 45–66.
33. Duby, *Warriors and Peasants*, p. 91.
34. ibid., p. 215.
35. *Recueil des chartes*, no. 3071 (IV, 254).
36. Duby, *La société*, p. 278.
37. Toubert, *Les structures du Latium*, I, 611; A Graboïs, 'L'abbaye de Saint-Denis et les Juifs sous l'abbatiat de Suger', *Annales E. S. C.*, XXIV (1969), 1188.
38. *Memoriale Guilielmi Venturae civis Astensis* xxvi, in *Rerum italicarum scriptores*, ed. L. Muratori, vol. XI (Milan, 1727), 192; cited by Brentano, *Rome Before Avignon*, p. 54.
39. *Recueil des chartes*, no. 4069 (V, 419–21), no. 4143 (V, 490–505), no. 4205 (V, 548–51). Cf. P. Deguerce, 'Cluny, étude d'évolution urbaine', *Etudes Rhodaniennes* (1936–37), 121–34. For Tournus, see P. Juénin, *Nouvelle histoire de l'abbaye royale et collégiale de Saint-Filibert et de la ville de Tournus*, 2 vols. (Dijon, 1733); documents in Vol. II.
40. *Recueil des chartes*, no. 3606 (IV, 765–8), no. 3806 (V, 153–5), no. 4054 (V, 408–409); Duby, *La société*, pp. 267, 270–4. *Bibliotheca Cluniacensis*, c. 1662.
41. *Libellus de diversis ordinibus et professionibus qui sunt in aecclesia* ii, ed. and tr. G. Constable and B. Smith (Oxford, 1972), p. 18.
42. W. Urry, *Canterbury under the Angevin Kings* (London, 1967), pp. 23–39.
43. John of Salerno *Vita s. Odonis* i.16 (*PL*, CXXXIII, 51); *Chronicon monasterii de bello*, ed. J. S. Brewer (London, 1846), pp. 51–2.
44. B. H. Rosenwein, 'Feudal War and Monastic Peace: Cluniac Liturgy as Ritual Aggression', *Viator*, II (1971), 132.
45. N. Hunt, *Cluny Under Saint Hugh, 1049–1109* (London, 1967), pp. 82–3; *NCE*, VI, 1141–2; Knowles, *Monastic Order*, pp. 425–6, 713–14.
46. W. Jorden, *Das cluniazensische Totengedächtniswesen vornehmlich unter den drei ersten Abten Berno, Odo und Aymard (910–54)*, Münsterische Beiträge zur Theologie, Heft 15 (Münster in Westf., 1930), pp. 78–84; Bishko, 'Liturgical Intercessions', pp.

53–76; C. Erdmann, *Die Entstehung des Kreuzzugsgedankens,* Forschungen zur Kirchen- und Geistesgeschichte, VII (Stuttgart, 1935), 51–85.

47. *Monastic Agreement,* pp. 5, 13, 14, 16, 20, 21, 22, 23.

48. *Antiquiores consuetudines Cluniacensis monasterii* iii.24 (*PL,* CXLIX, 766); cf. *Monastic Agreement,* pp. 61–2.

49. For the different types of the *anniversarium,* see *Consuetudines cenobii Cluniacensis,* ed. M. Herrgott, *Vetus disciplina monastica* (Paris, 1726), pp. 246, 272, 278.

50. *Statuta sancti Hugonis abbatis Cluniacensis pro Alphonso rege Hispaniarum tanquam insigni benefactore* (*PL,* CLIX, 945–6).

51. Mollat, *Etudes sur l'histoire de la pauvreté,* I, 25, 91–2, 145, 151–2, 214, 448.

52. Suger, *Oeuvres complètes de Suger,* ed. A. Lecoy de la Marche, Société de l'histoire de France (Paris, 1867), pp. 159–78; Jocelin of Brakelond, *The Chronicle of Jocelin of Brakelond Concerning the Acts of Samson, Abbot of the Monastery of St. Edmond,* ed. and tr. H. E. Butler (London, 1949). Another great twelfth-century abbot was Walter de Luci of Battle: 'The abbey itself, whose government he had undertaken in unprosperous times, he protected from the violence of its adversaries with all his might, and those things of which it had been despoiled, he vigorously in the subsequent season of tranquillity recovered.' *Chronicon* (ed. Brewer, pp. 134–8).

53. Voss, *Heinrich von Blois,* pp. 114–15, 118. For the sale of gold and silver from reliquaries at Battle Abbey to get cash for purchasing land, see *Chronicon* (ed. Brewer, pp. 57–8).

54. Duby, 'Economie domaniale', pp. 164–9, and *La société,* p. 280.

55. Letter 130 (*LPV,* I, 327–30).

56. Letter 131 (ibid., 332): 'Inde est quod Cluniacus debitores multos, benefactores habet paucos.'

Chapter 5: The new Egypt

1. Letter 124 (*LPV,* I, 317–18).

2. Letter 127 (ibid., 323–4).

3. J. Leclercq, 'L'érémitisme en Occident jusqu'à l'an mil', in *L'Eremitismo in Occidente nei secoli XI e XII,* Miscellanea del Centro di Studi Medioevali, IV (Milan, 1965), 27–44.

4. *Petri Damiani Vita Beati Romualdi* i–viii, ed. G. Tabacco, *Fonti per la Storia d'Italia,* XCIV (Rome, 1957), 13–28.

5. *Vita Romualdi* xxi, xxii, xxvi (ibid., pp. 46–8, 65).

6. G. Tabacco, 'La data di fondazione di Camaldoli', *Rivista di Storia della Chiesa in Italia,* XVI (1962), 451–5.

7. G. Tabacco, 'Romualdo di Ravenna e gli inizi dell'eremitismo camaldolese', in *L'Eremitismo,* pp. 73–119.

8. L. Schiaparelli and F. Baldasseroni, eds., *Regesto di Camaldoli,* I, *Regesta Chartarum Italiae,* II (Rome, 1907), #86, pp. 35–6.

9. *Vita Romualdi* lxiv (ed. Tabacco, pp. 104–5): 'Taliter autem tunc in Sitria vivebatur ac si ex similitudine non solum nominis sed etiam operis altera denuo Nitria videretur.'

10. J. Mittarelli and A. Costadoni, eds., *Annales Camaldulenses Ordinis Sancti Benedicti* (Venice, 1758), III, 512–18.

11. John of Lodi *Vita Petri Damiani* i (*PL,* CXLIV, 115–16); for Peter's early life and conversion, see M. M. McLaughlin, 'Survivors and Surrogates: Children and Parents from the Ninth to the Thirteenth Centuries', in *The History of Childhood,* ed. L. de Mause (New York, 1974), pp. 103–105; and L. K. Little, 'The Personal Development of Peter Damian', in *Order and Innovation in the Middle Ages: Studies*

in Honor of Joseph R. Strayer, ed. W. C. Jordan, B. McNab, and T. F. Ruiz (Princeton, 1976), pp. 317–41.

12. John of Lodi *Vita Petri* iv (*PL*, CXLIV, 120).

13. G. Spinelli, 'La data dell'ordinazione sacerdotale di S. Pier Damiani', *Benedictina*, XVII (1972), 595–605.

14. *Opusculum LIII* iv (*PL*, CXLV, 793–6), *Ep*. i.8 (*PL*, CXLIV, 212); see Herlihy, 'Treasure Hoards', pp. 4–5, on this general attitude among the leading reformers.

15. *Ep*. iv.12 (*PL*, CXLIV, 324).

16. ibid., 503.

17. *Vita Romualdi* vi (ed. Tabacco, p. 26).

18. *Contra clericos regulares proprietarios* vi (*PL*, CXLV, 490).

19. *Opusculum XI* (ibid., 231–52).

20. *De vili vestitu ecclesiasticorum* (ibid., 517–22).

21. *Opusculum XI* i (ibid., 232).

22. ibid., 251–91, 334, 358, 362.

23. ibid., 873–4.

24. *Ep*. vi.5 (*PL*, CXLIV, 378).

25. *Laus eremiticae vitae* (*PL*, CXLV, 247).

26. *Opusculum XII* iv (ibid., 255).

27. *Laus eremiticae vitae* (ibid., 248).

28. Atto *Vita S. J. Gualberti* i–v (*PL*, CXLVI, 671–3). On the sources for Gualbert and for Vallombrosa, see S. Boesch Gajano, 'Storia e tradizione vallombrosane', *Bulletino dell' Instituto Storica Italiano per il Medio Evo*, LXXVI (1964), 99–215.

29. Atto *Vita Gualberti* ix–x (*PL*, CXLVI, 675).

30. Atto *Vita Gualberti* xii (ibid., 676).

31. K. Hallinger, 'Woher kommen die Laienbrüder?', *Analecta Sacri Ordini Cisterciensis*, XII (1956), 1–104; on Vallombrosa, see pp. 29–32. Cf. Southern, *Western Society and the Church*, pp. 257–9.

32. Atto *Vita Gualberti* xli (*PL*, CXLVI, 684–5).

33. Geoffrey *Vita Beati Bernardi Tironiensis* i–iv (*PL*, CLXXII, 1373–89). On the French hermits, one should still consult J. von Walter, *Die ersten Wanderprediger Frankreichs*, 2 vols., Studien zur Geschichte der Theologie und der Kirche, IX (Leipzig, 1903–6). Cf. H. Grundmann, *Religiöse Bewegungen im Mittelalter*, 2nd ed. (Hildesheim, 1961), pp. 38–50.

34. Geoffrey *Vita Bernardi* v–vi (*PL*, CLXXII, 1392–7).

35. Geoffrey *Vita Bernardi* vi (ibid., 1397).

36. *Vita Bernardi* viii (ibid., 1406, 1409).

37. *DHGE*, VIII, 754.

38. *Vita Bernardi* viii (*PL*, CLXXII, 1411): 'Multi etiam monachi, viri sancti et religiosi, ex diversis monasteriis, fama sanctitatis illius permoti, ad eum concurrere festinabant, ut novum Antonium in eremo residentem viderent, atque paupertatis illius vestigiis inhaerent.'

39. *Vita Bernardi* i, iii, vii (ibid., 1375, 1380, 1404); cf. L. Genicot, 'L'érémitisme du XIe siècle dans son contexte économique et social', in *L'Eremitismo*, pp. 68–9.

40. *Vita Bernardi* iv (*PL*, CLXXII, 1384).

41. G. G. Meersseman, 'Eremitismo e predicazione itinerante dei secoli X e XI', in *L'Eremitismo*, pp. 164–79, esp. 169–71.

42. *Vita Bernardi* vi (*PL*, CLXXII, 1398).

43. *Vita Bernardi* iii (ibid., 1380): 'altera Aegyptus'.

44. Baldric of Dol *Vita B. Roberti de Arbrissello* i (*PL*, CLXII, 1047–9).

45. Baldric *Vita Roberti* ii, iv (ibid., 1050–1, 1055).

46. Baldric *Vita Roberti* iii (ibid., 1051–2); Andrew the Monk *Vita altera Roberti* iii (ibid., 1063).

47. Baldric *Vita Roberti* iv (ibid., 1055).
48. Andrew *Vita altera Roberti* vi (ibid., 1073).
49. 'Lettre de Robert d'Arbrissel à la comtesse Ermengarde', in *Bibliothèque de l'Ecole des Chartes*, 3rd series, V (1854), 228.
50. *Vita venerabilis viri Stephani Muretensis* i–x, in *Scriptores Ordinis Grandimontensis*, ed. J. Becquet, *Corpus Christianorum, Continuatio Mediaevalis*, VIII (Turnhout, 1968), 105–110.
51. See the articles on Stephen by J. Becquet in *DHGE*, XV, 1252–3, and *Dictionnaire de Spiritualité*, IV, 1504–14.
52. *Regula venerabilis viri Stephani prologus* (ed. Becquet, p. 66).
53. *Liber de doctrina* (ibid., pp. 3–62). The title *Liber Sententiarum* may indicate a conscious attempt to associate Stephen with the Desert Fathers; or, on the other hand, it may be a scholastic influence, brought to bear only later in the twelfth century.
54. *Vita Stephani* xxii, xxviii–xxix (ibid., 116–17, 120); Gerard Ithier *Conclusio vitae Stephani* viii (ibid., p. 324).
55. *Liber de doctrina* xxii, xxviii (ibid., 19–20, 24); *Vita Stephani* xii (ibid., p. 112).
56. *Liber de doctrina* i (ibid., p. 6).
57. *Regula* vi, 'De bestiis non habendis', (ibid., p. 74).
58. *Institutio seu consuetudines ordinis Grandimontis* lviii (ibid., p. 524).
59. *Liber de doctrina* i (ibid., p. 6).
60. *Liber de doctrina* (ibid., pp. 5–6).
61. *Ep.* vi (*PL*, CLXXI, 1484).
62. *Ep.* cclvi (*PL*, CLXII, 260–2).
63. The theme receives full discussion in an essay by G. Miccoli, in his *Chiesa Gregoriana: Ricerche sulla Riforma del secolo XI*, Storici antichi e moderni, XVII (Florence, 1966), 225–99. For Ivo and Reginald, see pp. 285–8.
64. G. Morin, 'Rainaud l'ermite et Ives de Chartres: un épisode de la crise du cénobitisme au XIe–XIIe siècle,' *Revue Bénédictine*, XL (1928), 99–115.
65. J. Leclercq, ed., 'Le poème de Payen Bolotin contre les faux ermites', ibid., LXXIII (1958), 52–84.

Chapter 6: The new monastery

1. *DHGE*, X, 951–4 and *Dictionnaire de Spiritualité*, II, 705–10. For the lives of Bruno, see *Vita S. Brunonis* (*PL*, CLII, 481–92), *Vita Altera* (ibid., 491–526), and *Vita tertia* (ibid., 526–52). On the relationship of the Carthusians to other eremitic and monastic reform groups, see B. Bligny, 'L'érémitisme et les Chartreux', in *L'Eremitismo*, pp. 248–63. On the settlement of Chartreuse, see Bligny, *L'Eglise et les ordres religieux dans le royaume de Bourgogne aux XIe et XIIe siècles* (Grenoble, 1960). For a charter confirming the original grant by Hugh of Grenoble, see Bligny, ed., *Recueil des plus anciens actes de la Grande-Chartreuse (1086–1196)* (Grenoble, 1958), pp. 3–8, #1.
2. *Consuetudines* (*PL*, CLIII, 631–758). Guigo also wrote a life of Bishop Hugh of Grenoble (ibid., 761–84). On the early priors, see A. Wilmart, 'La chronique des premiers chartreux', *Revue Mabillon*, XVI (1926), 77–142. For a contemporary description of life at the Grande Chartreuse, see Guibert of Nogent *De vita sua* i.11 (*PL*, CLVI, 853–6).
3. Bligny, ed., *Recueil*, pp. 53–8, no. 21.
4. *Consuetudines* lxxviii–lxxix (*PL*, CLIII, 751–4).
5. *Consuetudines* prol.2 (ibid., 637–8).
6. *Consuetudines* xx.1, xxviii–xxxi, lxxx (ibid., 673–4, 693–704, 755–6).
7. For examples, see Bligny, ed., *Recueil*, p. 52, #20; p. 106, #38; and p. 161, #57.

8. *Consuetudines* vii.4–5 (*PL*, CLIII, 649–50).
9. Adam Scott *Liber de quadripertito exercitio cellae* xxxvi (ibid., 880–4, esp. 883): 'Ut quia ore non possumus Dei verbum manibus praedicemus.'
10. *Consuetudines* xxviii.2–3 (ibid., 693–4).
11. *Consuetudines* xvi (ibid., 667–8).
12. *Consuetudines* xlii, lxxiii–lxxiv (ibid., 723–6, 745–8).
13. *Consuetudines* l.2 (ibid., 729–30).
14. Bligny, ed., *Recueil*, p. 80, #28; p. 124, #43 (cited by Duby, *Rural Economy*, p. 203).
15. *Consuetudines* xl.1 (*PL*, CLIII, 717–18): 'Ornamenta aurea vel argentea, praeter calicem et calamum, quo sanguis Domini sumitur, in ecclesia non habemus, pallia tapetiaque reliquimus.'
16. *Consuetudines* xiv.3 (ibid., 659–60).
17. *Consuetudines* xli.4 (ibid., 721–2): 'Nomen vero cujusquam in suo non scribent Martyrologio, nec cujusquam anniversarium ex more facient.'
18. *Consuetudines* xxii–xxiii, xxv, xxxv, (ibid., 681–8, 691–2, 709–10); the novice's vow begins thus: 'Ego frater *ille* promitto stabilitatem et obedientiam et conversionem morum meorum....'
19. *Consuetudines* xix.1 (ibid., 671–2).
20. *De vita sua* (*PL*, CLVI, 855).
21. *Meditationes* v (*PL*, CLIII, 609): 'insana cupiditate', and *Consuetudines* xix.1 (ibid., 671–2): 'vitiotae avaritiae'.
22. 'Sermo de contemptu divitiarum' (ibid., 569–70): 'Qua in re datur intelligi quam difficile sit de ventre avaritiae hominem avarum vel extrahi vel separari posse.' *Consuetudines* xli.1 (ibid., 719–20): 'Cupiditatis occasiones nobis et nostris posteris, quantum Deo juvante possumus, praecidentes, praesentis scripti sanctione statuimus, quatenus loci hujus habitatores, extra suae terminos eremi nihil omnino possideant, id est non agros, non vineas, non hortos, non ecclesias, non caemeteria, non oblationes, non decimas et quaecunque hujusmodi.'
23. Pounds, *Historical Geography*, p. 396.
24. *Consuetudines* xx.1 (*PL*, CLIII, 673–4).
25. *Vita Norberti Archiepiscopi Magdeburgensis*, known as the *Vita A* (*MGH, SS*, XII, 663–706); *Vita S. Norberti*, known as the Vita B (*PL*, CLXX, 1253–1344).
26. On Norbert's conversion, see P. Lefèvre, 'L'épisode de la conversion de s. Norbert et la tradition hagiographique du *Vita Norberti*', *Revue d'histoire ecclésiastique*, LVI (1961), 813–26. On Norbert's preaching, see von Walter, *Die ersten Wanderprediger*, II, 118–29. For the Council of Fritzlar, *Vita A* iv (*MGH, SS*, XII, 673) and Mansi, XXI, 178.
27. *Vita A* iv–v (*MGH, SS*, XII, 673–5).
28. *Vita A* ix (ibid., 677–80).
29. F. Petit, 'Pourquoi saint Norbert a choisi Prémontré', *Analecta Praemonstratensia*, XL (1964), 5–16.
30. Hermann of Laon *De gestis venerabilis Bartholomaei episcopi et S. Norberti* iii.4 (*PL*, CLVI, 992).
31. *Vita B* viii (*PL*, CLXX, 1291).
32. *Vita A* xvi (*MGH, SS*, XII, 690–91).
33. *Vita A* xviii–xx (ibid., 693–700).
34. *PL*, CLXX, 1330.
35. Hermann of Laon *De gestis Bartholomaei* iii.6 (*PL*, CLVI, 994).
36. On such general history of the order, see F. Petit, *The Order of Canons Regular of Prémontré*, tr. and rev. B. T. Mackin (De Pere, 1961).
37. F. Petit, 'L'ordre de Prémontré de saint Norbert à Anselm d'Havelburg', in *La Vita Comune del Clero nei secoli XI e XII*, 2 vols., Miscellanea del Centro di Studi Medioevali, III (Milan, 1962), I, 466–71.

38. Adam of Dryburgh *De ordine, habitu et professione canonicorum ordinis premonstratensis* vii, xiii, (*PL*, CXCVIII, 496–507, 580–93).

39. *Libellus de diversis ordinibus* v (ed. Constable and Smith, pp. 56–73).

40. Hermann of Laon *De gestis Bartholomaei* iii.3 (*PL*, CLVI, 991).

41. Anon. *Vita Roberti Molismensi* i.3–6, ii.8–10 (*AASS*, April, III, 677–9).

42. *Vita Roberti* ii.11–12 (ibid., 679).

43. The problem is fully discussed in two articles: J. Othon, 'Les origines cisterciennes', *Revue Mabillon*, XXII (1932), 133–64, 233–52, XXIII (1933), 1–32, 81–111, 153–89; and R. Folz, 'Le problème des origines de Cîteaux', in *Mélanges Saint Bernard* (Dijon, 1954), pp. 284–94.

44. William of Saint-Thierry *et al. Vita prima S. Bernardi* (*PL*, CLXXXV, 225–368). For two brief but very perceptive and sensitive essays, see D. Knowles, 'Saint Bernard of Clairvaux: 1090–1153', in *The Historian and Character* (Cambridge, 1963), pp. 31–49; and J. Leclercq, *St. Bernard et l'esprit cistercien* (Paris, 1966). Several useful essays appear in these two commemorative volumes: *Saint Bernard théologien, Analecta Sacri Ordinis Cisterciensis*, IX (1953), and *Saint Bernard, homme d'Eglise* (Bruges, 1953).

45. For charts of filiation and excellent maps, see F. van der Meer, *Atlas de l'ordre cistercien* (Paris, 1965). Cf. L. Janauschek, *Originum Cisterciensium*, I (Vienna, 1877); A. Pexa, 'Die Cistercienser in Oesterreich', in *Festschrift zum 800-Jahrgedächtnis des Todes Bernhards von Clairvaux* (Vienna, 1953); M. Cocheril, 'L'implantation des abbayes cisterciennes dans la péninsule ibérique', *Anuario de estudios medievales*, I (1964), 217–87; R. A. Donkin, 'The Growth and Distribution of the Cistercian Order in Medieval Europe', *Studia Monastica*, IX (1967), 275–86.

46. *MGH, SS*, XVI, 636. The reference is given by J.-B. Mahn, *L'ordre cistercien et son gouvernement des origines au milieu du XIIIe siècle, 1098–1265*, 2nd ed. (Paris, 1951), p. 141, n. 3.

47. J.-B. van Damme, 'Formation de la constitution cistercienne: esquisse historique', *Studia Monastica*, IV (1962), 111–37.

48. Ordericus Vitalis *Historia ecclesiastica* viii.26 (ed. Le Prevost, III, 435–6): 'Nos fratres charissimi, secundum norman S. Patris Benedicti professionem fecimus. Sed, ut mihi videtur, non eam ex integro tenemus. Multa, quae ibi non recipiuntur, observamus, et de mandatis ejus plura negligentes intermittimus.'

49. *Vita Roberti* ii.8 (*AASS*, April, III, 678).

50. *Instituta monachorum cisterciensium de Molismo venientum* (*PL*, CLXVI, 1507).

51. Mahn, *L'ordre cistercienne*, p. 253; also, see below, n. 64.

52. J. Leclercq, 'L'érémitisme et les cisterciens', in *L'Eremitismo*, pp. 573–6.

53. *Sermo* i.3 (*PL*, CLXXXIII, 505–6). This and other references in J. Leclercq, 'S. Bernard prêcheur, d'après un exemple inédit', in *Mélanges offerts a M.-D. Chenu*, Bibliothèque thomiste, XXXVII (Paris, 1967), 345–62.

54. P. Deseille, 'Théologie de la vie monastique selon saint Bernard', in *Théologie de la vie monastique: Etudes sur la Tradition patristique* (Paris, 1961), pp. 503–25, especially p. 514.

55. *Ep.* i (*PL*, CLXXXII, 77); *Sermones super Cantica canticorum* xxiii.6, xliv.4 (*SBO*, I, 142; II, 46–7).

56. *Vita prima* i.7 (*PL*, CLXXXV, 217).

57. *Ep.* cvi (*PL*, CLXXXII, 242); cf. *Ep.* ii (ibid., 86), where he chides a man who renounced his vow to become a regular canon: 'What are you doing in the city, who have chosen the cloister?' The formal opposition Bernard makes between city and cloister is noteworthy because regular canons were so often urban dwellers.

58. *Ep.* i.73 (*PL*, CCII, 520).

59. Slicher van Bath, *Agrarian History*, pp. 153–5; Duby, *Rural Economy*, p. 199.

60. Knowles, *Monastic Order*, p. 675.

61. Jones, *CEH*, I 359
62. Toubert, *Les structures du Latium*, I, 234–5, 272.
63. Sister James Eugene Madden, 'Business Monks, Banker Monks, Bankrupt Monks: The English Cistercians in the Thirteenth Century', *Catholic Historical Review*, XLIX (1963–4), 341–64; cf. C. C. Graves, 'The Economic Activities of the Cistercians in Medieval England (1128–1307)', *Analecta Sacri Ordinis Cisterciensis*, XIII (1957), 3–60.
64. Duby, *Rural Economy*, p. 235, and document #83, pp. 436–7. Clichés about the extensive role played by the Cistercians in opening up new land in the twelfth century will have to be modified to accommodate the many cases where Cistercians took over lands already under cultivation and sent away the local population. See the studies by R. A. Donkin, 'Settlement and Depopulation on Cistercian Estates in the Twelfth and Thirteenth Centuries, especially in Yorkshire', *Bulletin of the Institute for Historical Research*, XXXIII (1960), 141–65, and 'The Cistercian Order in England: Some Conclusions', *Transactions and Papers of the Institute of British Geography*, XXXIII (1963), 181–98; G. Despy, 'Les richesses de la terre: Cîteaux et Prémontré devant l'économie de profit aux XIIe et XIIIe siècles', *Problèmes d'histoire du christianisme*, V (1974–5), 58–80.
65. Duby, *Rural Economy*, pp. 149–50, 264–5.
66. For an example from a standard and highly influential work, see Knowles, *Monastic Order*, pp. 689–90.
67. J. Othon, 'Les origines cisterciennes', *Revue Mabillon*, XXIII (1933), 6.
68. *Ep.* ccccxi (*PL*, CLXXXII, 619).
69. Deseille, 'Théologie de la vie monastique', p. 521.
70. *Ep.* ccviii (*PL*, CLXXXII, 375).
71. *Ep.* ccix (ibid., 376).
72. V. Mortet and P. Deschamps, eds., *Recueil des textes relatifs à l'histoire de l'architecture* (Paris, 1929), II, 34.
73. *Ep.* xcv (*PL*, CLXXXII, 228).
74. *Apologia ad Guillelmum S. Theoderici abbatem* (*SBO*, III, 81–108).
75. Mortet and Deschamps, *Recueil de textes*, II, 156–8. See the discussion in W. Horn and E. Born 'The Barn of the Cistercian Grange of Vaulerent (Seine-et-Oise), France', *Festschrift Ulrich Middeldorf*, ed. A. Kosegarten and P. Tigler (Berlin, 1968), pp. 24–31, pls. XIV–XIX. I am very grateful to Professor Horn for bringing this text to my attention.
76. *Vita prima* i.6 (*PL*, CLXXXV, 242).
77. *Vita prima* ii.5 (ibid., 284).
78. *Vita prima* ii.5 (ibid., 285).
79. *Ep.* ccxxxviii (*PL*, CLXXXII, 430): 'Quis mihi det, antequam moriar, videre Ecclesiam Dei, sicut in diebus antiquis, quando apostoli laxabant retia in capturam, non in capturam argenti vel auri, sed in capturam animarum?'

Chapter 7: The regular canons

1. Four of the most important works on the canonical reform include excellent introductions covering the history of the priesthood from the early church up to the eleventh century. These are L. Hertling, 'Kanoniker, Augustinusregel und Augustinerorden', *Zeitschrift für katholische Theologie*, LIV (1930), 335–59; J. C. Dickinson, *The Origins of the Austin Canons and their Introduction into England* (London, 1950); C. Dereine, 'Chanoines réguliers', in *DHGE*, XII, 353–405; and J. Siegwart, *Die Chorherren- und Chorfrauen-Gemeinschaften in der deutschsprachigen Schweiz vom 6. Jahrhundert bis 1160; mit einem Überblick über die deutsche Kanonikerreform des 10. und 11. Jh.*, Studia Friburgensia (Fribourg, 1962). Also

indispensable on the canonical reform are the following: C. Dereine, 'Vie commune, règle de Saint Augustin et chanoines réguliers au XIe siècle', *Revue d'histoire ecclésiastique*, XLI (1946), 367–406; and the collection of essays in *La Vita comune del clero nei secoli XI e XII*, 2 vols., Miscellanea del Centro di Studi Medioevali, III (Milan, 1962). P. Toubert, 'La vie commune des clercs aux XIe–XIIe siècles: un questionnaire', *Revue Historique*, CCXXXI (1964), 11–26. On Augustine, see Possidius *Vita S. Augustini prol.* xi (*PL*, XXXII, 42).

2. *Regula canonicorum* iv (*PL*, LXXXIX, 1101).
3. Dickinson, *Origins of the Austin Canons*, pp. 16–20.
4. *PL*, CV, 805–954.
5. G. Duby, 'Les chanoines réguliers et la vie économique des XIe et XIIe siècles', in *La Vita comune del clero*, I, 73–4.
6. ibid., pp. 72–81.
7. *Epistolae et decreta* li (*PL*, CXLIII, 665–6).
8. *De communi vita canonicorum* (*PL*, CXLV, 503–512).
9. *Contra clericos regulares proprietarios* (*PL*, CXLV, 479–90).
10. A. Werminghoff, 'Die Beschlüsse des Aachener Concils im Jahre 816', *Neues Archiv*, XXVII (1902), 669–71.
11. Mansi, XIX, 898. The text is discussed and altered slightly by O. Hannemann, *Die Canonikerregeln Chrodegangs von Metz und der Aachener Synode von 816 und das Verhältnis Gregors VII* (Griefswald, 1914), p. 66.
12. Mansi, XIX, 1025.
13. C. Dereine, 'S. Ruf et ses coutumes aux XIe et XIIe siècles', *Revue Bénédictine*, LIX (1949), 161–82; A. H. Duparc, 'Un joyeau de l'église d'Avignon', in *La Vita comune del clero*, II, 115–28.
14. C. Dereine, 'Coutumiers et ordinaires de chanoines réguliers', *Scriptorium*, V (1951), p. 108; cf. Dickinson, *Origins of the Austin Canons*, pp. 40–5.
15. P. F. Kehr, ed., *Italia Pontificia*, I (Berlin, 1906), 22–6.
16. Dereine, 'Coutumiers et ordinaires', pp. 109–10; cf. Dickinson, *Origins of the Austin Canons*, pp. 46–8.
17. ibid., p. 49.
18. ibid., pp. 45–6; cf. Dereine, 'Coutumiers et ordinaires', pp. 111–12; and P. Classen, 'Gerhoch von Reichersberg und die Regularkanoniker in Bayern und Oesterreich', in *La Vita comune del clero*, I, 325–32.
19. Dickinson, *Origins of the Austin Canons*, pp. 91–162; idem, 'English Regular Canons and the Continent in the Twelfth Century', *TRHS*, I (1951), 71–89.
20. Dereine, 'Vie commune', pp. 392–401; Siegwart, *Die Chorherren*, pp. 258–61. Cf. C. Giroud, *L'ordre des chanoines réguliers de Saint-Augustin et ses diverses formes de régime interne: Essai de synthèse historico-juridique* (Martigny, 1961).
21. *Ep.* ccxi (*CSEL*, LVII, 356–71).
22. *PL*, XXXII, 1449–52; also Dickinson, *Origins of the Austin Canons*, pp. 273–4.
23. ibid., pp. 274–9. For further discussion of these rules, but with attention to a different way of numbering them, see the edition of Jordan of Saxony's *Liber Vitasfratrum* by R. Arbesmann and W. Huempfner (New York, 1943), pp. lxxviii–lxxix, 489–504.
24. C. Lambot, 'Un *ordo officii* du 5e siècle', *Revue Bénédictine*, XLII (1930), 77–80; C. Lambot, 'Saint Augustin a-t-il rédigé la règle pour moines qui porte son nom?' *Revue Bénédictine*, LIII (1941), 42–60.
25. Dickinson, *Origins of the Austin Canons*, p. 69.
26. C. Dereine, 'L'élaboration du statut canonique des chanoines réguliers, spécialement sous Urbain II', *Revue d'histoire ecclésiastique*, XLVI (1951), 534–65. Cf. Siegwart, *Die Chorherren*, pp. 233–4.
27. J. Mois, *Das Stift Rottenbuch in der Kirchenreform des XI.–XII. Jahrhunderts* (Munich-Freising, 1953).

28. *PL*, CLI, 338.

29. J. H. Claxton 'On the Name of Urban II', *Traditio*, XXIII (1967), pp. 489–95.

30. Dereine, 'S. Ruf et ses coutumes', and A. Carrier de Belleuse, *Abbayes et prieurés de l'ordre de Saint-Ruf* (Romans, 1933).

31. *PL*, CLVII, 718–19. Cited by Dickinson, *Origins of the Austin Canons*, p. 7.

32. C. Dereine, 'Enquête sur la règle de Saint Augustin', *Scriptorium*, II, (1948), pp. 28–36.

33. C. Dereine, 'Les coutumiers de Saint-Quentin de Beauvais et de Springiersbach', *Revue d'histoire ecclésiastique*, XLIII (1948), 411–42.

34. As with monastic history, one needs to look beneath the level of rules to that of the customaries of individual communities of canons. The task of editing such customaries has barely begun; for manuscripts see Dereine, 'Coutumiers et ordinaires de chanoines réguliers', *Scriptorium*, V (1951), 107–13; XIII (1959), 244–6. J. Siegwart, *Die Consuetudines des Augustiner-Chorherrenstiftes Marbach im Elass (12. Jahrhundert)*, Spicilegium Friburgense, X (Fribourg 1965) is an exemplary edition of a customary.

35. Duby, 'Les chanoines réguliers et la vie économique', pp. 73–5. The life of canonesses remained quite insensitive to social change; at Cologne in the twelfth and thirteenth centuries, 97 per cent of the canonesses were recruited from the nobility, which was still entirely rural; see F. M. Stein, 'The Religious Women of Cologne, 1120–1320', Yale University, Ph. D. dissertation, 1977, pp. 19–34, 281. I am grateful to Dr Stein for letting me cite his work.

36. C. Dereine, 'Discorso conclusivo', in *La Vita comune del clero*, I, 483–8.

37. E. Magnou, 'Le chapître de la cathédrale de Saint-Etienne de Toulouse (fin XI-début XII siècle)', in *La Vita comune del clero*, II, 110–114.

38. E. Griffe, 'La réforme canoniale en pays audois aux XIe et XIIe siècles', *Bulletin de la littérature ecclésiastique de Toulouse*, XLIV (1943), 76–92, 137–49.

39. E. Kittel, 'Der Kampf um die Reform des Domkapitels in Lucca im XI. Jahrhundert', in *Festschrift A. Brackmann* (Weimar, 1931), pp. 207–47. R. Schuman, *Authority and the Commune, Parma 833–1133*, Fonti e studi, 2nd series, VIII (Parma, 1963), 297–302.

40. Dickinson, *Origins of the Austin Canons*, pp. 244–5.

41. F. Poirer de la Coutansais, 'Saint-Denis de Reims jusqu' au milieu du XIIe siècle', in *La Vita comune del clero*, II,104–6. For the grip a family could hold on a cathedral chapter, see W. M. Newman, *Le personnel de la cathédrale d'Amiens (1066–1306). Avec une note sur la famille des seigneurs de Heilly* (Paris, 1972).

42. P. Delhaye, 'L'organisation scolaire au XIIe siècle', *Traditio*, V (1947), 221.

43. J. Becquet, 'Les chanoines réguliers en Limousin aux XIe et XIIe siècles', in *La Vita comune del clero*, II, 107–9.

44. A. d'Haenens, 'Moines et clercs à Tournai au début du XIIe siècle', in *La Vita comune del clero*, II, 90–103.

45. *Opusculum de aedificio Dei* xxv (*PL*, CXCIV, 1259).

46. *Vita Norberti* xvii–xx (*MGH, SS*, XII, 695–700).

47. On the relationship between religious reform, missionary activity, and the eastern frontier, see for example H.-D. Kahl, *Slawen und Deutsche in der brandenburgischen Geschichte des zwölften Jahrhunderts* (Cologne, 1964), 106–66, 438–41. Some German cathedral chapters such as Brandenburg and Havelberg were occupied by canons of Prémontré.

48. J. Leclercq, 'La spiritualité des chanoines réguliers', in *La Vita comune del clero*, I, 117–35.

49. *Epistola Roberti ad Liezelinum canonicum* (*PL*, CLXX, 667). For a discussion of the relative merits of Michael and Peter, see Honorius of Autun *Liber duodecim quaestionum* (*PL*, CLXXII, 1177).

50. *Dialogus inter Cluniacensem monachum et Cisterciensem*, ed. E. Martène and U. Durand,

Thesaurus novus Anecdotorum, 5 vols. (Paris, 1717), V, 1614: 'Velint, nolint omnes qui illam regulam professi sunt, monachi sunt. Aut enim monachi sunt, aut de nullo ordine sunt.'

51. For a study that gives great precision to this point, notably by showing that the canons shared an unconscious 'sense of responsibility for the edification of their fellow men', while the same sense was virtually absent from monastic writings, see C. W. Bynum, 'The Spirituality of Regular Canons in the Twelfth Century: a New Approach', *Medievalia et Humanistica*, n.s. IV (1973), 3–24.
52. A Carrier de Belleuse, ed., *Coutumier du XIe siècle de l'ordre de S. Ruf* (Sherbrooke, 1950), p. 97. Cf. F.-J. Schmale, 'Kanonie, Seelsorge, Eigenkirche', *Historisches Jahrbuch*, LXXVIII (1959), 33–63.
53. Anon. *Vita B. Giraldi de Salis* i (*AASS*, October, X, 74–5).
54. *Ep.* ccxiii (*PL*, CLXII, 216–17).
55. *PL*, CXLV, 486–7.
56. *Ep.* lxix (*PL*, CLXII, 88–9).
57. *Epistola apologetica pro ordine canonicorum regularium* (*PL*, CLXXXVIII, 1128–9).
58. *Ep.* clxxxix (*PL*, CLXXXII, 355).
59. John of Salisbury *Historia Pontificalis* xxxi, ed. and tr. M. Chibnall (Edinburgh, 1956), pp. 63–4.
60. *Ep.* cxcv-cxcvi (*PL*, CLXXXII, 361–3).
61. Walter Map *De nugis curialium* i.24, ed. M. R. James (Oxford, 1914), p. 40.
62. *Historia Pontificalis* xxxi (ed. Chibnall, pp. 64–5).
63. Otto of Freising *Gesta Friderici I Imperatoris* ii.28 (ed. Waitz, p. 134).
64. P. Classen, *Gerhoch von Reichersberg: eine Biographie, mit einem Anhang über die Quellen, ihre handschriftliche Überlieferung und ihre Chronologie* (Wiesbaden, 1960). A. Lazzarino Del Grosso, *Società e Potere nella Germania del XII secolo: Gerhoch di Reichersberg* (Florence, 1974).
65. *De aedificio Dei* xxxii, xliii (*PL*, CXCIV, 1278, 1302).
66. *De aedificio Dei* iv (ibid., 1209).
67. *De aedificio Dei* xlv (ibid., 1306).
68. *De aedificio Dei* xlii (ibid., 1299).
69. *MGH, Libelli de lite*, III, 205, 208.
70. *De quarta vigilia noctis* (*MGH, Libelli de lite*, III, 503–25); discussed by Classen, *Gerhoch von Reichersberg*, pp. 292–8, 426–7.
71. *MGH, Libelli de lite*, III, 509–10.

Chapter 8: The Humiliati, Waldensians, Beguines and Cathars

1. *Chronicon Laudunense* (*MGH, SS*, XXVI, 449).
2. G. Tiraboschi, ed., *Vetera Humiliatorum monumenta*, 3 vols. (Milan, 1766–68), II, 119–22.
3. *Chronicon Laudunense* (*MGH, SS* XXVI, 449–50).
4. Ilarino da Milano, 'Il *Liber supra Stella* del piacentino Salvo Burci contro i catari e altre correnti erecticali,' *Aevum*, XVII (1943), 127.
5. *Chronicon Laudunense* (*MGH, SS* XXVI, 449–50).
6. H. Grundmann, *Religiöse Bewegungen im Mittelalter*, 2nd ed. (Hildesheim, 1961), pp. 61, 64–6.
7. Mansi, XXII, 476–8.
8. Grundmann, *Religiöse Bewegungen*, pp. 67–9. On the expansion of the holdings of the Brera, see Tiraboschi, II, 126–7.
9. Tiraboschi, II, 136, 140–1. Cf. Grundmann, *Religiöse Bewegungen*, p. 76.
10. *Ep.* ii. 228 (*PL*, CCXIV, 788–9). Cf. B. M. Bolton, 'Innocent III's Treatment of the *Humiliati*', in *Studies in Church History*, VIII, ed. G. J. Cuming and D. Baker (Cambridge, 1971), 73–82.

11. L. Zanoni, *Gli Umiliati nei loro rapporti con l'eresia, l'industrie della lana ed i comuni nei secoli XII e XIII* (Milan, 1912), pp. 352–70.

12. Tiraboschi, II, 139–48; discussion of oaths is on pp. 145–6.

13. For the second order, Tiraboschi, II, 135–8; for the third order, ibid., 128–34.

14. This is prescribed in the rule (ed. Zanoni, *Gli Umiliati*, p. 366) and hence applies to both orders, except that Innocent specifically exempted the first order as noted above.

15. Tiraboschi, II, 131–2.

16. ibid., pp. 132–3.

17. ibid., 133–4. Cf. Grundmann, *Religiöse Bewegungen*, pp. 80–2; Chenu, *Nature, Man, and Society*, pp. 249, 260.

18. Tiraboschi, II, 198–200.

19. Zanoni, *Gli Umiliati*, p. 351.

20. *Historia Occidentalis* xxviii (*HO*, pp. 144–5).

21. Grundmann, *Religiöse Bewegungen*, p. 159.

22. B. M. Bolton, 'The Poverty of the Humiliati', *Franziskanische Forschungen*, XXVII (1975), 52–9.

23. *Historia Occidentalis* xxviii (*HO*, pp. 145–6); *Ep.* i (*LJV*, p. 73).

24. Quoted in Zanoni, *Gli Umiliati*, p. 262.

25. F. Borlandi, ' "Futainiers" et futaines dans l'Italie du Moyen Age', in *Eventail de l'histoire vivante: Hommage à Lucien Febvre offert par l'amitié d'Historiens, Linguistes, Géographes, Economistes, Sociologues, Ethnologues*, 2 vols. (Paris, 1953), II, 133–40.

26. ibid., p. 137.

27. Zanoni, *Gli Umiliati*, pp. 145–99. G. Bascapé, 'Sigilli degli Umiliati', in *Mélanges offerts par ses confrères étrangers à Charles Braibant* (Brussels, 1959), pp. 17–18.

28. *Ep.* i (*LJV*, p. 73).

29. Bonvicinus de Ripa *De magnalibus urbis Mediolani* iii.3, 7, ed., F. Novati in *Bulletino dell'Istituto Storico Italiano per il Medio Evo*, XX (1898), 78, 81.

30. Tiraboschi, III, 270–73.

31. A. Kleinclauz, *Histoire de Lyon*, 3 vols. (Lyons, 1939), I, 113–72; L. Bégule and M.-C. Guige, *Monographie de la cathédrale de Lyon* (Lyons, 1880), p. 7.

32. M.-C. Guige, ed., *Obituarium lugdunensis ecclesiae: Nécrologue des personnages illustres et des bienfaiteurs de l'Eglise métropolitaine de Lyon du IXe au XVe siècle* (Lyons, 1867). See pp. 180–82 for the division of the church's revenues among the canons for 1187; for an example of a canon's will, see pp. 184–5.

33. 'Through all Gaul and Germany', according to the anonymous chronicler of Laon, *Chronicon Laudunensis* (MGH, *SS*, XXVI, 447); cf. F. Curschmann, *Hungersnöte im Mittelalter. Ein Beitrag zur deutschen Wirtschaftsgeschichte des 8. bis 13. Jahrhunderts*, Leipziger Studien aus dem Gebiet der Geschichte, VI, 1 (Leipzig, 1900), p. 84.

34. *Chronicon Laudunensis* (MGH, *SS*, XXVI, 447).

35. ibid. See the discussion about this date in K.-V. Selge, *Die ersten Waldenser*, 2 vols. (Berlin, 1967), I, 238–9. Richard of Poitiers gave the date as 'around 1170'. See G. Gonnet, ed., *Enchiridion Fontium Valdensium*, I (Torre Pellice, 1958), 165. Many of the important sources are here gathered by Gonnet and will be cited accordingly. For Gonnet's discussion of Waldensian sources, see his 'Waldensia', *Revue d'histoire et de philosophie religieuses*, XXXIII (1953), 202–54. Cf. G. Koch, 'Neue Quellen und Forschungen über die Anfange der Waldenser', *Forschungen und Fortschritte*, XXXII (1958), 141–9. For a handbook of early Waldensian history, see J. Gonnet and A. Molnar, *Les Vaudois au moyen âge* (Turin, 1974).

36. *Chronicon Laudunensis* (MGH, *SS*, XXVI, 447).

37. ibid., pp. 447–8.

38. ibid., p. 448.

39. Stephen of Bourbon in *Anecdotes historiques, légendes et apologues tirés du recueil inédit d'Etienne de Bourbon*, ed. A. Lecoy de la Marche (Paris, 1877), pp. 290–3.

40. ibid., pp. 291–2.

41. Grundmann, *Religiöse Bewegungen*, pp. 161–4.

42. Richard of Poitiers, in Gonnet, *Enchiridion*, p. 165.

43. *Chronicon Laudunensis* (*MGH, SS*, XXVI, 449).

44. *Anecdotes historiques* (ed. Lecoy de la Marche, p. 292).

45. *Chronicon Laudunensis* (*MGH, SS*, XXVI, 449).

46. *De nugis curialium* i.31 (ed. James, p. 61).

47. P. Pouzet, 'La vie de Guichard, abbé de Pontigny (1136–1165) et archevêque de Lyon (1165–1181)', *Bulletin de la Société littéraire, historique et archéologique de Lyon*, X (1929), 117–50. Y. Congar, 'Henri de Marcy, abbé de Clairvaux, cardinal-évêque d'Albano et légat pontifical', *Studia Anselmiana*, XLIII, *Analecta monastica*, V (1958), 1–90, esp. 30–2.

48. J. Leclercq, 'Le témoinage de Geoffroy d'Auxerre sur la vie cistercienne', *Studia Anselmiana*, XXXI, *Analecta monastica*, II (1953), 174–201, esp. 194–5.

49. Geoffrey of Auxerre *Super Apocalypsim*, in Gonnet, *Enchiridion*, p. 46.

50. A. Dondaine, 'Aux origines du valdéisme: Une profession de foi de Valdès', *Archivum Fratrum Praedicatorum*, XVI (1946), 191–235.

51. C. Thouzellier, *Catharisme et valdéisme en Languedoc à la fin du XIIe et au début du XIIIe siècle*, 2nd ed. (Louvain, 1969), pp. 35–6.

52. Geoffrey of Auxerre, in Gonnet, *Enchiridion*, p. 46.

53. Stephen of Bourbon, *Anecdotes historiques* (ed. Lecoy de la Marche, p. 292).

54. Mansi, XXII, 476–8.

55. See the map in Selge, *Die ersten Waldenser*, end of vol. I.

56. Bernard of Fontcaude *Liber adversus Waldensium sectam* prol. ii (*PL*, CCIV, 793–4). Thouzellier, *Catharisme et valdéisme*, p. 50, specifies the date as between 1185 and 1187.

57. L. Verrees, 'Le traité de l'abbé Bernard de Fontcaude contre les Vaudois et les Ariens', *Analecta Praemonstratensia*, XXXI (1955), 5–35. Also discussed by Thouzellier, *Catharisme et valdéisme*, pp. 50–7.

58. Gonnet, *Enchiridion*, pp. 91–4.

59. ibid., p. 91.

60. Caesar of Heisterbach *Dialogus miraculorum* v. 20, ed. J. Strange, 2 vols. (Cologne, 1851), I, 299–300.

61. Innocent III *Ep*. ii.141 and 142 (*PL*, CCXIV, 695–9). Cf. Grundmann, *Religiöse Bewegungen*, pp. 97–100.

62. *Chronica Albrici monachi Trium Fontium* (*MGH, SS*, XXIII, 878).

63. Selge, *Die ersten Waldenser*, I, 204.

64. Salvo Burci *Liber supra Stella*, ed. Ilarino da Milano in *Aevum*, XIX (1945), 309–41. The editor discusses this work in a group of articles in *Aevum*, XVI (1942), 272–319; XVII (1943), 90–146; and XIX (1945), 218–309. See also the summa thought to be by Peter Martyr, ch. xxvi, 'De pauperibus leonistis', in T. Kaeppelli, 'Une Somme contre les hérétiques de s. Pierre Martyr(?)', *Archivum Fratrum Praedicatorum*, XVII (1947), 333–4. Cf. Thouzellier, *Catharisme et valdéisme*, pp. 170–73.

65. For the text of the Rescriptum, see Gonnet, *Enchiridion*, pp. 171–83. Cf. Thouzellier, *Catharisme et valdéisme*, pp. 176–9.

66. Anon. of Passau *Liber contra Waldenses* iv, ed. J. Gretser, *Opera omnia*, 17 vols. (Regensburg, 1734–41), XII2, 27.

67. *Liber antiheresis*, ed. Selge, *Die ersten Waldenser*, II; for analysis of this text, see ibid., I, 35–127, and Thouzellier, *Catharisme et valdéisme*, pp. 60–79. On the association of Durand with Huesca (in Aragon), see ibid., pp. 213–14.

68. Ed. Selge, *Die ersten Waldenser*, II, 60–2, 72, 74–6, 96, 98–9.

69. M.-H. Vicaire, 'Rencontre à Pamiers des courants vaudois et dominicain (1207)', in *Vaudois languedociens et Pauvres Catholiques*, Cahiers de Fanjeaux, II (Toulouse, 1967), 156–94. Peter of Vaux-de-Cernay *Hystoria Albigensis* ii. 48, ed. P. Guébin and E. Lyon, 3 vols. (Paris, 1926–39), I, 43–4. Cf. Gonnet, *Enchiridion*, pp. 126–8.
70. See the dated but still useful study by J. B. Pierron, *Die katholischen Armen. Ein Beitrag zur Entstehungsgeschichte der Bettelorden mit Berucksichtigung der Humiliaten und der Wiedervereinigten Lombarden* (Freiburg, 1911). Cf. Grundmann, *Religiöse Bewegungen*, pp. 100–18; and Selge, *Die ersten Waldenser*, I, 193–225.
71. Innocent III *Ep.* xi.196 (*PL*, CCXV, 1510–13).
72. Innocent III *Ep.* xiii.78 (*PL*, CCXVI, 274–5).
73. Innocent III *Ep.* xiii.94 (ibid., 289–93). Cf. Grundmann, *Religiöse Bewegungen*, pp. 118–27; and Selge, *Die ersten Waldenser*, I, 188–93.
74. Innocent III *Ep.* xiii.94 (*PL*, CCXVI, 292).
75. J. J. I. von Döllinger, *Beiträge zur Sektengeschichte des Mittelalters*, 2 vols. (Munich, 1890), II, 301.
76. *De nugis curialium* i.31 (ed. James, p. 61).
77. *Ep.* i (*LJV*, pp. 74, 77).
78. Potthast, *Regesta*, no. 9212, I, 788.
79. *Ep.* i (*LJV*, pp. 72–3).
80. ibid.
81. *Vita Mariae Oigniacensis* (*AASS*, June, V, 542–72).
82. S. Berger, *La Bible française au moyen âge: Etude sur les plus anciennes versions de la Bible écrites en prose de langue d'oïl* (Paris, 1884; photo reprint, Geneva, 1967), pp. 49–50.
83. J. Grevin, *Die Anfänge der Beginen. Ein Beitrag zur Geschichte der Volksfrömmigkeit und des Ordenswesen im Hochmittelalter*, Vorreformationsgeschichtliche Forschungen, VIII (Münster i. W., 1912), pp. 158–78; cf. J. B. Russell, *Dissent and Reform in the Early Middle Ages* (Berkeley and Los Angeles, 1965), pp. 90–6.
84. *Chronica Albrici monachi Trium Fontium* (*MGH, SS*, XXIII, 855).
85. On the career of John of Nivelles, see E. W. McDonnell, *The Beguines and Beghards in Medieval Culture, With special emphasis on the Belgian scene* (New Brunswick, 1954), pp. 40–5.
86. L. J. M. Philippen, *De Begijnhoven, Oorsprong, geschiedenis, inrichting* (Antwerp, 1918), pp. 40–126. Philippen's argument is summarized by McDonnell, *Beguines*, pp. 5–6.
87. Philippen, *Begijnhoven*, p. 304.
88. T. J. Lacomblet, ed., *Urkundenbuch für die Geschichte des Niederrheins oder des Erzstifts Cöln, der fürstenthümer Jülich und Berg, Geldern, Meurs, Cleve und Mark, und der Reichsstifte Elten, Essen und Werden*, 4 vols. (Düsseldorf, 1840–58), II, 288, no. 512.
89. Philippen, *Begijnhoven*, pp. 89–126.
90. D. Phillips, *Beguines in Medieval Strasburg: A Study of the Social Aspect of Beguine Life* (Palo Alto, 1941), p. 145; Stein, 'Religious Women of Cologne', pp. 78–9.
91. E. G. Neumann, *Rheinisches Beginen- und Begardenwesen: Ein Mainzer Beitrag zur religiösen Bewegung am Rhein* (Meisenheim am Glan, 1960), pp. 76, 19–20.
92. McDonnell, *Beguines*, pp. 224–33.
93. *Histoire de Saint Louis*, ed. Natalis de Wailly (Paris, 1868), p. 258.
94. McDonnell, *Beguines*, pp. 59–70.
95. J. von Döllinger, *Beiträge zur politischen, kirchlichen und Cultur-geschichte der sechs letzen Jahrhunderte*, 3 vols. (Vienna, 1862–82), III, 197.
96. Sources for this are relatively late; McDonnell, *Beguines*, p. 71, n. 5.
97. Stein, 'Religious Women of Cologne', p. 87; Phillips, *Beguines in Medieval Strasburg*, p. 27.
98. Etienne Baluze, *Vitae paparum Avenionensium*, ed. G. Mollat, 4 vols. (Paris, 1914–27), III, 354.
99. Grundmann, *Religiöse Bewegungen*, pp. 352–3.

100. *Historia Occidentalis* xv (*HO*, p. 117); cf. *Vita Mariae* prol. (*AASS*, June, V, 547).
101. *Vita Mariae* v (ibid., pp. 557–8).
102. Thomas of Çantimpré *Bonum universale de Apibus* ii.54.18, ed. G. Colvenerius (Douai, 1627), p. 529.
103. Thomas of Cantimpré *Vita Mariae Oigniacensis, Supplementum* i (*AASS*, June, V, 574).
104. McDonnell, *Beguines*, p. 153.
105. James of Vitry *Vita Mariae* ii (*AASS*, June, V, 552).
106. *Vita Mariae* prol. (ibid., p. 548).
107. *Die Wundergeschichten des Caesarius von Heisterbach*, ed. A. Hilka, 3 vols. (Bonn, 1933–37), III, 26–7.
108. A Borst, *Die Katharer*, Schriften der Monumenta Germaniae Historica, XII (Stuttgart, 1953).
109. Historiographical surveys: Borst, *Die Katharer*, pp. 1–58; R. Morghen, 'L'eresia nel Medioevo', in *Medioevo cristiano*, 4th ed. (Bari, 1965), pp. 204–81; J. B. Russell, 'Interpretations of the Origins of Medieval Heresy', *Mediaeval Studies*, XXV (1963), 26–53; R. I. Moore, 'The Origins of Medieval Heresy', *History*, LV (1970), 21–36.
110. For socialism, see K. Kautsky, *Die Vorläufer des neuen Sozialismus* (Stuttgart, 1895); for liberty, see B. Croce, 'Il materialismo storico e le eresie medievali', *Quaderni della Critica*, no. 5 (1946), 119–21; for dissent, see R. I. Moore, *The Origins of European Dissent* (London, 1977).
111. Borst, *Die Katharer*, p. v.
112. E. Delaruelle in J. Le Goff, ed., *Hérésies et sociétés dans l'Europe pré-industrielle, 11e–18e siècles*, Civilisations et sociétés, X (Paris, 1968), p. 118.
113. M.-D. Chenu, ibid., p. 12.
114. For the eleventh century, see Ilarino da Milano, 'Le Eresie popolari del secolo XI', *Studi Gregoriani*, II, 43–89.
115. Adhémar of Chabannes *Historiarum libri III* iii.49 (*MGH, SS*, IV, 138).
116. ibid.
117. Mansi, XIX, 423–60, esp. 423–5, 459–60.
118. Landulf Senior *Historia Mediolanensis* ii.27, ed. A. Cutolo, *Rerum Italicarum Scriptores*, IV2 (Bologna, 1932), 67–9.
119. Anselm of Liège *Gesta episcoporum Leodiensium* ii.62–4 (*MGH, SS*, VII, 226–8).
120. Lampert of Hersfeld *Annales* (*MGH, SS*, V, 155); Hermann der Lahme of Reichenau *Chronicon* (ibid., 130).
121. Anselm of Liège *Gesta episcoporum Leodiensium* ii.63 (*MGH, SS*, VII, 227).
122. T. Gousset, ed., *Les actes de la province ecclésiastique de Reims*, 4 vols. (Reims, 1842–44), II, 239–47.
123. Guibert of Nogent *De vita sua* iii.17 (*PL*, CLVI, 951).
124. Guibert of Nogent *De vita sua* iii.17 (ibid., 952–3).
125. G. Bourgin, *La commune de Soissons et le groupe communal soissonais*, Bibliothèque de l'Ecole des Hautes Etudes, Sciences historiques et philologiques, fasc. 167 (Paris, 1908), pp. 1–89.
126. Bernard *Ep.* ccclxxii (*PL*, CLXXXII, 677).
127. Bernard *Sermones super Cantica canticorum* lxv (*SBO*, II, 172–7). Cf. *Annales Brunwilarensis* (*MGH, SS*, VI, 727).
128. Bernard *Ep.* ccclxxii (*PL*, CLXXXII, 678).
129. Bernard *Ep.* ccclxxii (ibid., 677, 679).
130. Bernard *Ep.* ccclxxii (ibid., 677).
131. Bernard *Ep.* ccclxxii (ibid., 677–8).
132. Bernard *Ep.* ccclxxii (ibid., 677).
133. Bernard *Sermones* lxv.2, 4 (*SBO*, II, 173–4).
134. Bernard *Sermones* lxv.4, 5, 8 (ibid., 175–7).

135. Bernard *Ep.* cccclxxii (*PL*, CLXXXII, 677).
136. *Epistola ecclesiae Leodiensis ad Lucam papam II*, in E. Martène and U. Durand, eds., *Veterum scriptorum et monumentorum historicum, dogmaticarum, moralium amplissima collectio*, 9 vols. (Paris, 1724–33), I, 776–8. There is no date on the letter and the pope is identified only by the letter 'L'. Nearly all scholars agree that the letter was addressed to Pope Lucius II (1144–5). While J. B. Russell, in *Dissent and Reform*, p. 198, claims the letter went to Pope Leo IX (1048–54), he considerably softens his argument on p. 307, n. 42. Cf. Moore, *Origins of European Dissent*, pp. 171–2.
137. *Heriberti monachi epistola de haereticis Petragoricis* (*PL*, CLXXXI, 1721–2).
138. Mansi, XXII, 157–68.
139. Anon. *De heresi catharorum*, ed. A. Dondaine in 'La hiérarchie cathare en Italie', *Archivum Fratrum Praedicatorum*, XIX (1949), 280–312, text on pp. 306–12; also Anselm of Alexandria *Tractatus de hereticis*, ed. by Dondaine in a continuation of the same article, *Archivum Fratrum Praedicatorum*, XX (1950), 234–324, text on pp. 308–324.
140. A. Dondaine, 'Les actes du concile albigeois de Saint-Félix de Caraman: Essai de critique d'authenticité d'un document médiéval', in *Miscellanea Giovanni Mercati*, V, Studi e testi, CXXV (Vatican, 1946), 324–55; for more recent views see Y. Dossat, 'A propos du concile cathare de Saint-Félix: les Milingues', in *Cathares en Languedoc*, Cahiers de Fanjeaux, III (Toulouse, 1968), 201–14; and F. Sanjek, 'Le rassemblement hérétique de St-Félix-de-Caraman (1167) et les églises cathares au XIIe s', *Revue d'histoire ecclésiastique*, LXVII (1972), 767–99.
141. *De fide catholica* i (*PL*, CCX, 307–78); the work is discussed by Thouzellier, *Catharisme et valdéisme*, pp. 83–94.
142. Ed. C. Thouzellier, *Une somme anti-cathare: le 'Liber contra manicheos' de Durand de Huesca*, Spicilegium sacrum Lovaniense, Etudes et documents, fasc. 32 (Louvain, 1964). For the *Manichei moderni*, see ch. vi (ibid., p. 147).
143. *Un traité néo-manichéen du XIIIe siècle: le Liber de duobus principiis, suivi d'un fragment de rituel cathare*, ed. A. Dondaine (Rome, 1939), pp. 81, 84, 93, 99–109, 121, 126.
144. 'Un recueil cathare: Le manuscrit A.6.10 de la Collection vaudoise de Dublin, I: Une apologie', ed. T. Venckeleer, *Revue belge de philologie et d'histoire* XXXVIII (1960), 815–34, text on pp. 820–31; the definition of the church is in ch. i (p. 820).
145. A Latin version of the ritual is published by Dondaine in his edition of the *Liber de duobus principiis*, pp. 151–65. A Provençal version is found in L. Clédat, ed., *Le Nouveau Testament traduit au XIIIe siècle en langue provençale, suivi d'un rituel cathare* (Paris, 1887), pp. ix–xxvi. The most thorough study of the Catharist religion, with respect to both theology and ritual, is H. Söderberg, *La religion des cathares: Etude sur le gnosticisme de la basse antiquité et du moyen âge* (Uppsala, 1949).
146. 'Un recueil cathare: Le manuscrit A.6.10 de la Collection vaudoise de Dublin, II: Une glose sur le Pater', ed. T. Venckeleer, *Revue belge de philologie et d'histoire*, XXXIX (1961), 759–93, text on pp. 762–85.
147. Ritual in Dondaine ed. of *Liber de duobus principiis*, pp. 157–65; the phrase *veri cristiani docti ab ecclesia primitiva* occurs on p. 162. On the similarities of the consolamentum and early Christian baptism, see Söderberg, *La religion des cathares*, pp. 218–37.
148. Ritual in Dondaine ed. of *Liber de duobus principiis*, pp. 163–4.
149. Ritual in Clédat ed. of New Testament, pp. xxii–xxvi.
150. Söderberg, *La religion des cathares*, pp. 251–2, 254.
151. Ritual in Clédat ed. of New Testament, pp. ix–xi.
152. C. Thouzellier, 'La Bible des cathares languedociens et son usage dans la controverse au début du XIIIe siècle', in *Cathares en Languedoc*, pp. 42–57.
153. Y. Dossat, 'Les cathares dans les documents de l'inquisition', ibid., pp. 85–7.
154. Lynch, *Symoniacal Entry*, pp. 27–36.

155. Rainerius Sacconi *Summa de Catharis et Pauperibus de Lugduno*, in Dondaine ed. of *Liber de duobus principiis*, p. 68.
156. James Capelli *Summa contra haereticos*, ed. D. Bazzocchi, *La eresia cathara: Saggio storico filosofico con in appendice* Disputationes nonnullae adversus haereticos, *codice inedito del secolo XIII della biblioteca Malatestiana di Cesena* (text in appendix volume, published separately, Bologna, 1920), p. CLVII.
157. ibid., pp. CLVII–CLVIII.
158. ibid., pp. CXXXVIII–CXXXIX.
159. Anselm of Alexandria *Tractatus de hereticis* i (ed. Dondaine, p. 308).
160. G. Koch, *Frauenfrage und Ketzertum im Mittelalter. Die Frauenbewegung im Rahmen des Katharismus und des Waldensertums und ihre sozialen Wurzeln (12.–14. Jahrhundert)*, Forschungen zur mittelalterlichen Geschichte, IX (Berlin, 1962), pp. 13–155.
161. Mundy, *Liberty and Political Power*, p. 79; idem, 'Noblesse et hérésie. Une famille cathare: les Maurand', *Annales E. S. C.*, XXIX (1974), 1211–23.
162. Caesarius of Heisterbach *Dialogus miraculorum* v.24 (ed. Strange, I, 307–8).
163. James Capelli *Summa contra haereticos* (ed. Bazzocchi, p. CL).
164. *Historia occidentalis* xxxiv (*HO*, p. 165).

9: The Franciscans and Dominicans

1. Thomas of Celano *Vita prima S. Francisci* (hereafter cited as *1 Cel.*, just as the second life of Francis by Thomas will be referred to as *2 Cel.*) viii, in *AF*, X, 10–11. This is the passage, cited again below, that tells of his going to sell the cloth at Foligno, 'where he customarily went to sell all his merchandise' (*ibi ex more venditis omnibus quae portabat*).
2. *1 Cel.* iv–v; *2 Cel.* vi (ibid., 8–9, 133–4).
3. *1 Cel.* vi (ibid., 9–10).
4. *1 Cel.* viii–ix (ibid., 10–11).
5. *1 Cel.* xi (ibid., 12–13).
6. *1 Cel.* xii–xiv (ibid., 13–14).
7. *1 Cel.* xv (ibid., 14–15).
8. *1 Cel.* xvi–xviii, xxi (ibid., 15–17, 18).
9. *1 Cel.* xxii (ibid., 19).
10. *1 Cel.* xxiii–xxv (ibid., 19–21).
11. *Reg. prima* i, ed. H. Boehmer in *Analekten zur Geschichte des Franciscus von Assisi* (Tübingen and Leipzig, 1904), pp. 1–2; *1 Cel.* xxiii (*AF*, X, p. 20).
12. *Testament* iv (ed. Boehmer, p. 37).
13. *1 Cel.* xxiv–xxv, xxix–xxx, xxxii–xxxiii (*AF*, X, 20–7). One official they met in Rome was Cardinal John Colonna, a Benedictine, who suggested that Francis and his friends become monks or hermits. *Legend of the Three Companions* lii (*AASS*, October, II, 737).
14. *1 Cel.* xviii–xx, xxxvi–xxxvii (*AF*, X, 16–18, 29–30).
15. *1 Cel.* xxxix (ibid., 31–2).
16. *Ep.* i (*LJV*, pp. 75–6).
17. *Scripta Leonis* lxxix, ed, and tr. R. B. Brooke, *Scripta Leonis, Rufini et Angeli, Sociorum S. Francisci* (Oxford, 1970), pp. 226–7.
18. *Ep.* vi (*LJV*, pp. 131–2).
19. *Chronica Fratris Jordani*, ed. H. Boehmer (Paris, 1908); Thomas of Eccleston *De adventu Fratrum Minorum in Angliam*, ed. A. G. Little (Paris, 1909).
20. On the general history of the order in the thirteenth century, see J. Moorman, *A History of the Franciscan Order: From its Origins to the Year 1517* (New York, 1968).
21. Innocent III *Ep.* vi.81 (*PL*, CCXV, 84); discussed by Thouzellier, *Catharisme et*

valdéisme, in a chapter on Innocent III and heresy in France, 1204–1208, pp. 183–212.

22. Innocent III *Ep.* vi.243, vii.76, 210 (*PL*, CCXV, 273–4, 358–60, 525–6).
23. Jordan of Saxony *Libellus de principiis ordinis Praedicatorum* iv, x–xii, xv, ed., H.-C. Scheeben in *MOPH*, XVI, 27, 30–4.
24. Jordan *Libellus* xvii (ibid., pp. 34–5). Cf. Peter of Vaux-de-Cernay *Hystoria Albigensis* ii.20 (ed. Guébin and Lyon, I, 21).
25. Peter of Vaux-de-Cernay *Hystoria Albigensis* ii.20–21 (ibid., 22–3); cf. the account by Robert of Auxerre, who also stresses the Cistercian failure and the central role played by Diego, *Chronica* (*MGH, SS*, XXVI, 271).
26. Jordan *Libellus* xx (ed., Scheeben, p. 36).
27. Peter *Hystoria Albigensis* ii.21 (ed. Guébin and Lyon, I, 23–4).
28. Peter *Hystoria Albigensis* ii.21, 26, 47 (ibid., pp. 24, 28–9, 41–3); cf. Jordan *Libellus* xxi–xxii (ed. Scheeben, p. 37) and William of Puylaurens *Cronica* viii, ed. Beyssier in *Bibliothèque de la Faculté des Lettres de Paris*, XVIII (Paris, 1904), 128.
29. Jordan *Libellus* xxi (ed. Scheeben, p. 37).
30. Innocent III *Ep.* ix.185 (*PL*, CCXV, 1025).
31. For a full discussion and references to others who have studied the problem, see C. Thouzellier, 'La pauvreté, arme contre l'Albigéisme en 1206', *Revue de l'histoire des religions*, CLI (1957), 79–92.
32. Peter *Hystoria Albigensis* ii.47–48 (ed. Guébin and Lyon, I, 41–4); cf. William of Puylaurens *Cronica* x (ed. Beyssier, p. 129).
33. Peter *Hystoria Albigensis* ii.48–54 (ed. Guébin and Lyon, I, 43–65); Jordan *Libellus* xxviii (ed. Scheeben, p. 39).
34. *Historia diplomatica S. Dominici*, 4, ed. M.-H. Laurent in *MOPH*, XV, 22–3. Most of the material in this volume has been re-edited by V.-J. Koudelka, *Monumenta diplomatics S. Dominici*, in *MOPH*, XXV; whenever possible, the latter volume will be cited. *Monumenta diplomatica*, #5 (ibid., pp. 13–15). Jordan *Libellus* xxxvii (ed. Scheeben, pp. 43–4).
35. *Monumenta diplomatica*, #8 (ed. Koudelka, pp. 16–18).
36. Jordan *Libellus* xxxi–xxxiv (ed. Scheeben, pp. 40–2).
37. Innocent III *Reg.* xi.26 (*PL*, CCXV, 1354–8); cf. *Reg.* xi.27–9, 32–3 (ibid., 1358–62).
38. Mansi, XXII, 785.
39. *COD*, pp. 239–40.
40. *Monumenta diplomatica*, #63 (ed. Koudelka, pp. 56–8).
41. *COD*, p. 242.
42. Jordan *Libellus* xl–xliv (ed. Scheeben, pp. 45–7).
43. *Monumenta diplomatica*, #77 (ed. Koudelka, pp. 71–6).
44. *Monumenta diplomatica*, #79 (ibid., pp. 78–9). See Koudelka's study of the matter of how the papal text at first read *predicantibus* and was shortly afterwards, before being sent out, changed to read *predicatoribus*: 'Notes sur le cartulaire de S. Dominique', *Archivum fratrum praedicatorum*, XXVIII (1958), 92–100, especially p. 95.
45. *Monumenta diplomatica*, #86 (ed. Koudelka, pp. 86–7).
46. Jordan *Libellus* xlvii (ed. Scheeben, p. 48). For the date, see Stephen of Salagnac *De quatuor in quibus Deus praedicatorum ordinem insignivit* ii.3, ed. T. Kaeppeli in *MOPH*, XXII, 15.
47. Jordan *Libellus* xlvi–xlvii (ed. Scheeben, pp. 47–8); C. N. L. Brooke, 'St Dominic and His First Biographer', *TRHS*, XVII (1967), 35–6.
48. Jordan *Libellus* lv (ed. Scheeben, p. 51).
49. For the early history of the order, see W. A. Hinnebusch, *The History of the Dominican Order*, I (New York, 1965).
50. *Scripta Leonis* xiv (ed. Brooke, pp. 112–13).

51. Brentano, *Two Churches*, p. 333. Brentano uses these two writers to serve the contrast he is drawing between the English and Italian churches, but he points out (p. 334) that they could as well illustrate differences of personality, psychological type, economic structure, and, as in the present case, religious life.

52. *Chronica Fratris Jordani* iv–v (ed. Boehmer, pp. 4–6).

53. *Ep.* vi (*LJV*, pp. 131–2).

54. *2 Cel.* lviii (*AF*, X, 166).

55. *Monumenta diplomatica* #79 (bull of 21 Jan. 1217) and #86 (bull of 11 Feb. 1218) (ed., Koudelka, pp. 78–9, 86–7).

56. Jordan of Saxony *Epistolae* #1, 14, 19, 20, 26, 32, 34, 39, 40, 42, 50, ed. A. Walz in *MOPH,* XXIII, 4, 16–17, 23–4, 30–1, 38, 41, 44–7, 58.

57. J. B. Freed, *The Friars and German Society in the Thirteenth Century*, The Mediaeval Academy of America, Publication No. 86 (Cambridge, Mass., 1977), p. 336.

58. Salimbene de Adam *Cronica* (ed. Scalia, pp. 52–8). Cf. Brentano, *Two Churches*, pp. 334–5; and R. B. Brooke, *Early Franciscan Government, Elias to Bonaventure* (Cambridge, 1959), p. 46.

59. J. A. Weisheipl, *Friar Thomas d'Aquino: His Life, Thought, and Work* (Garden City, 1974), pp. 12–36.

60. *Scripta Leonis* xxviii (ed. Brooke, pp. 138–41).

61. *Scripta Leonis* xix (ibid., pp. 120–1).

62. *1 Cel.* xxiv (*AF*, X, 21).

63. Constantine of Orvieto *Legenda s. Dominici* xxi, ed. H.-C. Scheeben in *MOPH,* XVI, 301, told of the pope's dream of the collapsing church held up by Dominic, an apparent borrowing from the parallel story of Francis in *2 Cel.* xvii (*AF*, X, 141).

64. *1 Cel.* xxxiii (ibid., 26–7).

65. Thomas of Spalato *Ex historia pontificum Salonitanorum et Spalatensium*, ed. H. Boehmer, *Analekten*, p. 106.

66. *Reg. prima* xvii; *Reg. secunda* ix (ibid., pp. 16, 34).

67. Moorman, *History of the Franciscan Order*, pp. 123–39.

68. *Reg. secunda* v (ed. Boehmer, p. 32).

69. *Constitutiones* prol. ii, ed. H.-C. Scheeben, *Die Konstitutionen des Predigerordens unter Jorden von Sachsen*, in *Quellen und Forschungen zur Geschichte des Dominikanerordens in Deutschland*, XXXVIII, 49.

70. *Epistolae* xiii, in *Opera omnia Bonaventurae*, VIII (Quaracchi, 1898), 336.

71. Jordan *Libellus* xlii (ed. Scheeben, p. 46).

72. Jordan *Libellus* lxxxvii (ibid., p. 67) and *Constitutiones* IIa dist., XXVI, 1–2 (ed. Scheeben, *Die Konstitutionen*, p. 76).

73. *2 Cel.* lviii (*AF*, X, 166).

74. John of Navarre (*AASS*, August, I, 638).

75. *Constitutiones* IIa dist., XXXI (ed. Scheeben, *Die Konstitutionen*, p. 77).

76. *2 Cel.* lxv–lxvi (*AF*, X, 170–2).

77. Reg. prima viii–ix; *Reg. secunda* iv (ed. Boehmer, pp. 8–9, 31–2).

78. *Reg. prima* x (ibid., p. 11).

79. *Reg. secunda* iv (ibid., p. 32).

80. M. D. Lambert, *Franciscan Poverty: The Doctrine of the Absolute Poverty of Christ and the Apostles in the Franciscan Order, 1210–1323* (London, 1961), pp. 84–102.

81. *Reg. prima* i; *Reg. secunda* i (ed. Boehmer, pp. 1–2, 29–30).

82. *Speculum perfectionis* lxviii, ed. P. Sabatier, I (Manchester, 1928), 196; cf. *Scripta Leonis* cxiv (ed. Brooke, pp. 286–9).

83. *Reg. prima* v (ed. Boehmer, p. 5).

84. Humbert of Romans *Expositio super constitutiones fratrum Praedicatorum*, ed. J. J. Berthier, *Opera de vita regulari*, 2 vols. (Rome, 1889), II, 46.

85. *Historia Occidentalis* xxvii (*HO*, pp. 142–4).
86. *Historia Occidentalis* xxxii (ibid., p. 158).
87. *Historia Occidentalis* xxxii (ibid., pp. 158–63).
88. Stephen of Salagnac *De quatuor* iv.1–4 (ed. Kaeppeli, pp. 170–83).
89. Humbert of Romans, *Expositio super constitutiones* (ed. Berthier, II, 38–9).
90. A German might understandably think of the Waldensians as originating in Italy, since the movement came into Germany from Italy. That Burchard stressed the connection between the Humiliati and the Preachers, without even suggesting the possible tie between the canons and the Preachers, is perhaps explained by his being a Premonstratensian canon and therefore peculiarly sensitive to the more original aspects of Dominican spirituality.
91. Burchard of Ursperg *Burchardi et Cuonradi Urspergensium Chronicon* (*MGH, SS*, XXIII, 376–7).
92. *Scripta Leonis* lxxx (ed. Brooke, pp. 228–9). L. Pellegrini, 'L'esperienza eremitica di Francesco e dei primi francescani', in *Francesco d'Assisi e Francescanesimo dal 1216 al 1226* (Assisi, 1977), pp. 281–313.

Chapter 10: Scholastic social thought

1. Leclercq, *Love of Learning*, pp. 87–96.
2. Benedict of Nursia *Regula monachorum* iv. 68 (*CSEL*, LXXV, 33), where, among the tools of good works, he advises, 'not to love contention' (*contentionem non amare*).
3. Chenu, *Nature, Man, and Society*, pp. 310–30. Cf. R. Klibansky, 'Standing on the Shoulders of Giants', *Isis*, XXVI (1936), 147–9.
4. Chenu, *Nature, Man, and Society*, pp. 270–309.
5. M.-D. Chenu, *La théologie comme science au XIIIe siècle*, 3rd ed. (Paris, 1957); A. Giuliani, 'La logique de la controverse et le droit chez les romanistes du XIIe et XIIIe siècle', *Studia et Documenta historiae et iuris*, XXXIV (1968), 223–48.
6. L. Vereecke, 'History of Moral Theology', *NCE*, IX, 1120; M.-D. Chenu, *L'éveil de la conscience dans la civilisation médiévale* (Paris, 1969); O. Lottin, *Psychologie et morale aux XIIe et XIIIe siècles*, IV3 (Louvain, 1954), 310–54.
7. See above, the final paragraph and final note of Chapter 3.
8. J. W. Baldwin, *Masters, Princes, and Merchants: The Social Views of Peter the Chanter and His Circle*, 2 vols. (Princeton, 1970); for commerce, see I, 261–311.
9. M.-M. Dufeil, *Guillaume de Saint-Amour et la polémique universitaire parisienne, 1250–1259* (Paris, 1972), pp. 3–9, 14–17, 23–35.
10. C. W. Bynum, 'The Spirituality of Regular Canons in the Twelfth Century: A New Approach', *Medievalia et Humanistica*, n.s., IV (1973), 3–24.
11. James of Vitry, though, was particularly astute at recognizing such originality in others. The same is true of Innocent III, whom Baldwin cautiously suggests (op. cit., I, 343) might have been a student of Peter the Chanter.
12. On scholastic social thought, see B. Jarrett, *Social theories of the Middle Ages, 1200–1500* (London, 1926); T. P. McLaughlin, 'The Teaching of the Canonists on Usury (XII, XIII and XIV Centuries)', *Mediaeval Studies*, I (1939), 81–147; II (1940), 1–22; B. N. Nelson, *The Idea of Usury: From Tribal Brotherhood to Universal Otherhood* (Princeton, 1949; 2nd ed. Chicago, 1969); G. LeBras, 'Usure', *DTC*, XV (1950), 2336–72; Le Goff, *Marchands et banquiers*, pp. 70–98; J. T. Noonan, *The Scholastic Analysis of Usury* (Cambridge, Mass., 1957); the works of J. W. Baldwin cited above in n. 8 and below in nn. 18 and 26; J. Ibanès, *La doctrine de l'Eglise et les réalités économiques au XIIIe siècle: l'intérêt, les prix et la monnaie* (Paris, 1967); J. Gilchrist, *The Church and Economic Activity in the Middle Ages* (New York, 1969); R. W. Southern, 'Medieval Humanism', in *Medieval Humanism and Other Essays* (Oxford, 1970), pp. 29–60; J. F. McGovern, 'The Rise of New Economic

Attitudes—Economic Humanism, Economic Nationalism—During the Later Middle Ages and the Renaissance, A. D. 1200–1550', *Traditio*, XXVI (1970), 217–53; R. de Roover, *La pensée économique des scholastiques, doctrines et méthodes* (Paris, 1971); and *Business, Banking, and Economic Thought in Late Medieval and Early Modern Europe: Selected Studies of Raymond de Roover*, ed. J. Kirshner (Chicago, 1974).

13. Southern, *Medieval Humanism*, pp. 53–4.

14. Noonan, *Scholastic Analysis*, p. 29.

15. *Summa theologiae* 2a 2ae, q. 66, art. 2, in *Opera omnia*, III (Parma, 1853), 247–8.

16. G. Post, 'The Naturalness of Society and the State', in his *Studies in Medieval Legal Thought: Public Law and the State, 1100–1322* (Princeton, 1964), pp. 494–561.

17. K. S. Cahn, 'The Roman and Frankish Roots of the Just Price of Medieval Canon Law', *Studies in Medieval and Renaissance History*, VI (1969), 1–52.

18. J. W. Baldwin, *The Medieval Theories of the Just Price: Romanists, Canonists, and Theologians in the Twelfth and Thirteenth Centuries*, Transactions of the American Philosophical Society, n.s., XLIX4 (Philadelphia, 1959), p. 54.

19. G. Post, K. Giocarnis, and R. Kay, 'The Medieval Heritage of a Humanistic Ideal: "Scientia donum dei est, unde vendi non potest" ', *Traditio*, XI (1955), 209–10.

20. J. Le Goff, 'Temps de l'Eglise et temps du marchand', *Annales E. S. C.,* XV (1960), 417–33.

21. R. W. Southern, *Western Society and the Church in the Middle Ages* (Harmondsworth, 1970), pp. 278, 294.

22. Noonan, *Scholastic Analysis*, pp. 52–3, 56–7, 110, 144–5.

23. J. Le Goff, 'Métiers licites et métiers illicites dans l'occident médiéval', *Etudes historiques, Annales de l'Ecole des Hautes Etudes de Gand*, V (1963), 46–7.

24. Baldwin, *Masters, Princes, and Merchants*, I, 262–3.

25. Thomas of Chobham *Summa confessorum*, ed. F. Broomfield, Analecta mediaevalia namurcensia, XXV(Louvain, 1968), p. 301.

26. *Ennarratio in Psalmum LXX (PL*, XXXVI, 866–7); cf. J. W. Baldwin, 'The Medieval Merchant Before the Bar of Canon Law', *Papers of the Michigan Academy of Science, Arts, and Letters*, XLIV (1959), 287–99.

27. Baldwin, *Medieval Theories of the Just Price*, p. 63.

28. *Summa theologiae* 2a 2ae, q. 77, art. 4, in *Opera omnia*, III (Parma, 1853), 279.

29. Baldwin, *Medieval Theories of the Just Price*, p. 48. Cf. *DTC*, VI2, 1980–81.

30. *Summa theologiae* 2a 2ae, q. 66, art. 7, in *Opera omnia*, III (Parma, 1853), 250. Cf. R. W. Southern, *Medieval Humanism*, p. 54; and G. Couvreur, *Les pauvres ont-ils des droits? Recherches sur le vol en cas d'extrême nécessité depuis la 'Concordia' de Gratien (1140) jusqu'à Guillaume d'Auxerre (†1231)* (Paris, 1961).

31. Noonan, *Scholastic Analysis*, pp. 133–53; Baldwin, *Masters, Princes, and Merchants*, p. 289.

32. Noonan, *Scholastic Analysis*, pp. 19–20.

33. ibid., pp. 44–5, 49, 53–4; *Summa theologiae* 2a 2ae, q. 78, art. 2, in *Opera omnia*, III (Parma, 1853), 281.

34. Nelson, *The Idea of Usury*, pp. 3–28.

35. Noonan, *Scholastic Analysis*, pp. 105–9.

36. *Le traité 'De Usura' de Robert de Courçon*, ed. and tr. G. Lefèvre, Travaux et mémoires de l'Université de Lille, X, mémoire no. 30 (Lille, 1902).

37. Baldwin, *Masters, Princes, and Merchants*, I, 284; Noonan, *Scholastic Analysis*, pp. 115–16.

38. ibid., pp. 109, 117–18.

39. *Tractatus de usuris*, published as Opusculum 66 of Thomas Aquinas, *Opera omnia*, XVII (Parma, 1864), 413–36.

40. *Tractatus de usuris* prooemium, p. 413. Cf. Noonan, *Scholastic Analysis*, p. 62.

41. *Tractatus de usuris* vi–viii, pp. 419–22.

42. ibid., vii, p. 420.
43. ibid., xiii, pp. 429–30.
44. E. Longpré in *Catholicisme*, I, 307–8.
45. A. M. Hamelin, ed., *Un traité de morale économique au XIVe siècle: le* Tractatus de usuris *de Maître Alexandre d'Alexandrie*, Analecta mediaevalia namurcensia, XIV (Louvain, 1962).
46. ibid., pp. 32–4.
47. Noonan, *Scholastic Analysis*, p. 64.
48. Hamelin, *Un traité*, para. 54–71, pp. 144–52.
49. Noonan, *Scholastic Analysis*, pp. 154–70.
50. Hamelin, *Un traité*, para. 136–48, pp. 180–6. Probably the first writer to do so was another Franciscan, Francis of Meyronnes, whose career spanned the latter part of the thirteenth century and the first quarter of the fourteenth; see P. Michaud-Quantin, 'Aspects de la vie sociale chez les moralistes', in P. Wilpert, ed., *Beiträge zum Berufsbewusstein des mittelalterlichen Menschen*, Miscellanea Medievalia, III (Berlin, 1964), 40.

Chapter 11 : A reformed apostolate

1. *Opera omnia in universum vetus et novum testamentum*, 7 vols. (Venice, 1600), I, 14, col. 1.
2. *Verbum abbreviatum* i (*PL*, CCV, 25).
3. *Expositio super constitutiones fratrum praedicatorum* viii (Berthier, II, 29).
4. *De eruditione praedicatorum* xxi (Berthier, II, 432).
5. *Historia Occidentalis* xxvii (*HO*, p. 143).
6. *De adventu fratrum minorum in Angliam* vi, vii, ed. A. G. Little (Paris, 1909), pp. 27, 48.
7. W. A. Hinnebusch, *The Early English Friars Preachers* (Rome, 1951), pp. 286–8; R. F. Bennett, *Early Dominicans* (Cambridge, 1937), p. 80.
8. G. Tiraboschi, ed., *Vetera Humiliatorum monumenta*, 3 vols. (Milan, 1766–8), II, 133–4; Thomas of Celano *Vita Prima S. Francisci* xxxiii (*AF*, X, 26–7).
9. *Comm. in Joannem* xxi.8, in *Opera Omnia*, VI, 521.
10. *De eruditione praedicatorum* viii–xii (Berthier, II, 399–407).
11. *Opera omnia*, II, 272, col. 2.
12. L. de Kerval, ed., *Sancti Antonii de Padua vitae duae, Collection d'études et de documents sur l'histoire religieuse et littéraire du Moyen Age,* V (Paris, 1904), 23–52.
13. *Les opuscules de Saint François d'Assise*, ed. D. Vorreux *et al.* (Paris, 1955), p. 224.
14. Salimbene de Adam *Cronica* (ed. Scalia, pp. 813–14). For Berthold's career, see *DHGE*, VIII, 980–7.
15. *Comm. in evang. S. Lucae* xii.11, in *Opera Omnia*, VII, 315.
16. *De eruditione praedicatorum* vii (Berthier, II, 395).
17. *Councils and Synods with other Documents Relating to the English Church*, ed. F. M. Powicke and C. R. Cheney, II, 2 parts (Oxford, 1964), part II, 901.
18. J. Le Goff, 'Ordres mendiants et urbanisation dans la France médiévale', *Annales E. S. C.*, XXV (1970), 931–2; Bennett, *Early Dominicans*, pp. 79–80.
19. *Determinationes Quaestionum circa Regulam Fratrum Minorum*, pars ii, qu. xix, in *Opera Omnia*, VIII, 370.
20. *De modo prompte cudendi sermones* i.72, ed. P. Despont, *Maxima bibliotheca veterum patrum*, XXV (Lyons, 1677), 491; see the discussion in Le Goff, 'Ordres mendiants', pp. 929–30.
21. *S. Antonii Legenda prima* xiii (L. De Kerval, p. 47).
22. *De eruditione praedicatorum* xxviii (Berthier, II, 444).
23. *Peter Abelard's* Ethics, ed. and tr. D. E. Luscombe (Oxford, 1971), pp. 14–15.

24. ibid., pp. 88–9.
25. P. F. Palmer, 'Sacrament of Penance, 1. Dogmatic Aspects', *NCE*, XI, 73–78.
26. *Peter Abelard's* Ethics (Luscombe, pp. 98–101).
27. Chenu, *Nature, Man, and Society*, p. 284.
28. D. E. Luscombe, *The School of Peter Abelard: The Influence of Abelard's Thought in the Early Scholastic Period*, Cambridge Studies in Medieval Thought and Life, Second Series, XIV (Cambridge, 1969), pp. 278–80.
29. Alain de Lille *Liber Poenitentialis*, ed. J. Longère, 2 vols., Analecta mediaevalia namurcensia, XVII, XVIII (Louvain, 1965), II, 39–123.
30. Robert of Flamborough *Liber Poenitentialis* i.2, ed. J. F. Firth, Pontifical Institute of Mediaeval Studies, Studies and Texts, XVIII (Toronto, 1971), 58–62.
31. *COD*, p. 245.
32. Hinnebusch, *Early English*, p. 282.
33. P. Simson, *Geschichte der Stadt Danzig*, IV (Danzig, 1918), 5–6.
34. *Bullarium Franciscanum*, I (Rome, 1759), 59.
35. Robert Grosseteste *Ep.* lviii, ed. H. R. Luard, *RS*, XXV, 179.
36. MP, IV, p. 511.
37. *De eruditione praedicatorum* xxi (Berthier, II, 432).
38. *De eruditione praedicatorum* xliv (*ibid.*, II, 479).
39. Moorman, *History of the Franciscan Order*, p. 274.
40. *S. Antonii Legenda prima* xiii (L. de Kerval, p. 49).
41. A. Teetaert, *La confession aux laïques dans l'église latine depuis le VIIIe jusqu'au XIVe siècle: étude de théologie positive* (Bruges, Paris, 1926), pp. 256–74.
42. *De eruditione praedicatorum* xliv (Berthier, II, 479).
43. H. Caplan, *Mediaeval Artes praedicandi: A Hand-list* (Ithaca, 1934), and *A Supplementary Hand-list* (Ithaca, 1936); idem, *NCE*, I, 853.
44. idem, 'Classical Rhetoric and the Medieval Theory of Preaching', *Classical Philology*, XXVIII (1933), 73–96.
45. *Summa de arte praedicatoria* (*PL*, CCX, 109–98).
46. S. H. Thompson, *The Writings of Robert Grosseteste, Bishop of Lincoln, 1235–1253* (Cambridge, 1940), p. 121; M. Powicke, introduction to D. A. Callus, ed., *Robert Grosseteste, Scholar and Bishop* (Oxford, 1955), p. xvii.
47. Ed. Despont, *Maxima bibliotheca veterum patrum*, XXV (Lyons, 1677), 456–567.
48. J. T. Welter, *L'exemplum dans la littérature religieuse et didactique du moyen âge* (Paris, 1927), pp. 135–6.
49. Caplan, 'Classical Rhetoric', p. 78; L. Duval-Arnould, 'Trois Sermons Synodaux de la Collection attribuée à Jean de la Rochelle', *Archivum Franciscanum Historicum*, LXIX (1976), 336–400; LXX (1977), 35–71, especially pp. 47–8, 57–9, 63–6.
50. P. Michaud-Quantin, 'Guy d'Evreux, O. P., technicien du sermonnaire médiéval', *Archivum Fratrum Praedicatorum*, XX (1950), 213–33.
51. R. H. and M. A. Rouse, 'The Verbal Concordance to the Scriptures', ibid., XLIV (1974), 5–30.
52. *The* Exempla *or Illustrative Stories from the* Sermones vulgares *of Jacques de Vitry*, ed. T. F. Crane, Folk-Lore Society, XXVI (London, 1890); cf. Welter, *L'exemplum*, pp. 118–23. Caesar of Heisterbach *Dialogus miraculorum*, ed. J. Strange, 2 vols. (Cologne, 1851); cf. Welter, *L'exemplum*, pp. 113–18. A. M. Friend, 'Odo of Cheriton', *Speculum*, XXIII (1948), 641–58; cf. Welter, *L'exemplum*, pp. 124–7.
53. *Anecdotes historiques* (ed. Lecoy de la Marche); cf. Welter, *L'exemplum*, pp. 215–23.
54. *Liber de dono timoris*, or *Tractatus de habundancia exemplorum*, discussed in J. A. Herbert, *Catalogue of Romances in the Department of Manuscripts in the British Museum*, III (London, 1910), 98–100, and Welter, *L'exemplum*, pp. 224–8.
55. ibid., pp. 228–30.
56. ibid., pp. 230–3. This collection of biblical exempla shades off into the genre of

the *Biblia pauperum* and was at one time attributed to St Bonaventure and included in *Bonaventurae Opera Omnia*, ed. A. C. Peltier, VIII (Paris, 1866), 483–642.

57. Welter, *L'exemplum*, pp. 233–6. For still other collectors of exempla, see ibid., pp. 236–89, and S. L. Forte, 'A Cambridge Dominican Collector of Exempla in the Thirteenth Century', *Archivum Fratrum Praedicatorum*, XXVIII (1958), 115–48.

58. *Liber Exemplorum ad usum praedicantium*, ed. A. G. Little, British Society of Franciscan Studies, I (Manchester, 1908); cf. Welter, *L'exemplum*, pp. 290–4.

59. J. T. Welter, *La 'Tabula exemplorum secundum ordinem alphabeti': Recueil d'exempla compilé en France à la fin du XIIIe siècle* (Paris, 1926); cf. Welter, *L'exemplum*, pp. 294–7.

60. P. Michaud-Quantin, *Sommes de casuistique et manuels de confession au moyen âge (XII–XVI siècles)*, Analecta mediaevalia namurcensia, XIII (Louvain, 1962).

61. Thomas of Chobham *Summa*, ed. Broomfield, pp. XII–XVII; cf. G. LeBras, 'Pénitentiels', *DTC*, XII1, 1160–79.

62. Thomas of Chobham *Summa*, ed. Broomfield, p. 3.

63. Thomas of Chobham *Summa*, ed. Broomfield, pp. 240, 346–53, 504–18.

64. ibid., p. XXV, where the editor exaggerates the 'popular' nature of this work.

65. *Summa de Poenitentia*, ed. Benedictine Fathers, Bibliotheca Casinensis, IV (Monte Cassino, 1880), 191–215.

66. Michaud-Quantin, *Sommes de casuistique*, pp. 24–6; P. Mandonnet and M.-H. Vicaire, *Saint Dominique, L'idée, l'homme et l'oeuvre*, 2 vols. (Paris, 1938), I, 249–69.

67. *Summa de poenitentia* (Rome, 1603).

68. Bloomfield, *Seven Deadly Sins*, p. 124. On Raymond's influence, see A. Teetaert, 'Quelques *Summae de Poenitentia* anonymes dans la Bibliothèque nationale de Paris', in *Miscellanea Giovanni Mercati*, II (Vatican, 1946), 311–43.

69. Michaud-Quantin, *Sommes de casuistique*, pp. 39–40.

70. ibid., p. 36.

71. ibid., pp. 40–2. On Adam, see F. Valls Taberner, 'La *Summula Pauperum* de Adam de Aldersbach', in *Gesammelte Aufsätze zur Kulturgeschichte Spaniens*, VII (1938), 69–83.

72. On John of Freiburg's career, see M.-D. Chenu in *DTC*, VIII, 761–2 or W. Hinnebusch in *NCE*, VII, 1051. Cf. L. Boyle, 'The *Summa Confessorum* of John of Freiburg and the Popularization of the Moral Teaching of St. Thomas and of some of his Contemporaries', in *St Thomas Aquinas, 1274–1974: Commemorative Studies*, 2 vols. (Toronto, 1974), II, 245–68.

73. ibid., and Michaud-Quantin, *Sommes de casuistique*, pp. 44–50.

74. Boyle asserts that the author was Guy of Evreux, 'The *Summa Confessorum* of John of Freiburg', p. 260, and cites, n. 49, an article of Michaud-Quantin (see above, n. 50) published in 1950. But Michaud-Quantin in his book, *Sommes de casuistique*, p. 48, published in 1962, says that beyond the name Guy and his membership in the Order of Preachers the author remains unidentified.

75. Boyle, 'The *Summa Confessorum* of John of Freiburg', p. 258, says: 'it may prove not to be an exaggeration to state that the *Summa confessorum* was the most influential work of pastoral theology in the two hundred years before the Reformation.' Cf. Michaud-Quantin, *Sommes de casuistique*, pp. 52–7.

76. Reflection on these matters should take into account the studies being carried on by E. L. Eisenstein. Her persuasive arguments on behalf of the revolutionary significance of printing need eventually to be integrated with the findings of Rouse, so that one could gain a coherent view of the propagation of written material over the period 1150–1600. See E. L. Eisenstein, 'The Advent of Printing and the Problem of the Renaissance', *Past and Present*, no. 45 (1969), 9–89; 'The Advent of Printing in Current Historical Literature: Notes and Comments on an Elusive Transformation', *American Historical Review*, LXXV

(1969–70), 727–43; 'L'avènement de l'imprimerie et la Réforme', *Annales E. S. C.*, XXVI (1971), 1355–82.

Chapter 12: Urban religious life

1. For the monks in the first feudal age, see B. H. Rosenwein, 'Feudal War and Monastic Peace: Cluniac Liturgy as Ritual Aggression', *Viator*, II (1971), 129–57; for a parallel argument concerning the monks and the friars, see B. H. Rosenwein and L. K. Little, 'Social Meaning in the Monastic and Mendicant Spiritualities', *Past and Present*, no. 63 (1974), 4–32.
2. P. Riché, *Education et culture dans l'Occident barbare, 6e–8e siècle*, 2nd ed. (Paris, 1967), pp. 158, 517–18.
3. See above, chap. X, n. 2.
4. *Regula monachorum* vi.8 (*CSEL*, LXXV, 39).
5. Alan of Lille *Summa de arte praedicatoria* xli (*PL*, CCX, 187–8); cf. *Revised Medieval Latin Word-List from British and Irish sources*, ed. R. E. Latham (London, 1965), pp. 9, 324.
6. J. T. Welter, *Un nouveau recueil franciscain d'Exempla de la fin du XIIIe siècle* (Paris, 1930), p. 52.
7. *Fasciculus Morum*, MS, Oxford, Bodleian, Bodley 332, f. 254r.
8. Ibanès, *Doctrine de l'Eglise*, p. 74.
9. Thomas of Spalato *Ex historia pontificum Salonitanorum et Spalatensium* (ed. Boehmer, *Analekten*, p. 106).
10. R. Davidsohn, *Forschungen zur Geschichte von Florenz*, IV (Berlin, 1908), 85.
11. *Scripta Leonis, Rufini, et Angeli, Sociorum S. Francisci* xliii, ed. and tr. R. B. Brooke (Oxford, 1970), pp. 166–7.
12. M. D. Lambert, *Franciscan Poverty: The Doctrine of the Absolute Poverty of Christ and the Apostles in the Franciscan Order, 1210–1323* (London, 1961), p. 39.
13. Peter Ferrand *Legenda sancti Dominici* i, ed. M.-H. Laurent in *MOPH*, XVI, 248.
14. *Sacrum Commercium S. Francisci cum Domina paupertate* (Quaracchi, 1929); the reference to it as the *Commercium Paupertatis* is in the *Chronica XXIV Generalium, AF*, III (Quaracchi, 1897), 283.
15. Anthony of Padua *Sermones dominicales*, ed. A. M. Locatelli, 3 vols. (Padua, 1895–1907), I, 28–32, 57; II, 18, 30, 114–16; III, 4, 98, 313.
16. Bonaventure *Defense of the Mendicants* xii.6, tr. J. de Vinck in *The Works of Bonaventure*, IV (Paterson, 1966), 260.
17. *De eruditione praedicatorum* xxxii (Berthier, II, 452).
18. ibid., iv (Berthier, II, 383).
19. ibid., xx (Berthier, II, 429–30).
20. J. H. Crehan, 'Indulgences', *A Catholic Dictionary of Theology*, III (London, 1971), 84–90.
21. MP, V, 599.
22. ibid., p. 742.
23. *Historia Anglorum*, ed. F. Madden, 3 vols., *RS*, XLIV3, 51–2.
24. A. Vauchez, 'Les stigmates de saint François et leurs détracteurs dans les derniers siècles du moyen âge', *Mélanges d'Archéologie et d'Histoire*, LXXX (1968), 614.
25. Dufeil, *Guillaume de Saint-Amour*, pp. 223–5, where the author analyses William's *De periculis novissimorum temporum*.
26. *De eruditione praedicatorum* xxi (Berthier, II, 432–3).
27. ibid., p. 432. Cf. *Expositio super constitutiones* ix (ibid. p. 32).
28. *De eruditione praedicatorum* xii (ibid. 433).
29. *De eruditione praedicatorum* (ibid., p. 383)

30. *Testament* v (ed. Boehmer, *Analekten*, pp. 37–8).
31. See above, chap. XI, n. 19.
32. *Anecdotes historiques* (ed. Lecoy de la Marche, p. 124).
33. Frederick was, though, a close friend of Brother Elias; see T. C. Van Cleeve, *The Emperor Frederick II of Hohenstaufen, Immutator Mundi* (Oxford, 1972), pp. 438–9. Also, there was some collaboration between Frederick and the friars where heresy was concerned from 1221 to 1245, the latter being the date of Frederick's second excommunication, when Innocent IV engaged the friars in his campaign to destroy the Hohenstaufen; see Freed, *The Friars and German Society*, pp. 138–50.
34. Letter sent by Frederick in 1246 to his fellow princes of Christendom, ed. J. Huillard-Bréholles, *Historia Diplomatica Frederici Secundi*, VI₁ (Paris, 1860), 391–3.
35. F. D. Swift, *The Life and Times of James the First of Aragon* (Oxford, 1894), pp. 109, 164.
36. R. I. Burns, *The Crusader Kingdom of Valencia: Reconstruction on a Thirteenth-Century Frontier*, 2 vols. (Cambridge, Mass., 1967), p. 199.
37. ibid., p. 197.
38. ibid., p. 200.
39. ibid., pp. 200, 198.
40. Swift, *James the First*, pp. 109, 164.
41. A. G. Little, *Studies in English Franciscan History*, pp. 35–9.
42. L. K. Little, 'Saint Louis' Involvement with the Friars', *Church History*, XXXIII (1964), 134–5.
43. *HF*, XX, 94.
44. ibid., XXIII, 426.
45. L. K. Little, 'Saint Louis' Involvement', p. 135.
46. A. Guerreau, 'Rentes des ordres mendiants à Mâcon au XIVe siècle', *Annales E. S. C.*, XXV (1970), 956–65.
47. J. Moorman, *Church Life in England in the Thirteenth Century* (Cambridge, 1946), p. 371.
48. Burns, *Crusader Kingdom*, pp. 200–1, 205–6.
49. See above, n. 46.
50. C. L. Kingsford, *The Grey Friars in London: Their History with the Register of their Convent and an Appendix of Documents* (Aberdeen, 1915), pp. 27–35, 145–50.
51. Freed, *The Friars and German Society*, p. 46.
52. Burns, *Crusader Kingdom*, pp. 200–1, 205–6.
53. Cf. Guerreau, 'Rentes', p. 965.
54. Quoted by Southern, *Western Society and the Church*, p. 247.
55. G. Meersseman, 'L'architecture dominicaine au XIIIe siècle. Législation et pratique', *Archivum Fratrum Praedicatorum*, XVI (1946), 136–90.
56. R. Branner, *Gothic Architecture* (New York, 1961), p. 43.
57. *Determinationes quaestionum crica regulam fratrum minorum*, pars I, qu. VI, in *Opera Omnia*, VIII (Quaracchi, 1898), 341–2.
58. *Abbot Suger on the Abbey Church of Saint-Denis and Its Art Treasures*, ed. and tr. E. Panofsky (Princeton, 1946). Cf. Brentano's analysis of the contrasts between 'twelfth-century' and 'thirteenth-century' historians in *Two Churches*, pp. 327–32.
59. Burns, *Crusader Kingdom*, pp. 200–1.
60. G. G. Meersseman, *Ordo Fraternitatis: Confraternite e pietà dei laici nel medioevo* 3 vols., Italia Sacra, Studi e documenti di storia ecclesiatica, 24–6 (Rome, 1977).
61. *1 Cel.* xxxvii (*AF*, X, 30).
62. *S. Francisci Opuscula, Bibliotheca Franciscana Ascetica Medii Aevi*, I (Quaracchi, 1904), 87–98.
63. *Bullarium Franciscanum*, IV (Rome, 1768), 94–7.

64. ibid., I (Rome, 1759), 8.
65. ibid., p. 20.
66. M. Bihl, 'Elenchi Bononiensis Fratrum de Poenitentia S. Francisci, 1252–88', *Archivum Franciscanum Historicum*, VII (1914), 227–33, especially 229–30; cf. Moorman, *History of the Franciscan Order*, pp. 216–25.
67. Burns, *Crusader Kingdom*, p. 201.
68. P. Guerrini, 'Gli Statuti di un'antica congregazione francescana di Brescia, *Archivum Franciscanum Historicum*, I (1908), 544–68.
69. See above, n. 61.
70. *NCE*, XIV, 93–6.
71. G. Meersseman, 'Etudes sur les anciennes confréries dominicaines, II: Les confréries de St-Pierre Martyr', *Archivum Fratrum Praedicatorum*, XXI (1951), 58.
72. ibid., pp. 91–2.
73. G. Meersseman (as in n. 71), III: 'Les congrégations de la Vierge', ibid., XXII (1952), 5–176; and IV: 'Les milices de Jesus-Christ', ibid., XXIII (1953), 275–308.
74. G. Meersseman (as in n. 71), I: 'Les confréries de Saint-Dominique', ibid., XX (1950), 5–113. The text of the letter appears on pp. 65–6.
75. MS, Bergamo, Biblioteca Civica, MIA, XL, 937, ff. 1r–12r.
76. Burns, *Crusader Kingdom*, pp. 201, 206.
77. *NCE*, IX, 57–8.
78. H. E. J. Cowdrey, 'Unions and Confraternity with Cluny', *Journal of Ecclesiastical History*, XVI (1956), 152–62. On the advice of St Norbert of Xanten to Count Theobald of Champagne about how the latter might live a spiritually valid existence without abandoning his secular condition, see *Vita Norberti Archiepiscopi Magdeburgensis* xv (*MGH, SS*, XII, 688).
79. G. Meersseman, *Le dossier de l'ordre de la Pénitence au XIIIe siècle*, Spicilegium Friburgense, VII (Fribourg, 1961), p. 11.
80. ibid., pp. 180–7.
81. ibid., p. 38.
82. H. A. R. Gibb, *Mohammedanism*, 2nd ed. (New York, 1975), pp. 103–4.
83. M. Fougères (Marc Bloch), 'Entr'aide et piété: Les associations urbaines au moyen âge', *Mélanges d'histoire sociale*, V (1944), 106.
84. *Bertholds Predigten*, ed. F. Göbel (Regensburg, 1905), p. 282.
85. M. Becker, 'Towards a Renaissance Historiography in Florence', in *Renaissance Studies in Honor of Hans Baron*, ed. A. Molho and J. A. Tedeschi (Florence, 1971), pp. 143–71.
86. ibid., p. 151.
87. ibid., p. 152.
88. W. Hinnebusch, *NCE*, XII, 667–70.
89. L. White, jr., 'Medieval Borrowings from Further Asia', *Medieval and Renaissance Studies*, V. (1971), 17–18. Bernard Gui describes how, in the ceremony of the melioramentum, the believer kneels and clasps his hands together; *Manuel de l'Inquisiteur*, ed. and tr. G. Mollat, 2 vols., *Les Classiques de l'histoire de France au moyen âge*, VIII, IX (Paris, 1926–27), I, 20–1. While some argue that the new posture came into use earlier and came from the ceremony of homage, the histories of liturgy indicate that the new way gained general currency only in the thirteenth century. Thus the Indic thesis is as plausible as the homage thesis; neither is proven. See L. Gougaud, *Dévotions et pratiques ascétiques du moyen âge* (Paris, 1925), pp. 20–9; and G. Ladner, 'The Gestures of Prayer in Papal Iconography of the Thirteenth and Early Fourteenth Centuries', in *Didascaliae: Studies in Honor of Anselm M. Albareda*, ed. S. Prete (New York, 1961), pp. 245–75.
90. E. Guidoni, 'Città e ordini mendicanti: Il ruolo dei conventi nella crescita e nella progettazione urbana del XIII e XIV secolo', *Quaderni medievali*, no. 4 (1977), 69–106.

91. See for example A. Vauchez, 'Une campagne de pacification en Lombardie autour de 1233: l'action politique des ordres mendiants d'après la réforme des statuts communaux et les accords de paix', *Mélanges d'Archéologie et d'Histoire*, LXXVIII (1966), p. 534.
92. *COD*, p. 223.
93. ibid., pp. 328–30.
94. G. Le Bras, 'Usure—Sanctions', *DTC*, XV 2, 2365–71.
95. Ibanès, *Doctrine de l'Eglise*, p. 25.
96. K. T. Erikson, *Wayward Puritans: A Study in the Sociology of Deviance* (New York, 1966), pp. 3–29.
97. Le Goff, *Marchands et banquiers*, p. 95.
98. Ibanès, *Doctrine de l'Eglise*, p. 94.
99. *Summa theologiae* 2a 2ae, q. 78, art. 1, ad 3, in *Opera omnia*, III (Parma, 1853), 279–80.
100. Ibanès, *Doctrine de l'Eglise*, p. 95.
101. J. Lestoquoy, *Les villes de Flandre et d'Italie sous le gouvernement des patriciens (XIe–XVe siècles)* (Paris, 1952), p. 210.
102. B. J. Nelson, 'The Usurer and the Merchant Prince: Italian Businessmen and the Ecclesiastical Law of Restitution, 1100–1500', *Journal of Economic History*, VII (1947), Supplement, pp. 104–22.
103. ibid., pp. 115–17.
104. Lestoquoy, *Les villes*, pp. 204–11.
105. Humbert of Romans *De modo prompte cudendi sermones* i.72, ed. Despont, *Maxima bibliotheca*, XXV, 491–2.
106. J. Le Goff, *FEH*, pp. 78–9, 100; the text discussed by Le Goff is found in J. B. Schneyer, 'Alberts des Grossen Augsburger Predigtzyklus über den hl. Augustinus', *Recherches de théologie ancienne et médiévale*, XXXVI (1969), 100–47.
107. ibid., p. 112; cf. p. 116.
108. ibid., p. 112; cf. p. 118.
109. ibid., p. 118.
110. ibid., p. 123.
111. ibid., pp. 135, 141, 145.
112. Bonvicinus de Ripa *De magnalibus urbis Mediolani*, ed. F. Novati in *Bulletino dell'Istituto Storico Italiano per il Medioevo*, XX (1898), 67–114.
113. Bonvicinus *De magnalibus* iv.18 (ibid., pp. 113–14).
114. *The Golden Legend of Jacobus de Voragine*, tr. G. Ryan and H. Ripperger, 2 vols. (New York, 1941), I, vi.
115. Reginald of Durham *Libellus de Vita et Miraculis S. Godrici, Heremitae de Finchale*, ed. J. Stevenson, *Surtees Society*, XX (London, 1847).
116. *Bibliotheca sanctorum*, IX, 1173–5.
117. A. Vauchez, 'Sainteté laïque au XIIIe siècle: la vie du bienheureux Facio de Cremone (v.1196–1272),' *Mélanges de l'Ecole Française de Rome, Moyen Age-Temps modernes*, LXXXIV (1972), 13–53.
118. ibid., p. 37.
119. ibid., p. 39.
120. *Bibliotheca sanctorum*, VII, 997–1001.
121. Little, 'Saint Louis' Involvement', pp. 125–48.
122. P. Ariès, 'Richesse et pauvreté devant la mort', in *Etudes sur l'histoire de la pauvreté (Moyen Age-XVIe siècle)*, ed. M. Mollat, 2 vols. (Paris, 1974), II, 524; P. Veyne, 'Panem et Circenses: l'évergétisme devant les sciences humaines', *Annales E. S. C.*, XXIV (1969), 804–5; J. Le Goff, 'Les mentalités: une histoire ambiguë', in *Faire de l'histoire*, ed. J. Le Goff and P. Nora, 3 vols. (Paris, 1974), III, 78; and Duby, *Warriors and Peasants,* p. 259 (although note that the key phrase, 'at the approach of death', is omitted in the translation).

123. Davidsohn, *Florenz*, pp. 81–9.
124. ibid., pp. 84, 87.
125. Brentano, *Two Churches*, p. 195.
126. These remarks came from sermons preached elsewhere; cited by D. Herlihy, *Pisa in the Early Renaissance: A Study in Urban Growth*, Yale Historical Publications, Miscellany, LXVIII (New Haven, 1958), p. 167.
127. Davidson, *Florenz*, pp. 85, 87.
128. ibid., p. 87.

Conclusion

1. *Bibliotheca Cluniacensis*, col. 520.
2. Caesar of Arles *Sermones* ccxxxiv, ed. G. Morin, *Corpus Christianorum, Series Latina*, CIV (Turnhout, 1953), 993; Peter Damian *Ep.* vi.3 (*PL*, CXLIV, 374); Anselm of Canterbury *Ep.* iii. 102 (*PL*, CLIX, 140); William of Malmsbury *De gestis pontificum anglorum* iv (*PL*, CLXXIX, 1612–13); Nicholas of Clairvaux *Sermo in festo S. Nicolai* v (*PL*, CLXXXIV, 1058).
3. Brentano, *Two Churches*, p. 337, n. 159.
4. MP, II, 511; IV, 346; V, 529.
5. Petrus de Bosco *Summaria brevis et compendiosa doctrina felicis expedicionis et abreviacionis guerrarum ac litium regni francorum*, ed. H. Kämpf, *Quellen zur Geistesgeschichte des Mittelalters und der Renaissance*, IV (Leipzig and Berlin, 1936; photo reprint, Stuttgart, 1969), 50.
6. Scheneyer, 'Alberts des Grossen Augsburger Predigtzyklus', p. 146.
7. Davidsohn, *Florenz*, pp. 86–8.

INDEX